MW00777627

BL RICHEY PUBLISHING
P.O. BOX 393
PARK FOREST, ILLINOIS 60466

www.emmetttills-secretwitness.com

This book is the compilation of a scholarly work, based on the author's raw research. All people, places and incidents described herein were obtained from documentation or disclosed to the researcher by persons directly involved in the case. These facts have been novelized to allow the readers to take this journey in a smooth and engaging manner.

ISBN – 97809896978-1-1
Copyright © 2013 by Bonita Blue LLC

EMMETT TILL'S SECRET WITNESS:

FBI CONFIDENTIAL SOURCE SPEAKS

BONNIE BLUE

CONTENTS

DEDICATION

This book is first and foremost dedicated to my Father, who continues to carry me through this long and challenging adventure.

Each step of my journey is dedicated to the two most loving, intelligent and strong willed women in my life. These women are my blessed mother, Blanche and my beloved aunt, Edna Mae. Both women I lovingly call M.O.M. (Mama Onna Mission).

Integrity, love and determination will always put a well-deserved period at the end of one's life. A lesson well learned. Thank you M.O.M.'s

To all of those whose voices were stolen as a result of distorted political, social and moral norms; I send you my purest love in remembrance that you passed this way for a reason.

ACKNOWLEDGEMENT

The following people had been a great source of encouragement and had supported me through the 36 years that it has taken me to research and complete this book.

It is my firstborn, Chuckie, whose unconditional love allowed me to feel the depth of a mother's love for her child that died to soon. To Shelly, Michael and Alyssa, my children that continue to walk with me; I give the biggest thanks and appreciation. These darling children have selflessly shared their mother with a child that was lynched decades before their births. Alyssa, my youngest daughter, has never known life without Emmett Till. To her, I thank with a wink and kiss. I love them all the way to heaven and beyond.

My brothers, Bruce and Marlon along with my sisters, Beverly (Dobbie), Barbara, and Marilyn have continued to be as supportive as only a family can.

My dear Aunt Joyce Richey, had been my champion from the very beginning and continues to do so through her own personal challenges, no matter how long my journey. My father-in-law, WV and mother-in-law, Malinda P., had lovingly guided and supported me and my children throughout the years. My precious brother-in-law, Leon was invaluable in assisting me in my research. My dear friend Aaron Hamb had been my consistent voice of caring reason and unconditional support and guidance. My lifelong friend Chuck Beckley had selflessly guided and encouraged me into and through my adult life. My caring friend, Shirley Bledsoe had consistently shown me the love and support of any mother-friend. Father Howard Tuite has been my spiritual inspiration through the rocky times. Bishop Arthur M. Brazier, encouraged me to stay true to the story when I wasn't sure what I should disclose and what I shouldn't. David Ter Molen, and Lawyers for the Creative Arts, had been invaluable encouragement and legal advisors during this process.

Countless others had crossed my path during my challenging lifelong journey to uncover the truth surrounding the lynching that changed the face of a nation. To you all, I extend my most sincere gratitude.

Most of all, I must acknowledge the willingness of Emmett Till's family who supported me in my quest for the truth. His mother, Mrs. Mamie Till-Mobley, and his grandmother, Mrs. Alma Spearman took me into their homes and hearts for many years. I must also extend a very special thank you to Emmett's cousin, Wheeler Parker, for his unshakable faith in my work. Their support had never wavered and they continued to encourage me to tell that truth, whatever it turned out to be. I promised them that I would; and I have.

INTRODUCTION

Social and political changes in America's racial dynamics prior to 1955, created an undercurrent of distrust and unrest among segments of her population. This trend was nothing new. Throughout history, when any degree of change threatened the political norm, social upheaval usually followed.

In 1863, President Abraham Lincoln penned the famous Emancipation Proclamation. The purpose of this document was to unite the nation in the midst of the Civil War and to end slavery; the legal tyranny and inhumanity against people, kidnapped from their homes in Africa for the sole purpose of free labor.

Two years after the ink from Lincoln's quill tipped pen dried, Southern states (Confederates) continued to fight feverously against the Northern states (Union) over the question of slavery. The country was still in its infancy in 1865 when the final shot was fired, ending the Civil War.

The Proclamation and end of legalized free labor in America bit deeply into the economic power of the South. Consequently, Southern states developed a mechanism which gave the illusion of adhering to the new law while maintaining their pre-Civil War way of life; the *Black Code*.

The *Black Code* and later, *Jim Crow* laws were shallow modifications of the *Slave Code* wherein, race was defined by blood, and Blacks were legally valued as only 3/5 human (Article 1 Section 2 of the Constitution's 13th Amendment).

Under the *Black Code,* White Southerners created vagrancy laws, which mandated that the newly freed Black people were to work for the White population or face legal prosecution. Blacks could not assemble without the presence of a White man. Segregation of all public facilities was the norm. With few exceptions, Blacks could not own real estate, and had no right to testify in court. Freedmen were not taught to read or write, though some were forced to make their mark (sign an x) on contracts requiring them to work for a meager salary or forced to work on chain gangs. The list goes on.

Failure by the freedmen to comply with any of these laws would result in severe whippings and like their pre-Civil War condition, branded or put to death by lynching.

In 1955, many White Southerners continued to cling desperately to the remnants of the pre-civil war south. This was the undercurrent in which Emmett Till committed his social 'offense'.

Unfortunately, in 2013, the '*code*' still exists in varying degrees. One has but to listen for the 'code words' and the true meaning behind those words will make themselves, crystal clear.

The struggle for social and economic equality may differ across geographic boarders, but the universal message is unmistakable. One has only to examine our global history to see that nothing can stifle the resolve of the human spirit to live free.

Racist are not sick people or ignorant (not knowing that all people hold the same value), nor are they just insecure, or merely hold excessively strong political views. Simply put, racism is an evil, and it is a choice. There is not enough sugar to hide its bitterness, not enough reasoning to validate its existence, and the code words which some believe are so clever and undecipherable are as hard and clear as crystal.

Racism is the degradation and attempt to dehumanize a people whose culture was stolen and destroyed for the sole purpose of free labor; a means to satisfy the greed of their White captors in the United States.

There were less affluent Whites, who took great pleasure in brutalizing these enslaved people, for the sole purpose of elevating their own diminished self-worth and insecurities. This practice went on for hundreds of years after the first 20 kidnapped Africans were sold in Virginia in 1619.

It is imperative to acknowledge that the overwhelming majority of White Americans today are not racist. Most, in fact, abhor the implication and history of slavery and racism. Freedom for enslaved African-Americans was won in part, with the assistance from a select group of Jewish and White-Americans.

Their decisions to standup for the rights of all Americans posed a real threat to their own lives. Some, in truth, gave their lives in valiant attempts to fight against this horrific wrong.

The American term, 'nigger' is not just a combination of letters that creates a word or a bad word or an insulting word. It is not 'just' a word at all. 'Nigger', stirs deep unsettling emotion. The manner in which it was used then and now, is a searing attempt to break the spirit of the survivors of kidnapped African enslaved people. 'Nigger' is designed to degrade and sever an African-American from their very home and birthright which, according to modern-day scientist, is the cradle of humankind.

Those who choose to use the term lightly are showing a blatant disregard for the pain and torture which enslaved people were forced to endure for hundreds of years. It also makes light of the racism which African-Americans continue to struggling against today. Frivolous usage of this term puts a stamp of approval on the residue of the brutality and inhumanity of the slave trade which is; racism.

The word, 'N-G-R', was the original title for Ancient Egyptian Pharaohs. These Pharaohs, who were Africans, saw black skin as sacred and a direct blessing from the sun god. It is also important to note that 'N-G-R' (pronounced, En-Ger,) was the Ancient Egyptian word for 'God'.

Over the ages, mutations of the pronunciation due to language translations had been expected and accepted. However, the intent of recent history misinterpretations may give one cause to wonder: is the American term 'nigger' a mutation? Was the sole purpose of mutating this 'word', a malicious ruse to take an historic identifier and twist it into an ugly and degrading description of a lazy, unintelligent beast of burden? Many believe that it is a distinct possibility that the misrepresentation of the word En-Ger was an attempt to inflict self-hatred instead of great pride.

1980 – Money Mississippi
Bonnie Blue in front of Roy Bryant's
store

Photograph restoration courtesy of
The Chicago History Museum
Carol Turchan, Conservator and John Alderson,
Photographer

ABOUT THE AUTHOR

My relationship with the Emmett Till lynching, evolved over 36 years and has traveled with me through many personal plateaus.

In 1970 I did as many of my friends did; married right out of high school. But unlike my friends, becoming pregnant was not easy. For months, I made bi-monthly trips to my doctor. When I finally got the news that I had a baby on the way, I ran directly to the department store to load up on maternity clothes, began my pregnant lady waddle and ordered an entire set of Childcraft Encyclopedias; all before my 20-year-old husband came home from his job at the supermarket.

Ten months after my first born, Chuckie, arrived, my bubbly daughter, Shelly, made her appearance and she was followed, 16 months later by my baby boy, Mikey.

By 1975, I was a 24-year-old divorced mother of three small children, working full time and attending Kennedy-King College pursuing a degree in broadcasting. Life was challenging but exciting until winter break of 1976 this was when my soul was fractured.

During a road trip with my siblings, we encountered a major snow storm and my small car hit a patch of ice. Ultimately, Shelly and Mikey escaped without a scratch. However, Chuckie, my 4 year-old firstborn was killed instantly.

In the fall of 1977 I returned to school, with a new determination to work harder to make life better for my two surviving children.

My interest had settled on radio. It was my intent to bring history to life through the same vein as producers had done for radio shows such as Masterpiece Theater.

Other students signed on and we went about moving into the library to find little known historical events that impacted the evolution of African Americans. One of my classmates kept mentioning the name, Emmett Till. I was misunderstanding what he was saying. I thought that he was saying, 'immaterial'. I kept asking him what was immaterial. He finally convinced me that he was talking about a boy named Emmett Till.

I must admit that at that time, I was not at all interested. I had never heard of that person before. It was not until he pulled the story up on microfiche that I understood his insistence. The first photos that I saw were the holiday pictures of Emmett Till and his mother just 8 months before his lynching. However, it was the second picture that changed my life. It was the photo of Emmett's body; a testament of what racial hatred in its purest form looked like. After a sleepless night, I was hooked. That was 36 years ago.

Researching the Emmett Till lynching nearly became an obsession with me. I could not accept that such an atrocity could be allowed to lay as silent and buried as its victim. It seemed almost a secret, that the hell this child endured was the actual catalyst that sparked the social explosion of the Civil Rights Movement.

For months, I reviewed newsreels and combed the resources available in Chicago's main library and the Woodson Regional Library in Chicago. Eventually, I sent for FBI files and compiled documents from other agencies and organizations around the nation. After months of searching, I finally located and met Mrs. Mamie Till-Mobley.

From the beginning, I was amazed at the unshakable faith and strength embodied in this very small woman. She had the ability to take the horrific lynching of her only child and create something positive.

At that time, Mrs. Mobley was a teacher in the Chicago Public Schools. She made it her mission to keep the philosophy of Dr. Martin Luther King Jr. alive by teaching students to recite his speeches at school assemblies and for church programs. She named this group of students, 'The Emmett Till Players'.

Mrs. Mobley and Emmett's grandmother, Mrs. Alma Spearman, met with me many times, prior to meeting with Emmett's other relatives. The meeting with Emmett's mother, his grand-mother, and his cousins that witnessed the whistling incident and kidnapping was not only enlightening for me, but also for Emmett's mother and grand-mother. Mrs. Spearman informed me that this was the first time the family actually come together to discuss the events that led to Emmett's lynching.

My relationship with the family extended over many years. However, after I discovered how Emmett actually died, it was very difficult to sit and talk with Mrs. Mobley. For me, omission of the truth was the same as lying. Mrs. Mobley, along with the rest of the world was under the impression that Emmett had been shot. Having lost my own first born, I could not imagine deepening her pain. I was not able to bring myself to disclose the torture that her baby had actually endured.

After dissecting countless documents and incorporating the family's oral history, the story was still far from complete. I knew that I had to, not only locate involved individuals from Mississippi, but more importantly, finesse my way into their trust if I hoped to get a more detailed account of the story.

Presenting myself, a young Black woman from the North, to dig into one of the deepest darkest periods in the South, was going to be challenging.

Through the early years, research came easy. No one was interested in the case, so when I found people that were involved, they were willing to talk. Their reactions varied from discomfort, to relief that they had the opportunity to talk about one of the most important events in their lives.

Interestingly enough, these people were not only open to speaking with me, but also directed me to others that were involved.

Even though the lynching occurred over 20 years earlier, most of my meetings were covert. Prior to interviewing them I had to promise, that if asked, I would deny any knowledge of them. It was through this method that I was led to the whereabouts of J.W. Milam; the leader of the lynch mob.

My interviews with J.W. Milam were some of the few conducted via telephone. We had at least four such conversations. I must admit that after I got over the initial uneasiness of actually hearing his voice, he did not seem very intimidating. That fact, in itself, is terrifying. It was not until we began discussing Emmett Till, politics and how his life changed since the lynching that I, even hundreds of miles away, experienced actual fear.

J.W. Milam asked me to contact him when I planned my next trip to Mississippi so that he could take me step by step to the locations of; where the beatings took place, where Emmett was eventually killed, where they actually disposed of his body and where Emmett's clothes were buried. To say that I found this unnerving would be a gross understatement. It was never my intent to become one of Mississippi's 'Peculiar Fruit'.

I could only imagine the reception that I would have received had I appeared smiling at his front door with luggage in hand.

J.W. obviously assumed that I was a young White woman. And believing such, he apparently felt safe talking to me. Years later, the FBI agent that I was working with, informed me that J.W. died of cancer just months after our last interview.

As time went on, media interest began to grow; Columbia pictures, James Earl Jones, Lonnie Elder III (Sounder and A Lady called Moses) - Muhammad Ali, Richard Durham, author of (The Greatest: biography of Muhammad Ali, and Birds of an Iron Feather), among others.

It seemed that many in the industry were interested in doing something with the materials and interviews that I had collected. However, things were moving too fast for me, and being young, I became nervous. I faded back to my little comfort space and continued working.

Life and time went on. I saw Mrs. Till-Mobley at many affairs including the dedication and renaming of 71st Street in Chicago to Emmett Till Road. I was very proud of her and the work that she had done in her son's name, but still, I was saddened that I could not reveal to her all that I had found from my research without disclosing Emmett's cause of death.

The last conversation that I had with Mrs. Till-Mobley was November 23, 2003. She was supervising the preparation of her birthday dinner and was happy to hear from me. I had made up my mind that I would attempt to disclose this information to her. We decided to get together after the Christmas holidays. Again, I froze. I could not tell this little woman, who had spent fourteen years raising her son and forty-eight years mourning him, the true brutality and torture that ended in his death.

Shortly after our conversation, I picked up a newspaper and read that she had passed away. Mixed with my deep sadness, was the comfort in knowing that this little warrior had closed her eyes and was finally reunited with her beloved son.

There is much debt owed, not only to Emmett Louis Till Jr. and Mamie Till-Mobley, but to numerous other known and unknown heroes that sacrificed to make this country as free as it is today.

I categorize *'Emmett Till's Secret Witness'*, a non-fictional novel, because it was important for me to not only disclose the facts in the case, but it was equally important for the reader to experience, as intimately as possible, the evolving social cultures of African Americans and Southern White traditionalist. I must admit, that the imagery is cutting and at times, ugly. But then again, racial hate is ugly.

For the purpose of this work, 'racist' refer to White hatred towards African Americans, although racism is found worldwide.

In 2008, as I stood in line at the county courthouse to cast my ballot for president, I noticed a petite, elderly, African-American woman with a small oxygen tank, being pushed in a wheel chair by her granddaughter. With tears in her eyes, she just kept saying softly, "God is good". It sounded as an echo of slaves; long since dead. I have no doubt, that this scene was repeated in polling places all over our nation.

At the publishing of this book, America continues to maintain its position as the political giant of the free world, and at its helm, Barack Hussein Obama, America's first African-American President. In 2013, 150 years after the emancipation of African enslaved people, President Barack Obama was re-elected and once again, took the oath of office to serve a 2nd term as President of the United States of America.

It will be years before the true history is written on the journey taken by President Obama during his residency in the White House. Was it a matter of political differences or raw racism that caused the President's proposals to be so aggressively struck down by members of Congress? This is not to say that everyone that disagrees with the president is racist. In fact, there has never been a full agreement of presidential policy by every member of Congress in American history. However, with the vigorous attempts to block any proposal from this president, no matter the consequence, one has to wonder if these same blocking tactics are taken from the 1954 White Citizens Council Handbook?

The White Citizens Council was a conservative group which was formed in 1954 after the Supreme Court ruled that segregation of public schools, was a violation of the United States Constitution and that all schools had to be desegregated by 1955 (Brown vs The Board of Education). It was also during this time that the NAACP was active in encouraging and assisting African Americans in voters registration drives in the South. The purpose of the White Citizens Council was to block any attempts by African Americans to obtain equal civil rights.

The role that racism played in American politics during the 8 years of President Barack Obama's two terms in office, is a question which will be debated for years.

Unfortunately, the evil of racism is still very much alive in 2013. It is my belief, that only through the efforts and persistence of the spiritually, intellectually and socially evolved citizens of the world, that the evils of racism can be annihilated.

It is my hope that the difficult lessons learned in the last century will become common sense in this one.

BOOK ONE

SUMMER VACATION DON'T COME EASY!

The summer of 1955 was one of the hottest in many years. An inevitable political burn also hung heavily in the air, evident by the growing sea of stoned faces.

State Street, usually one of the busiest veins in Chicago, was choked to a near halt. Only a trickle of traffic was ushered through by exhausted police officers. They tried, unsuccessfully, to contain the mourners that flooded out into the street, behind the barricades.

Jimmy Hicks, seasoned reporter for the *Baltimore Afro-American newspaper,* stood a block away from the massive throng leaning against his rented mint green 1954 Buick; legs crossed, watching.

Jimmy was one of a handful of elite Black newspaper men that had traveled the country to cover stories. Sure, he'd seen murdered bodies before. His line of work made him privy to a host of devious fashions in which man could destroy his brother.

He pushed his hat back from his forehead before walking towards the multitude of mourners. The majority of which were honestly saddened, but some were curiosity seekers, sprinkled with others that just felt the need to look on the face as a reminder of the fate that they or a family member could encounter at any time, while living Black in White America.

Yes they were all there, each submerged in their own realities. He doubted that anyone in this crowd of strangers which moved down the police lined streets actually knew the child. Yet they stayed for what seemed hours in near hundred degree heat; sweat dripping from their chins and clothes sticking to their skin.

Mothers held their children close to them as if to protect them from the strangers within arm's reach.

"What the hell could they be thinking?" Jimmy mumbled as he slowed his pace.

A young girl cried as she tried to pull away from her mother's grasp. "Mama please don't make me go! The monsters gonna get me!"

"It's not a monster. It's a little boy. Now stand up here and be still!"

"Yeah that makes a hell of a lotta sense lady," he muttered as he quickly made his way past the crying child. "Give the poor kid nightmares for the rest of her life."

Jimmy had no idea why he was so angry with the crowd. All he knew was that it intensified as he marched past the slow moving masses.

This was one story that had affected him more than any of the others; maybe because it was a child or perhaps because it so boldly represented the clash of innocence and the evil of racism.

The little girl was right. The bloated entity in the glass covered, oversized coffin did look to be more a monster than some mother's child.

Jimmy loosened his neck tie and checked his pocket for the press pass.

His composure was returning. He had to file a human interest story with his newspaper before the day's end.

Interviewing mourners before they went into Robert Chapel, where the body lay in state, wasn't difficult. Everyone it seemed had an opinion. But as he made his way to the other side of the building and the exit door, the mood grew heavier. Most children and adults alike, were sobbing.

Off to the side of the building, an officer was assisting a young White minister who was vomiting violently.

Suddenly, he heard a commotion just inside the exit door of the church.

"Naw! Naw! Mama! That ain't him! I'm tellin' ya that ain't Bobo! They tellin' a big ol' story! I'm tellin' ya, he's still lost down there!" a young boy screamed as he jerked away from his mother's hand and bolted back towards the oversized coffin.

The child was caught by his mother, but it took a number of men to contain him.

Naw! Bo! It ain't you!" he cried out angrily. "That can't be..." The child looked up and searched his mother's tear smeared face.

"I'm sorry Brucie."

"But Mama, why? He ain't done nothin'! He ain't never done nothin' ta nobody!"

"Boy!" One of the men that held the child firmly said. "He ain't gotta *DO* nothin'. All he had to do was *BE* Negro."

Brucie stared up at the man. A steady stream of salty tears poured from his swollen eyes. His mother held him tighter to her bosom.

"Bobo was a good boy and a good friend," she whispered "Only God knows why it happened. He's with the Lord now."

As the group of men that aided the woman led them out the door, Jimmy rushed over and asked, "Is your boy all right, ma'am? Is there anything I can do?"

She paused and looked up with disgust at this stranger, who was obviously a newspaper man looking for a story.

"No! He's ain't all right! Take a look around you Mister! Ain't nothin' all right!"

They looked at each other for a moment and the group walked away in silence, leaving Jimmy standing alone.

Bonnie Blue

* * *

Two weeks earlier the sun beamed so intensely down on the pavement that at an angle, waves of heat were actually visible.

On almost every city block, children played ball, jumped rope, sat on their porches shooting marbles or played Jacks. It seemed like all of the children were outdoors enjoying the last weeks of summer vacation, everyone that is, except fourteen year-old, Emmett Till Jr.

Emmett, or Bobo as his cousins and friends called him, lay around the house brooding as he attempted to devise a plan that would change his mother's mind about letting him go to Mississippi with his cousins. Time was running out, and she would be coming in from work before long. He wanted to be ready, but nothing he thought of seemed any good.

Emmett found temporary refuge by stretching out on the living room floor and watching the *Kukla, Fran, and Ollie* puppet show on television. Soon after the program was over, a news announcer began reporting on the possible effects on Southern Whites when enforcement of the Federal school desegregation law became a reality in the fall.

Emmett pushed back the large green area rug that covered the hardwood floor, emptied the small blue bag that held all of his cat-eye marbles and began practicing his shooting skills.

He often thought about his father and wondered what it would be like if he hadn't been killed. He knew that if his father was alive, he wouldn't treat him like a baby. He would let him travel with the other boys. But his father, Emmett Louis Till Sr., died while in the military when Emmett was barely a toddler.

Mamie knew how badly Emmett wanted to go down to her Uncle Moses' farm in Mississippi, which was why she was in no hurry to return home. She expected Emmett's long pitiful face and constant whining to meet her at the door. It wasn't that she was concerned that her only child wouldn't be cared for. She

4

was just not prepared to let her baby go anywhere outside of touching

Summer Vacation Don't Come Easy!

distance. Besides, she was looking forward to her vacation from her position as a voucher examiner for the armed services. She planned to take Emmett with her to visit Viola, one of her favorite cousins that lived in Nebraska.

Mamie had stopped by the market to stock up on groceries for the week and to also allow herself some extra time before heading home.

Finally, she pulled her car up to the curb in front of their neatly manicured two-flat apartment building in Chicago's Black Belt. She glanced around to see if Emmett or his cousin Wheeler was nearby, but neither was in sight. Relieved, she scooped up both bags, kicked the car door shut and ascended the concrete stairs to the front door.

As she bumped the vestibule door open with her shoulder Mike, Emmett's puppy, darted in from behind her leaping and whirling around her legs.

Mamie struggled with the heavy grocery bags as she climbed the remaining three steps that led to her second floor apartment, careful not to trip over the excited puppy. When she reached the landing; she shifted her bag to position her keys for the lock. She lost her grip and they slipped from her fingers, making a loud clank as they fell to the floor.

"Oh for Pete's sake." she said as Mike hopped up and licked her face when she knelt to retrieve her key chain.

Emmett heard all the commotion in the hall, scrambled from the floor and flung open the door.

"GGG...Get back boy!" he yelled as he stomped his foot to chase the puppy into the apartment.

Emmett quickly caught the bags tilting out of his mother's arms and carried them back into the kitchen.

"Mama, why do you always try to do everything by yourself? You sss...shoulda called me, blown the horn or somethin'."

5

"Well," Mamie called as she closed the door and followed him into the kitchen, "they really aren't that heavy."

"They felt heavy to me." Emmett mumbled.

Bonnie Blue

Just then the telephone rang out from the living room and Emmett ran to answer it.

"Who is it?" Mamie called as she began unpacking the groceries.

"Grandmama." Emmett said as he came back into the kitchen. "She said to call her back when you get a chance."

"Dog-gone it! I knew I was going to forget something! Emmett, go around to the corner store and pick up a loaf of bread. I'll finish putting everything else away. Look in my purse and get that quarter."

"Okay. Mama, can I get...?"

"Forget it mister. There are cookies and donuts already here. You don't need any more sweets and bring me back my change."

"How'd you know www...what I was gonna ask?"

"I know *you*." she said as she punched him playfully in the arm.

"Oh! And baby, come right back. I want to get dinner out of the way so I can get a cool bath and relax."

"Yes ma'am," Emmett said, "I'll stop by MMM...Miss King's first though and see if she needs anything. C'mon Mike! Here boy!"

"Alright, but remember what I told you. I'm tired and want to get through. Get those marbles up off of that floor and fix that rug back before you leave!" she called as Emmett rushed towards the front door. "Wait a minute Emmett! I told you not to let that dog out by himself until after I get his tags!

"He musta slid out through the screen door again. But I'll keep an eye on him!"

"Well you'd better or you're going fool around and not have a dog!"

* * *

Emmett ran over to the elderly woman's apartment in the next building, rang the doorbell and waited. Finally, he noticed Mrs. King peering through the delicate white lace curtain.

Emmett liked his neighbor and felt sorry for her. He couldn't remember a day when she wasn't dress as though she was preparing for company. It didn't seem right to him, that this nice little lady

Summer Vacation Don't Come Easy!

didn't have family around her more often. Although, he did have a sneaking suspicion that the parade of pictures of relatives, long since dead, might have something to do with it.

"It's just me Miss King!" Emmett called. "I'm goin' to the store. Do you want me to pick up anything fff...for you?"

She disappeared from the window and quickly swung the door open. A blast of heat, mixed with the thick delicious aroma of Southern peach cobbler, poured onto the porch.

"No I don't think so baby. But I *am* trying out a new recipe." she whispered. "My cousin in Kentucky thinks her cobbler is better than mine. She even had the nerve to send me her recipe," Mrs. King said quietly as she looked down at the crumpled letter in her hand. "No matter," she smiled. "I made both. Would you like to stay a while and be the judge?"

Emmett wanted to stay, but he reluctantly declined. "No, thank you ma'am. Mama told me to come straight home. But I'll ask if I can come back later. But are you sss...sure you don't need anything?"

"No dear, but thanks for stopping by." She smiled and patted him gently on his hand. "How is your Mama?" She asked, flashing a warm smile.

"Oh, she's okay. She just got home a little while ago."

"Well, tell her I said hello. You go on now and do like your Mama told you."

As Emmett started down the stairs, he heard a familiar voice calling his name. He stopped when he saw Wheeler running down the side walk, his catcher's mitt tucked securely under his arm.

Before Wheeler and his mother Hallie moved into the neighborhood from Argo, a suburb of Chicago, Emmett was very shy. As a toddler he was afflicted with polio, which caused him to stutter much of the time and left him with weak muscles in his legs that usually caused him pain when he walked. But now, with his sixteen year-old cousin who also happens to be his very best friend living right next door, he felt much more secure and mostly stuttered when he was upset or excited.

Bonnie Blue

"Hey Bo, you wanna go play some ball?"

"Yeah, but first I gotta go to the store for Mama."

"You walkin' all the way to the Hi-Lo?"

"Naw, just over to Turners."

"Okay, I'll go with you."

They passed the school yard where the other boys were playing ball. One of the boys caught sight of them and yelled, "Say Bobo! Wheeler! Boy am I glad ta see ya'll! C'mon! They're killin' us out here! We need some heavy hitters!"

"What's the score?"

"Just get over here! We need some help!"

Brucie Stewart ran over to the gate where Wheeler and Emmett were standing. "It's one ta four, an' they got that new boy up ta bat."

Emmett didn't remember any new family moving into the neighborhood.

"Ya know, Marlon Turner!" Brucie said after seeing the bewildered look on his friend's face. "They call him Rico. His family moved in the Baxter's old place over on Drexel just last weekend. Ol' man Turner's his uncle. Boy! We won't never have ta pay for candy again! This guy don't know it yet, but he's my new best friend! I'm gonna stick ta him like Bazooka Joe on the bubble gum wrapper!"

Their conversation was interrupted by the loud crack of a ball off the bat. Brucie suddenly turned in the direction of the other players. The batter dropped his bat and dashed to first base. He hesitated to see if the ball had been caught before he rounded second and headed to third. Emmett's friends in the outfield scrambled after the ball. Chubby Darwin Gilbert finally caught it and clumsily tossed it to Ralph who stumbled and fell as he threw it to Lewis, the pitcher, who in turn threw it towards home base, but it was too late. He was safe.

Brucie turned back to Wheeler and Emmett, who were still watching the game.

"Well anyway, this boy can hit anythin' ya throw at him! He's really good! C'mon guys! Ya gotta help out! This is embarrassin'! He ain't just beatin' us, he's hurtin' my feelin's, for real!"

Summer Vacation Don't Come Easy!

"Dag! He *is* good!" Wheeler said as he peered around Brucie to get a better look at the new boy. "But I think we can cool his heels. C'mon Bo, let's send this guy home, crying to his Mama."

The idea was appealing, but Emmett knew that he had to hurry home with the bread before he found himself in trouble.

"Go on Wheeler!" he yelled as he started running. "I'll be back in a minute! C'mon Mike! Here Mike! C'mon boy! Hey Wheeler, did you see him?"

"Don't worry about that ol' dumb dog! Just get back here before the games over!" he yelled.

Emmett ran the rest of the way to the store, bought the bread, and started running past the school yard.

As he did, Brucie called out to him, "C'mon Bo! It's your turn! Ya up ta bat right now!"

Emmett hesitated and looked down the street in the direction of his home. Thinking that it would take only a minute to play, he ran around the fence to the baseball diamond, laid the bread on the bench, strolled over and grabbed the bat.

The team cheered as the ball cracked off the bat and shot across the field. The score was now three to five. They were still losing, but the gap was tightening.

* * *

Emmett had completely forgotten about the bread, but Mamie hadn't.

Her once steaming bowl of mashed potatoes sat stiff and lifeless. The creamy simmering gravy, which just a short time ago

9

filled the air with appetizing fragrant hints of smothered green peppers, onions and pork chops, now lay dead and cold; edges flaking and pulling away from the skillet. The telephone rang out from the living room.

"Where's that boy?" she said as she hurried into the living room.

"Hello?" Mamie answered, pulling the cord of the telephone as close to the living room window as it would go.

"Hello dear." It was Alma, her mother.

Bonnie Blue

Mamie stretched out of one of the small opened side windows to see if she could catch a glimpse of Emmett coming up the street.

"Mamie, are you there?"

"Oh, I'm sorry Mother. I was looking for your grandson." she said as she paced around the living room.

"Do you know I sent that boy to the store over an hour ago and he hasn't gotten back yet?"

"Now don't you go getting all upset." Alma warned. "He probably ran into some of his little friends and..."

"Mother, I told that boy to come straight home. You know he doesn't have any business running around out there. Now, I told him what to do, but if he took it upon himself to go fooling around out there with those boys and ends up hurt...forget it Mother, just forget it."

She was becoming even more irritated because her mother was, once again, finding excuses for Emmett.

"Mother let me call you back in a little while, alright?"

"Mamie, sometimes you're entirely too hard on that child. Emmett's fine. He's a big boy and you know he can take care of himself."

"I know Mother. But friends or no, he didn't do what I told him to do. I'll give you a call a little later." She hung up the phone and headed out the door to find him.

* * *

Time had passed so quickly that Emmett hadn't even noticed that he had been gone for nearly two hours.

10

The score was now six to five in their favor, and home was the last thing on his mind, until someone on the other team yelled, "Hey Bo, ain't that ya Mama?"

Startled, Emmett turned around and sure enough, Mamie was making her way down the sidewalk. He could tell that she was steaming.

Wheeler ran over to where he was standing.

"Uh oh Bo, looks like the games over now, for real!"

"Dag!" Emmett said as he glanced down at his wristwatch. "I didn't know I www…was gone that long."

Summer Vacation Don't Come Easy!

He dashed over to retrieve the smashed brown paper bag that housed the loaf of bread which someone conveniently used as a cradle for their catcher's mitt.

"Man, she's ggg…gonna have a fit." He said as he knocked the mitt on the ground and attempted to straighten out the deformed loaf.

Mamie caught sight of him and marched around to the inside of the school yard where the boys were playing.

"Emmett Louis Till! Come here to me *NOW!*"

Emmett tried to hide the smashed bag behind his back, but Mamie saw it. His legs were sore from all the running he had done, but he couldn't let her see that either. He was in enough trouble.

Emmett quickly and carefully walked over to her and attempted to explain what happened but, before he could, a leather belt seemingly appeared from nowhere.

"I thought I told you to come right home!" she yelled, swinging the belt through the air.

He couldn't believe it. She was actually whipping him, and in front of his friends. He said nothing but ducked quickly out of her way and ran home.

Mamie was still fussing when she finally came into the apartment behind him and slammed the door.

Emmett tried once again to explain as he took the lopsided loaf of bread out of the bag.

11

"MMM...Mama," he took a deep breath to gain control of his words.

"Emmett, slow it down and whistle to untie your tongue." Mamie instructed, aggravated, but still concerned. "Now try it again."

He took another deep breath, blew a long low whistle and continued, "Mama, I know I sss...should have come home first, and I started to, honest, but the ggg...guys were in trouble and needed help. I know III...I was wrong. But Mama," he asked more chastising than fearful. "Did you really have to emmm...embarrass me in front of all the guys?"

Bonnie Blue

"Look little boy, I'm tired and I told you to bring your hind quarters right home and you chose not to!" Frustrated, she looked around, threw her hands on her hips, and cocked her head to the side. "And where's the dog?"

"I ggg...guess he got away from me again." Emmett answered quietly.

"Well you'd better hope he comes dragging back in here before dark. Now go on and get washed up for dinner."

Emmett's legs were hurting and he tried to cover it up as he walked into the bathroom to wash his face and hands. He knew that he had really messed up. If she found out that he kept playing while he was in pain, there was no way that she would ever consider letting him go on a trip without her.

* * *

The next morning, Mamie left for work in a much better mood. She had just a few more days left before her two week vacation would begin. The events of the previous evening hadn't crossed her mind, but Emmett was still bothered. He knew that the kids would tease him about it, but that really didn't worry him too much.

Emmett wanted to do something special for his mother to make up for his behavior. He didn't have any money left over from his allowance to buy her anything, so he decided to bake a cake. He'd tried it before, and it turned out pretty good, of course Mamie was standing nearby to help.

He looked around the kitchen and gathered all the ingredients on the table.

"Let me see. I think I got everything; eggs, milk, sugar, salt, butter, vanilla and flour. I think I'm missin' somethin'."

Looking at his collection lined up like little soldiers on the table, he snapped his fingers and said, "Oh yeah! Baking powder!"

He searched through the cabinets but there was none. Then he remembered that there was a box of baking soda. The bright gold box with the muscular arm and sledgehammer logo had been opened and long since forgotten in the back of the refrigerator.

Summer Vacation Don't Come Easy!

"Baking soda. Well it's baking' somethin'. There can't be that much difference." He said as he began mixing the ingredients.

"Hey there Betty Crocker! Whatcha doin'?"

Emmett jumped. It was Wheeler, standing right behind him. He was so preoccupied with his concoction, that he hadn't noticed him come through the back door.

"Real funny Wheeler! Boy, you better make some noise instead of sneakin' up on somebody like that!"

"I thought I'd better peek in first." Wheeler laughed, "I didn't wanna run into your Mama. Here friend, have a seat." he said as he pulled the chair out from the table. "Or is your rear end still sore?"

"I didn't get a www...whipping." Emmett said as he looked out the corner of his eye.

"I'm sorry," Wheeler said as he covered his mouth and attempted to muffle a snicker. "But you look like some kinda nut standin' there talkin' to yourself. What is that stuff anyway?"

"I'm makin' a cake for Mama." Emmett answered as he reached in the cabinet over the sink to get a large mixing bowl.

"Oh yeah? Well if you didn't get a whipping what happened? I didn't see you after you ran home."

"Nothin'. I stayed in and www...watched television. You know, I don't know what's wrong with Mama lately." Emmett said quietly as he dumped a stick of butter into the bowl. "She's tired all the time and kinda cranky."

Wheeler frowned as he watched Emmett crack the eggs and let the slimy gunk plop into the bowl and slide down the mound of butter.

"She might just be excited about goin' to Nebraska. I know *you* can hardly wait!" he teased, nudging Emmett in his ribs.

Emmett eased his hand into the canister, grabbed a fist full of flour, flicked it in Wheeler's face and ran out the back door.

When he got to the yard, he started for the back gate, but Wheeler caught up and tackled him before he reached it. They wrestled around on the grass until Wheeler pinned him.

Bonnie Blue

"You give?"

Emmett looked up at him and couldn't help laughing. "You look like one of Grandmama's giant bbb...biscuits!"

"You wanna laugh? I'll give you somethin' to laugh at."

Wheeler tried to get him in a position to tickle him, but Emmett rolled over with a hard jerk.

Wheeler tumbled to the ground and Emmett shot back up the stairs. By the time he reached the back door, Wheeler was right on his heels and grabbed his shirttail before he could get inside.

"Okay! Okay! I quit! My leg's hurting. Now, ccc...cut it out!"

"You shoulda thought about that before you made me look like some kinda crazy."

"I'm sorry, are you alright?" Emmett asked as he tried to look remorseful.

"Yeah, but boyyy ..."

Emmett could hold it no longer. He burst into uncontrollable laughter as he ran into the house and dashed in the bathroom with Wheeler right behind.

Wheeler grabbed Emmett by the arm and pulled him back into the kitchen.

"Wheeler, no! Stop! Look boy, you're ggg...gonna get me in trouble!"

Wheeler grabbed a handful of flour.

"Wheeler, c'mon...!"

It was too late. Wheeler threw it right in his face.

"Now! You're a bigger biscuit!" Wheeler said as he pointed at his flour covered cousin and fell laughing into the chair.

"Dag Wheeler! Look what you did! Mama's gonna hit the roof! You know I'm already in trouble!" Emmett, said wiping the flour from his eyes. "Now you have to help me ccc...clean this up before she gets home!"

They crowded into the bathroom, washed the flour off of their faces and brushed their clothes off.

"Your legs really hurt?"

"Naw!" Emmett said as he wiped the white powder from the table and chairs. "I was just foolin' with you!"

Summer Vacation Don't Come Easy!

"Bo, you need to stop playin' like that!" Wheeler said as he grabbed the broom and began to sweep the flour into a pile. He had always been protective of his little cousin and worried about him being in pain.

"Do you really think she'll let you go down South with us, or have you even asked her about it again?"

"Heck, I don't know. You saw how she was yesterday and III...I didn't wanna take any chances, so I guess I'll just have to wait until she's in a better mood."

"Don't wait too long. You'd better come up with something pretty soon," Wheeler said, "or you just might find yourself in Nebraska!"

"That ain't fff...funny. I'm gonna come up with something. I ggg...got to!"

"Well, I gotta get back to the house and finish cleaning up my room," Wheeler said as he popped Emmett playfully on the head and walked towards the back door, "or Mama won't let me go either. Don't forget to save me some cake!"

"Oh yeah," Wheeler teased as he brushed a spot of flour from his jeans, "I think there's a chisel and sledgehammer in the basement. You're gonna need it!"

"Boy I don't know what you're talkin' about." Emmett said, pouring the batter into a floured cast iron skillet.

"BBB...Betty Crocker couldn't make it this good! And I betcha, Mama'll feel so good after she has a nice big chunk of this cake, that she'll let me go down to Uncle Moses', or maybe even drive me down there herself!"

"Yeah, either that or she'll wring your neck after she breaks a tooth on that brick," Wheeler called grabbing a donut from the breadbox.

"Don't worry. I'll save you a ppp...piece," Emmett said as he scratched a stick match and got on his knees to ignite the pilot light at the bottom of the oven.

"Okay! See you later, alligator!" Wheeler said as he waved and hurried out of the door.

"After while, crocodile!" Emmett called, sticking the flame into the oven.

Bonnie Blue

* * *

Soon, the sweet aroma of vanilla perfumed every corner of the apartment. Emmett was feeling quite proud of himself. He could hardly stand the suspense; constantly checking the timer as he cleaned the house. Twice he started to open the door to see how it was coming along and twice he changed his mind.

Finally, the timer rang. He dashed to the kitchen, threw the oven door open, and peered in. His heart sank.

Not only had the cake not risen, but it held a strange resemblance to a moon crater. He carefully removed the large skillet from the oven and placed it on the wooden block that sat in the middle of the table. Emmett sat staring, his face in his hands, trying to figure out where he went wrong.

Suddenly, he heard keys rattling in the hall. Mamie was home. He quickly shoved the cake back into the oven.

"Umm Emmett, something sure smells good!" She called as she closed the door. "I can smell it all through the hall!"

"Oh, hi Mama," Emmett said rushing into the living room to greet her. "Don't let your nose fff...fool you."

"Alright baby. What do you mean?"

"Well, I was ttt...trying to bake you a cake, but it didn't ccc...come out right."

"A cake, for me? That is so sweet!"

Mamie removed her pale blue hat and laid it with her purse on top of the upright Kimball piano that sat just inside of the archway which separates the living room from the dining room. She smiled and followed him back to the kitchen.

Emmett pulled the cake back out of the oven and placed the lopsided object on top of the stove.

Mamie's brow shot up. But then she smiled and said, "Well, Emmett, really...I mean...it smells really very good. Um, and you know, you can't always judge by how it looks."

Emmett eased down in the chair and moaned. "MMM...Mama, you know it's bad. I don't know www...what happened! I put everything in that I was supposed to!"

Summer Vacation Don't Come Easy!

Mamie took a knife from the drawer. "Let's see." She said holding the knife level on the cake, trying to push it down. The knife barely penetrated the edge. She tried sticking the point of the knife into the center of the concaved creation. It slid easily into the gooey middle.

"Well baby, you tried. That's the important thing."

"For whatever good it does," Emmett whined as he started out of the room.

"Now wait a minute. Let's figure out what happened. What'd you put in it?"

Emmett sighed, came back to the table and rambled off the makings of his catastrophe. When he got to the baking soda, Mamie winced.

"You used baking soda?"

"There wasn't any bbb...baking powder. They do the same thing, don't they?"

Mamie tried to suppress the smile that was coming across her lips because Emmett looked so disappointed, but her dimples

17

deepened. "No baby, they don't quite work the same. But that's all right. The thought was there."

"I'm sorry I made you mad yesterday." Emmett said. "I just www...wanted to make up for it."

"Well, you have to do what I tell you. Look Emmett, I tell you to do things for a reason. Not just to be mean. You're a young man and you have to be more responsible."

Emmett started to ask her about the trip, but thought he'd better not push; not yet anyway. Instead, he apologized again, gave her a peck on the cheek, and went out the back door to visit Wheeler.

* * *

Mamie finished preparing dinner and sat reading the evening paper when the doorbell rang. She leaned out the window and saw that it was her mother. She rushed down the front stairs.

"Mother! What are you doing out in this heat? You come right on in here and sit by this fan," Mamie said as she led her mother back into the kitchen. "I don't know what I'm going do with you!"

Bonnie Blue

"What do you have cold to drink? The heat isn't that bad, but the air is just so heavy. My God, I can hardly breathe." she said as she leaned against the kitchen table.

Mamie moved the large oscillating fan, which sat in the middle of the open back door, closer to her mother and quickly poured her a tall glass of cold lemonade. "Here Mother, drink this. Sit right here and I'll be right back."

She hurried into the bathroom, saturated a face towel with cold water, and called out, "What are you doing out in this heat anyway? You know your blood pressure! This can't be good for you!"

She rushed back into the kitchen and handed her mother the cool cloth.

"Thank you baby. This is exactly what I needed." She removed her glasses and slowly wiped the streams of sweat from her smooth vanilla skin.

18

"Girl, don't tell me that you had this oven on! It's as hot as blue blazes in here!"

"It was Emmett. He baked a cake for me. It was sweet, but the heat darn near knocked me over when I opened that door. You know how he is."

"That's my baby," Alma said beaming with pride. "Well where is it? I've got to at least take some home with me."

"Trust me Mother," Mamie said as she peered out the back door, "you really don't want to try this. And you haven't answered my question," Mamie said as she poured a glass of lemonade for herself.

"Well, I stopped by Willa Mae's on the way over here and my dear, I think you're in for a time." Alma turned the glass up, draining it. "Baby fill this again," she said as she handed the empty glass to Mamie.

"What do you mean?"

"Well, do you remember James, Cousin Earnestine's husband?"

"Yes. I think so," she said as she gave her mother a refill. "Wasn't he going back and forth to the hospital for something?"

"Well he was bedridden for almost a year. Poor soul! He had some kind of something or other they couldn't cure. You know

Summer Vacation Don't Come Easy!

baby, sometimes a soul just gets too tired to fight. He died last night."

"Oh Mother, I'm really sorry to hear that!"

"Well, Earnestine's been saying for the longest that he wanted to go back to Mississippi. It's a shame they couldn't get him down there in time. I believe that if he was able to get back home, his passing wouldn't have been so hard on him." She sighed heavily, staring at the ice cubes swirling lazily in the glass. "He was a good, God fearing man. It's a shame he had to suffer so, before the Lord called him to Glory." Alma said as she wiped tiny beads of perspiration from her nose and upper lip.

"I talked to Andrew last night. He said that he wouldn't be able to come up, but Mose is coming for the funeral."

"Oh boy," Mamie mumbled.

"I know! Where's my little shugga wugga now?"

"Next door," Mamie said. "Mother, you know he's been on me about letting him go down South with Wheeler and Curtis, but I just can't do it. A two week stay is entirely too long to be away from home by himself. I keep telling that boy that we're going to Omaha to see Viola and her kids. You know they haven't seen each other in a long time."

Alma sat back in her chair and crossed her arms as she listened to the ravings of her overly protective daughter.

"What are you looking at me like that for? You know it's the truth."

"Baby," Alma said as she rose and attempted to seek a breeze through the screen door. "Emmett is getting to be a big boy. Before you know it, he's going to be grown and on his own. I don't care how hard you try to keep him a baby, one day you're going to have to just let him go. Besides," she said as she turned to look her daughter squarely in the face, "I really don't see what the big to do is. He wants to spend some time with his cousins down there. You know they're going to take good care of him. And you know he'll have a good time. You just said yourself that Emmett hasn't seen Viola's children for a long while. They wouldn't know each other if they knocked each other over on the street."

"Mother, don't you start!"

Bonnie Blue

"All right, I won't say another word about it. But you're still wrong," she mumbled as she opened the refrigerator to retrieve the pitcher of lemonade. "You hold such tight reins on that boy that it almost takes an act of Congress to get permission for him to spend a weekend a few blocks from home, in Argo!"

Mamie decided to ignore her mother's remarks. They weren't going to change her mind anyway.

"When is Papa Mose coming?" Mamie asked, pulling a box of donuts from the flowered breadbox.

"Well, the funeral is in a couple of days and according to Andrew, Mose is on his way up here now. He'll be coming in tomorrow afternoon on the City of New Orleans. I'm driving Willa Mae downtown to the Illinois Central Station to pick him

20

up. I've got to tell you, that girl is so excited. I believe she said she hasn't seen her daddy for at least a year!"

* * *

While Mamie and Alma were inside talking, Wheeler and Emmett came outside and sat on the front stoop.

"Bo, if you keep chickenin' out, you won't be goin' nowhere."

"I told you," Emmett said as he picked a small pebble from the step and tossed it across the sidewalk, hitting a new sapling. "I'm tryin' to wait until she's in a better mood."

"Well you just keep right on waitin' and I'll be sendin' you a postcard."

The boys had been inside Wheeler's apartment shooting marbles, when Alma arrived and they didn't notice her large blue Buick right away. Suddenly, Emmett caught sight of it.

"Aw man! Grandma!" he yelled excitedly.

"Where?" Wheeler asked as he stood and looked around the street.

"She's parked right there!" Emmett pointed excitedly. "I bet she'll help me! She's the only one that can talk to Mama!"

"What makes you so sure? She hasn't said anything about it yet, has she?"

Emmett shot a glance over at him and said, "Wait here, I'll be right back."

Summer Vacation Don't Come Easy!

He ran around to the side of the building and up the back stairs. When he reached the back porch, he stopped, tucked in his shirt-tail, which was hanging half way out of his crisp creased jeans, and walked calmly through the back door.

"There's my baby! Come give Grandmama some sugar!"

Emmett felt he was too big for this sort of carrying on. But he adored his grandmother and since none of the guys were around, he felt comfortable giving her a tight hug and kiss on the cheek. She'd always been very loving towards him and rarely denied him anything. He hated to ask for her help with this but, he could see no other way.

"Emmett, go get washed up. Dinner's ready," Mamie said as she took the Blue Willow dinnerware from the cabinet.

21

Emmett kept the bathroom door opened as he washed his hands.

"Mother, you're staying for dinner, aren't you?" Mamie asked as she set the table for three.

"Baby, you know how much I love your liver and onions," she said pinching off a piece of liver to taste. "But I promised Willa Mae I'd help her get everything together for Moses' arrival tomorrow."

When Emmett heard this, he quickly rinsed his hands and whispered to himself, "Uncle Mose?! Aw naw! He's coming?"

"How long is he staying?" Mamie asked.

"Only a couple of days. Just until after the funeral I imagine. You know how he hates to be away from the house. Curtis started packing as soon as he heard his granddaddy was coming. It would be so nice if they could all go back with him," Alma said as she rose to go.

"Forget it Mother," Mamie mumbled, walking her mother out the front door.

Emmett waited until he heard them leave before he shot out of the bathroom and down the back stairs.

When he reached the yard, he called softly, "Wheeler! Wheeler! Back here!"

Bonnie Blue

Just at that moment, Mamie and Alma emerged from the vestibule.

"Hi Wheeler. How're you doing, sweetie?" Alma asked as she started down the steps.

"I'm fine Miss Alma," Wheeler replied as he stood to greet them.

"Is Hallie home?"

"Oh no ma'am, not yet. But she'll be home in a few minutes though. You want her to call you?"

"That's alright baby," She said checking her purse for her car keys, "I'll talk to her later on this evening and Mamie, I'll call you after I find out more about the arrangements."

"Mother, please try to stay out of this heat as much as you can and make sure all the windows are rolled down."

Alma waved over her shoulder. "I'm fine baby. You worry way too much. You just think about what I said!"

"There's nothing else to think about."

Mamie turned sharply and rushed back up the stairs to her apartment.

As Alma walked to her car, Emmett whispered again, louder.

Wheeler leaned back, looked down the gangway and saw Emmett waving wildly.

"Boy, what's the matter with you?" Wheeler asked when he finally walked back to where Emmett was standing.

"Did yyy...you know Uncle MMM...Mose is comin' to town ttt...tomorrow?" Emmett whispered excitedly.

"Naw boy, he ain't comin' up here! Uncle Andrew's coming to get us. We're takin' the train back down there with him, remember? And what're you whisperin' for?"

"WWW...Will you listen to me?" Emmett said firmly. "I'm ttt...tellin' you, Uncle Mose is ggg...gonna be here tomorrow!"

"Well, if you're right, you better start workin' on your Mama!"

Summer Vacation Don't Come Easy!

Their conversation was interrupted by Mamie, who was leaning over the banister. "Emmett, I thought I told you to get ready for dinner!"

"I was jjj...just on my way back up Mama!"

"Wheeler, have you had your dinner yet? You're more than welcome to join us."

"No thank you. Mama said she was gonna stop and pick up some 'Chicken in the Box'."

"Boy, I need to go over yyy...your house for dinner," Emmett said as he placed his arm around Wheeler's shoulders.

Mamie laughed and said, "Mr. Till, get yourself up here. Your liver awaits."

23

"Liver?"

Turning to Wheeler, Mamie said, "Tell Hallie to call me when she gets in. Emmett Louis Till! Up these stairs...*now!*"

When Mamie disappeared and he heard the screen door close, Emmett turned back to Wheeler. "Well, you heard. I better go, but I'll be over after I finish eatin'."

"Okay! See you later alligator!"

"After while, ccc...crocodile!"

For the remainder of the afternoon, Emmett didn't bring the subject up at all.

* * *

Later that evening, Emmett sat on Wheeler's back porch, waiting for him to come back outside. He watched the large orange sun descend behind the jagged skyline of Chicago's South Side.

A light cool breeze moved in to replace the day's sea of wavy heat; relaxing him further as it caressed his damp skin.

"Man, is it hot in there!" Wheeler said as he sat down on the step next to him.

Emmett remained silent, looking out over the rooftops.

"Bobo, you know your Mama's gonna let you go. You just gotta ask her again."

Emmett looked slowly over at him. "We're talkin' about my MMM...Mama, remember? You know when she makes up her mind, that's it. NNN...Nothin's gonna change it."

Bonnie Blue

"I thought you were gonna have Miss Alma talk to her for you."

"I was, but I didn't get a chance yet. BBB...Besides, I wanna talk to her without Mama bein' there. Now she's out in Argo, at Aunt Willa Mae's."

They sat silently looking out at the sunset, ignoring the ambulance siren squealing down 63rd street, when the telephone rang out from his open door. Wheeler started to get up, but then he heard his mother answer it. He sat back down on the step and looked over at Emmett, who continued to hold his head in his hands. They paid little attention to the conversation which drifted out to the porch until Wheeler noticed she was talking about him.

"Listen," he whispered as he nudged Emmett.

They slid up on the top step to hear better. They were sure from snatches of conversation that Wheeler and Curtis would be leaving for Mississippi with Mose the morning after the funeral.

They listened intensely as the conversation became more detailed.

A new surge of urgency washed over Emmett. He ran down the stairs and over to his house.

Mamie sat relaxing in the living room talking on the telephone when Emmett burst through the back door and ran into the living room.

"MMM...Mama! PPP...Please! You gotta let me go!" he pleaded.

Aggravated, Mamie held her hand over the receiver and whispered, "Emmett, what's the matter with you little boy? Don't you see I'm on the phone? Now you just wait until I get off!"

He dragged himself into his bedroom and plopped down on the bed. "She's nnn...never gonna let me go," he mumbled to himself.

When Mamie placed the receiver back in its cradle, she called for him. "Emmett, come in here for a moment please!"

His legs were aching, so he limped slowly with his hands dug deep in his blue jean pockets.

Summer Vacation Don't Come Easy!

"Ma'am?" he answered dryly as he appeared in the doorway.

"Okay little boy. Exactly when and where did you lose your mind? You know better than to interrupt me when I'm on the phone unless it's important."

"I kkk...know. I'm sorry, but WWW...Wheeler and Curtis are gonna be leavin' soon. Mama, ppp...please, can't I go too?"

"No!" she said as she rose from the couch. "I told you, you're not going all the way to Mississippi by yourself. You're not old enough. Now the subject is closed."

Emmett followed close behind as she walked out of the room.

"BBB...But, MMM...Mama..."

"I told you no! Now that's it! I don't want to hear another word about it!"

Frustrated, Emmett took a deep breath and blew a long whistle to clear his stuttering. He wanted to be flawless and remind her that he was no longer a little baby. He wanted to point out that he would hardly be alone, not with five cousins and a great-uncle and great-aunt with him. But he thought better of it and went to his room and moped for the rest of the evening.

* * *

The next morning, when Wheeler came over, Emmett wasn't his usual playful self.

When they arrived at the schoolyard, his friends were already choosing teams. Emmett wandered over to an empty bench and sat alone staring down at the groove he was digging in the dirt with his favorite Red Ball Jets, sneakers.

"C'mon Bo! Are ya gonna play or what?!"

"Leave him alone," Wheeler said defensively.

"What's eatin' him?" Brucie asked as he joined Wheeler.

"Nothin'. He just don't feel like playin' is all."

No one said anything else to Emmett as they completed selecting sides. He watched the game without enthusiasm and soon wandered home.

Bonnie Blue

Emmett ignored the dull pain in his legs as he came through the back gate, dragged up the stairs, and sat on his back porch, angry and disheartened. "It's just not fair," he mumbled.

Mike had been wandering around the neighborhood and finally made his way back home. Emmett looked through the banister and saw the puppy scratching up the dirt in Mamie's flower garden.

"Mike! Get away from there! Mama's ggg...gonna kill me if you mess up her fff...flowers!"

26

The puppy looked up at him, barked, and trampled deeper into the colorful jungle.

Emmett whistled for him. "Here Mike! C'mon boy! I got a nice bone for you! CCC...C'mon Mike! Here it is! It's yummy yummy!"

Mike's head popped up in the middle of the mums patch. He scampered up the stairs to Emmett, jumped in his lap, and licked his face.

"GGG...Go on, you ol' ddd...dumb dog," Emmett said as he pushed him aside.

But the more Emmett pushed him away, the faster the puppy would jump back on his lap. Frustrated, he got up and marched into the house. Mike slipped past the screen door behind him.

Emmett went into his bedroom and stretched out across the bed. Mike hesitated in the doorway before walking timidly over to the bed. Emmett lay so still that the puppy wasn't sure what he should do. He crept around to the other side and sat between the chest of drawers and the bed, staring sadly up at Emmett.

"C'mon buddy," Emmett said as he patted the bed. "Even you ggg...get to go anywhere *you* want to."

Mike leaped up on the bed and curled up next to him. "What am I gonna do boy?" Emmett asked as he stroked Mike's head.

* * *

Alma and Willa Mae left the heat of the early afternoon sun and entered the coolness of the Illinois Central Station.

Summer Vacation Don't Come Easy!

A relic of the past, it stands conspicuously apart from the other structures in Chicago's downtown area. The massive limestone building stands majestically; covering an entire city block. Large, Roman like concrete pillars supported the huge canopy that loomed overhead, protecting the oversized solid oak doors.

Inside, red caps scurried to and fro across the gray marble floor; amid the mass of travelers and their friends and family. Among the latter were Willa Mae and Alma, seated on one of the many long wooden benches which garnish the huge waiting area.

As is often the case, the train was late. Finally, after nearly an hour and a half, a distorted voice boomed throughout the huge hall as the powerful steel locomotive rumbled its way down the iron tracks into the station.

"City of New Orleans! Now arriving on track 3!"

"Well, it's about time," Alma said as she stood and gathered her belongings. "Why they even bother with schedules is beyond me!"

Willa Mae looked up at her, shook her head and said, "Now Auntie, don't make no sense gittin' yuhseff worked up. They ain't nevah been on time."

"I know, but it's still frustrating all the same. Well, come along. We might as well go see if we can spot your daddy."

Red caps rushed to aid the sea of White passengers who emerged first from the 'Whites Only' section of the train. Moments later, Negroes, many with tattered luggage, most with remnants of fried chicken in grease stained brown paper bags, disembarked from the rear passenger car of the train.

Mose was one of the first to step off the Jim Crow section of the train. Even at the age of sixty-five, his lean five-foot, nine inch black frame stood perfectly erect, giving the appearance of a much taller man. Draped in his best Sunday go-to-preachin' suit,

Bonnie Blue

which showed signs of wear over the long train ride, he retained the look of a dignified country preacher.

Mose stood with his single suitcase, scanning the faces of those that came to greet fellow travelers. Suddenly, he saw Alma and his daughter making their way through the bustling crowd. He waved and began to weave his way towards them.

"Theah he is!" Willa Mae shouted as she waved wildly.

"Where?" Alma asked, straining to see around the rushing waves of bodies. "Never mind, I see him. Just keep walking. I'm right behind you."

Willa Mae skillfully dodged the oncoming travelers rushing towards her. When she reached her father, she embraced him tightly and kissed him on the cheek.

"Oh, Papa! It's so good tuh see yuh! How's Mama an' the boys?"

"Fine, fine. Evahbody workin' hard is all. Ain't gittin' no easier. 'Specially since White folks dun got all riled 'bout..."

"Mose Wright!" Alma said as she stood smiling with her hands on her ample hips. "If you don't hush up and come over here and give me a hug...!"

"Alma, how yuh been gurl? Nevah mind. Ain't no need in askin'!" He laughed and embraced her. "Yuh look jist fine!"

"Well, I don't know about that, but just look at you! God's sure been good to you."

"Yes ma'am, we all been blessed. Whut 'bout the youngins? Ah kain't wait tuh see 'em!"

Willa Mae took his arm as they walked towards the exit.

"Oh Papa, Curtis is so excited. He ain't lemme have uh minutes rest. Yuh know he's had them bags packed fuh ovah uh week!"

"Wheeler's all set to go," Alma said. "And I know Emmett wants to go along too. But you know Mamie. She's planning to take him out to Omaha with her."

"Oh, that should be nice. Goin' up tuh see Ward's gurl, Ah 'spect. Them two was thick as thieves comin' up. If yuh sent Mamie, then it was fuh sho that gurl was right close b'hind! Ah ain't seent Ward mahseff since when, 1947 or maybe '48' fuh sho," Mose laughed as they entered the hot streets of Chicago.

Summer Vacation Don't Come Easy!

* * *

Mose Wright was the patriarch of the family and it had been a great many years since the last time that he came to Chicago.

During his short visit, Mose stayed with his daughter and her family in Argo. The house quickly filled with relatives and layers of delicious scents. Cakes and pies, peach cobbler, and

29

candied sweet potatoes, pots of turnip and mustard greens, baked ham, potato salad and fried chicken, garnished every corner of the dining room table and eye on the kitchen stove. Uncle Moses' visit was a holiday for the entire family, even under such unfortunate circumstances.

* * *

For a brief time, Emmett felt that he had enough support to ensure his vacation south. But, even with the persuasive arguments of cousins, friends and other members of the family, Mamie refused to reconsider. Mose respected her decision and requested that everyone else do the same.

* * *

The day before Mose was to leave for Mississippi, Emmett spent most of his time alone, lying quietly in his bedroom. He wanted to be on that train so bad that it hurt.

Emmett knew that Wheeler hadn't returned from shopping with his mother, but he decided to wait on the front stoop for his best friend or inspiration, whichever crossed his path first.

He played over and over in his mind what it would be like, traveling alone with just the guys. Eating whatever you wanted. Talking guy talk and doing guy stuff. Emmett didn't know what guy stuff was, but he knew that it wasn't your mother telling you to tuck in your shirt and wash your hands or worse yet, giving you that *look* to stop doing whatever it was that you were doing. And then there was the rest of the summer; a time that seems much longer if you had to spend it with people you didn't know, in a place that you've only seen on a map.

* * *

Gene Mobley, a family friend and Emmett's barber, came to visit later that afternoon. He had been attracted to Mamie for a

Bonnie Blue

long while and had attempted to express his feeling for her many times, but she always changed the subject before he could clearly state his intentions.

After being married twice; widowed once and divorced once, she really didn't want to chance another heartbreak. She was happy with the relationship as it was; comfortable. Gene didn't understand what she was doing or why, but he didn't want to scare her off and was content with just being a friend.

Mamie had called him the night before and they talked for over an hour about Emmett and her resolve to keep her vacation plans. Gene had found that there was no way to change Mamie's mind, once it was made up. He knew that she wanted him to agree with her unconditionally, and so he said, 'Yes', you're right' and 'I know what you mean,' in the appropriate places. But he also felt the young boy's pain.

* * *

When Gene turned his large black Chevy around the corner, he saw Emmett sitting alone on the stoop. He had an idea, and drove past the house without acknowledging him.

Mamie had just returned home after completing her last day of work before her vacation. She was changing out of her shirtwaist dress, when the doorbell rang.

"Emmett, get the door!" Mamie called out from her bedroom. "Emmett!" She didn't hear him stirring. "Little boy, did you hear me!" She poked her head out of her door. There were no sounds other than the doorbell ringing again.

She threw on her robe and rushed down the steps.

"Oh, hi Gene! I wasn't expecting you, but I'm glad you came by anyway."

He gave her a quick hug and whispered, "I went by the Woolworth Five & Dime, to pick up a little something for Emmett."

"Oh, I see," she said playfully, heading back up the stairs. "And what about me? Do I get a gift too?"

"Yes." he said, half-jokingly, "My undying love."

"Okay, I'll take that," she said as she closed the door behind him.

Summer Vacation Don't Come Easy!

"Where's the little man?"

"Gene, I just don't know what to do with him. When I got home, he was just sitting outside by himself. I know he was waiting for Wheeler to come home."

"I didn't see him out there. Where's he now?" Gene asked as he walked through the living room towards the kitchen.

31

"In his room, with his comic books I'm sure."

"Let me talk to him alone," Gene said, stopping just outside of Emmett's closed bedroom door.

"Well, good luck," she said as she waved her hand and returned to her bedroom to finish changing her clothes.

Gene knocked softly on Emmett's bedroom door as he slowly pushed it open.

"Hey Emmett. What's goin' on man?"

Emmett's attention didn't waiver from his Superman comic book that he was merely thumbing through.

Gene cleared his throat loudly, leaned against the door way and asked, "Am I interrupting anything? Because if I am, I'll catch you later."

Emmett looked up and saw Gene standing there with his brimmed hat cocked slightly to the side, smiling his warm 'I know what you're goin' through, little man' smile.

Emmett liked Gene a lot. He was the coolest man that he knew.

"I picked up something for you that I think you'll like."

Emmett jumped from his bed just in time to catch the package as Gene tossed it to him. He smiled as he ripped the wrapping from the small box.

"Oh boy! This is just what I been www...wantin'," Emmett said as he excitedly opened the clear plastic box containing the leather wallet. He just knew that a train ticket had been tucked into the bill holder as a surprise. He searched every compartment but only came up with the picture of a White woman in the photo album section that came with all new men's wallets.

He politely thanked Gene and put it in his chest of drawers.

Bonnie Blue

Gene was a little surprised and asked, "What's the matter? You don't like it?"

Emmett nodded his head. "Yes, I like it. Thank you." he said walking slowly back to his bed.

"Look Emmett, I know you're disappointed man, but everything will work out alright. You can come down and help me at the barbershop! You'll have a few bucks to put in your new wallet and we can take in a Negro League game! Maybe we can catch Sam Jones pitching another no hitter! What'd you think?"

Emmett looked quietly up at him, attempted a small smile, and said, "It's okay. I'm alright."

Gene nodded and left his room.

"Mamie!" he called through her closed bedroom door, "I've got to get back to the shop. I've got appointments lined up back to back and you know how Booker gets when I'm not around. He'll fool around and try givin' one of those Cats a conk and take all their hair out! Then they'll be ready to kill him!"

Mamie opened the door, wearing the yellow flowered house dress that he'd given her for Christmas.

He smiled as he looked down at her. She didn't look like the 33 year-old woman that she actually was. She looked more like a young girl with dimples set deep in her round cheeks.

"You can't stay for dinner? It won't take that long. You really don't need to be living off that greasy stuff at that little nasty restaurant."

He wanted to hold her, but instead gave her a quick kiss on the cheek.

"Girl, you're a mess." he laughed as he walked through the living room to the front door. "If you think about it, there's no difference between fried chicken, mashed potatoes and gravy and 'chicken in the box' with fries and hot sauce."

He looked down at her, smiled and cocked the brim of his hat down further. "Emmett's in bad shape now, but he'll be alright in a day or two. Just leave him alone and let him get it out of his system."

Summer Vacation Don't Come Easy!

"Mamie," he said as started down the front stairs, "I know you don't want to hear it, but he's not a little boy anymore. He just turned 14 last month. He's a teenager now."

Mamie walked him down the front steps to the vestibule.

"Gene, I just don't know what to do! I know he's growing up," she said, wringing her hands. "And maybe I'm making too much of this, and maybe I am being unfair. I mean, Hallie's letting Wheeler go and Willa Mae lets Curtis go all the time, but Emmett isn't familiar with the South. I trust my family, but with Emmett's condition. And besides, you know how crazy some of those White people are down there. They just as soon beat you as say hello, if you do or say anything they think is out of line. But then again, I know that Emmett is a good boy and minds his manners. And I know if there are any bullies down there that want to pick on my baby, he's got enough cousin's to protect him. And I know that Elizabeth doesn't allow the boys to mingle with girls outside the family. He's almost at that age, you know."

Gene nodded and opened his mouth to comment but Mamie continued. "He's actually already had a 'near' date with one little girl from school. I mean, I dropped them off at the show and picked them up. Of course, he offered to pay her way, but she had her own money. And then he also..."

Gene stepped in front of her pacing path, held her shoulders and looked into her large brown eyes.

"Mamie, this is your decision. I wish I could stay and help you, but it's totally up to you. Besides, I gotta get down to the shop. I'll call you later. Are you going to be okay?"

"I'm fine and Emmett's going to be alright. You just go on!"

She gave Gene a quick hug and watched as he hurried down the steps to his car.

Mamie looked up the stairs and sighed before climbing slowly back to her apartment.

* * *

Later that evening, Mamie and Emmett sat at the kitchen table, silently picking through dinner. It seemed that the yellow daisy clock, which hung over the stove, had the volume of a

Bonnie Blue

grandfather clock with seconds, resonating throughout the apartment.

34

Mamie sat perfectly still, subconsciously, tapping her fork on her patty of hot water cornbread, staring at her baby and best friend. He had never been away from her for so long. She already felt the burn in her heart from the decision that was stubbornly invading her mind. All of her motherly instincts said, as they had since Emmett's birth, 'keep your baby with you'. But then, as she watched him sitting across the table, pushing black-eyed peas from one side of the plate to the other, she reluctantly accepted that he was no longer a baby in need of pampering.

Without his father to guide him into manhood, Mamie did her best to raise him to be an independent and strong young man. He would one day be a man, making his own decisions. This would be a big step towards that independence. And as painful as it was for her, she had to succumb to her own growing pangs. She had to let go.

"Alright Emmett. What is it? Are you just not hungry, or did I flunk out on your dinner?"

"Huh?" Emmett asked as he looked up from his plate. "Aw, no ma'am. It's good," he said, scooping some peas up into his spoon.

"Well that's good," Mamie said as she rose from the table and poured another glass of grape Kool-Aid. "I would hate for you to be on that train all day tomorrow with a nasty taste in your mouth."

She hesitated. "I really doubt that I'll have time to fix a large breakfast in the morning. I mean, between making sure that you have everything you'll need and frying chicken for you to eat on the train, a quick breakfast may be all that I'll have time to make."

Mamie braced herself for the explosion of excitement, but again, he remained silent.

Emmett propped his head in the palm of his hand and chewed at the few peas in his mouth.

A glimmer of hope flickered in her mind. He had changed his mind and was satisfied with staying at home! She turned back to face him.

Summer Vacation Don't Come Easy!

"Emmett! Get your elbows off that table," she said as she sat back across from him.

Emmett remained lost in the clutter of his dinner.

Reluctantly, Mamie continued. "I don't think there's much that we need to do before you boys pull out, do you?"

"Huh?" Emmett looked up for the first time.

"'Huh?' Little boy, I hope you don't go down there with those manners. Folks'll think you were raised in a cave."

Emmett's eyes bulged. He jumped out of the chair, nearly knocking over the table.

Mamie grabbed at the glasses of Kool-Aid as they went crashing to the floor. Emmett caught the plates, but he was so excited that he couldn't hold onto them, and they joined the rest of the dinner that laid in a tangled mess on the floor.

"MMM...Mama! Are you fff...for real? You're really lll...letting me go?"

Mamie smiled as she handed him the yellow and white kitchen towel. "Not before you clean up this mess, mister."

He grabbed the towel and dropped it to the floor over the spilled drinks then grabbed his mother and hugged her tighter than he ever had before.

Mamie wiggled to loosen his grip. At five feet, six-inches tall, her baby was looming over her. She was suddenly aware that at some time between birth and now, her baby had become nearly as tall as a grown man.

"Emmett! Baby, please! I've got to be in one piece if I'm going to get you to that train!"

"Mama! You're the bbb...best Mama in the whole wide www...world!" Emmett said as he held her a little tighter and gave her another little squeeze. "I ppp...promise, I'll never ask for anything else for the rest of the summer! And I'll write every day! And I'll watch my mmm...manners, and I'll..."

"Baby, if you just let go, I'll be satisfied."

"Oh, III...I'm sorry," he said as he released her and gave her his biggest grin. "And MMM...Mama, don't www...worry about the kkk...kitchen," he said as he quickly kneeled down and began scooping the food on the floor, into a pile.

Bonnie Blue

36

Mamie knelt beside him and busied herself with the cleanup, all the while trying to hold back the burn of tears, which threatened to expose her true feelings.

"Slow it down baby. Remember what I told you. Take a deep breath and one long, low whistle."

Emmett looked over at his mother kneeling next to him, sopping grape Kool-Aid into her clean yellow and white towels. He thought he saw her eyes dampened. He sat up straight, took an exaggerated deep breath and blew out a low whistle.

"Mama, I'm sorry for how I've bbb...been acting," he said slowly and carefully.

"That's alright baby." She quickly wiped away a tear with the back of her hand. "Lord, it's hot. We've got to hurry and finish."

She smeared another tiny tear with the stream of sweat across her cheeks. "You need to start packing!"

"I'll clean it up Mama," Emmett said as he took the towel slowly from her hand.

She hesitated for a moment before returning to the sink to wash the dishes. She looked back at him and smiled to herself. At that time, he did indeed remind her of his father and her first love.

* * *

Mamie and Louis had met as teenagers in Argo; a suburb of Chicago. Louis was the most handsome boy that Mamie had seen. His 6 foot 3 inch muscular body was draped in smooth chocolate skin. His light brown eyes sparkled whenever he caught a glimpse of her and occasionally, she would catch herself with a grin stuck on her lips when the thought of his smile flashed through her mind.

Mamie wanted to spend the rest of her life with him. However, Alma had other plans for her only child. She was to attend Wilson Teachers College as soon as she graduated from high school. Alma had no intentions of allowing anyone or anything deter Mamie from her goal.

One blistery winter morning, Mamie lay curled up in her bed with her stuffed animals, clutching her favorite bear,

Summer Vacation Don't Come Easy!

Teddybear Linda. Trees held steady against the relentless winds which tossed the bare branches against her window. This would be the day that she would tell her mother. Mamie would be an adult soon and there was no need to wait. Yes, she and Louis could get married now. If her mother brought up the cost of a wedding she would simply tell her that they could get married at city hall. And if her mother flat out refused, they would elope.

Mamie had never defied her mother and she wasn't sure that she could do it now. But, she loved Louis and they wanted to be together. Yes…she could do this! And today would be the day!

Mamie squeezed Teddybear Linda and whispered to her, "Well, this is it." She looked over at the beautiful mountainous design crystalizing on the bottom of her window pane as the branches seemed to hit a little harder. The strong scent of coffee percolating on the stove seeped under her bedroom door. Mamie scooted further down in her nest, pulled the covers tightly over her head and whispered over and over again, "I can do this…I can do this." She waited a moment to muster up more nerve than she's ever had in her life and crept out from under the blanket.

Her mother had just put, 'Amazing Grace' by Mahalia Jackson, on the record player and immediately, Alma's own rich voice blended with the artist. Mamie knew that it wouldn't be long before her mother would come to her room to get her up for Sunday school.

Mamie reached over to her nightstand and gingerly held the picture that she and Louis had taken in front of her house; just before the beginning of the current school year.

"It's now or never." She said as she grabbed her robe and slid her tiny feet into her house slippers. Very soon, she would be eighteen, a grown woman, so she might as well start acting like it and stand up for herself.

"I can do this." She whispered again. "After all, this is my life and I'm old enough to make my own decisions."

The closer she got to the door, the larger it seemed to become. By the time she took the few steps to reach it, she felt more like Alice in Wonderland, falling through the hole after the rabbit, than a young woman declaring her independence.

She paused before cracking the door open and peering down the hall to see where her mother was. Alma wasn't in sight, but she could hear her humming in her bedroom. Mamie took a nervous deep breath and entered untraveled territory. Confrontation with her mother!

"Good morning Mother," she said as she walked quickly into her mother's bedroom and flopped down on her bed. "I've got something important to talk to you about."

"Well good morning to you too. Now hurry and get those curlers out you hair. I think you can throw those out. They're looking really greasy. You can make new ones when we get back this afternoon. It's probably easier to pin curl anyway." Alma said as she threw her bold floral house coat over her slip and raced to the kitchen.

"Mother!"

"Oh Lord, we've got to hurry! Baby, we only have time for a little oatmeal and toast! Did you hear me?"

"Yes Ma'am!" Mamie called after her. She began untying the homemade curlers made from strips of brown paper bags.

"I can do this." She mumbled softly as she followed Alma into the kitchen and continued to unwrap her hair.

"Mother I really do need to talk to you about something."

"Little girl you know better than to fool with your hair in the kitchen while I'm cooking! Look at the time! Go get washed!"

Mamie obeyed and called out over the running water, "Louis is going to meet us at church today! Isn't that great?"

Only the popping of oatmeal bubbling in the small pot drifted from the kitchen.

"I invited him back here for dinner! I hope that's alright! Mother?"

Summer Vacation Don't Come Easy!

Alma sat at the kitchen table and stared at the glass bottle of milk. "That Till boy." She mumbled. She was very uncomfortable with the amount of attention and time that her daughter spent with Louis. He was nice enough and came from a good, God fearing family. Actually, it really didn't matter who he was or where he came from, he was a distraction for her daughter and college.

"Mother, did you hear me? Louis is going to church with us and I invited him back here for Sunday dinner. You don't mind, do you?"

Alma didn't speak, but instead rose from her chair and set the table.

"Your record's gone off. I'll turn it over on the other side for you. Okay?"

Mamie rushed into the living room, turned the vinyl disc record on the flip side and gently placed the needle at the beginning. The crackling of the needle edging through the grooves of the record preceded the rich warm tones of another Mahalia Jackson gospel tune.

"Don't worry about cooking dinner," Mamie said as she went to the refrigerator where her mother stood. She kissed her mother on the cheek, moved her gently aside and looked into the ice box. "I've got that taken care of." She removed a frozen chicken, placed it in the sink, took a deep breath and held it for what seemed hours, before she spoke.

"Louis needs to get used to my cooking if we're going to get married." There! She said it. The words actually fell from her mouth! But now, she was afraid to turn and face her mother.

Alma whirled around with her arms crossed firmly over her bosom and stared at the back of her, now very silent, child.

"Mamie," she replied softly. "I think it's nice that Louis is coming to our church today and I don't mind him coming over for dinner. I think you know that I really like him. He's always been nice and nothing but respectful. But baby, it stops there. Do you understand me? What you really need to do is

40

stop seeing so much of him. Spring will be here before you know it and you'll be looking at college. You don't have the time to get caught up

Bonnie Blue

in a close friendship, much less marriage. What you need to do is…"

Mamie turned to face her mother. There were no surprises in what her she had said.

"Mother, Louis and I have already discussed it."

"Oh you have, have you?"

"Yes ma'am. Oh Mother, please hear me out!" She whined.

"Okay," Alma pulled a chair out from the table and sat, her arms again, crossed. "I'm listening. Now, what can you tell me?"

Suddenly, the doorbell chimed in the hall. Alma sat as stiff as stone and stare at her. Mamie was almost afraid to move. She had gotten this far and was absolutely sure that her mother wouldn't hear any more about it until after graduation if their conversation was interrupted at this point.

The bell chimed again.

"The door isn't going to answer itself."

Defeated, Mamie walked rapidly down the hall to the front door. She looked out the window and her heart felt as though it would stop. The tall snow-covered figure waved at her as she pulled the curtain back to see who it was.

"Oh my God! Louis!" she quickly opened the door, pulled him in and whispered, "What are you doing here? I was just talking to my mother about you and right now she's not too happy with you or me."

He flashed his silly grin and gave her a peck on the cheek.

"Let me talk to her," he said as he easily slid past her and made his way down the hall.

"Mamie, who's at the door?"

"Good morning Mrs. Spearman." Louis said as he entered the kitchen. "I hope you don't mind, but since I was going to be with you and Mamie at church, I thought maybe we

41

should just go together. My folks thought that it was too early, but I know that you all get started early. Oh, and my folks wanted me to say, hello and to thank you for the invitation."

Summer Vacation Don't Come Easy!

"Good morning Louis," Alma said as she looked past him to Mamie who seemed to be hiding. "Tell your parents it's our pleasure. Actually Louis, we were just having a talk that involved you and I think it only fair that you get your say in as well."

She got up. "Here, have my seat. Mamie, you sit over there."

"About me?" he said as he rubbed his hands together and slowly lowered himself into the red and white vinyl kitchen chair.

"It's nice and warm in here." He said flashing a nervous smile. "I didn't know it was going to be this cold today. Oh Mrs. Spearman, did I tell you that my folks send their best?"

"Yes baby, you did. And you make sure you tell them I said hello when you go home."

'Oh no!' Mamie thought, 'She's going to kick him out!' Mamie lowered her head and tried not to cry. Many people were intimidated by her mother's strong personality, but Louis sat firm with that charming smile plastered on his face.

"I've been wanting to talk to you about your church and minister for a while."

Once again, Alma firmly positioned her arms across her bosom. "Oh really? And what would like to talk about…exactly?"

Mamie quickly looked up at her mother and over to Louis. Her mother was wound up and he had no clue that she had even mentioned their plans to marry.

"Louis, Mother and I were just beginning to talk about our future; yours and mine."

Alma tilted her head and pierced his eyes with an unyielding stony stare. "Yes young man. Tell me about your future with my daughter."

42

Louis planned to have both sets of parents together before they discussed a wedding. They were both under age and would need their parents to sign. Mamie had only a few months before

Bonnie Blue

her 18th birthday, but he still had 2 years to go before he could sign for himself.

He glanced over at Mamie who was wiping a tear from her eyes. Gently, he pulled her hand from her face and whispered softly, "It'll be fine. Don't worry."

"No, I don't think it will be fine young man. It's a far, far cry from fine."

Alma lowered herself into the chair across from Louis. "Little girl, you don't need to be crying now. Save those tears for when you don't have any food to eat and no roof over your head. Then you can cry all you want."

"Mrs. Spearman, I plan to have money to take care of my family. I would never do anything to hurt her."

"What kind of job can you get to take care of a family? You know the babies come quick! You don't have a college education, and if Mamie marries anyone right now, she won't get a college education! Now where does that leave the both of you? Nowhere, that's where! Now look Louis, I don't have anything against you. But I only want the best for my daughter, and getting married isn't the best thing for her right now."

Alma hesitated for a moment then rose to finish dressing for church.

"With all due respect Mrs. Spearman, I am joining the Army in the spring and I will be able to have my allotment sent home to Mamie. I want her to follow her dreams and if college is one of them, then it's my job to make sure that she does it."

Louis stood, looked down at her and said, "As God is my witness, Mamie will never have to do without."

Alma admired his 'spunk' and it seemed that he had a plan. There was no doubt that he loved her daughter. She smiled up at him, patted him on the hand and said in as stern a voice as she could, "You may be big, but you're still a child. I

43

don't know what your folks have planned for you or if you have even told them anything about all this. But for Mamie, the plan is set. There will be no marriage."

Alma looked over at her daughter, who looked like she wanted to say something but thought better of it and lowered her

Summer Vacation Don't Come Easy!

head. "Now, if you'll excuse us, we have to finish dressing for church."

Louis returned a few days later with Army enlistment papers which included the forms that Mamie would have to complete as his wife.

Eventually, Alma surrendered to Louis' natural charm and determination: she gave her approval for their marriage. Mamie and Louis were married in the spring.

* * *

Later that night, while Emmett was going through his jewelry box, looking for cufflinks for his dress shirts, he came across his father's ring.

It was among Louis' personal effects that were sent to Mamie after he died during World War II. She was saving the ring to give to Emmett when he was big enough to wear it.

Emmett took the ring from the box and re-read the inscription that was deeply engraved into the silver metal, 'LT - May 5, 1943'.

He looked at his reflection in the mirror and turned his head from side to side, seeking the resemblance that his mother said he shared with his father.

Mamie kept the few pictures of her first love, safely in her photo album on the top shelf of the closet in her bedroom. Most of the images were too small or faded to make out features, but there were two photographs of his parents as teenagers that were very clear.

His father was very tall and handsome, and his mother, at only five-feet, one-inch tall, looked like a little girl standing next to him. Mamie would point out the traits and physical features that he shared with his father; his sense of humor, his light-brown

44

eyes, his ears, his smile and even his knees. How she figured that one, he wasn't sure, but it made him feel more connected to his father.

Emmett continued to look straight into the mirror, trying to find the image of his father in his own reflection. But all that he could see was his same old face.

Bonnie Blue

"Emmett!" Mamie called from the living room.

"Ma'am?"

"You'd better take your braces in case your legs start acting up!"

"Okay, Mama!"

"And don't go down there trying to do a whole lot and don't lift anything heavy!"

"Mama, don't worry. I'll take care of myself!"

He turned his attention back to the ring. Previously when he'd tried it on, he wrapped layers of tape around it to make it fit securely. Mamie made him put it away until he could wear it without the tape. But now, Emmett squeezed it tightly in his fist before sliding it easily on his finger.

"Hot dog!" he said as he hurried into the living room.

"Mama, look! It almost fits! Can I ttt...take it with me? I promise I won't lose it. I won't even take it off my finger. Mama ppp...please!"

"Emmett, that ring is still entirely too big for you."

He held his hand out to her so that she could see how it fit his finger.

"Well, it's still a little loose." She looked up at him as a sad smiled slid across her lips. "I guess you really aren't my little baby anymore. It seems like you sprang up overnight."

"Mama," he said as he grinned down at her, straightening his back and squaring his shoulders. He took a deep breath. He didn't whistle this time but spoke very carefully. "I'm fourteen years-old, and I've been taller than you since I www...was ten. Beside, you're just around me every day and didn't see it comin'."

"I get the picture," she said as she patted him playfully on the cheek.

"Does that mean you're gonna let me www...wear it?"

"Sure, okay. But you're going to have to wrap it with string or something so that it fits snug. Emmett, I'm warning you, if you lose..."

"Mama," Emmett said as he quickly pecked her on the cheek, "I'll never take it off. I'm taking my marbles too. And Mama don't be mad," he said as he ran back into his room to finish packing, "but I haven't seen Mike in a while."

Summer Vacation Don't Come Easy!

Emmett poked his head out of the door. "You don't think the dog ccc...catcher's got him do you? Boy, I hope he's alright."

Mamie sank back into the overstuffed flowered chair and propped her feet up on the small hassock. "I'm sure he's fine," Mamie sighed. Her thoughts weren't with the dog.

"Mama, have you seen my red ppp...plaid shirt? You know, the one you got when you and Grandmama went shoppin' up on 63rd last weekend. It ain't in here."

"It 'Ain't.' Are you sure it 'Ain't?'"

"It isn't."

"That's better. Look behind your pants hanging in the back of the closet!" she said lifting herself exhaustedly from the chair. "Never mind, I'll get it."

She went to his crowded closet, reached in and pulled the shirt from the pole. "You never look any further than your nose. I really bought this for school," she said as she draped it across his suitcase.

"Come over here and sit down," she said seriously. "I need to talk to you."

Emmett was afraid that she was going to change her mind again, and he started to remind her that he wouldn't be alone and it was only going to be for a couple of weeks. But before he got a chance to speak, Mamie began, "Look baby, I know how much this trip means to you and I'm not trying to be a wet blanket, but like you just pointed out, you're a big boy now. No, I take that back. You're a young man. You aren't just going to Mississippi. You're going to a whole new world; a new way of life."

Emmett listened intensely and nervously, waiting for her to give the final word that she had changed her mind and he couldn't go.

"There are so many White people down there that dislike Negros. Now I'm not saying that they're crazy about us up here, but there are just so many down there that would hurt you without any provocation at all."

Emmett sat staring at the floor, twisting the ring on his finger. "I gotta sss...stay home, right?"

Bonnie Blue

"No." She took his hand in hers, looked him in the eyes and said very sternly, "What I'm saying is, just be careful. Be very careful. Stay out of their way and avoid trouble at all cost. Remember to say "Yes sir" and "No sir.""

Mamie's tone changed. Anger rose in her voice, her hand locked tighter around his fingers.

"Don't look them in the eye! I mean for you to get down on your hands and knees if necessary to avoid trouble!"

"YYY...Yes ma'am," he replied quietly.

"I'm telling you Emmett, Mississippi is nothing like Argo or Chicago. Do you understand? Talk to me! It's very important that you realize that there is a great difference!"

Emmett was listening, but all of this was foreign to him, especially coming from his mother. What she was telling him to do was going against everything that she had taught him all of his life; about being a man and standing up for his principles. He wanted to question her, but because he knew that he was still on shaky ground as to whether or not he would actually catch that train in the morning, he didn't argue the point.

"Yes ma'am, I understand."

The train was scheduled to depart from the Illinois Central Station at 7:05 in the Chicago Loop.

Gene was at the house before dawn. Right before they left the house, Emmett remembered his new wallet and ran back to his bedroom to retrieve it from his drawer. Before he left his room, he grabbed the picture of his grandmother that he had

47

stuck in the frame of his dresser mirror and inserted it into the album section.

Time was rapidly slipping by and before long it was time to meet the others.

* * *

Mose, Wheeler and Curtis were already waiting on the platform when the Colored conductor, standing in the door of the Jim Crow section called, "We fixin' tuh pull outta heah! Ya'll folks bes' be boardin' if yuh goin'!"

Mose took one last glance down the platform to see if he could spot Emmett or Mamie. He didn't see them and assumed that they weren't coming and boarded the train.

Summer Vacation Don't Come Easy!

At that very moment, Emmett, Gene and Mamie rushed into the station. When they got near the entrance to the platform, they heard the rumble of the 'City of New Orleans' pulling out down the tracks. A redcap told them that the train would be stopping at the Stony Island Avenue Station, and if they hurried, they might catch it there.

They sped through the nearly deserted streets of Chicago's downtown area, and barely made it to the station in time. The train was loading the last of the passengers when they arrived.

Emmett quickly boarded the 'Colored' car, and found where the others were seated. The boys excitedly planned what they were going to do when they reached Mississippi.

BOOK TWO

MONEY MISSISSIPPI SURE AIN'T CHICAGO!

The strong fragrance of fresh percolating coffee drew Mose from his peaceful slumber. His eyes remain closed as the whimsical tones of the boys' snoring blended with the familiar concerto of crickets and birds drifting in from the predawn morning. For Mose, this was unwavering evidence that being a sharecropper didn't hinder him from being a very wealthy man.

His timeworn body would have appreciated a few more moments of relaxation. But the anticipation of taking his place of

49

reverence behind the pulpit drove him from his pillow. His membership isn't large, but they are loyal.

Moses' knees cracked as he stood erect beside the bed and slid his feet into his leather slippers. He held the small of his back as he bent to retrieve his denim overalls, which lay across the family's splintered cedar chest.

The sweet breath of baked teacakes, still lingered throughout the house as he made his way down the hall towards the dim light shining from the kitchen. He hoped that maybe there was just one left but with six hungry boys in the house, he doubted it.

Money Mississippi Sure Ain't Chicago!

Elizabeth's ample body fluttered between placing the large cast iron pot of water on the wood burning stove and jabbing another small log into the fire beneath.

"Mo'nin'," Mose said, flashing a hungry smile while surveying the kitchen for any sign of his coveted teacakes. The only thing that came close was a large ball of biscuit dough sitting at the end of the table, surrounded by specks of flour.

"Well good mo'nin' yuhseff," his wife said as she smiled and grabbed a handful of flour. "Ah sho ain't 'spect fuh yuh tuh be stirrin' yet. Ain't got nothin' ready. Wid them boys horsin' 'round 'til all hours of the night, it's uh wonda mah feet hit the flo' when they did!"

Her chunky vanilla hands dusted another light coating of flour over the mound of dough as she repeatedly folded and forced the heel of her hand into the light spongy dough.

"Breakfust be ready terectly. Yuh was ti'ed sho 'nuff. Sleepin' so hard, Ah had tuh keep nudgin' yuh jist tuh make sho yuh was still among the livin'."

Mose poured the steaming black coffee into his favorite old cup, sat at a clear space at the end of the table, and slowly slurped his brew with a spoon. He'd kept this chipped cup with its broken handle for so long that he couldn't even remember where it came from.

"Liz'bit," he said as he took one last look around the kitchen, "ain't yuh got no mo' of them teacakes hid 'round heah?"

Elizabeth looked down at him with a sympathetic smile. "Well," she said as she scraped the dough from between her fingers. "Ah do know mah boys."

She reached behind the holiday dishes at the top of the cupboard and carefully scooped a bundle of loosely wrapped wax paper from a bowl. "They jist like uh pack of hongry locus'," she said. "Eat evahthang in they way."

She placed his treasured teacakes on the table next to his coffee cup.

"This'll hold yuh fuh uh bit, but Ah'll make yuh some up fresh aft'a church," Elizabeth said as she began rolling the wooden rolling pin across the bread dough.

Bonnie Blue

Mose invited his favorite food into his mouth and cautiously sipped directly from the stemming cup. "Oooh, that's good," he said as he smacked his lips and reared back in his chair. "Kain't nobody come close tuh mah Miz Liz'bit's pot shakin'."

"Aw, gowan away from heah now." Elizabeth smiled as she sprinkled more flour on the flattened dough.

With the precision of an assembly line, she twisted the mouth of a Mason jar into the dough, forming perfectly circular biscuits. Her thick fingers quickly removed the newly formed pastry and placed them into the iron skillet, pressing each one lightly into place.

"Ah tells yuh God's own truth. It's good tuh go visit folk, but it's sho betta tuh be back home, in yuh own. Liz'bit, yuh wouldn't b'lieve whut all them folk got up theah." He took another careful slurp of coffee from his spoon. "They got big evahthang. Lawd knows it's betta tuh be in yuh own shack than somebody else's mansion. Right heah's big 'nough fuh me."

Being in the bosom of his family always soothe Moses' spirit. He could have very well sat at the kitchen table for hours, but as he glanced through the screen door he could see the first signs of sunrise weaving its way through the branches of the persimmon trees in his front yard.

51

"Ah bes' git on down tuh the church. Make sho evahthang's ready fuh service," Mose said as he shoved the last of his teacakes into his mouth. "Ain't God nor day gonna wait fuh me," he called back as he hurried down the hall to their bedroom.

* * *

The screen door bounced shut behind Mose as he stepped out onto the porch and into the beautiful call of a 'Bob White' quail cluster that nestle in the nearby underbrush.

The soft sweet mist of morning dew caressed his leathered ebony skin as he moved leisurely across the yard, pausing briefly to glance up at the fading night sky; dotted with tiny flicks of light.

Mose smiled and entered the unpainted shed to survey the condition of his tools. As he expected, everything was in its proper place. Anytime that he had to be away from his family, he would check to make sure that his sons had shown the proper respect to

Money Mississippi Sure Ain't Chicago!

the tools and home that nurtured the family.

Sweet Potato, the family's old sooner, followed lazily behind him, barely able to wag her drooping tail with what was left of excitement.

"C'mere gurl!" Mose called as he hurried across the yard and opened his car door. "Good tuh know yuh been takin' care of the family whilst Ah was away,"

Sweet Potato's age dimmed eyes looked up at her friend of many years. Mose sadly realized that she simply didn't have enough energy to climb into the car.

"That's alright gurl," Mose said as he cradled the dogs face in both of his hands. "Yuh jist hold down the fort. Ah'll be back terectly."

* * *

Mose drove slowly down the winding gravel road to his tiny whitewashed church in East Money. His eyes sparkled as the remaining night skies gave way to a magnificent mauve and powder blue horizon which landscaped the eastern sky.

"The Father sho do good work," he snickered lightly to himself. "Ah thank Ah'll tell 'Im so when Ah see 'Im."

52

The soft tapping of pebbles against the bottom of his car turned to light crackles as he rolled into the churchyard.

He had missed his Mississippi. A slight heaviness came to his heart as his eyes became misty. It was difficult for him to understand how anyone that spends all of their lives surrounded by the concrete of the big city could ever feel a real closeness to the Father.

Mose stepped from his car into a soothing symphony of gentle breezes and light fragrances tickling all of his senses. Here at home he felt an absolute kinship to all of God's creations, great and small.

He wasn't aware of how long he had actually stood gazing over the outstretched manicured rows of cotton, until he was distracted by the subtle crackling of gravel dancing beneath nearly bald tires.

Bonnie Blue

He turned and saw his close friend and church deacon, Jess Taylor, driving up behind him blowing his horn and calling out.

"Preacha! Hey! It sho is good tuh see yuh," Jess called excitedly as he jumped from the cab of his pickup truck.

"When'd yuh git back?" he asked in his husky voice as he grabbed Moses' hand and shook it heartily.

Smiling, Mose slapped him on the back and said, "Last evenin'! An' lemme tell yuh, it sho is good bein' home! Ah kain't tell yuh how good!"

"Well, whut yuh preachin' on dis mo'nin'?"

"Ah don't rightly know. Whutevah the good Lawd brangs tuh mind." After pausing for a moment, Mose walked up the two rickety wooden steps that led to his sanctuary.

"Yuh know, Ah was thankin' jist this mo'nin' 'bout folks up yonda in the city an' even some folk down heah. It seem tuh me, there're times when folk don't even know they bein' blessed! Ah thank it's 'bout time we all reflect on the plentiful blessin's that befalls us daily; blessin's seen an' 'specially them blessin's unseen. It look like tuh me, that the Lawd is doin' some of His bes' work when we ain't payin' no 'tention. Brother Taylor, Ah b'lieve that's whut Ah'll be preachin' on this mo'nin'."

Jess shook his head and gave a robust, "Amen!"

* * *

Back at the house, Elizabeth was putting the finishing touches on a large black cast iron pot of hominy grits while a skillet of red-eyed gravy simmered on the old wood burning stove.

Wheeler and his 16 year-old cousin, Kelvin were the first to be awakened by the heavy aroma of fried fatback, biscuits, and warm pear preserves, which rolled from the kitchen into the back rooms.

Wheeler's eyes remained shut as he whispered, "Kelvin, you awake?"

"Why ain't yuh open up yuh eyes tuh see?"

Wheeler parted his eyes ever so slightly and peered over at his cousin, who was propped up on his elbow grinning, looking Wheeler squarely in the face.

Money Mississippi Sure Ain't Chicago!

"Boy, you know you're goofy." Wheeler said as he threw the sheet over his head and turned away laughing.

"Hey, yuh wanna do somethin?" Kelvin whispered as he tugged at Wheeler's sheet.

The mischief in his cousin's voice sparked Wheeler's interest. "Oh boy!" he said as he threw the covers back.

Kelvin was already quietly creeping out of the bed towards the other side of the room, where the younger boys lay sleeping peacefully. Wheeler quickly caught up with him.

"What we gonna do?"

"Git that sock ovah theah!" Kelvin whispered.

They tiptoed over to the unsuspecting boys. Carefully, they held the dirt caked sock over Curtis, letting the sock barely touch the tip of his nose. He twitched his nose and rolled over. Wheeler and Kelvin covered their mouths to quiet giggles which threatened to escape their lips.

54

After composing themselves, they began their assault on Emmett. They lowered the sock just under his nose, careful not to let the fabric touch. The sour smell of the sock caused Emmett to sneeze, waking him from his sleep. Laughter exploded from the bedroom as the younger boys became aware of what had happened.

Elizabeth hurried down the hall to bring order to the tumbling group of young, somewhat smelly bodies, that rolled around on the floor.

She had allowed them to stay up much later than usual last night in honor of their visiting cousins. Now, they were obviously awake and ready to begin their day. She stood in the door for a short time smiling, waiting to see how long it would be before they noticed her. They didn't. And it wouldn't be long before Mose would return and they would have to leave for church.

"Ya'll git up offa that flo' like that! Actin' like yuh was raised in uh cave."

It took a moment before they realized she was there, and pulled themselves together.

Bonnie Blue

"Mama," Kelvin called as he stumbled to his feet, "Ah was jist gittin' ready tuh...."

"Boy, befo' uh lie as big as hell itself fall outta yuh mouf, ya'll jist c'mon in this kitchen, eat yuh breakfust an' start gittin' yuh chores dun! We ain't got no time fuh foolishness!"

* * *

After the boys finished eating, Wheeler and Curtis began their work in the cotton fields with Kelvin, while fourteen year-old Ollie and 10 year-old Alfie, slopped the hogs and fed the chickens. Elizabeth kept Emmett in the house to help her wash dishes in the large tin tub, sweep the wooden floors and spread homemade patchwork quilts over the beds.

Emmett worked quickly so that he could join the older boys in the cotton field. He planned to stash away a handful of cotton bolls to show his friends back home. But, by the time he made it outside, the other boys had come back from the field and were playing in the yard.

A cloud of dust, led by a 1946 black Chevy, moved down the tiny road and turned into the yard. It was Mose.

"Whut ya'll doin' out heah foolin' 'round? Ya'll bes' be gittin' ready fuh church!" he called as he got out of the car.

"Yes suh," they called back almost in unison.

The boys looked at each other and burst into a roar of laughter. Mose shook his head and went inside.

"Liz'bit, why ain't them boys in the house gittin' ready? Yuh know we gotta git outta heah befo' long. It ain't fittin' fuh the preacha an' his kin tuh be late fuh worship."

"They jist finishin' up they chores," Elizabeth said as she went to the door to call them into the house.

"Mose, we got plenty time. Yuh gotta stop gittin' so riled 'bout evah lil' thang. One of these days, yuh gonna drop dead from pure worrah."

"Plenty time ain't 'nough time when yuh ain't doin' whut yuh suppose tuh," Mose mumbled as he hurried down to their bedroom to get dressed.

Money Mississippi Sure Ain't Chicago!

Elizabeth stuck her head out the screen door and bellowed, "Kelvin, ya'll! C'mon in heah an' git dressed! We gotta git started now! Ya'll stop foolin' 'round out theah an' c'mon!"

Elizabeth followed Mose down to their bedroom and closed the door behind her.

Mose sat on the edge of the bed in his crinkled undershorts and sleeveless tee shirt holding one sock in his hand.

"Anythang the matt'a?" she asked quietly.

He sighed heavily and stared down at the fraying tassels on the small tattered rug which protected his bare feet from splinters in the floorboards.

"Mose?"

He looked up at her, smiled an unconvincing smile and slid a sock onto his waiting foot. "Ain't nothin'," he said lightly. He slid the other sock on and stood to retrieve his one good suit from the closet. "Jist been uh long week is all."

She looked at him and without saying another word, left the room.

Emmett came back into the house to unpack his Sunday suit. When he returned to the bedroom, he attempted to fluff up the flattened homemade pillows.

Elizabeth beamed when she looked in on him and said, "Ooh, it look right nice in heah. But ain't no need in tryin' tuh git no mo' puff in them old thangs. Yuh bes' be gittin' dressed now. We gonna be leavin' outta heah terectly, yuh hear?"

"Yes ma'am," Emmett said lightly as he quickly placed the pillows at the head of the bed. "I'm almost finished."

Turning to leave, Elizabeth called back to him, "Ah got wat'a heatin' on the stove so yuh boys kain git rid of yuh nightly dirt."

"C'mon when yuh ready!" She called back to him as she hurried down the hall.

It wasn't long before they were all suited up in their Sunday best and heading down the red clay road leading to Moses' little white church.

Bonnie Blue

* * *

By early afternoon, church was over and the Wrights were visiting Archie, Moses' older son from a previous marriage. He has twelve children in all. Curtis was to stay with his uncle Archie and his family for the remainder of his vacation.

Later that evening, clusters of bright stars lit the clear moonless sky. Mose and Elizabeth relaxed on the front porch, silently enjoying the light night breeze and gentle rustle of the persimmon trees.

"Ah'll prob'bly stay heah fuh the rest of mah days." Mose said as he looked thoughtfully over at his wife. "This heah is livin'. Workin' the earf an' bein' close tuh the Lawd."

* * *

57

Over the next two days, the boys fell into a regular routine. Wheeler picked cotton in the field with Mose, Ollie, and Kelvin, while Emmett did most of his work in the house and in the family garden, with Elizabeth and Alfie.

She expected him to put up a fuss since he wasn't out doing 'man's work' with the older boys, but he didn't complain.

For Emmett, housework in the country was an adventure. Pumping water from the well, heating it on the wood burning stove, scrubbing the bare floors and chopping wood was no problem for him. He always managed to finish quickly so that Mose would let him spend some time picking cotton in the field with Wheeler and the other boys.

Elizabeth was so impressed with Emmett's behavior that she wrote her sister, Alma, a letter to let her know how he was doing. She complemented her on how well behaved he was and how much he was willing to help out. She also assured her that she was keeping an eye on him to make sure that he didn't hurt himself.

* * *

Early the next afternoon Jess came by and picked Mose up for bible study. But before he left, he gave the boys their list of chores. Without being there to oversee things, he was sure that there would be more playing than working.

Money Mississippi Sure Ain't Chicago!

Elizabeth spent a good part of the afternoon in the house preparing a special dinner of Moses' favorites. Even though this summer's heat was exceptionally hot, she kept cut wood crackling in the oven. Mustard and turnip greens were already done and she made sure there was plenty salt pork and turnip bottoms in the pot. Fresh chow-chow was on the table; corn had been gathered, shucked, and in the pot, boiling; three chickens had been selected from the coop, killed, plucked, and fried to a beautiful brown and she had put four jugs of water with tea leaves in the sun for sun tea. Finally, she turned her face away to defend herself from the blast of heat, as she pulled the oven door open. Quickly, she removed the iron skillet of cornbread from the oven and shoved two top ground potato pies, into the open mouth of the oven.

Elizabeth wiped the sweat that dripped from her face with the rag that she kept in her apron pocket and rushed out to have the boys bring in 2 watermelons from her garden.

She stepped out from the screen door and called, "Kelvin! Ollie! Wheeler! Ya'll!"

Sweet Potato raised her head from her spot on the porch and sluggishly thumped out a greeting with her tail. When Elizabeth ignored her, the old dog unceremoniously lay her head back down on the gray planks and closed her eyes.

"Kelvin, Ollie, ya'll! C'mere, Ah say!" she hollered as she stepped down from the porch and walked around to the back of the house.

Tools were scattered on the ground, trash was burning in a pile unattended, and a swarm of huge horseflies all but covered the slop bucket for the hogs, which still sat full of old table scraps.

She stood, jaw dropped, when she saw Emmett, Kelvin and Wheeler disappearing up the gnarled, knotted branches of one of the older cottonwood trees with the other boys close behind.

"Wheeler, Kelvin, ya'll! Git up outta that tree right now! Ollie, Alfie, ya'll know betta than tuh be swangin' from them trees an' yuh got work tuh do! Don' let yuh Papa come back heah an' see this yard lookin' like the devil hadda fit in it! Ya'll know betta!"

Bonnie Blue

Elizabeth hurried out to the clothesline and began snatching clothespins from the two rows of clean sheet's that stretched between young cottonwood trees. "Alfie, git yuh lil' tail ovah heah an' take these thangs in the house! An' yuh betta not drag 'em eith'a! Ah ain't 'bout tuh warsh them clothes again!"

"Yes ma'am," Alfie said as he rushed to his mother's side. He looked back at his big brothers who, it seemed to him, were taking their sweet time at that tree. "Whut 'bout Kelvin an' them?" he asked as he gathered the linen in his arms.

"Yuh jist stop whinnin' an' do whut *you* suppose tuh do," she said as she swished her husband's church shirt around in the washtub of Argo Starch and flicked the water from her hand. Then, she grabbed the remaining linen and hurried back into the house.

Wheeler and Ollie quickly began picking up the hoes, axe, and rake that lay abandoned across the yard as Emmett and Kelvin climbed down to the last branch and jumped to the ground.

"Hey Bo," Kelvin called as he took an empty bucket to the water pump, "gowan ovah yonda an' git that slop pail! We kain slop the hogs an' git 'em fresh wat'a whilst they try an' gatha them chickens back in the coop befo' Papa gits back!"

Emmett looked over at the bucket swarming with flies. "You do it," he said as he ran and grabbed the clean water bucket. "I ain't touchin' that nasty thing! I'm ttt...tellin' you that right now!" Emmett said, rubbing his father's ring on his shirt. "Mama'll ring my neck if I ggg...get my daddy's ring all messed up. Besides, I ain't goin' near those hogs! I've seen how they go chhh...chargin' anybody with anything that looks or smells like food!"

"Bo, lemme see that rang," Kelvin said as he pulled at Emmett's hand. "That ain't nonna yuh Papa's rang. Yuh Papa been dead befo' yuh was born. Yuh ain't nevah even seent 'im."

"Boy, you don't know what you're talkin' about! I don't remember seeing him because I was little but, I did see him and he saw me before he died. That's enough," he said as he held up his ring clad finger. "See," he said, shoving it closer to his cousin's curious eye. "LT, that's my ddd...daddy! Louis Till." Emmett gloated as he stroked the ring with his thumb.

Money Mississippi Sure Ain't Chicago!

Kelvin surrendered the clean water pail and rushed to the slop pail. "Okay Bo," he said as he waved the swarm away and strained to pick up the heavy slop bucket with both hands. "Ah'ma let yuh git 'way wid it this time but, next time, yuh gonna do it!"

"Aw naw," Ollie laughed dragging the rake across a small patch of yard. "Bobo's scared of a little bacon ya'll!"

"All ya'll uh bunch of chickens an' ain't nonna yuh city slicka's worth yuh weigh in slop!" A voice called from behind the trees bordering the Wright's yard and the cottonfield.

The boys stopped and looked toward the matted footpath that cut through the tall wall of weeds to the fields.

"Who's that?" Emmett whispered to Kelvin.

"Grab that shooter ovah yonda," Kelvin called as he smiled, put down his bucket, and ran to retrieve one of the other slingshots near the tree that they were just climbing.

"Whoevah yuh is...yuh betta git ready! This heah chicken fixin' tuh fry ya'll up preacha brown. Show yuhseff or git tuh runnin'!" Kelvin called as he looked around the ground for a small rock or piece of bark.

No one appeared. The other boys crouched down low and ran toward the trees, which stood as lookouts to the pathway.

Suddenly, the screen door slammed and Alfie stomped down off of the porch. "Kelvin, Ollie, ya'll! Mama said yuh betta not be out heah playin'!"

Ollie ran back towards him. "Shuddup boy! Yuh tells too dawg gawn much!"

Alfie squint his eyes, stuck out his tongue and called back towards the house, "Mama, they ain't doin' they work! They out heah playin'!"

He ran up the stairs and called through the screen door to his mother who was in the kitchen checking on her pies. "Mama! They ain't doin' they work!"

When he didn't get a response, he opened the door. "Ah'm tellin'! Mama!" he yelled as he disappeared behind the screen door.

"Dag," Kelvin said as he loaded his slingshot and ran towards the path. "Oooh, that boy gits on mah natural nerve."

Bonnie Blue

They all converged on the path and quickly looked around, behind, and up the trees but saw no one.

Alfie held the screen door for Elizabeth as she appeared on the back steps, armed with a fly swatter.

"See Mama! They still playin'!"

"Hush up boy an, gowan back in the house. Yuh jist worrah 'bout foldin' them clothes."

"Yes ma'am," he mumbled with just a pinch of frustration as he headed back through the open door. He wanted to see them get popped with the swatter; instead he was rewarded with a pile of sheets and pillowcases to fold.

"Yuh say somethin' boy?"

"No ma'am!" he said as he quickly disappeared behind the screen door.

"Boy, don't yuh know," she called in to him, "Ah'll knock the livin' daylights outta yuh now, an' ask the Lawd tuh fuhgive me later!"

Elizabeth's attention returned to the boys playing in the trees and weeds. "Ya'll thank Ah'm playin' wid yuh?" she asked as she stepped down onto the yard. "Ain't no hogs gittin' slopped!" she yelled, pulling the hand mower from the middle of the yard. "Chickens runnin' all ovah the place! Ya'll ain't eatin' nor drinkin' 'til your chores is dun, an' Ah mean that! An' don't thank Ah ain't gonna let yuh Papa know how ya'll out heah showin' out!"

The boys looked back toward the house and saw their mother heading toward them.

Suddenly, nineteen year-old Adolphus Harper and his eighteen year-old sister, Liga Mae, ran around from the side of the house and plopped down on the step.

"Hey Antee," Adolphus laughed as he looked out at his cousins just seconds away from a swatting.

"Got 'em good this time," he laughed so hard, he fell off the step. "Whut ya'll lookin' fuh?" he called as he pointed a finger at them. "Ain't gonna find no hogs tuh slop out in them weeds!"

Money Mississippi Sure Ain't Chicago!

"That yuh out heah stirrin' up all this foolishness?" Elizabeth asked as she waved her fly swatter at him. "Ya'll need tuh git out theah an' help 'em."

Then she turned to the group that was running up to greet the new comers, shaking the swatter at them. "Ya'll hold on theah now! The day near gone an' this yard look worser than it did befo' yuh got started! Ah mean fuh ya'll tuh git this mess cleaned up, an' Ah mean right now!"

"Yes ma'am," they said as they scattered around the yard to complete their tasks.

Elizabeth knew that the fly swatter didn't even sting when it hit their legs, and so did the boys, but no one ever let on. They would holler and squeal like the angel of death, was dragging them down.

The truth was that they didn't want Elizabeth to tell Mose. They were really afraid of what he would do. Moses' bark was so harsh that nobody ever wanted to see what his bite would be like. He would work your fingers down to the white meat for sure.

"Ya'll gowan an' help 'em wid they chores, since yuh helpin' 'em git in trouble."

"Yes ma'am," Liga Mae called as she ran out towards her cousins. "C'mon Adolphus," she called as she picked up the rake that leaned against the side of the house. "Yuh ain't nobody special!"

Adolphus ignored his sister and followed his aunt inside. Although he had eaten before he left home, the combined aromas of his aunt's cooking drew him straight to her bowl of fried chicken while her back was turned to remove the pies from the oven.

"Adolphus, yuh know yuh ought not git them boys in trouble. They do uh good job of that all by theyseff."

"Aw Antee. Ah was jist messin' wid 'em." He shoved the chicken leg into his mouth and pulled out a nearly clean bone. "Truth is," he said as he wiped the grease from his mouth on the back of his arm and reached for another piece, "Ah come out heah tuh see if Ah kain take 'em out tuh town."

"Adolphus, befo' yuh go anoth'a furtha, Ah b'lieve Ah'ma hafta make yuh go back out theah an' catch me anoth'a chicken,"

Bonnie Blue

Elizabeth laughed as she placed the last top ground potato pie into the oven.

"Ah'm sorrah, but Ah jist kain't help mahseff! Yuh always make the bes' yardbird!" He bit down into another leg. "This heah the last one. Ah ain't gonna git no mo' Antee," he mumbled as he finished off the chicken leg. "When yuh comin' down tuh the house an' show Ma how tuh cook like this heah?"

"Yuh bes' git on away from heah." She laughed as she placed two of the pies on the table to cool.

She pulled out a chair, and for the first time since sunrise, sat and rested. "Now, whut yuh talkin' 'bout goin' tuh town this late up in the day. Kelvin an' them kain make it, but Ah don't know 'bout Emmett."

"Aw Antee," Adolphus said as he lifted the top from her pot of greens and inhaled deeply. "That boy ain't no baby. Ain't nothin' but 'bout three miles or so up the road."

"Boy, yuh uh mess. Git uh bowl an' stop sniffin' ovah mah food." She rose and handed him a bowl from the cupboard. "Ah b'lieve Ah put in quite 'nough meat tuh satisfy yuh Un'ka an' the boys. Ah don't need yuh droppin' nothin' in mah pot from yuh nose."

He flashed a wide grin at her as he scooped a large fork of greens into his bowl.

"Mmmm," he moaned as he slowly slid the fork from between his lips. "Antee, Ah kain eat them greens right down tuh the pot likka! Ah do b'lieve yuh do good tuh open yuh own café."

"Boy, git up outta mah kitchen befo' Ah make yuh go out back an' pick me some mo' dandylion greens fuh the pot," she said as she pulled the car keys from the wooden peg next to the door. "Ah guess yuh Un'ka won't mind yuh usin' the car. Ah 'spect Emmett's Mama don't allow 'im tuh do that kinda long walk."

Adolphus slurped the last mound of greens from his fork and reached for the keys.

"All they chores gotta be dun befo' ya'll go anywheah."

"Yes ma'am," he said as he clutched the keys in his fist. "We jist goin' tuh the gen'ral sto' fuh chips, gum, an' such. Ain't gonna be gone tuh long. Town'll be closed befo' long anyway."

Money Mississippi Sure Ain't Chicago!

"See that yuh ain't," Elizabeth called as he hurried out the door calling out to his cousins and waving the keys.

"If ya'll hurry up an' finish, we kain go tuh the sto' in town!"

* * *

Money is a tiny hamlet, carved in a clearing in the Mississippi Delta. The town is sandwiched between the snakelike Tallahatchie River, which runs approximately a mile behind the town, and railroad tracks where freight trains made frequent stops to receive their cargo of cotton. The largest structure in the town is the cotton ginning mill, which sits about a quarter mile down the road, just past a dense wooded area. The 'business district' is mostly composed of single story buildings which includes, Ben Roy's gas station, a tiny bank, a feed and hardware store, cafe and the general store, which was run by Roy and Carolyn Bryant.

The Bryant's are a struggling young White couple who reside in the living quarters at the rear of the red brick store. For the most part, their patrons are Black fieldhands, sharecroppers, and tenant farmers. Their meager earnings had lessened since the Federal Government began giving poverty stricken residents some of the foods they previously had to purchase. To make ends meet, twenty four year-old Roy Bryant did interstate deliveries for his brothers.

Roy was the youngest son of a combined family. The first set of children that his mother had was Milam children. The second set was Bryant. She had eleven children in all. Their family consists of four girls and seven boys. They are a close knit, hardworking family, with Mama Eula at the head. In keeping with the tradition of the Milam-Bryant men, Roy had joined the army when he was seventeen.

Carolyn, Roy's twenty two year-old wife, was fifteen when they met. Her mother died when she was a young girl. Her father owned a small farm on the outskirts of Indianola in the Mississippi Delta and could only afford a very few Colored men to work the cotton fields with him.

Bonnie Blue

65

One hot, sticky day, Roy came home on leave and went out to the farm to surprise Carolyn. When he arrived, he caught her flirting with one of the young Colored fieldhands. Roy flew into a violent rage, beating the teenager until he was nearly unconscious. Then he turned on Carolyn, smacking her to the ground.

Her father emerged from the barn with a bag of feed slung over his shoulder, and saw Carolyn sprawled on the ground. He threw the bag from his back, ran into the house, and came back out with his double barrel shotgun.

"Boy, Ah dun raised that gurl," he yelled. "An' Ah'm the only one gotta right tuh beat hur! Now yuh bes' lissen tuh me good, 'cuz Ah ain't repeatin' mahseff! If yuh evah set anoth'a hand on mah lil' gurl, it'll be yuh last act on God's green earf! Now git offa mah land!"

"But suh!" Roy exclaimed as he backed away towards his truck. "Didn't yuh see 'im? Didn't yuh see that niggah pawin' all ovah hur. Ah know yuh don't want no filthy niggah hands on yuh own daw'der!"

"Ah seent whut was goin' on! That one thar! He's uh good niggah! Know'd 'im all his life! Know'd his Pa too! He gotta right tuh be on mah land! He workin' fuh me! Now yuh heard me, boy! Ah said git offa mah land befo' they hafta come an' carry yuh ass off!"

"Ah'm sorrah Car'lyn!" Roy yelled as he stood with one leg in the open door of his truck. "Ah sweah! Ah didn't mean tuh hit yuh! As God is mah witness, Ah ain't nevah gonna touch yuh in uh unlovin' way! Fact is, Ah come out tuh ask yuh tuh marry up wit me! Please. Ah'm sorrah," he pleaded quietly. "It's jist...Ah love yuh so much Car'lyn. The thought of anoth'a man touchin' yuh, an' well, Ah jist kain't take it." He glared over at the teenager that still lay sprawled in the mud, afraid to move. "But uh niggah, sniffin' 'round yuh like uh damned dawg, jist lookin' tuh git put down!"

Even though she still sat on the ground where she landed, her face red and stinging from where he struck her, she looked over at her father and ran to Roy.

The following year, Roy was dischared and they were married.

* * *

With the help of his family, Roy and Carolyn moved out on their own and started their small business. Roy's family was molded in the tradition of the White South. Women were never left alone when the men were away.

Roy had been on the road, driving one of his brother's trucks, delivering shrimp from New Orleans to San Antonio and Brownsville Texas.

It was Juanita Milam's day to stay at the store with Carolyn.

Juanita parked in front of the store. As was always the case her husband, J.W. Milam, kept a .38 colt automatic under the front seat of their pickup truck.

Carolyn was alone in the store, rearranging the few staples on their nearly empty shelves, while Juanita was busy in the living quarters chasing their four toddlers around with a washrag; attempting to clean the dirt from their faces.

When Adolphus and the kids arrived, they saw some boys that they knew, already playing checkers on the faded checkerboard that was painted on the wooden porch floor of the store. He jokingly inched the car closer and closer to the elevated wooden walkway.

Liga Mae reared up from the back seat and yelled, "Boy, yuh must be stone outta yuh mind! Yuh kain act uh fool an' wreck Un'ka Mose car if yuh want tuh!"

"Aw gurl, jist shuddup an' git out the car," Adolphus said as he opened the door.

The neighborhood boys waved and ran over to the car as soon as they saw the new faces. It wasn't often that outsiders visited their little community.

Adolphus emerged with newfound authority. From the reaction of the locals, one would have thought that royalty had surely arrived in Money.

Johnny B. Washington, one of the largest Colored men in the area, worked at the cotton-ginning mill at the edge of town. He had the unconditional respect of many Colored folks in the area because he seemed to be on the inside of the White circle. The White population trusted him to give them accurate information on what was happening in the Colored arena.

The day had been long and he'd been at the mill since just before daybreak. Because of his size, Johnny B. had always been delegated the heaviest duties.

His dingy, sleeveless, tee shirt clung tightly to his bulging black chest, moving while he walked, as a second skin. Sweat glistened as it rolled unencumbered down his muscular arms.

"Hey Homma," he bellowed back to his co-worker, Homer Jackson. "goin' tuh da sto tuh git uh couple of sody pops! Yuh wan' somethin'?"

"Yeah! Brang me back some of dem grape sody pops an' some chewin' t'bacca!"

Johnny B. threw up his hand and started down the road towards the store.

Billie Smith, Alfie's ten year-old friend, and a couple of other area boys were flinging rocks and looking curiously out the corner of their eyes at the newcomers when Johnny B. caught their attention.

"Uh oh ya'll," Billie called as he ran to hide behind Adolphus. "Heah come Mista Johnny B.!"

"Hush up yuh mouf, boy," Liga Mae said, turning to see Johnny B. heading towards them.

"Wow! Who's that?" Wheeler asked, as he turned to see who Billie was referring to. "Man! That is one big greasy dude."

"Yeah! An' he's mean too! Ah heard mah Pa say he choked uh mule wid his bare hands," Billie said as he scooped up another handful or rocks to pitch at the large cottonwood tree across the road.

"Come on," Emmett said, watching the massive figure lumbering towards them. "I know you can't believe that. He mmm...may be big, but look at..."

Money Mississippi Sure Ain't Chicago!

Liga Mae hurried over to Emmett and grabbed his arm tightly, holding it down to his side to keep him from pointing. "Yuh betta hush up befo' he heah yuh. Then yuh find out fuh yuhseff whut he kain do."

They watched in silence as Johnny B. took long strides towards them. Checkers bounced chaotically around the board as he pounded up the two steps to the porch and entered the store.

"Mo'nin' Mz. Car'lyn. How ya'll?"

"Whut yuh needin'?" She asked as she pushed her damp hair from her sweaty forehead.

"Some snuff, Prince Alber' t'bacca, an' some cold dranks," he said as he reached over into the soft drink bin. "Is ya'll got any mo' dem grape sody pops? Ah really like dem."

She watched as his massive, coal black arms submerged further down past the large chunks of ice. "Ah b'lieve we got some out back, but they ain't got no chill on 'em. Yuh bes' jist git some of them cola's outta thar. Who's all them lil' niggahs out front thar? Some of 'em, Ah ain't nevah seent befo'. Yuh know whar they out from?"

"No ma'am, but Ah'll sho find out fuh yuh," He said as he loaded four bottles of soda pop on the counter.

"Naw. Don't matt'a," she said as she listed this purchase to his bill. "Jist thought yuh knew is all."

"Don't yuh worrah none Mz. Car'lyn. Ah'll keep uh watch on 'em so dey don't git in no devilment," he said as he took his purchase and headed out the door.

Emmett stood leaning against the doorway watching the player's reassemble their checkers and didn't immediately notice Johnny B. hovering over him.

"Boy, don't yuh see people tryin' tuh git pass," Adolphus said as he shoved Emmett out of the way.

"Say! What'd you think you're doin'? You don't just go knockin' people..."

Bonnie Blue

The stale odor of aged funk settled down around him. Emmett's face contorted into a frown. He turned around, looked straight up and saw Johnny B. standing with a mouth full of brown snuff leaking from the corners of his full black lips.

"I...uh...eee...excuse me sir." Emmett said, pulling himself together and all but falling over to get out of the big man's path.

"Who dis heah niggah 'long tuh? Ah knows he ain't from 'round heah no wheah!"

"That theah's mah cousin, Mista Johnny suh. He don't mean no harm. Jist come down tuh stay uh while wid us befo' school start back. He out from Ch'caga," Kelvin said with a hint of pride. "That one theah, he mah oth'a cousin. He's out from Ch'caga too."

"Shoulda knowd," he grunted. "Nawthn niggah's all act like dey own de damn worl'."

Johnny B. turned and looked down with disgust at Emmett. "Niggah, yuh bes' go right on back tuh yuh big city 'til yuh Mama learnt yuh some mannas."

He pounded down the steps and shot a stream of brown juice from his mouth, before making his way back down to the mill.

Billie stuck his tongue in his lower lip, pretending to have it full of snuff, swung Emmett around and mocked him in as deep a tone as his young voice could get. "Niggah! Git yuh some manna's. Ain't yuh mammy learnt yuh nothin' yet?"

They burst into laughter.

Liga Mae smacked Adolphus on the back of the head. "Yuh's the oldest an' heah yuh is actin' uh bigga fool than they is. Ya'll betta leave that man alone. Yuh know dawg-gawn well, he be dun whupped the livin' daylights outta yuh. An' Lawd knows all ya'll be deservin' of it too!"

"Look, yuh ol' no account gal," Adolphus said as he pushed her out of his way, "why don't yuh stop tryin' tuh act like yuh somebody's Mama. He ain't heard nothin', ain't seent nothin' eith'a. An' yuh betta stop cussin' fuh Ah tell Ma!"

Money Mississippi Sure Ain't Chicago!

"Dag!" Emmett said as he sat on the step and watched Johnny B.'s thick, muscular arms sway, rocking his body from side to side. "That ggg...guy's as big as a tree. I don't know what his Mama fff...fed him when he was a baby, but we ain't got nothing that big up in Chicago."

"Ain't nobody dat stinky nowheah," giggled Billie.

"Yeah," Wheeler said as he positioned himself back on the porch floor to begin a new game of checkers, "I bet he could have knocked out that mule. Actually Bobo, he looked like he was ready to knock your block off too!"

"Heck," Adolphus said as he shoved Emmett in his arm, almost knocking him off balance, "all he had tuh do was raise his arm. The funk alone woulda knocked yuh out!"

"Ah dun told yuh," Liga Mae said as she stood over him with her hands on her hips.

"An' Ah dun told *you*!" Adolphus glared at her. "Yuh ain't nonna mah Mama! Now yuh kain jist shut yuhseff up befo' yuh end up walkin' home!"

Moses' sons remained silent. The one thing they knew for sure was that whatever Liga Mae saw with her eyes she would quickly let fall from her mouth into her Uncle Moses' ears. It had happened all too many times.

Billie was a different story all together. This was his chance to perform.

"Liga Mae gotta boyfriend," Billie taunted as he ran in front of her, shaking his rear end. "Ya'll bes' leave Mz. Johnna B.'s husban' 'lone." He teased as he once again pretended to have a lower lip full of snuff.

"Billie, yuh betta git yuh lil' b'hind outta mah face boy, befo' Ah tells 'em 'bout that lil' ol' pissy tail gal yuh call yuhself like'n ovah in Itta Bena, wid hur skinny, funny lookin' seff!"

Billie jumped off the porch and started chasing her. "Dat ain't nonna mah gurlfriend!" he yelled as she easily put more distance between them.

"Liga Mae!" Adolphus called as she ran laughing past him. "That boy ain't gonna be uh runt all his life. One of these days, that boy gonna catch yuh an' beat the livin' mess outta yuh! Billie, c'mere boy! All she want yuh tuh do is chase aft'a hur."

Bonnie Blue

Billie slowed to a trot and called after her, almost in tears. "Don't yuh worrah none 'bout who mah gurlfriend is. Ah ain't got no gurlfriend. Least it ain't big ol' stankin' Johnna B.!"

"Don't pay hur no mind," Adolphus said as he briskly rubbed across the small boy's curly hair.

Inside, the store was smoldering and business was slow, so Carolyn returned back to the living quarters, where Juanita was making sandwiches for the children.

"Willy," Juanita called to her four year-old son, "go see if them boys got that bread in they room."

"Lawd knows it's hot," Carolyn drawled as she pulled her thick black hair up off the nape of her neck.

"Looks tuh be rainin' befo' too long," Juanita said as she leaned back and looked into the children's bedroom to see if her toddler had found anything.

"How long they been lyin'? Ah b'lieve them science folks kain make it rain if they really needed it fuh theyseffs. Git rid of so mucha heat too, if they uh mind tuh."

"Willy, hurry up boy an' brang me whutevah yuh fount! Car'lyn, yuh need tuh stop them boys from sneakin' food an' hidin' it in that room. Ain't no wonder the cocka-roaches runnin' yuh out!"

Willy came out of the bedroom dragging a half empty bag of Wonder Bread that had been ripped opened in the middle with Harvey, his two year-old brother, following close behind.

Carolyn snatched the bag, spilling the remaining slices onto the floor and yelled, "Lil' Roy! Thomas Lamar! Ya'll git ovah heah right now! Ah'ma beat yuh!"

Three year-old Roy Jr., and his two year-old brother Thomas Lamar, appeared bashfully in the doorway.

"Git heah tuh me, Lil' Roy! Yuh old 'nough tuh know betta!" she yelled.

He walked slowly towards her, his thumb shoved firmly in his mouth. She grabbed him by the arm and shook him until his shrill screams pierced the air.

Money Mississippi Sure Ain't Chicago!

"Shuddup!" she screamed as she shook him harder. "Shuddup, Ah say! Ah dun told yuh ain't no thievin' in this house! Boy, Ah'ma beat the..."

Juanita pulled the toddler away from her. "Car'lyn, leave the boy alone. The chil'ren was prob'bly hongry. 'Side, boys always gonna git intuh somethin'. Gowan out front an' take uh pack of cigarettes. Roy ain't gonna be back fuh uh long while. Ah need tuh git somethin' in they stomachs 'til we git back tuh the house."

"Lil' Roy," she said to the baby who stood rocking himself and crying silently next to the stove, "Gowan ovah thar an' sit wit yuh brotha."

Carolyn was relieved that she didn't have to deal with her crying children and that her sister-in-law, allowed her to smoke a cigarette in secret. Roy forbade her to smoke. He'd slapped her around the last time he even smelled smoke on her clothes.

She rushed to pick out a pack of Lucky Strikes as she passed through the store.

"Evenin' Mz. Car'lyn, ma'am," the children chimed as she stepped out on the porch where the boys were playing checkers.

She paused momentarily, glanced suspiciously at the group of boys, then turned away and calmly lit her cigarette, blowing the smoke slowly between her thin pale lips. There was only a hint of a breeze, but it didn't matter to her. She leaned against the wooden pillar and deeply inhaled the white smoke.

A light breeze began to rattle the large leaves that covered the cottonwood trees across the road. She smiled ever so slightly as she felt the tensions of the day drain from her body. She allowed herself to be drawn into the tiny world of two baby gray squirrels as they chased each other around the large tree, zigzagging up and down the thick rugged trunk.

Johnny B. and Homer took a break and rested on the tailgate of a junked pickup truck; abandoned in the field next to the train tracks. The shadows from a cluster of trees stretched long across the

Bonnie Blue

road, protecting them from the late afternoon sun while they gulped down their cold bottles of soda pop.

"Damn!" Homer said, "She sho 'nuff is uh purty lil ol' thang."

"Niggah, yuh crazy! Br'ant'll beat hell outta yuh an' hur too if he heard how yuh talkin' 'bout his woman." Johnny B. tossed his bottle up to his open mouth, let it drain, and forced a tremendous belch from his stomach.

"Damn, dat was good!" he said as he looked down at the empty bottle and flung it into a pile of junk in the bed of the truck. He looked down towards the store then back at Homer.

"Ah know yuh ain't doin' nothin' but talkin' shit. But Ah'm tellin' yuh, let 'im eben thank yuh looked at dat woman. He go crazy on yuh ass!"

Johnny B. jumped off the back of the truck, reached for Homer's other soda pop, pried the cap off with his teeth and turned it up. Homer was irritated but said nothing.

"Yuh know whut dey say 'bout dem White boys," Johnny B. said as he laughed and took another swig from the bottle, "ain't got nothin' in dey drawzs but ass air! Dat's why he skeered uh niggah gonna come 'long an' git hur!"

Johnny B. sucked the last gulp from the bottle, belched and said as he nodded towards the store, "Wid dat one dere, Ah'm tellin' yuh, he crazy as hell! Coal black! Snow white! Don't make no diff'rence! Ah seent dat foo' beat dat po' woman so bad! Shit! One day, he musta gotta notion dat she kept hur eye on some Boy too long, 'cuz when Ah went in da sto', Ah seent hur mouf all blooded up! Ah started tuh help hur, but shit man...Ah leff outta dere real quick like! Whutn't 'bout tuh be standin' 'round dere fuh 'im tuh start in on me!"

Homer slapped his leg and doubled over laughing.

"Ah'm tellin' yuh whut Ah seent! Dat lil' woman ain't big as uh gnat's ass! She had tuh stay in da house 'til da swellin' went down at least tuh da size of uh mushmelon! Ah'm tellin' yuh, he had dat ol' crazy devil look in dem ol' evil eyes of his! Ah be damned if Ah was gonna dance wid *dat* devil!"

Money Mississippi Sure Ain't Chicago!

"He ain't got it all sho 'nuff. But ain't no way in da worl' dat wild man ever be crazy 'nough tuh raise uh hand at yuh, big as yuh black ass is!"

"Shit man, bullets don't give uh damn who yuh is nor how big yuh is. Yuh ass gonna hit da dirt fast as uh lil' niggah. Make no difference."

The boys played quietly until Carolyn went back inside and was out of sight.

"Ah be back," Johnny B. said as he finished off the last drop of soda. "Ah gotta keep uh eye on dem youngins. See whut dey up tuh."

"Yeah, dere's uh bunch of 'em sho 'nuff. Who all down dere anyway? Ah seent some of ol' Preacha's boys an' da lil' youngin' runnin' 'round. Ain't dat one of Big Teddy's boys?"

"Yeah, Ah b'lieve so," Johnny B. said as he hopped off the tailgate. "Ah bet dem two 'portant niggahs from up nawth full of big talk."

"Well don't find yuh home down theah! Bossman say we gotta git dat ol' blow fan outta de wall befo'..."

Homer's attention was immediately drawn towards the crackling of wide rubber tires rolling over new rocks. He jumped from the truck.

"Dere she be! Musta talked hur up sho 'nuff! Sho will be uh blessin' tuh have one dat work!" Homer laughed as he started across the road. "Ah be 'spectin' tuh look dead in da eyes of da devil hisself it be so damn hot in der!"

"Yuh is one dumb ass niggah. Dat new fan'll make it 'bout as cool as de ol' one. It ain't no blowin' in air fan. All it gonna do is..."

"Don't make me no difference," Homer said as he hobbled stiffly towards the side entrance of the mill. "Gotta be better'n whut we got now!"

* * *

Meanwhile, Adolphus, Wheeler and a couple of the older boys started bragging about their girlfriends; real and imagined.

Bonnie Blue

"Man, you ought to see my girl," Wheeler said as he put his arm around Adolphus's shoulders. "Built like a Coca-Cola bottle. And got that good hair! All the guys were trying to talk to her, but *you* know," he said as he ran his finger across his imaginary mustache.

"The guys always talkin' about how lucky I am to have a girl with a face that's fine enough to melt butter."

"Yeah," Emmett said as he picked up a twig from the ground. "Her legs are about ttt...this big! At home, they call her 'Bird-leg Betty'!"

Wheeler laughed and pretended to leap towards him. Van, another local teenager, had been leaning silently with his back against the rough wooded beam, taking in and disapproving of everything that Emmett said and did.

"Yuh thank yuh so high an' mighty, don't yuh?" he said as he walked up to Emmett. "Well, Ah thank yuh all talk. Yuh ain't nothin' but uh lil' sissy. Yuh mammy's baby boy. Betcha ain't nevah eben had no gurlfriend yuhseff. Seems like tuh me youse skeered of 'em. Yuh kain't even talk right. How yuh thank we suppose tuh b'lieve yuh gotta gurl when yuh kain't eben say 'how ya'll' tuh no gurl widout soundin' kkkkk...krazy?"

"Ooooh!" Billie's mouth dropped; surprised that Van was bold enough to smart off at the new boys. Both city boys wore store bought clothes, starched stiff with sharp creases that never wavered. They were rich. They had to be! And if they were rich, they didn't have to lie. It didn't matter if they talk right or not!

76

Embarrassed, Emmett tried to regain some of the respect that he'd just lost in the eyes of his peers. He really didn't have a girlfriend, but he couldn't let them know that, and someone teasing about his stuttering was nothing new. His friends never did, but kids that didn't know him always made fun of him.

"Oh don't you worry about it. I ggg...gotta girl, my friend," he said as cocky as he could without much stuttering. "GGG...Go on Wheeler. Tell him." He said looking at Wheeler to back him up.

Money Mississippi Sure Ain't Chicago!

Wheeler stood next to Emmett, put his arm around his shoulder, and boldly lied. "He ain't lyin' man! He got more girls lined up than any of the Cats I know!"

"I told you, I ain't gotta lie," Emmett said smugly. "To tell you the truth, if you saw my girl, you couldn't ttt...take it. She's so pretty, you'd just roll over and die."

"Wa-al, dat dere sho yuh jist whut Ah was talkin' 'bout," Van said as he came closer to Emmett, challenging him further, not caring that he was alone and the foreigner was protected by kinfolk.

"Tain't nevah heard of uh body dyin' from lookin' at purty. Nossah, purty ain't nevah killed nobody, but ugly'll do it fast as lightnin'. Is yuh gotta picture? Sich uh thang kain speak fuh itsself."

Emmett's defense was sorely lacking. If he was exposed as a liar, he would never be able to hold his head up again.

"Her picture is way too big to carry in a little billfold. I got it at home, hangin' on the www...wall in my bedroom. Her face is the last thing I see at night and the fff...first thing I see in the mornin'."

After seeing that the others were taking all of this in as fact, Emmett decided to do more coloring. He walked up to Van and stood staunch before him.

"She's real light skinned and got long ppp...pretty hair. She's got a face like an angel. All the guys try to talk to her but, like I said; she's my girl."

77

Wheeler loved to watch his little cousin in action. There were times when he preferred watching Emmett weave a story, over television.

"Ah b'lieve youse lyin' thru yuh teefs. Dese fools kain sit heah takin' in yuh dawg-faced lies, but de way Ah figger, yuh ain't got no gurlfriend, tain't held no gurl's hand, an' tain't nevah kissed no gurl, but maybe yuh Mama on the cheek. Talkin' 'bout yuh gotta gurlfriend! Ya'll city slicka's figgerin' on comin' down heah makin' up stuff an' we'se suppose tuh lap it up like uh hawg in slop! Ah'ma tell yuh right now! Ah ain't movin' mahseff offa dis spot 'til yuh proves it tuh me! Ah 'spect yuh ain't gonna keep me waitin' 'til da Lawd come agin, is yuh?"

Bonnie Blue

The others started laughing. Even his kinfolk snickered and waited to see how Emmett was going to meet his new challenge.

"I don't have to ppp...prove anything to the likes of *you*. But," Emmett said as he turned his back and sauntered the few steps to the wooden pillar. "I will tell you this mister. There *are* a lot of girls in Chicago that wanna bbb...be my ggg...girlfriend. They're always callin' me up on the telephone, wantin' me to come over to their house and watch ttt...television or wantin' me to go to the show with them. But I picked this one super-cute girl. I'll get to the rest of them later. If you don't wanna believe me, tough!"

"Okay, yuh ol' big shot! Ah want tuh see fuh mahseff yuh ain't lyin'! Lemme see yuh gowan in an' talk wid hur!"

"With who?"

"Yuh seent dat White gal in da sto'?"

"Naw boy. That's a grown lady," Emmett said as he threw his hand at him and walked away.

Adolphus stood up and said, "Ain't nobody gotta prove nothin' tuh yuh ol' dusty b'hind. Yuh jist mad 'cuz theah ain't uh gurl in this world or the next that'll go tuh uh dawg fight wid yuh, ugly as yuh is! Don't pay him no mind Bobo. C'mon, it's yuh turn," he said as he sat back down and set up the checkers. "Whut yuh want? Black or red?"

With his support intact, Emmett patted Van on the shoulder. "I'll play you in a minute. I just gotta teach this boy

78

something," Emmett said as he dug down in the back pocket of his blue jeans, checked his wallet for money, and went inside.

He wasn't sure what he would say or if he would say anything at all. After staring down into the homemade display case at the sparse selection of snacks available, he said, "Hi! Can I get 10 pieces of Bazooka bubble gum, a pack of Red-Hots, and a bag of potato chips, please?"

Carolyn had never been around Colored people from the North, but she had always heard that they were bold and had to be watched closer because they had no respect for White women. She could tell from his speech and his neatly pressed store bought clothes that he was definitely a foreigner.

Money Mississippi Sure Ain't Chicago!

The other boys were looking through the window and peering around the corner of the door giggling.

Alfie followed Emmett into the store, afraid he would do something wrong and get in trouble.

Emmett surveyed his goods on the counter as he handed her a dollar bill. She hesitated before gingerly taking it from his grasp, careful not to touch his hand, and laid his change on the counter.

"Thank you," he said, scrapping his coins into his hand and collecting his goodies

"C'mon. We gotta go," Alfie whispered as he grabbed Emmett by the arm and started pulling him towards the door.

When Emmett saw all eyes peering in at him with a mixture of disappointment and anticipation he called back to her, "Good-bye!"

When they reached the door, Emmett sounded a wolf-whistle.

"Boy, yuh know betta'n that," Adolphus said nervously.

Johnny B., half hidden on the side of the store, came around front when he heard all the commotion.

Enraged, Carolyn ran from behind the counter. "Goddamn! Black ass niggah!" she yelled as she headed for the door.

"Heah she come!" Someone screamed.

79

"She's goin' fuh uh gun!"

"Hurry up! Let's git outta heah!" Liga Mae screamed as she jumped into the car.

Carolyn ran out to the pickup truck to retrieve the gun from under the front seat. But she was so shaken, that by the time she fumbled around the crowbar and other tools underneath the seat and found it, the local boys had scattered in different directions and Emmett and his cousins were pulling off down the road.

Johnny B. quickly ran over to her. "Mz. Car'lyn! Is yuh alright? Yuh wants me tuh round 'em up fuh yuh?"

Carolyn stood trembling, watching the dust from the car as it fishtailed down the road.

"Mz. Car'lyn," Johnny B. continued as he drew nearer to her, "Ah knows who dey is, if yuh wants me tuh go aft'a 'em!"

Bonnie Blue

She ignored him as she shouted curses at the car, long since out of earshot and stomped back into the store. He started to run after them, but heard Homer calling as he ran down the road from the mill.

"Johnny B.! Bossman say git yuh ass down heah so he kain git dat fan up!"

Carolyn marched straight back to the living quarters and plopped down on the tattered couch, held up by cinder blocks. Juanita ignored her. She was too busy washing the dishes in the tin tub that sat in the middle of the wobbly kitchen table.

"Goddamn niggah's!" she yelled as she jumped back up and paced the kitchen floor.

"Gurl, whut's wrong wit yuh now?" Juanita asked as she tossed the rag into the washtub. She was irritated that her young sister-in-law was doing nothing to help with her own children. Irritated, but not surprised.

"One of them uppity ass niggah's from up nawth smarted off at me is all! Kain yuh 'magine the nerve of that damn niggah! Didn't yuh hear 'im whistlin' at me? Like Ah was one of them nasty niggah bitchs! Wait 'til Roy gits home! He'll teach 'im fuh sho!"

Juanita grabbed her firmly by her arm. "Gurl, hush up!"

She quickly glanced down the short hall into the store to make sure that no one was within earshot and whispered firmly, "Don't be no fool. Yuh know yuh kain't tell Roy nothin'. Not aft'a all that trouble he was in last year. Yuh know he almost ended up in jail then!"

"But Ah kain't let that niggah git away wit this! It ain't right! Ah mean, who the hell he thank he is anyway?"

Frustrated, Juanita released her, sat on the couch and held her head in her hands. She knew that if Roy thought it was 'justified', her own husband would be there to back him up.

"Gurl, Ah'm tellin' yuh," she pleaded, "keep yuh mouf shut. Don't tell nobody. Yuh know how Roy is. Furst thang'll fall out his mouf is it's yuh own fault. Sayin' yuh most likely grinnin' all up in the niggah's face. Talkin' tuh yuh while he's beatin' all hell outta yuh!"

Money Mississippi Sure Ain't Chicago!

"Juanita, yuh wrong 'bout 'im! Yuh jist plain wrong! Roy knows Ah love him. He don't do nothin' tuh nobody less they do somethin' tuh wrong 'im. He knows Ah would only speak the truth 'bout sich uh thang. Thar ain't no reason fuh 'im tuh doubt mah word! Roy's uh good man!"

Juanita looked up from the couch at Carolyn, whose lip still displayed a small, permanent reminder of Roy's love. She was tired of Carolyn's flirting and vying for more of Roy's attention, even at the risk of getting beaten herself.

"Car'lyn, honnay do as Ah say an' save yuhseff uh beatin'. Yuh know he'll snatch yuh befo' he thank 'bout doin' anythang tuh that niggah. 'Sides, if Roy git in any more trouble wit the law, the family's gonna have one mo' thang tuh hold against yuh."

Carolyn turned silently away. She knew that Juanita was speaking a burning truth.

She remembered last summer when Roy and a couple of his friends were hanging around the mill after hours, guzzling illegal moonshine, which flowed so freely in this dry county.

When they finally ran out, they piled into the truck and headed out to Hillard's Barn for a few more jars.

* * *

The moon hung aloof amid the starless night, fully lighting the tree lined, rock covered, dirt road. The truck wove from side to side, as they came upon a lone figure walking along the edge of the road just ahead of them.

"Hey ya'll! See whut Ah see up yonda way uh piece?" Roy yelled to his buddies as he stuck his head out the window and pointed.

Leo and Hubert, who were sitting in the bed of the pickup, fumbled as they attempted to stand. They fell when the truck lurched forward.

"Goddamnit, Roy! Who the hell taught yuh tuh drive? Stay in the middle of the damned road boy!" Leo yelled as he laughed and sat back up.

Roy struggled with the steering wheel as he hung halfway out the window. "Looks like we gonna have some fun tuhnight! Looka whut's up ahead!"

Bonnie Blue

Leo crawled over the empty Mason jars, to the side of the truck and peered down the road. "Yep, barely, but Ah see 'im! C'mon Roy! Let's see whut we got!"

Eugene Plummer never liked walking these roads at night, but he had received word that his younger sister was giving birth to her first child and was having a dangerously hard time. Out of the twelve children that his parents had, Eugene and his sister Sharon were the youngest. They were always very close. After she married and became pregnant, she made him promise that he would be there when the baby was born.

The local midwife feared that she wouldn't survive the night and had sent word to Eugene. He had no car and he refused to wait until morning when he could get a ride. The dawning of the new day may find his sister and her baby dead. So he set out on foot.

Eugene moved quickly over the rocks when he saw the headlights coming up behind him.

"Yeah, Ah b'lieve we dun foolt 'round an' caught us uh coon, boys," Roy yelled as he forced the gas pedal to the floorboard; the ball of his hand grinding into the horn.

Eugene jumped out of the way as the truck roared towards him. Rocks pounded wildly as Roy pressed the accelerator to its limit. He drove too close to the edge of the road and started sliding sideways into the ditch. He slammed on the brakes. The truck skidded on the rocks and flipped over on its side, sending empty Mason jars flying into the air. Leo and Hubert jumped to safety before the truck slid to a halt in the ditch. No one was seriously injured including Roy; until he noticed a small trickle of blood escaping from a split in his lip.

"That black sonna-bitch!" He screamed as he attempted, unsuccessfully, to climb through the open window. His voice was thick with moonshine and his jello-like muscles made the simplest operation a major undertaking. "Leo! Huber'! Ya'll git me the hell outta this goddamned truck!"

Hubert attempted to pull himself from the muddy hole where he was thrown. After sliding around, he finally made his way to the

Money Mississippi Sure Ain't Chicago!

truck where Leo had already maneuvered Roy out through the window.

"Ah'ma kill 'im!" Roy screamed as he snatched away from his friends. "Whar'd he go?"

"C'mon! Ah thank he ducked through this way!" Leo called as he stumbled over fallen branches and layers of damp, dead leaves.

The further they went into the woods the more dense it became.

"Shhhh. Be still. Wa-ait jist one minute," Roy whispered, stretching his arms up to silence the others. "Ah know Ah heard somethin'."

They stopped and stood perfectly still. Amid the natural night noises, a loud crackling of a dry branch breaking drew the hunters' attention back to an area that they had already covered.

"Wa'al Ah'll be damned," Hubert whispered. "Smart ass niggah dun doubled back on us."

"Damn coon fryin' tuhnight!" Roy screamed as he ran awkwardly in the direction of the sound.

They tried to see their way through the maze of trees by the light from the moon, gleaming through gaps in the cottonwood tree branches.

"Thar he goes...headin' fuh the road!"

Eugene was living every Colored man's nightmare. He had heard stories, knew of people who disappeared, and even witnessed a friend's body being pulled from the river, but he had always been careful not to cross any barriers which might cause him to be killed. Yes, he'd been beaten, but there weren't many Colored men that he knew who hadn't. And now, they were after him.

His heart pounded with such force that he could feel it fighting against his chest. Sweat rolled endlessly from his brow, partially blinding him. Or were they tears. He didn't know, didn't care.

Branches tore through his clothes, biting into his skin as he fought fiercely to get back on the road for help. Their voices echoed all around him. Nearer and nearer they came. The

Bonnie Blue

throbbing of blood coursing through his veins battered his ears. He prayed as he darted wildly towards the patch of moonlight he knew was the open road. Suddenly he was down.

He muffled an agonizing scream as a sharp pain shot up his leg. Frantically he tried to stand, but it was no use. He could tell that his leg was broken. Knowing he would never make it to the road before being caught, he tried to drag himself into the shadows of a large dead tree. As they drew closer, he held his breath, afraid that they would hear his short raspy breathing or at the very least, feel the pounding of his heart as it attempted to escape his chest.

"Spread out!" Roy bellowed as they unknowingly approached him.

"Aw, c'mon Roy. Fuhgit it," Hubert said as he headed back towards the road. "That niggah's long gone by now."

"Shuddup!" Roy yelled, his body trembling in anger. "Jist shut yuh fuckin' mouth an' do like Ah tell yuh! Ah'll be

84

goddamned if Ah let uh niggah git the bes' of me! Ah don't give uh damn if we gotta stay out heah all night! He ass is still heah goddamnit, an' he's mine!"

Hubert hunched his shoulders and started off in one direction as Leo and Roy checked in another area.

"Hey, Huber'!" Leo laughed. "Don't yuh git off too far by yuhseff now, less yuh thank yuh part hound dawg!"

"Aw, go tuh hell," Hubert mumbled to himself as he walked away.

Hubert hadn't gone far before he noticed, gleaming in the moonlight, a small swatch of blue plaid material trapped on a twig. He crept over for a closer look. As he slowly reached to retrieve it, his attention was drawn to the scraping of dead weight.

Eugene choked back the excruciating pain as he dragged his broken leg closer to his body.

Hubert straightened up slowly and cocked his head to one side to listen more intensely. Except for the normal wooded area noises, all was quiet.

Eugene had pressed himself firmly against the tree. Jagged, prickly bark dug deeply into his flesh. But it didn't matter. He didn't dare move.

Money Mississippi Sure Ain't Chicago!

Hubert drew closer, squinting as he surveyed the shadowy figures around him. A smile slid across his lips as he spotted their prey. "C'mon out Boy," he said, almost in a whisper. "Ah know yuh ovah thar so yuh might as well c'mon out whar Ah kain see yuh."

Hubert feared confronting this Colored man alone. Not taking a chance on being attacked, he began backing away and yelled, "Hey, Roy! Ya'll! Ah do b'lieve the trap dun sprung on yuh coon! Roy! Yuh heah me? Ah got yuh niggah cornered ovah heah!"

Panicked, Eugene tried one last ditch effort to gain his freedom. His leg pulsated with pain as he struggled to stand; propping himself against the tree. He summoned all of his strength and lunged towards the end of the wooded area and possibly, his salvation.

The crunching of dead leaves and small branches under their brogans became louder and faster until; they were upon him.

"Niggah, looka whut yuh dun tuh me!" Roy yelled as he stumbled up to the frightened man who crouch a breath away from the moss covered ground. "Yuh black mutha' fucka, yuh drew mah goddamn blood!" he screamed. "Yuh drew mah goddamn blood!"

Eugene raised his arm ever-so-slightly from over his eyes to catch a glimpse of the men stalking him. Bright rays of light filtered through the thick forest, lighting a large enough patch of Roy's face to strike a fear in his heart that he had never known.

"Ah'm sorrah sah! Ah ain't dun nothin' sah!" Eugene cried as he balled himself tighter in a knot.

"Niggah! Git yuh stankin' black ass up!" Roy slurred as he dug his fingers into Eugene's thick curly hair, pulling him to his feet.

"Ah sweah sah. Ah ain't dun nothin'," he mumbled through the pain and fear.

Roy swung wildly, missing his intended target, scraping his knuckles against the jagged skin of the tree. He screamed as he cradled his wounded fist in the pit of his stomach.

No one budged or spoke as Roy raised his head and shoved his face so close to the terrified traveler that, for a brief

Bonnie Blue

moment, he breathed in the same air that escaped the trembling lips of his prey. He glared into the Eugene's watery eyes.

"Niggah," he growled, showering foul rot gut mist into Eugene's face "Yuh black sonna-bitch, Ah'm sending yuh ass straight tuh hell tuhnight!"

"Ah'm sorrah, sah!" Eugene whimpered. "Ah sweah Ah'm sorrah. As God is mah witness, Ah ain't mean no harm sah. Ah was jist goin' tuh see mah sistah, sah. She's in uh powerful bad way, sah. Ah sweah Ah ain't mean no harm."

Hubert looked at his friend's face in the moonlight, but it didn't seem the same. For a moment, he was afraid. "Aw shit," he murmured.

Roy buried his white knuckled, blood glazed fist into Eugene's abdomen. Eugene doubled over. Leo caught him before he could fall and held his arms behind his back.

"Git the hell outta mah way!" Roy yelled. He pushed Leo away and continued to pound the wounded man.

Roy's anger fueled his insatiable appetite to destroy this object of his blind resentment. He continued to beat, and beat at the nonresponsive flesh until the others pulled him away.

"C'mon Roy! Yuh jist wastin' time," Leo said as he tugged at his arm. "Don't make no sense workin' up uh sweat onna corpse!"

A satisfied smirk slid across Roy's face as he looked down at the limp bloody body.

"Whut we gonna do wit 'im?" Hubert asked quietly as they stood in a huddle around the still body.

"Hell, Ah already dun whut Ah had tuh do wit his black ass," Roy said as he kicked damp dead leaves in Eugene's face. "Thar now. Yuh feel betta?" He asked sarcastically to Hubert. "He dun had uh right propp'a burial. D'yuh mind if we git outta heah now? Ah need uh drank."

A night owl screeched in the distant shadows, unnerving them all. They moved quickly through the woods, skillfully dodging low hanging branches, stumbling occasionally over dead undergrowth and long forgotten stumps.

Money Mississippi Sure Ain't Chicago!

They had forgotten that the truck lay on its side in the ditch, until they emerged from the thicket.

"Shit man, how the hell're we suppose tuh git that damned thang back on the road?" Leo asked wiping the sweat from his brow on his rolled up sleeve.

"Fuck it," Roy yelled as he waved his arms in the air. "Niggah drew mah goddamned blood! An' look at mah goddamned hand! Black sonna-bitch an' the devil kain fry tuhgetha!"

He cradled his hand and staggered down the road. "C'mon, let's go git that drank."

* * *

Eugene finally regained consciousness. He lay still as he listened for any sign of his attackers. Slowly, he managed to drag himself far enough out of the woods to be seen from the

87

road; before the remnants of life drained from his body. Bright morning rays trickled through the leaves to dance oddly on the dead man's face; now cradled in dried dog manure and blood.

Later that morning, when Deputy Ed Cochran went out to investigate a report of a dead body near the side of the road, he immediately recognized the truck lying a quarter mile away from the corpse.

Ed had lost his bid for High Sheriff of LaFlore County but accepted the position of deputy. He'd been a part of the law in this area for a short while, but was already making his mark as a man that upholds the law for all of the citizens in his domain. He was very familiar with the Milam-Bryant clan and wasn't surprised to learn that this disabled vehicle belonged to Roy. Ed attempted to bring him up on a murder charge, but the little evidence that he could gather, wasn't nearly enough to formally charge him with the crime.

* * *

Adolphus sped over the road; pebbles popping wildly underneath. They fishtailed on rocks as he struggled to regain control of the car.

Bonnie Blue

"Adolphus!" Liga Mae screamed. "Slow this dawg gawn car down befo' we end up in uh ditch! Yuh know we'll be in some sho 'nuff trouble then!"

He eased his foot off the accelerator and pulled off to the side of the road. They sat silent for a moment, more shaken than even they realized.

"We kain't tell Papa," Kelvin said almost in a whisper. "He'll skin us alive."

"Bobo, yuh jist kain't go doin' that ol' crazy stuff down heah." Adolphus said, "These White folks'll whip yuh up worsened than uh dawg."

The thought of his mother and the conversation that they had as he packed, all came rushing back to him.

"PPP...Please don't tell on me. If Mama fff...finds out, she'll nnn...never let me go anyplace else. MMM... Maybe I should just leave, go home eee...early. Just don't ttt...tell on me," he pleaded as he looked wide eyed over to Wheeler.

"I don't know Bo. Maybe," Wheeler replied softly, looking up from his hands, which were pressed firmly on his knees in an attempt to stop their trembling. "Maybe we should both go back home now."

Liga Mae looked at Wheeler, surprised that apparently he didn't understand. "Maybe nothin'! Boy, yuh betta git yuh tail out from down heah! Ain't no tellin' whut that man'll do tuh yuh! Whup yuh up good, fuh sho! An' Kelvin, whut yuh talkin' 'bout, not tellin' Un'ka Mose? He gonna find out any ol' way! Then, way aft'a while, when somebody else tells 'im, he gonna be double mad 'cuz we ain't let 'im know tuh begin wid! Yuh know dawg gawn well yuh bet not brang no shame down on Un'ka Mose, accident or on purpose! He'll plant some sho 'nuff pain wheah yuh b'hind use-ta-be! Suppose that man come out tuh the house an' talk wid Mista Fredricks? Then whut yuh gonna do?"

She turned around to face Emmett, who sat wide eyed in the back seat. "Lissen, Bobo", she said nervously. "Ah ain't tryin' tuh skeer yuh, but that's jist how it is. Ah don't know. Maybe up yonda it ain't nothin', but White folks down heah jist lose they natural born mind ovah nothin'. We gotta let Un'ka Mose know soon as we git tuh the house."

Money Mississippi Sure Ain't Chicago!

Adolphus shifted nervously in his seat; hands clutched tightly on the steering wheel, with his eyes fixed on Emmett in the rear view mirror.

"Okay Liga Mae," Adolphus said, nodding his head. "But Ah thank we outta tell Antee furst. She's uh lot easier. Yuh know we ain't gonna hafta worrah 'bout whut White folks gonna do aft'a Un'ka Mose find out."

"Boy, you're crazy," Wheeler said to Adolphus as he flashed a nervous grin over to Emmett. "You're actin' like you're more afraid of Uncle Mose than those stupid White people."

"Ah am!" Adolphus said as he pulled the car back onto the road and continued towards the Wright house.

Wheeler looked closely at Emmett. In an attempt to lighten the situation, he jabbed him playfully in the arm saying, "Hey buddy, we're partners. We came here together, and we're

89

gonna leave together. We can have a ball on that train by ourselves. Besides, there're a lot of things we can do at home. And we still got plenty time before school start."

Emmett looked to Wheeler for any sign of their normal reality. But his cousin's thinly cloaked fear of Southern White folks couldn't be hidden. True enough, he had never whistled at any girls, young or old, but he had no idea that he could get into real trouble. After all, it was just a whistle.

Emmett's head began to ache. The lecture that his mother was so serious about just a few days before flooded his mind. Maybe she wasn't just over-reacting. His mother was known for reading more into people and situations then there actually was. But now, on this country road, in this different world, her words made perfect sense. He knew that Mamie would never let him hear the last of this, and it was a pretty fair bet that he could forget about going anywhere else without her. But right now, at this moment; that didn't seem like such a bad idea.

"I'm going home," Emmett said just above a whisper.

They sat again, silent and shaken, as the car slowly turned onto the red dirt road leading to the Wright's shotgun house.

"Liga Mae, yuh don't thank Papa'll send him home tuhday do yuh?"

Bonnie Blue

"Alfie, quit whinin'," she said as she stared out the open window.

"Look, Ah been thankin'," Adolphus said. "Ah b'lieve it's bes' not tuh say nothin' tuh nobody."

Liga Mae sat bolt straight up and yelled, "Adolphus! Is yuh crazy? Un'ka Mose gonna find out 'bout it! Then we all in big trouble!"

Adolphus angrily jerked the car to the side of the road again and turned to face his sister. "Shuddup Liga Mae! Jist shuddup an' lissen! All ya'll, lissen! Weren't nobody around, an' she don't know who he is. We be gittin' in trouble fuh nothin'. All we gotta do is stay outta town. Ya'll jist stay down at the house. That way, yuh ain't gonna run intuh nobody."

"Yeah," Kelvin agreed. "Don't nobody say nothin'. 'Specially *you* Alfie!"

They all agreed to the uneasy pact.

* * *

Elizabeth sat content under the shade of a large persimmon tree in front of the house, singing old spirituals and shelling crowder peas. The chipped mixing bowl, which she skillfully balanced on her lap, tilted each time she dug a fist full of purple hulled peas from the bushel basket next to her. The familiar clatter of her husband's car drew her attention to the road. She peered through the cluster of trees and saw a timid cloud of dust nearing the tiny turnoff into her yard.

"Hey Kelvin, ya'll,' she yelled as they piled out of the car. "Gowan 'round back an'..."

"Mama!" Alfie interrupted as he darted ahead of the others. "Bo an' them ain't gotta go home do they?"

"They gotta go back tuh school baby. Yuh know that," she said as she scooped another handful of peas and dumped them into her mixing bowl.

"No'm. Ah mean, they ain't gotta go home right now! Not befo' they time?"

"Shugga whut yuh talkin' 'bout, goin' home? They jist got heah!"

Money Mississippi Sure Ain't Chicago!

The others sheepishly approached her.

"Whut this boy talkin' 'bout? Ya'll c'mon ovah heah."

Emmett inched his way closer to her, his hands crammed deeply into his pockets. Elizabeth reached out to him. He stretched his arm out to take her hand.

"Yuh gittin' homesick, ain't yuh baby? Yuh miss yuh Mama an' Granny?" She asked as she pulled him closer to her.

He glanced over his shoulder to the group for help. Elizabeth looked around him.

"Whut's the matt'a wid ya'll? Lookin' like the wolf dun got in the chicken coop."

Adolphus quickly stepped forward, picked up a pebble and threw it lightly at Alfie. "That boy pure city! Ah b'lieve he *is* homesick!" He smiled and punched Emmett playfully in the arm. "Ain't nothin' but uh big ol' baby!"

91

"Adolphus," Elizabeth scolded. "Let this chil' be. He's doin' jist fine. Now, ya'll gowan 'round back an' pull me some turnup bottoms. Liga Mae, ya'll pull yuh some tuh carry home tuh yuh Mama too!"

They raced around to the garden on the side of the house that Elizabeth grew for the family's use.

"See? Ah told ya'll!" Kelvin said. "Yuh ain't gotta thang tuh worrah 'bout. So, yuh might as well stop thankin' 'bout packin' yuh bags."

"Ah don't care!" Liga Mae said as she bent over and wrapped her hands around a base of turnip greens and pulled the root from the rich soil. "Ah jist don't feel right 'bout tellin' uh story tuh Antee. Ah still thank ya'll should take yuh tails right on back tuh Ch'caga."

"Yuh act like yuh want 'im tuh leave," Adolphus said as he jumped across three rows of greens to put distance between them. "'Sides, yuh need tuh stop bein' so dawg-gawn bossy! Always actin' like yuh evahbody's Mama! Truth is, yuh kain't tell nobody whut tuh do! So jist shuddup, an' leave us alone! Yuh dun got on mah last nerves now!"

Bonnie Blue

Wheeler pulled Emmett slightly to the side. "What'd you wanna do Bo? I'm tellin' you, if you wanna leave, we can both go tomorrow. We already got our tickets. All we have to do is tell the conductor that we decided to go home early. Takin' the train by ourselves won't be a big deal. But, it's up to you."

"I don't know. I ggg...guess I'll stay."

"Okay, but if you change your mind, just say the word."

Liga Mae stood with her hand on her hip like she had all the authority in the land as her shrill voice cracked through the air.

"Adolphus! Boy, ain't nobody studin' 'bout yuh! Kelvin, Ollie, ya'll! Whut yuh thank yuh doin'? Standin' 'round like yuh got broke backs; or is the ar-the-ritas whut gotcha all stiff standin'? Ah ain't playin'! Ya'll betta bend yuh b'hinds down

92

heah an' pull them bottoms like Antee told ya'll! Slavery days is ovah yuh know, an' Ah ain't nonna ya'll's!"

"Liga Mae!" Kelvin yelled as he mimicked her.

"Whut?"

"Shuddup!"

Emmett and Wheeler joined the others in the rows of greens. Liga Mae kept a watchful eye on them as they attempted to pull the leaves from the stems.

"Whut ya'll call yuhseff's doin'?"

"WWW...What does it look like we're doing? Pickin' turnups." Emmett was also beginning to get aggravated with his cousin.

"Ya'll pitiful!"

Adolphus crept up from behind where Liga Mae was kneeling and booted her in the rear with his foot, making her plunge face first into the dirt. Soon, the incident in town was forgotten.

* * *

In the dusk of the evening, Mose and Elizabeth sat on the front porch silently watching the large orange sun, the exhausted griot of the day, slide silently beyond the golden horizon.

A strong breeze rushed through the hall from the open doors, forcing the heavy air of the day out into the cool night.

Money Mississippi Sure Ain't Chicago!

The boys had gathered in Kelvin's bedroom for a marbles tournament. Wheeler and Ollie quickly cleaned out Alfie and Kelvin. Emmett fought valiantly to keep the last few cat-eye marbles that he'd brought from home. He struggled to position himself on the floor to shoot, but his stomach was cramping.

"C'mon, Bo! Shoot!" Wheeler said as he let his fist full of marbles roll from his hand into his small, purple cloth bag which held his collection. "I ain't got all day. Now if you wanna just give them to me, that's cool. Make it easy on yourself!"

Emmett shot his marble towards the largest blue cat-eye and missed. "Dang," he said as he rolled over on the floor. "I quit. My sss...stomach hurts."

Ollie threw a shoe at him and said, "Ah thought yuh knew how tuh play. If yuh take yuh Papa's big ol' rang off yuh fing'a, yuh might be able tuh hit somethin'! It don't matta! Yuh kain't play no betta than that lil' boy theah!"

"I'm serious! My stomach hurts bad!" Emmett moaned as he stood up and leaned against the footboard of the bed. "I gotta go to the bathroom for real. C'mon, Wheeler. Go with me."

Wheeler looked over at him laughed and said, "Boy, you'd betta go on and grab that slop jar or take a trip to the outhouse."

"When ya'll gonna gimme back mah marbles?" Alfie whined. "Yuh betta give 'em back tuh me or Ah'ma tell Papa."

"Shuddup boy," Ollie said as he gathered all of his marbles. "Why don't yuh gowan tuh the outhouse wid Bobo. Yuh gotta use it befo' yuh go tuh bed anyway."

Emmett looked hopefully over to Wheeler. "C'mon boy, Alfie's gonna go with us."

"If Alfie's going," Wheeler said as he looked up at Emmett, "I sure don't need to take that trip out there."

"All Ah need tuh use is the slop jar tuhnight. Ah ain't gotta booboo," Alfie said as he opened the jar of lightning bugs and grasshoppers that he'd caught, and dumped them in a small pile of grass on the floor. "Ya'll jist skeered. An' ya'll suppose tuh be so big an' brave. Humph!"

Bonnie Blue

"Alfie!" Kelvin called out when he saw the grasshoppers leaping across the floor. "Boy, yuh betta hurry up an' shut that door befo' Papa come back heah!"

Frightened, Alfie scampered across the room and slammed the door shut.

"Ugh!" Emmett said as he dodged out of the way of a grasshopper that leaped towards him. "Why'd you www...wanna play with those nasty things anyway?"

Ollie picked up one by the leg and flung it on him. Emmett almost tripped over himself as he jumped up, knocking the

94

grasshopper from his shirt. "Look at Bobo! Skeered of the dark an' runnin' from uh lil' ol' jumper!"

"I ain't afraid of no bugs," Emmett said as he opened the door. "I just don't like anything thrown on me."

"Well whatcha leavin' for?" Wheeler laughed. "I ain't never seen that boy move that fast. Your stomach sure got better in a hurry!"

"Aw go on boy," Emmett said. "You know I ain't afraid of no sss...stupid lll...little bug. And come to think of it! I haven't seen you go out to the outhouse by yourself in the dark or in the mmm...middle of the day. What's the matter? Afraid a snake might bbb...bite you on the butt?"

"Oooh!" Alfie said with his hand over his mouth. "Ah'ma tell Papa, yuh said uh bad word!"

The boys playfully grabbed the little tattletale and wrestled him to the floor.

All of this exercise really churned Emmett's stomach. He tried to slip quietly from the room and lie down, hoping to calm his urge until daybreak.

Wheeler caught sight of him easing out of the door.

"Hey Bo, wait up!" Grinning, he ran up to him, smacked him playfully on the back and said, "I was just kiddin'. You know I'm gonna go with you."

"Yeah," Kelvin laughed as he joined them. "We gonna go wit yuh too. Truth be told, don't nobody hardly evah go by theyseffs aft'a dark. Skeered of Banchees mos'ly."

Money Mississippi Sure Ain't Chicago!

That was all Emmett needed to hear to cement his decision to wait. "Aw naw, I aaa...ain't goin' out there. I'm gonna write Mama to see if I can get her to send mmm...my motor bike down."

"Bo, you're outta your mind. You know there's no way in the world she's gonna ship that bike all the way down here. You almost didn't get here yourself, so you might as well forget it. Besides, why'd you wanna ride it now? You've only taken it out of the basement a few times all summer!"

95

"Wow! Bobo! Yuh got one of them kinda bikes?" Ollie asked as he excitedly scooped up a handful of grass that was now scattered all across the floor, and shoved it back into the jar.

"Yeah, he's got it at home, and that's where it's gonna stay."

"We'll see," Emmett said smugly as he left the room.

He hurried to the back bedroom to find the stationary Mamie had packed in his luggage.

After he found it, he crammed the suitcase back under the neatly made bed and sat at the kitchen table to write.

An aura of peace and calm settled around the tin roofed shotgun house.

"This is all right," Emmett said to himself as he held his face in his hands, undisturbed by the muffled voices and occasional laughter that floated down the narrow hall from the rear bedroom.

With the exception of spending an occasional weekend with relatives in Argo, this was the first time that he'd been away from his mother. And now, sitting here hundreds of miles away from home with his great-aunt just outside the door, singing the old familiar hymns that his grandmother sang, he thought back to Spring Break; the beginning of 'Clean-up Week.'

* * *

Mamie and Alma sat at the dining room table folding winter clothes to pack away in boxes for the summer, when Emmett and Brucie came traipsing into the kitchen. Even though they had wiped most of the mud from their shoes on the porch mat, they still managed to track some into the house.

Bonnie Blue

"Emmett, I want you to do something for me," Mamie called when she heard them come through the screen door.

Emmett snapped his fingers. He was just coming in to get a cold drink before he and Brucie went back over to the schoolyard.

Today was a big day for them. The championship game between their school team, McCosh Elementary, and neighboring Parker Elementary, was scheduled to begin in a couple of hours.

His legs were already sore from practicing for so long. If Mamie found out about it, he knew that she wouldn't let him play.

The after effect of his bout with polio flared up more than he let his mother know. But, because she restricts his activities whenever she sees the slightest limp, he has learned how to walk carefully whenever he was in pain.

"Emmett, did you hear me?"

"Ma'am?"

"Come in here. There's something I need you to do for me."

Emmett went into the dining room, leaving Brucie in the kitchen gulping down a tall glass of grape Kool-Aid.

"I bought some paint for the garage. It's in the basement."

"Mama, I don't have to do it now, do I?" Emmett whined.

"That garage is a real eyesore and I'm tired of looking at it."

"But Mama, the game's today! In a little while; and I have to play!"

"Emmett, I don't recall asking if you would do it. I believe I told you. Now, bring your grandmother some Kool-Aid. It's hot as the dickens in here."

Alma started to suggest that he do it another day. After all, the entire summer was ahead of him. She decided not to interfere, instead, she looked sympathetically at him and continued folding sweaters.

Emmett went rapidly, almost running into the kitchen, not caring if Mamie saw him limping. He snatched a glass from the cabinet and closed the refrigerator door harder than he intended.

"Aw man!" he whispered angrily to Brucie. "She can sure pick some dumb times to make me do stuff!"

Money Mississippi Sure Ain't Chicago!

"I guess we're gonna have ta find someone ta take your spot, huh?"

"Naw, Brucie. We don't have to do that. Wait a minute," he whispered as he leaned against the sink staring blankly past the screen door.

"Meet me by the basement." He said his cheeks rising in a smile.

Brucie gulped down the rest of his kool-aid and rushed out the door.

Emmett filled the glass to the rim to make it look as though he was walking slowly to keep it from spilling. He didn't want to chance having to stay off of his feet for the rest of the day.

"Here you are Grandma!" he said as he placed it on the table next to her.

"Thank you baby."

"Mr. Till, I heard you in there acting out. Do you call yourself mad?" Mamie asked.

"No ma'am. That was Brucie. I'm getting started on it right now!"

"It's a good thing because we were just about to have a long talk, and you wouldn't have seen outside until school started!"

"Oh, no ma'am! I'll see you later Grandma!" he said as he backed out of the room.

As soon as he was out of eyeshot, he grabbed the large bag of Ginger Snaps from the pantry and hurried out to meet Brucie.

"C'mon!" he yelled as he pulled Brucie with him.

"Where're we goin'?"

"Don't worry about it. I'll tell you on the way. We ain't got much time before the game."

They half walked, half ran to the playground as he unfolded his plan. He met a few of his teammates on the way and had them gather the others.

When everyone was together, he filled them with cookies and made them an offer. "Look guys!" he said as they surrounded him. "We're a team, right? And we work together, right?"

Bonnie Blue

Most of his friends attempted to make confirmation noises through stuffed mouths.

98

"We gotta big game ahead of us and need all the energy we can get right?" Again they nodded and mumbled in agreement.

"So, what I'm gonna do is make us a bunch of sandwiches and Kool-Aid and stuff. But so I don't get in trouble, we'll do somethin' nice for my Mama, right? Who's with me?"

Ted Johnson, one of the younger but heavier boys, swallowed hard to free his mouth. "Wait a minute. We gotta do some work or somethin'?"

"Well, it ain't *really* work. We just gotta do somethin' so she won't get mad. And we'll be finished in plenty of time for the game."

"I don't know Bo. What kinda sandwiches you plannin' on makin'?"

"Peanut butter an' jelly and baloney. There's another big bag of cookies that Mama bought for church, but she can pick up some more before tomorrow. Are you with me or not?"

"Sounds alright to me!" Ted said as he licked his lips and looked around wide eyed at the others.

"What you got in mind?" Wheeler asked as he walked up through the crowd. Emmett was surprised to see him.

"Uh, hey, Wheeler! Where'd you come from?"

"Your house. I saw your Mama, and she said you were down in the..."

Emmett threw him a look and he knew right away that his little cousin had something in the works.

"All right, fellas. Follow me!" Emmett called as he led the troop down the street to his house.

When they were all rallied in the backyard, Emmett took his place on the steps and announced, "You see that garage?"

"Bo, you still ain't told us what we gotta do," Ted said as he plopped down on the step that Emmett was standing on.

"That's what I'm trying to tell you, if you'd hush up for a minute! Here, eat another cookie. Like I was saying, we're gonna paint that garage!"

Money Mississippi Sure Ain't Chicago!

The boys turned to look in the direction that Emmett had indicated, moaned, and headed toward the back gate.

"Boy, you crazy as a box of rocks. Ain't no way you gonna get us to paint that big ol' thing!"

"I told you Brucie," Emmett said as he flung his arm around Brucie's shoulder. "You try to help your buddies out and this is what you get. I guess they don't care if we lose."

Brucie shrugged his shoulders and vanished into the basement with Emmett.

Wheeler smiled as he watched his confidants mull over their dilemma.

For Ted, the choice was easy. "I don't know about ya'll, but Bo's my friend. And if he's thinking enough about us and the game to fix all them sandwiches, I think we should chip in and give him a hand. After all, he's doin' it for us! The team!"

"Yeah! We're pals and pals stick together!" they sang as they disappeared into the basement and emerged with cans of paint and paint brushes.

Emmett smiled victoriously as he carefully supervised the progress of his work crew.

Wheeler grinned in disbelief. "Hey, Bo!" he yelled.

Emmett strolled confidently towards him.

"I gotta hand it to you cuz. Either you're the slickest dude around, or they're the greediest bunch of Cats I've ever seen. Now, what're you planning to do about your part of the bargain? They'll have your head when they get through and you don't have any food."

"I've got it all under control! Your Mama still out in Argo?"

"Wait a minute Bobo. You said you're gonna feed 'em. Not me."

"Don't worry about it. I know what I'm doin'."

Emmett started up the stairs but stumbled when a pain stabbed his leg. He hesitated and glanced back to make sure no one noticed and listened intensely to make sure that his mother

Bonnie Blue

hadn't heard the noise. When he felt it was safe, he slipped back into the kitchen.

He peered in to make sure that his mother and grandmother were still in the dining room before seizing the opportunity to snatch the jars of peanut butter and jelly from the cabinet. A quick chill shook him as he shoved a pack of baloney and cheese from the refrigerator under his shirt; in his waistband. Finally, he left out the door with a loaf of Wonder Bread dangling from between his teeth.

After creeping down the steps of the building, he started up to Wheeler's back door.

"Hey! Where do you think you're going'?"

"C'mon, gimme a hand," Emmett mumbled through the plastic bag.

The kitchen took on the appearance of a cafeteria. They made all the sandwiches that they could. When they ran out of bread, he started unloading Wheeler's breadbox. It didn't take long to stuff their trusting friends and get them to finish painting the lower half of the garage.

* * *

Yes, Emmett was really proud of the way he'd pulled that one off. Suddenly, he missed them. He missed them all. He sat dreamy eyed as he remembered how his mother and grandmother came rushing out on the porch when they heard the commotion coming from the backyard. Mamie's mouth fell open, and Alma flashed the biggest smile that he'd ever seen on her as she nodded her approval when they saw the paint party below.

* * *

At that moment, the sounds, smells and very feel of home set a deep desire in Emmett's heart to be with his mother. He couldn't let her know in his letter that he understood the talk that they had before he left, without telling on himself. He wanted her to know, without being too mushy, that he missed her.

As he finished the letter, his stomach began to gripe violently. There would be no waiting. He had to face the Banshees,

Money Mississippi Sure Ain't Chicago!

snakes, and every other thing that lay in wait for him on the trail to the tiny outhouse at the edge of the trees.

Emmett crept carefully down the hall; past the bedroom where the voices of his cousins leaked from behind the closed door.

He peered out the screen on the back door, but the outhouse wasn't visible from that angle.

A strong wind violently whipped the upper branches of the trees as thick clouds rolled across the sky. Cautiously, he stepped down on the second and final step. He paused, but he couldn't hold it much longer. "Dag!"

He pressed his hands against the back of his pants, took a deep breath, and shot out across the backyard.

Soon, he emerged pain free. But now he had to get back to the house. Somehow, it seemed further away than when he first started. His legs were throbbing, but still, he broke into a full limp run until he made it close to the light from the house. He slowed to a brisk hop, afraid that the others would see him flying through the yard like a Banshee *was* after him.

Even though it had cooled off in the house and he wanted to be with his cousins, he couldn't chance playing around and having to make that trip to the outhouse again.

* * *

The clean night air and the powerful breeze made Emmett want to stay outside a while longer. He could hear his uncle and aunt on the front porch talking. He limped around to the front of the house.

"Hi," Emmett said as he mounted the porch.

"Hey boy! Why yuh out heah by yuhseff?" Mose asked as he packed tobacco in his pipe. "Gowan an' grab yuhseff uh seat."

Emmett perched on the edge of the porch; his feet dangling.

"Why ain't yuh back in the back wid the rest of the chil'ren?" Elizabeth asked, handing him a slice of pear that she was peeling.

"I'm tired of playing marbles," he said as he rolled a large marble in his hand, "and I wanted to write Mama."

Bonnie Blue

102

"That theah is a mighty fine marble yuh got. Hand it heah. Lemme take uh look at that." Mose said.

"Yes sir. It's my absolute favorite." He said proudly handing it to Mose. "It's my lucky marble. Just look at that navy blue cat-eye!"

"Yes suh! This heah is mighty fine. Whut yuh call it? Uh cat's eye?" Mose said as he held it up to admire in the moonlight.

"Yes sir. You can go on and keep that one. I have more at home." Emmett said crunching into his slice of pear.

"Yuh gonna give me this heah lucky cat's eye marble?" Mose asked.

"Yes sir." Emmett nodded and smiled.

"Well Ah thank yuh! This heah's mighty fine!" Mose said rolling it around in his hand. "Mighty fine indeed!"

BOOK THREE

MAMA! I SHOULD HAVE STAYED WITH YOU!

By the breath of the new day, Carolyn's emotions had grown from rage to raw fear. Being bred in the backwoods, she was aware that word was rapidly weaving its way through their rural community. It was just a matter of time before her in-laws got wind of the incident with the foreign Colored boy. Even the anticipation of Roy's return began to make her nauseous.

Only one fieldhand dared to enter the store for the entire day. When he did, he stood further back from the counter than usual.

"Mo'nin' ma'am." He mumbled softly, keeping his eyes cast down to his jagged toenails. "Ah come tuh pay on mah bill ma'am. And kain Ah git some chewin' to'bacca?" Juanita pushed the ledger across the counter for him to make his mark next to his name for his purchase.

He quickly laid the coins on the edge of the counter, keeping his eyes cast down, he scooped up the packet of chewing tobacco, and scrambled out the open door.

Even the poor White patrons, who were usually full of small talk and gossip, said little as they glanced back toward the living quarters, where they were sure Carolyn was hiding. They gave Juanita curious looks as they conducted their business.

104

After they closed the store, Carolyn and her children spent another evening in Glendora, at the Milam's home.

She lay awake for most of the night, while the soothing music of the boys' tiny snores danced off the walls, blending with the serenade of hidden songstress' of the night.

Well before dawn, she heard the crackling of large tires crushing the tiny pebbles that blanketed the entrance of the yard. Immediately, she slid out of the bed that she shared with her two small sons, tiptoed into the living room, and peered out the window. Just as she feared, it was the truck that Roy had been driving to make his deliveries. She hurried back to the bedroom and slid into the bed; careful not to wake her sleeping children.

Roy had been on the road for five days and most of the nights. After finally quieting the powerful engine, he dragged his weary body slowly through his brother's kitchen door. He was excited about the money that he'd earned and could barely wait to tell Carolyn. He opened the door where his young family was sleeping, went back to the living room and fell into an exhausted sleep on the couch.

* * *

Before daybreak, Carolyn and Juanita, left Roy asleep and drove back down to Money to open the store for business.

All morning, Carolyn jumped nervously whenever the crunching of tires rolled over the rock covered road or when she caught a glimpse of her husband's friends driving past in their pickup trucks.

Late that afternoon, J.W. dropped Roy off at the store and ushered Juanita back to their home.

Carolyn attempted to avoid her husband by cleaning the living quarters. He was so preoccupied with deciding what type of used truck he could get and how soon he could get it, that his wife's odd behavior escaped him.

Roy was alone in the store after pulling boxes of canned foods from the storage area. He had just begun stocking the near empty shelves, when Johnny B. came sauntering in.

105

"Aft'a-noon, Mista Br'ant, sah! Ain't seent yuh 'round lately! Was yuh out on da road widcher kin?"

Roy looked over his shoulder and returned his attention to restocking the shelves.

Even though Johnny B. was given a measure of respect by some Whites in the area, he left a bitter taste in Roy's mouth. His concern wasn't so much of how close Coloreds got, because he could always handle them. His main concern was that they not get too smart or too big. Johnny B., a 320-pound mass of coal-black muscle, was definitely not to his liking. Besides, he was a 'mite' too familiar.

"Whut'd yuh want, Boy?"

"Jist figgin' Ah'd help efen youse in need."

"Niggah, Ah don't need no help," Roy said dryly and continued stocking.

"Yassah," he replied wily. "Wa-al Ah'll jist be takin' mah leave, sah. Ah reckon yuh dun already heard 'bout dat niggah boy from up yonda when furst yuh got home. Ah'm surprised dat yuh ain't uh teenonchy bit mad wid 'im, whistlin' at yuh mizzus an' all."

A can of Pet Evaporated Milk slipped from Roy's hand and went crashing to the floor. "Whut's that yuh say, niggah?"

"Dat niggah boy from up in Ch'cagy...da one whut whistled at Mz. Car'lyn."

Blood flooded Roy's face as he jumped from the stepstool, rushed from behind the counter, and attempted to grab Johnny B. by the collar. "Yuh lyin' black sonna-bitch! Niggah, Ah'll kill yuh!"

For a moment, Johnny B. regretted being the first to tell him. Even though he was considerably larger in stature, he feared that Roy might fly into one of his fits and pull out a gun. But then, the sense of power that he felt from having any kind of control over Roy, however temporary, made him smile.

"Wa'al sah, Ah reckon Ah mus' be lyin' tuh muhseff den, too," he said as he easily removed Roy's slim white knuckled grip from his soiled tee shirt. "Muh eyes ain't seent whut Ah thought dey seent, an' Ah guess mah ears be dead, tuh-boot. Ah'm gonna

106

git on out yuh way now. Yuh got mah regrest fuh brangin' up de subjick." He turned to walk back out of the door.

"Wait uh minute!" Johnny B. was a niggah, to be sure, but he was a reliable niggah. Roy's body trembled as he bottled up his pride, bit his lower lip, and beckoned Johnny B. back inside.

"Ah jist mean fuh yuh tuh tell me evahthang."

Johnny B. smiled to himself and continued. "Wa'al sah, Ah was standin' up-side da sto' 'cuz Ah ain't like da way dey was lookin'. Dey was two of 'em...niggah boys down from Ch'cagy. Dey was wid dat ol' preacha's boys whut live up da road. Say dey some kin tuh 'em. Ah tells yuh, dat ol' uppity niggah moufed off at dat po' woman like he hadda right tuh! Den commenced tuh whistlin' at hur! Ah asked Mz. Car'lyn if she wanted me tuh git aft'a 'em, but Ah reckon she was waitin' fuh yuh tuh come home!"

"Car'lyn!!!" Roy bellowed as he bolted towards the rear of the store.

Carolyn began to panic as soon as she saw Johnny B. come in and heard them talking. She knew that there would be a fight. There would be no getting around it.

"Car'lyn! Whar yuh at?"

She emerged from the children's bedroom, where she was hiding.

"Roy, honay...Ah..."

"Why didn't yuh tell me?!" he screamed as he grabbed her by the hair. Her eyes widened as he drew his fist back. She threw her arm above her head to block the oncoming blow. "Shame me! Ah gotta hear 'bout some shit like that from uh niggah, 'cuz mah own damn wife don't tell me whut's goin' on in mah own goddamn house!" he screamed. "Maybe yuh didn't want me tuh know! Is that it?!"

"No Roy! That ain't so!" she screamed as his fist found its mark on the side of her face.

"Yuh was aft'a 'im wasn't yuh?! Always grinnin' up in them mutha fuckin' niggahs face! Makin' uh fool outta me in mah own goddamn house!"

Carolyn stumbled towards the back door. "Roy! Lissen tuh me baby! Ah love yuh baby...Ah would nevah..."

Mama! I Should Have Stayed With You!

Roy's hands trembled as he caught her by the throat and slammed her, against the wall. "One of them uppity Nawthn niggahs! Yuh worser than uh niggah whore! Ah'll kill yuh dead furst! Stomp yuh tramp ass intuh the ground befo' Ah let yuh shame me like this!" He flung her across the room. Her small frame crashed into the kitchen table, snapping the rickety wooden legs from their base.

Johnny B. leaned over the counter, trying to see what was happening, but no one was in sight. All he heard was yelling and furniture breaking, so he reached behind the counter, scooped out a handful of penny candy, grabbed two grape soda pops, and left.

Roy was unable to leave the store. They had no telephone or vehicle, and besides, it was collection day. Fieldhands were coming in all during the late afternoon and evening to settle their accounts.

* * *

Later that evening, Hubert came by just as Roy began closing the store. "Hey Roy! Yuh know Ah been hearin' 'bout yuh competition!" He laughed as he punched Roy playfully in the stomach. "Yuh make uh visit tuh Mz. Car'lyn's new sweetheart yet?"

"If Ah hadda truck, that niggah be dead already," Roy said as he knocked him away. "Ain't no niggah gonna disrespect me an' mine an' thank they gonna keep livin'. Nawthn niggahs got them White boys up yonda runnin' in circles, chasin' they own damn tails! Yuh know whose responsible fuh this shit don't yuh?"

Roy grabbed him by the arm and leaned in so close that Hubert could feel the heat of his breath and the light mist of saliva as he whispered, "It's them goddamned commies an' Nawthn lib'rals in cahoots tuhgetha! They dun took ovah the gov'ment. That's whut got them niggahs so fulla shit an' vinegar! Yuh kain see that kain't yuh?"

Hubert didn't try to release the grip on his arm or even step back. He simply and slowly nodded his head and answered softly, "Yeah, yeah, Roy. Ah...Ah see it."

Bonnie Blue

"Wa'al," Roy drawled, grinning as he released his friend's arm and returned to scanning the near empty shelves, "this lil' niggah ain't gonna git away wit that shit, wit me. Them Klan boys ain't the only ones that know how tuh take care of shit the right way! Stomp 'em out befo' they git started!"

"Yeah Roy, but some of 'em jist plain crazy," Hubert said as he rubbed his arm where Roy had grabbed him. "Some of the stuff they do jist ain't right, don't matt'a how yuh look at it!"

"Boy whut the hell's wrong wit yuh?" Roy yelled as his face reddened and he rushed across the dull wooden floor to defend his heroes. "They tryin' tuh do whut every red blooded White man need tuh do tuh protect the country from them damn commie lib'rals! Plantin' uh niggah when they ain't got the propp'a respect, is yuh 'sponsibility, is all they sayin'! An' Ah b'lieve 'em! They doin' the people uh service by gittin' rid of the trouble makers an' settin' thangs straight!"

"Ah kain go 'long wit them Citizens Council boys betta'n them Klansmen," Hubert said as he took a pickle from the large wooden barrel. "Hell, they both aft'a the same damn thang, but the Council do it the right way. They do it political."

"Since when yuh git so goddamn worldly smart? Wasn't that yuh wit me last year when we went coon huntin'?" Roy asked snidely "So yuh jist shuddup 'bout it! Yuh don't know whut the hell yuh talkin' 'bout! Ain't nothin' Ah kain do 'bout it tuhnight, noway. But yuh kain bet, Ah'ma damn sho take care of this thang!"

Roy and Hubert Clark had been friends since Hubert's family relocated to the Mississippi Delta area when he was nine years-old. He knew Roy would never let a thing like this pass. He had thought for a long time that Roy was a member of the Ku Klux Klan because many of his friends were, but he'd never asked him outright.

Hubert had nothing against the Coloreds; not really. Secretly, he feared them. He believed that they had some kind of mystical power. In fact, he was taught as a very young child to be careful and to not be around them without a grown white man present.

Mama! I Should Have Stayed With You!

His family had always warned that Colored folks could put a hex on you and make you go crazy. Legend had it that after you were hexed, you would do something terrible to yourself. And that was why the Klan worked in groups.

Hubert didn't know for sure, but he wasn't taking any chances. He stayed away from them, and was always careful not to confront any Coloreds, unless he was in a group.

* * *

Mose drove leisurely towards his sanctuary looking forward, as he always did, to his Deacon Board meeting. "Thank yuh Father," he whispered as he basked in the brilliant colors of the evening sky. "Beauty like this don't come by accident."

He stretched his onyx arm lazily out of the open window to receive the gentle moist caress of dew as it settled to cool the sun drenched ground.

Across the field, huddled behind a cluster of pine trees, a subtle glimpse of his small white structure could be seen. As he wove around the unmarked dirt road to his church he was surprised to be met by Brother Cleotha Hines, who was obviously troubled.

"Hey ya'll!" Mose called as he stepped from his car. "Yuh out heah kinda early ain't yuh?"

"Ah was hopin' tuh meet up wid yuh befo' da others got heah!" Cleotha exclaimed. "Ah been hearin' some talk Preacha', an' it sound like bad trouble fuh yuh, an' yuh family!"

Alarmed, Mose cautiously looked back down the road and grabbed Cleotha by his arm. "Wait," Mose whispered as he led him inside of the sanctuary. He pulled the door shut hard behind them.

"Whut? Whut yuh talkin' 'bout?"

"Now Ah gotta tell yuh, Ah been hearin' talk most all day.

110

Ah don't know if it's jist talk or not. But if White folk git wind of it, it might as well be da gospel."

"Whut yuh talkin' 'bout, Cleotha!" Mose said, his patience visibly ebbing away.

"Dere's talk dat one of yuh boys, out from Ch'caga, went down tuh Money an' sassed off at dat White gal down at de general sto'!"

Bonnie Blue

"Whut? One of mah boys? Ain't nobody said..."

"Ah'm jist tellin' yuh whut's goin' 'round. Now Ah don't know whut else tuh say."

"Yuh sho they say it's one of mah boys?" Mose asked quietly as he dropped his head and paced up and down the aisle.

"That's whut dey all sayin'," Cleotha said as he stepped out in front of his old friend. "Like Ah said, its one of yuh kin, outta Ch'caga. Dey say it was Wednesday evenin' past, whilst yuh was heah teachin' bible class. Anyway, dat's whut dey sayin."

"Ah need tuh find out whut's true an' whut ain't," Mose said, rushing to the door and jerking it open.

"Cleotha, Ah'ma need yuh tuh take ovah the meetin' fuh me, an' don't say nothin' tuh nobody, Ah gotta git back down tuh the house now!"

Mose was very familiar with J.W. Milam and his harsh hand. Grover C. Fredricks, owned the former plantation grounds where Mose and his family lived and sharecropped. At every harvest, when the sea of ripe cotton burst forth and the bean field was full, Fredricks hired the manned mechanical cotton combiners and bean scratchers that J.W. and other members of his family leased to farmers in the area.

Mose had watched for years as J.W. barked orders to the timid Colored workers on the backs of the mechanical beast or snatched them from the perched metal seats, slinging them to the ground if they didn't respond with the swiftness or as accurately that J.W. demanded. But now, his stomach churned in violent convulsions at the very notion that one of his young boys may had stepped unwittingly into the forbidden world of slavery's overseers.

As he left the church, Moses' thoughts were muddled. Anger, fear, and confusion, ricocheted aimlessly around in his mind. His drenched palms milked sweat, as he gripped the skinny steering wheel, all too aware that the calming dusk would quickly succumb to the ominous Mississippi blackness, hiding all things from sight.

Mama! I Should Have Stayed With You!

The ghostly cries of the night's train moving in the distance, drifted in on the shadows of the calming breeze. The rhythmic clacking of metal wheels against the steel rails, that had always stirred the sleeping boy in him, now appeared to cry out a warning as his ride home seemed to stretch endlessly before him.

"Kain't be mah boys. They know betta," he said to himself as his tires whizzed over the red dirt road. "'Sides," he rationalized as he attempted to calm himself. "If aira-one of them White boys been down tuh talk wid Mista Fredricks 'bout it, he woulda been dun sent down fuh me befo' now. Ain't nothin' but talk."

As Mose neared his home, he stared straight out into the brightly lit path that his headlights pared out of the now solemn night; feverishly fighting the powerful panic that raced his heart.

"Father, please protect mah family an' show me the way. Ah ain't nevah had nothin' like this tuh happen. Jist tell me whut tuh do."

His foot pressed harder on the accelerator as he came upon the familiar formation of trees that lined the road leading to his home; and the truth.

"Lawd, Ah know it ain't true. It kain't be true. But, if them youngins been down theah cuttin' uh fool, Ah'ma tear their b'hinds up!"

* * *

Brilliant twinkling stars decorated the black canvass of night as Elizabeth sat on the front porch, rocking rhythmically in her old wooden rocking chair, humming her favorite spiritual. Suddenly, she stopped, slowly stood and peered out at the headlights flickering through the trees, moving rapidly toward her.

She'd lived her entire life in the Delta, and unexpected visitors that came after dark was usually a sign of bad news. It was too soon to be Mose returning from the meeting and she wasn't expecting any company. Cautiously she began to back up to the screen door.

Bonnie Blue

The headlights quickly turned off of the dirt road and sped down the short drive which spilled into the yard. She ran back into her kitchen and pressed the hook into the latch of the screen door. As the car came closer, she could see that it was Mose. Relieved, she smiled, unlatched the screen and went out into the yard to meet him. "Whut? Yuh back heah already? Ah know the Deacon Board meetin' ain't..."

"We got trouble. Mista Fredricks ain't sent fuh' me, is he?"

"Naw Mose! Yuh know Ah'd tell yuh soon's Ah hear!" she exclaimed. "Oh Lawd, why yuh 'spect he be sendin' fuh yuh?"

"Ah don't rightly know yet." he said as he walked past her. "But them boys betta tell me somethin', or Ah'ma beat the livin' daylights outta all of 'em."

"Kelvin! Wheeler! Ya'll!" His voice boomed through the house. "All ya'll, git on out heah tuh me right now!"

The boys were shooting marbles on the floor in the back bedroom. When Moses' booming voice shook through the halls, they froze. They knew that they had been discovered. There was no time to make up a lie or even pray to God that Mose wouldn't whip them.

"Don't ya'll make me hafta come back theah!" he yelled as he stormed down the hall towards the tiny congregation.

"Aw man!" Kelvin whispered frantically as he collected his senses and rushed to the bedroom door. "Ya'll betta c'mon! He know!"

The boys crashed into Mose as they attempted to pile out the bedroom door. "Git back in theah!" he yelled pushing them back into the room. "Liz'bit, turn off them lights up theah an' watch! Lemme know if yuh see anythang up the road!"

"Mose, whut is it? Whut am Ah lookin' fuh'?"

"Don't matt'a. Jist call me if yuh see anythang movin' out theah!"

She rushed into the kitchen, pulled the chain to the ceiling light, took up a candescent spot next to the kitchen window and peer through the persimmon trees, towards the road.

Mama! I Should Have Stayed With You!

"Ya'll sit yuh tails down ovah theah!" Mose said angrily.

The older boys crowded quietly onto one bed. Emmett and Alfie quickly plopped on the floor next to them.

Terrified, Emmett mashed his back as far into the edge of the mattress as he could and slid his sight up to his cousins for any sign that his great uncle wasn't going to whip him and send him right back home, where another whipping would surely be waiting.

What he saw were three sets of frighten eyes, staring at Mose as he pressed the door shut.

"Papa, Ah wasn't in it!"

Mose closed his eyes as he held up his hand. "Kelvin, hush up boy."

He slowly opened his eyes, his voice low and unnaturally calm, "Don't give me nothin' but the God honest truth. Whut happened when ya'll went tuh town? Now, befo' yuh fix yuh mouf tuh lie, lemme tell yuh, Ah jist come from the church an' heard theahs been talk 'bout one of yuh boys causin' trouble in town."

"Papa, Ah didn't do nothin'," Kelvin replied. "That was Bobo an' them! It wasn't nonna me! Ah told 'em they shoulda told yuh but they didn't!"

"Oooh," Alfie said as he turned his serious little face around to confront his older brother. "Yuh jist sittin' theah tellin' tales! Yuh was the one whut told evahbody tuh hush up 'bout it! Liga Mae say we should tell Papa, an' yuh said 'No'!"

114

"Naw, that whutn't nonna me!"

"Whut the ham-fire wrong wid yuh chil'ren?" Mose growled as his angry eyes pierced past his furrowed brow. "This ain't no fun an' games! This heah serious bidness! Yuh bes' shut yuh mouf right now an' thank the Lawd fuh sendin' His angel tuh sit on mah shoulda! Ah'ma tell yuh the God's honest truth! If he didn't, Ah'd be snatchin' uh knot in yuh lyin' b'hind right now!"

"Granddaddy," Wheeler raised his hand to speak. "I'ma tell you what happened," he said as he looked around to the others. "It wasn't just Bobo. It was all of us."

Mose stood silent. His arms twined tightly across his chest as he listened to Wheeler solemnly relay the incident at the store.

"...and granddaddy, that's the whole truth. I swear."

Bonnie Blue

Mose looked down at Emmett, who was picking at the hole that he had worn in the toe of his sock. "Ah don't know whut tuh tell yuh boy. Ah know Mamie talked tuh yuh befo' yuh leff Ch'caga. That jist ain't somethin' we do down heah son. These peckawoods'll kill yuh dead. An' whistlin' at hur Emmett? Whut possessed yuh? Now Ah know dog-gone well yuh don't do no mess like that at home! Whut made yuh thank yuh could come down heah wid all that foolishness?"

Emmett cast his eyes down at his sock, shrugged his shoulder, and meekly said, "I ddd...don't know. I'm sorry. I ddd...didn't mmm...mean anything by it. Honest. WWW...We were just playin' aaa...around."

"Ya'll move ovah," Mose said as he made room for himself and Emmett to sit on the bed. "Horsin' 'round wid White folk down heah's dangerous. Ain't nonna ya'll goin' back in town whilst yuh heah. An' Ah ain't lettin' ya'll outta mah sight. Ah gotta send ya'll back. It's too late tuh do anythang tuhnight. Ah'ma check wid the train folk tuh see if Ah kain change ya'lls tickets an' git yuh outta heah on the next train. If Ah kain't change 'em in Batesville, Ah guess Ah'ma hafta scrape up some money an' buy yuh new tickets fuh the day aft'a. Them White boys mus' not of gone up tuh Mista Fredricks' tuh complain, 'cuz he ain't sent nobody down fuh me. But it don't matt'a. Ya'll still leavin' outta heah."

"WWW...Why?" Emmett took a deep breath and blew a short whistle to clear his stammer. "Why would MMM...Mr. Fredricks www...wanna talk to you? You didn't do anything."

"Don't matt'a. Ah told yuh. Thangs down heah...well they different. We ain't nothin' mo' than uh snap 'way from slavery days. Ah sharecrops from G. C. Fredricks. So if them White boys wanted tuh, they could take it up wid him, an' he could make us pay whutevah damages them boys say. Down heah, when Colored folk sharecrop or tenant farm from Whites, whoevah we rentin' from is responsible fuh' rightin' our wrong doin's. The problem is, any peckawood kain make up whutevah crime he want an'say uh Colored man dun it. Don't matt'a if fifteen other Colored folk an' God Almighty know yuh weren't no wheah 'round, yuh still gotta pay."

Mama! I Should Have Stayed With You!

"They want you to pay money for aaa...any and everything?"

"Yuh gittin' off good if all they want is money. They kain take it out on yuh hide, beat yuh 'til they feel betta 'bout the situation, send yuh tuh jail or the graveyard; don't matt'a."

Emmett swallowed hard. His mouth dropped as he looked into Moses' eyes.

"If they was gonna do somethin' 'bout it, Ah 'spect Ah woulda heard by now. Jist do as Ah say, an' evahthang gonna be fine. Ya'll kain still have uh good time whilst yuh heah. Lawd knows theah's 'nough of ya'll. But Ah gotta tell yuh," he warned as he stood to leave, "don't nary uh one of ya'll dare tuh open yuh moufs 'bout this tuh no body. Don't matt'a, kinfolk or no. This ain't nevah happen. An' Ah'ma work on gittin' ya'll back home soon's Ah kain. Lawd know, Ah ain't got uh cryin' dime tuh mah name right now, but Ah'ma do whutevah Ah hafta do tuh git ya'll outta heah by tuhmorrow; day aft'a at the latest."

* * *

In Chicago, Mamie was sound asleep when the late morning sun crept through the partially opened venetian blinds and danced brightly on her face. Small beads of sweat, which formed on her forehead and upper lip, glistened on her clear golden skin. Slowly, she opened one eye and groaned as she turned away from the glowing light and reached for the small alarm clock that sat on the bedside table.

"Eleven-thirty already?" She whined as she rolled over on her back, looked up at the ceiling and felt just how empty the house was without Emmett. "This just doesn't make any sense at all," she said as she threw the covers back and slid out of bed.

As she began straightening the sheets, the doorbell rang. "I'm coming!" she called as she threw on her robe and made her way down to the front door.

"Oh, good morning Mother. What are you doing out so early?" she asked as she yawned and walked back up to her apartment.

Bonnie Blue

"You mean good afternoon, don't you? And where have you been? I tried to call you last night. My God, child! Open these windows! It's hot as blue blazes in here!"

"Mother, please don't start. I heard the phone ringing, but I really wasn't in the mood for conversation."

"What's the matter baby? You've been locked up in this house ever since Emmett left. You should have been out to Viola's by now. What did you tell her? I know she's disappointed."

"Yes, I know. But I told her I was just going to wait until I heard from Emmett before I come out there. Uncle Mose really needs to go on and get a telephone. I think a party line is better than no line at all," she said as she opened the kitchen door.

"Now Mamie, that boy is having a ball and you know he's no trouble to Elizabeth. I got a letter from her just a couple of days ago. She said that Emmett was fine and behaving himself." Alma said as she searched the refrigerator for a cold drink. "If you had answered the telephone, you would have known that."

"I know. But, just the same, I'm going to wait until I hear from him." Mamie went back into her bedroom, finished making her bed and began to get dressed.

"You haven't been out of this house all week!" Alma called as she removed the pitcher of lemonade. "So I think we should go out and have a decent lunch before we go shopping!"

117

"I don't know," Mamie called, sliding her red and white poka-dot shirtwaist dress over her head. "Maybe later. I just need to do a little something around the house."

"Mamie, look around you! There's nothing left to do! Besides, we already made plans to go shopping for Emmett's school supplies. What you need to do is get out of this hot house. If you don't want to go to lunch with me, why don't you give Ruby a call?"

Ruby Hollis and Mamie had attended school together and had been best friends for years. She'd telephoned Mamie a few times already this week, but Mamie put off seeing her. Even Gene hadn't been able to coax her out of the house.

Mama! I Should Have Stayed With You!

"What is it? Why are you so dead set on getting me out? I just don't feel like being bothered!"

"All right. All right. Forget I said anything," Alma said as she retrieved a tall glass from the cabinet. Mamie sat quietly, waiting for her mother to get her last words in. "If all you want to do is take root in this stuffy house, there's nothing I can do about it!" she said as she carefully filled the glass, holding back the lemon slices with a spoon.

Mamie glanced up at the bright yellow kitchen clock. "Okay Mother, I'll give her a call later. But I just don't feel like being around a bunch of people," she said as she positioned the oscillating fan in the opened back door.

There was no breeze, but rather a bed of humidity that sat heavily in the air. Alma finished her drink while Mamie returned to her bedroom and took the paper curlers from her hair.

Alma finally convinced Mamie to walk down to Norman's, a homey neighborhood restaurant on 71st and Cottage Grove. The walk made her feel better, but she still missed her son.

When Mamie returned home, Emmett's letter was waiting in the mailbox. She stood at the foot of the stairs in the vestibule, ripped open the envelope, and smiled as she climbed briskly up the stairs.

Once inside, she sat on the sofa and gingerly unfolded the letter.

Hi Mama!

Having fun, but I miss you. You were right. It's a lot different down here than at home, but it's alright. In a way, I will be glad to get back home. I miss everybody. I'm out of money and can you please send my motorbike? I'll pay you back when I get home. Tell Grandmama hello for me and give her a kiss for me too. See you when I get home.

Love you, Emmett

Bonnie Blue

Mamie closed her eyes as she sat with the letter trembling in her hands. It was then, that   she decided to go to Mississippi and bring him home. She rushed into the bedroom for her telephone book.

Bernard Hunt, her cousin, was the traveler in the family. Before you could ask, "Hey Bernie, do you want to take a ride out to....," he was already packed and had the car's motor running. She hoped that he would drive down with her.

"Come on, Bernie. Please be home," she said as she dialed his number.

Bernard was just returning to Argo after attempting to talk one of his army buddies into driving to Mississippi with him for a few days. But as it turned out, his friend couldn't take the time away from his job.

Disappointed, Bernard returned home to cut his grass. He heard the telephone ring, as he pulled the hand mower from his garage. He bolted up the back steps, burst through the kitchen door and snatched up the telephone.

"Yeah! Hello? Hello?"

When there was no answer. Mamie hung up and sat looking out the living room window, wondering what she should do.

A group of Emmett's friends passed below, on their way to play ball in the schoolyard.

Brucie caught sight of her and called, "Hi Miss Bradley! Is Bobo home yet?"

"No baby, but he'll be back next weekend!"

"Oh, okay! Bye!" he said as they waved and continued down the street.

* * *

At dawn, Mose drove down to the tiny train station in Batesville, but he was unable to get the boys tickets changed. The clerk informed him that they could not make any ticket changes at their small station, but suggested that maybe he could get them changed in Memphis.

Mama! I Should Have Stayed With You!

For much of the day, Mose made his rounds to his friends, family and deacons; borrowing whatever money he could, to drive down to Memphis get their tickets changed, or purchase more tickets get the boys back home sooner. He was already aware that they were all in the same poverty condition that he was, and as much as they may have wanted to help, they couldn't loan what they didn't have.

* * *

In town at the Bryant's, Roy's anger was mounting. Different accounts of what had occurred days earlier with the Chicago boy continued to trickle in, and with each account the story grew. Roy was barely able to contain his rage. Waiting until one of his brothers came out wasn't an option. He started working on an old pickup truck that sat abandoned across the road, next to the train tracks.

Carolyn sat quietly in the splintered folding chair behind the counter, absorbing the momentary peace, when Billie came through the door. He had completely forgotten about the whistling incident as he stooped over and gazed wistfully at the individual boxes of Nut Chews, Mary Janes and other candies that now crowded the glass case. He was so quiet in fact, that Carolyn didn't noticed him until she saw his crown of curly hair, protruding just above the counter.

120

"Whut yuh want boy?"

"Oh, mo'nin' Mz. Car'lyn ma'am," he said with a start. "Mah Mama wants uh jug of Burr Rabbits molasses an' uh pack of Garrett's Snuff." He dug down into the pouch on the bib of his overalls, and piled all the coins on the counter as Carolyn filled his request.

Roy was working under the truck when Billie entered the store, but his attention was immediately turned to the porch when the screen door bounced as it closed. He only caught a glimpse of Billie as he came out; but a glimpse was all he needed.

"Car'lyn! Git out heah!" he yelled as he ran across the road. She almost instantly appeared before him.

"Git in the truck!"

Bonnie Blue

"Whar we...?"

"Shut the hell up, an' do like Ah tell yuh!" he said as he started back across the road.

Carolyn glanced back at the open door of their home and business with her children playing in the back, and followed her husband to the rusted truck.

Roy's eyes pierced unblinkingly into Billie's back. He beckoned for Johnny B. as he emerged from across the tracks, zipping his pants after peeing in the bushes. "Git in back! Hurry up an' grab that lil' niggah goin' up the road! Ah know he's one of 'em!"

Roy attempted to start the engine. It spat and choked before the grinding noise gave way to a loud revving. Johnny B. hopped on the open tailgate. Rocks propelled with tremendous force as Roy floored the accelerator.

Billie clung tightly to the copper coins, the change from his mother purchase, as he hugged the bottle of molasses. The unfastened metal clasp on the strap of his faded out overalls bounced freely on his back as he hurried up the road, stopping only occasionally to scrape loose pebbles, which stubbornly stuck to the bottoms of his bare feet.

Billie continued down the side of the road, unaware of the rusted pickup truck that rapidly approached him amid bellowing smoke. Suddenly, he heard the explosion of the motor backfire. Roy swerved towards him. The frightened boy fell to the ground as he leaped out of the way. The glass bottle of molasses broke into huge chunks as it crashed against the jagged rocks on the road.

Johnny B. jumped from the truck, lifted Billie effortlessly from the puddle of molasses, which was forming around his small face and chest, and pitched him in the back of the truck.

"Is this the niggah?" Roy asked as he clutched the steering wheel and stared fiercely through the windshield.

"Naw, Ah don't thank so," Carolyn said timidly as she turned all the way around in her seat to see what was happening in the rear of the truck. "Ah thank that's one of Big Teddy's boys."

Mama! I Should Have Stayed With You!

"Goddamnit! Ah'm ti'ed of this shit! Evahtime Ah turn around, some damned niggah grinnin' all up in yuh face! Ah ain't havin' it! Now woman, is that the niggah or not?"

"Naw Roy. Ah dun told yuh it ain't. This heah Big Teddy's boy. The other niggah is bigger an' from up nawth!"

Roy looked at her for a long moment and finally called back for Johnny B. to let the boy go. He grabbed the teary faced child by the arm and tossed him from the truck onto the broken glass.

Billie lay frightened with his eyes squeezed tight until long after he heard the truck rumble down the road. Finally he rose, sticky and bloodied from where his tooth broke and where a part of his ear was torn. He was more frightened than he had ever been in his young life.

Billie's trembling little legs barely held him as he ran down the road, hugging the edge of the ditch; constantly looking over his shoulder in anticipation of their return. When a tractor motor revved in the distance, Billie screamed and broke into a hard run; not stopping until he reached his home and the safety of his family.

* * *

122

J.W. Milam was one of the older sons in the Milam-Bryant clan. Most people who knew of 36 year-old J.W. either respected or feared him, particularly because his six-foot, three-inch frame and solid 285 pounds was decorated with scars from shrapnel wounds.

J.W. thought himself a God fearing patriot who held a strong love for Mississippi. He was proud of his military service and the medals that he was awarded during his tour of duty in World War II. Before his discharge, he was promoted to the rank of Commissioned Officer; Lieutenant.

When he returned from the service, he began renting Colored operated tractors and cotton combiners to area farmers. He had the reputation of kept his 'niggahs' in line as well as overseers did back in the days of slavery.

Bonnie Blue

At about 10:30 that night, J.W. drove out to Money to check on his younger brother and to let him know that their mother was expecting them the next day.

The frame of the screen door bounced as he knocked.

"Roy! Hey, Roy!"

Roy stumbled out onto the porch, his voice thick with moonshine. "Hey, Dub! Yuh come right on time! Ah need yuh truck! Ah need tuh make uh run!"

J.W. held his brother back at arm's length. "Goddamn, boy! How mucha that shit yuh been drankin'?" He laughed. "Yuh need tuh leave that shit alone befo' it burn uh hole in yuh gut. Yuh ain't drivin' mah damn truck nowhar. Ah come out tuh see if yuh need somethin' befo' Ah pick ya'll up tuhmorrow noon. Ah'm tellin' yuh now, Ah ain't makin' no extra trip out heah early mornin'."

"Naw...Naw...Naw...!" Roy said as he stumbled out to the pickup. "All Ah need is yuh truck fuh tuhnight. Ah don't need nothin' fuh tuhmorrow. Ah jist need tuh take care of this niggah right heah! Right now! Tuhnight! Yuh hear? Ah ain't takin' no mo' shit offa 'em! Come down heah disrespectin' mah

123

goddamned woman! Yuh disrepec' mah goddamn woman, yuh disrespectin' me!"

J.W. took his time and strolled over to his drunken brother as he fumbled with the truck door handle. "Roy, take yuh ass tuh bed. Ah'll be back tuhmorrow tuh pick ya'll up fuh' supp'a out at Ma's."

Roy then told him of the incident.

"Goddamn!" J.W. yelled as he slammed his fist on the truck's hood. "Why the hell didn't yuh git word tuh me earlier!"

"Shit, Dub," he slurred as he attempted to stand erect. "Ah told yuh! Ah jist fount out mah damn seff! Yuh know Ah ain't got no way tuh reach no damn body! That goddamn Johnny B.! That black ass sonna-bitch! That niggah told me!"

His eyes widened as he giggled. "Ain't that some shit? When uh niggah know 'bout whut's goin' on in yuh own damn house befo' yuh do?"

Mama! I Should Have Stayed With You!

His grin disappeared, his voice sank and eyes quickly filled with tears. "An' yuh own damn wife won't open hur goddamn mouf. Ah hate that damn niggah! If Ah had uh bullet big 'enough, Ah'd take his big black ass down! Him, *an'* that city niggah!" he screamed, staggering back to the truck. "Jist open up this goddamned door!" he demanded. "It's mah wife, an' Ah ain't 'bout tuh let no niggah come down heah an' make uh fool outta me in mah own goddamn house. Ah ain't gonna do it!"

J.W. shoved him solid against the side of the truck and held him by his tee shirt. "Roy," he said firmly "befo' Ah go anywhar, Ah got tuh be sho this ain't that rot-gut talkin'. Now straighten up!" he demanded between clinched teeth. "Whut happened?"

"Ah dun already told yuh! Now, Ah ain't gonna lie. Ah dun had uh drank uh lil' while ago, but Ah ain't drunk!"

J.W. pushed his younger brother towards the front porch and leaped into the cab of his truck. "Gowan, take yuh ass tuh bed an' sleep it off. Ah'll be back," he said, "Early!"

* * *

124

J.W. drove out to Minter City to meet up with his brother-in-law, Melvin Campbell. He and Melvin met while serving in the army when they were teenagers. They became fast friends after learning that they both came from neighboring counties in the Delta. Soon after they were discharged, J.W. met and married his sister, Juanita.

Melvin had already started closing the store, before J.W.'s truck pull up out front. It had been a long day and he was looking forward to being with his friends for their regular Saturday night of card playing, drinking and young women. He was surprised when J.W. came by earlier this afternoon and consented to playing cards with the boys.

It wasn't often that J.W. went out for anything that was recreational. This was the first opportunity that he's had in a long time to spend with 'the old' J.W.

"Ah'll be ready in uh minute. All the boys meetin' up out at Fred's."

Bonnie Blue

"Take yuh time. Ah'll wait in the truck," J.W. said as he turned to leave back out.

Melvin looked up from his ledger and knew from the stern look on his brother-law's face, that plans had changed. "Goddamnit, Dub! Ah knew yuh wasn't comin'! Boy, yuh gotta make time tuh have some fun!" he said lightly. "Whutevahs workin' yuh craw kain wait 'til tuhmorrow! We playin' cards tuhnight! Ah got uh nice lil' gal fuh yuh!"

"Ah said Ah'm waitin' in the truck!" J.W. called as he walked out the door and swung himself up into his new 1955 Chevy pickup.

J.W.'s head throbbed. He couldn't be sure if Roy's story was true or not. But for J.W., if it was true, not only had his family been violated, but the entire Southern way of life had been challenged. The longer he waited, the more intensely he thought about the changes that the government was forcing on him.

"Nawthn lib'rals, Commies, an' Jews." He mumbled. "They all tryin' tuh take ovah the goddamn country. They runnin' the whole damn fed'ral gov'ment, an' now they got these niggah's comin' down heah in mah own back yard tryin' tuh walk all ovah me an' mine, stealin' away evahthang we dun fought fuh. Freedom? Whut the hell they talkin 'bout freedom. They kain give all them niggah's up thar as much freedom as they want, but they bes' keep that shit right on up thar," he said angrily to himself. "Ah dun worked too damn hard an' long fuh this country!"

Melvin rushed out of his store and climbed into his own pickup.

J.W. started his motor and called through the open window, "Ah'ma need yuh tuhnight! Meet me out at Hillards! Ah gotta make uh stop!"

"Whut's goin' on?" Melvin called, as J.W. already began backing out from in front of the store.

* * *

Twenty nine year-old Henry Lee Login, his twenty year-old wife, Claire, and their three small children lived on one of the

Mama! I Should Have Stayed With You!

plantation-like farms managed by the Milam's. Henry Lee drove the mechanical cotton picker for J.W., and Claire worked as a fieldhand; picking cotton.

Henry Lee, Claire and thirty year-old, Levy 'Too Tight', Collins had known each other since childhood. Although married, Too Tight has a number of girlfriends. This is the reason for the separation from his wife, who lives in the Colored section of Glendora with their 4 young children.

The trio had worked on farms managed by the Milam's, for most of their lives. Too Tight sleeps on the worn sofa that sits off to the side of the wide room at the front of the house which doubles as a living room on one side and kitchen on the other.

126

Their quarters are cramped; only three rooms. All three of Henry Lee's young sons share a pallet in the smallest room adjacent to their parent's bedroom.

Henry Lee had repaired much of their secondhand furniture, using wooden planks from collapsed shanties. Too Tight did his share of chores around the house as well.

Claire also tended the small vegetable garden flourishing in the back of their home, which serves as provisions for the family. Most of her wares, she cans for the winter.

It was hot and humid this time of year. The cool night air was the only relief for these backwoods residents. Most people slept with only the screen door closed, if they were fortunate enough to have a screen door to keep the flies and mosquitoes out. Such is the case with the Logins' tonight.

It was well past midnight and the household had settled into a peaceful slumber, when J.W. approached the porch and banged on the latched, homemade screen door.

Claire sat up with a start. "Hen Lee," she whispered as she shook her snoring husband. "Hen Lee! Wake up Ah say!"

"Whut?" Henry Lee moaned as he reluctantly dragged himself from his sleep. "Whut yuh want Claire?"

Bonnie Blue

"Lawd, who yuh 'spect dat is dis time uh night?" she asked, snatching the crumbled sheet from the floor to cover herself. "Don't no good come when folks come callin' dis time uh night."

"Hurry up an' git yuh trifflin' asses' out heah!" J.W. yelled as he banged on the door again.

"Stay heah," Henry Lee whispered as he quickly got out of bed and snatched on his trousers.

Too Tight rolled off the ragged sofa in the living room, crawled across the floor, and peered through the darkness of the house. Immediately, he recognized the imposing silhouette

127

standing in the bright headlights of the truck. Henry Lee hugged the wall as he crept towards the kitchen.

"It's ol' Milam," Too Tight whispered.

The screen door bounced as J.W. banged on it again, and yelled, "Henry Lee! Too Tight! Ya'll heard me! Now git yuh asses' out heah!"

Henry Lee peered past the homemade curtain covering the small kitchen window, desperately searching his mind to pinpoint what he had done wrong. He took a deep breath and stepped out onto the porch. "Evenin' sah."

"Git Too Tight an' meet me at the truck! Hurry up! Ah ain't got all night!"

"Yassah," he said as he moved quickly back through the door into the darkness of the house.

"Did yuh see da look on his face?" Too Tight asked nervously.

Claire got up and whispered, "Who dat is? Dey some trouble fuh sho, ain't it?"

"Ain't no need in frettin'. Jist Mista Milam. Want us tuh help 'im wid somethin' is all," Henry Lee whispered as he glanced over to Too Tight.

"Mama?" Their oldest toddler cried, as he rubbed his sleepy eyes and stumbled out of the bedroom.

"Is yuh dun somethin' tuh make 'im mad? Is yuh in trouble? Lawd please tell me yuh ain't!"

Mama! I Should Have Stayed With You!

"Naw! Fuh sho Ah ain't! Now yuh jist gowan back an' check on dem youngins, an' git on back tuh bed yuh own seff. We fine."

As she turned to go, she said, "Ain't no good uh body kain do dis time uh night."

"Mama?" The toddler cried again as he stood in the middle of the floor.

Henry Lee took his young son by the hand and led him back to their bedroom.

Too Tight was already dressed and standing at the door when he returned.

J.W. leaned on the horn and yelled out the window, "Hurry up an' brang yuh black asses' outta thar! Ah said Ah ain't got all night!"

Too Tight stood back from the door, but he could still see J.W. sitting in the truck, cursing them. "Ol' low down cracka! Evah time dey gits ready tuh do dey dirt, dey come lookin' fuh uh niggah tuh help 'em."

Henry Lee grew more nervous. He and Too Tight both knew that J.W. was a cruel man and that there wasn't much that he was incapable of doing.

"C'mon," he said. "Let's go befo' he git the notion tuh come back again. Ah don't want Claire tuh git no mo' skeered den she already is."

Henry Lee felt her presence behind him. "Hen Lee, baby...Ah'm skeered fuh yuh," she whispered as she choked back the urge to cry. "Did yuh do somethin'?"

"Naw. We ain't dun nothin'," Too Tight said confidently as he walked to the open door.

Henry Lee took Claire into his arms attempting to reassure her.

"Gowan back tuh bed. We gonna be fine. Ain't nothin' happen. Ah'll be back tereckly." Without another word, he kissed her on the forehead and joined Too Tight as he headed out into the moonlit night.

Bonnie Blue

* * *

The trio rode in silence, down the long stretch of highway toward Roy's store in Money.

The countryside was beautifully calm. The night was so clear that the brilliant full moon looked close enough to reach up and touch.

From the open bed of the truck where he was seated, Henry Lee looked up into the night and prayed softly, "How long King Jesus...how long?"

129

Too Tight glared over at him and thought to himself, 'Prayin' ain't gonna help. Folks got dey mind set tuh do dirt, ain't nothin' gonna help'.

"Whut yuh 'spect he up tuh?" Henry Lee whispered.

"Ah reckon we'll fin' out soon 'nough."

* * *

At about that same time, Mose and his family were turning onto the dirt road that led to their driveway. He was finally able to get some money together, but it still wasn't enough to buy new tickets.

Since the boys were leaving soon, Mose and Elizabeth took them to pick up Curtis from Moses' eldest son, Archie. Most of their kinfolk from the surrounding areas came out to Greenwood for dinner and visited well into the night. The boys were exhausted and fell asleep shortly after they began the long ride home.

Mose pulled up in front of the house, and turned off the motor. He and Elizabeth sat quietly in the car amid the call of a hoot owl, and the snores of the boys propped up on each other in the back seat.

"Ah didn't want tuh say nothin' 'round the boys," Mose said softly, "but Archie pulled me aside tuhnight. Say he heard the same story Cleotha told me, 'bout some boys from up nawth an' that White gal down at the sto'."

"Oh Lawd," Elizabeth gasped quietly as she looked in the back seat at Emmett sleeping soundly. "Maybe it was some oth'a boys. Maybe some oth'a youngin's come aft'a they leff. Yuh

Mama! I Should Have Stayed With You!

know they ain't the only boys visitin' down heah from up nawth."

"Ah told yuh the boys dun already told me Emmett did it, but they all had uh hand in it." Mose said quietly.

Elizabeth inhaled deeply as she shook her head and whispered, "It's only through the Grace of God, that ain't nothin' happen."

Mose stared out the front window. The glow of the radiant moon illuminated the worry lines, etched in his face. "They gotta go back now," he said sternly. "An' Ah mean they

130

gotta go back right now! We goin' tuh Memphis in the mo'nin', tereckly aft'a church. Ah should have 'nough gas money by then tuh make it out theah. Maybe they kain change them train tickets out, since they kain't change 'em in Batesville. Eith'a way, we leavin' up outta heah tuhmorrow mo'nin'."

"Yuh know his Mama ain't nevah gonna let 'im come back down heah."

"Woman...whuts wrong wid yuh?" he replied in disbelief. "That boy don't need tuh be down heah if he don't know how tuh act 'round these peckawoods! Actin' out wid White folk! Whut kinda foolishness is that?" he mumbled as he left her in the car.

"Okay Mose. Ah'll see tuh it they bags is packed furst thang in the mo'nin'," Elizabeth said faintly, reaching over the seat to shake the child's knee closest to her. "Ollie, ya'll, wake up an' gowan in the house. C'mon now. We home. Ain't no suckin' titty babies out heah. Ah ain't carryin' no grown folks."

"Ah ain't 'sleep," Ollie yawned. "Ah was just restin' mah eyes. Wheeler an' them the ones sleepin'," he said as he yawned again and shook the other boys out of their drowsy state. "Wheeler' Bobo, ya'll! We gonna leave ya'll out heah!"

Slowly, everyone dragged themselves from the car.

Mose had already turned on the single light that hung in the middle of the living room and disappeared down the hall to his bedroom.

"Aw man!" Emmett said as he bumped into the large worn chair, which sat slightly to the side of the door. "I can sleep right here." He said softly. Nearly overcome with sleep, he plopped

Bonnie Blue

into the tattered but comfortable chair and cradled his head gently on the arm.

"Boy, you know you crazy," Wheeler said as he tried to pull Emmett from the chair. "Bobo, you better open up your eyes and walk your tail on to the back and go to bed like you got some sense."

"Wait a minute. I'm jjj...just getting' ready to get ready for bed."

"Bobo yuh jist come up wid stuff," Kelvin laughed as he popped Emmett on the back of his head. "Ah ain't nevah heard of nobody gittin' ready tuh git ready tuh do nothin'."

The small herd of exhausted boys trudged down the dark hall. "Mama," Alfie whined as he stumbled towards his mother, still heavy in sleep, propping his head on her breast. "Ah'm hongry. Kain Ah have uh teacake?"

"Baby, it's way too late up in the night tuh be talkin' 'bout eatin'." she said as she rubbed his head and pulled his arms from around her waist.

"Emmett," Elizabeth said as she turned him towards the hallway leading to the bedrooms, "take this boy on down tuh the back bedroom wid yuh. Ah don't want him wakin' up befo' day, tryin' tuh keep up wid his Pa."

"Yes ma'am," Emmett said as he pried himself from his comfortable nest, took his little cousin by the hand, and led him to the rear bedroom.

There was little talk in the bedrooms as the boys shed their trousers, shirts, and shoes and fell into their beds. Soon they were all asleep and a blanket of peaceful silence settled around the Wright house.

* * *

J.W. had just arrived back at Roy's store. Brilliant moonlight flooded the tiny town sculpted from the surrounding forestry. All semblance of peace was destroyed when J.W. slammed the door of the truck, stormed up the steps, and banged on the screen door.

"Roy! Roy!"

Mama! I Should Have Stayed With You!

Roy stumbled from the back in the living quarters, hugging a near empty Mason jar of moonshine. "Who the hell...?" he yelled as he peered through the darkness of the store to make out the silhouette of his brother. "Aw, hey!" he said as he struggled to unhook the screen.

132

"Boy, Ah dun told yuh tuh leave this shit alone!" J.W. commanded as he snatched the jar.

"Whut? Yuh come all the way back heah tuh take mah las' lil' swallow?" Roy giggled as he tried to grab the jar.

"Naw that's alright! Yuh gowan," Roy slurred as he pushed the jar to J.W.'s lips. "yuh mah big brotha! Heah! Gowan! Take uh sip! But don't kill it! Jist leave me uh lil' spider leg in the corner."

"Ah don't want none, an' yuh sho as hell don't need no mo'," J.W. said as he easily held his smaller brother at arm's length. "Yuh got tuh git yuh shit tuhgetha boy! We gonna go down an' take care of this niggah right now! Ah don't know why ain't nobody said nothin' tuh me 'bout this shit," he said angrily. "But heah 'bout it or no, it make the whole damn family look like we jist sittin' back takin' it!"

"Roy! Straighten up, boy! Yuh alright?" J.W. said, looking him square in the face.

"Yeah, yeah," Roy slurred as he attempted to stand straight, and look sober.

"Hurry up an' git dressed," J.W. said as he shoved Roy away from him and the Mason jar. "We gonna take care of this shit tuhnight! Right now!"

"Ah'm ready!" Roy said excitedly as he gave up on retrieving his moonshine and rubbed his sweaty palms down his dingy sleeveless undershirt. "Ah tell yuh, Ah'ma love beatin' the black offa that mutha fuckin' niggah!" he yelled.

Stale spit sprayed as his face distorted in rage, his moonshine wilted arms swinging wildly in the air at the imaginary figure before him.

"Ah tell yuh! Ah was fixin' tuh go out thar an' take care of that lil' niggah mah damned self! Ah kain jist see 'im now, struttin' 'round, thankin' he got away wit this shit! Hell, Ah was

Bonnie Blue

fixin' tuh walk down tuh that niggah preacha's place!" Roy yelled.

"Jist shuddup an' lissen!" J.W. yelled, his patience fraying at his younger brother's moonshine driven bravado.

"Naw...Naw...Lissen...Ah'm fine! Ah ain't drunk! Now lissen...lissen! Ah heah that 'ol preacha's gotta bunch of niggahs outta Ch'caga down at his place, an' Car'lyn, she know which one it is. All we gotta do is brang the niggah back heah tuh make sho we got the right one!"

"She goin' down thar wit us. We only makin' one trip."

"Whut 'bout mah boys'? They kain't stay heah by theyseffs."

"Don't matt'a! The preacha's down on Fredricks' jist up the road. Ain't gonna take no time at all," J.W. murmured angrily. "Now shuddup. Git Car'lyn, an' don't wake up them boys. We'll drop hur right back heah aft'a she show us which one it is."

"Good, good!" Roy exclaimed. "We kain swang by an' pick up Huber'. He come by earlier. Said he'd help if we need 'im."

"Okay, jist hurry it up!" J.W. said impatiently.

As they prepared to leave inside, Henry Lee looked around in the darkness and said almost in a whisper, "Tight, Ah feel right skeered; inside Ah mean."

* * *

On the way there, Too Tight rewound his actions of the last few days, trying to recall if he or Henry Lee could have done or said anything that landed them in this place. He knew that J.W. always had a bad taste in his mouth about him, but he also knew that, if this midnight ride was meant for him, he wouldn't be sitting in the back of his truck thinking about it now. It was only when they pulled up in front of Bryant's store that he remembered the rumor that he'd heard at the 'Juke Joint' in Glendora the night before.

Too Tight had worked in the fields, from 'kain't see, to kain't see'. He was tired and hungry, but he wanted to spend time with some of his friends.

Mama! I Should Have Stayed With You!

He had ventured down the back roads of Glendora to the Juke Joint. When he got there, a crowd of men were gathered

134

around a small table, devouring everything that came out of Johnny B.'s mouth.

"Ah tells yuh, dat niggah went in dere an' sassed dat woman like it weren't nothin'! Efen Ah knows Mista Br'ant, an' ya'll knows fuh sho we's tight, he gonna beat da black offin' dat uppity niggah! Serve 'im right too! Dem city niggahs thanks dey so damn much betta'n other folk! Ah fixed his ass though. Ah told Br'ant soon's Ah seen't 'im! Dat very mawnin' he come home! Ah sho told 'im!"

While the others listened to Johnny B. in total awe, Too Tight shook his head. "Damn fool," he said as he went back outside and sat on the steps in the coolness of the night.

The others were still inside when Ike Jackson, Too Tights drinking buddy, walked up.

"Whut yuh doin' out heah by yuhseff?" Ike asked as he walked to the entrance of the Juke Joint and glanced inside. Seeing no one that he had business with, he came back out and plopped down on the rickety step next to Too Tight. "Look like Johnny B. got dem ignunt niggahs b'lievin' his big talk again. Ah'm tellin' yuh man, one of dese days dat big cornbread fed, liva-lipted niggah's gonna be fount face down in da rivah by dem same crackas' he claim tuh be so damn tight wid."

Too Tight looked out the side of his eye at his buddy's cloaked boldness; especially since slim Ike had never said more than a handful of words in Johnny B.'s presence. "Ike, yuh need tuh take all dat ol' tough talk an' shove it in uh preacha's pocket." Too Tight laughed. "Yuh big talk's jist like preacha's money; won't nevah see da light of day!"

"Yuh sho right!" Ike laughed. "Ain't no preacha Ah evah heard of, dig too deep in dey pocket fuh nothin'! Skeered he might mess 'round an' touch uh Bo doll'a! Hafta knock de dust off fuh sho!"

Their laughter was interrupted by a large commotion filtering through the distant darkness. History had taught them to

Bonnie Blue

be silent and still. Out on the road, a pickup truck loaded with young White men passed and called out to them, "Hey, yuh

135

niggah's thar! It's dark out heah! Flash dem pearly whites fuh me one time, so Ah can see yuh propp'a!"

The vulgar laughter faded as the truck disappeared down the road. Too Tight spat and rose to leave.

"Ah hate dem damn crackas'."

Johnny B.'s voice rang out above the laughter that boomed from inside.

"An' dat ignunt mutha fucka...! Between dem low down crackas' an' niggahs like dat fool in dere..." He spat again and started walking slowly down the road, deeper into the night.

"Hey Tight!" Ike called after him. "Ain't nothin' new! Yuh know dat! Boy, yuh take thangs too serious! Wait uh minute!" He called as he ran out on the road to catch him. "Lemme git yuh uh drank!"

Too Tight continued to walk in silence into the night towards his home. He hated the life that he was forced to live, being treated like an animal by Whites and being belittled and sold out by his own people. But what he hated most was that there was little that he could do about either; if he wanted to remain alive.

By the time he arrived home, his head was cleared and he had dismissed the incident. He hadn't given it second thought until now.

"Ah thank Ah know whut dey's aft'a."

Henry Lee glanced over at him. He wanted to know, but was afraid.

"Last night at da Juke Joint, Johnny B. was jaw-flappin' 'bout..." Too Tight hesitated, thinking, hoping that he was wrong.

"'Bout whut?" Henry Lee whispered impatiently. "Whut yuh hear? It ain't us. We ain't got no trouble is we?"

Too Tight turned to him. "Yuh hear tell 'bout uh niggah boy from up nawth?"

Henry Lee shook his head slowly.

"Johnny B. was talkin' 'bout some Ch'caga niggah boy. Maybe he was tellin' da truth. Or at least told it in uh way dat ol'

Mama! I Should Have Stayed With You!

136

Br'ant b'lieved 'im. Dat niggah's mouf jist too damn big! He do anythang tuh git uh pat on da head from dem crackas'!"

Henry Lee's fear struck eyes suddenly inflated when J.W. and the Bryant's came out of the store. As they approached the truck, Henry Lee and Too Tight cast their eyes down and mumbled, "Evenin' sah."

Roy glanced back in their direction to see who belonged to the voices in the shadows of the truck. "Who all yuh got back thar Dub?"

"Couple of mah boys. We most likely gonna need 'em."

"We kain git Huber' out at the Gibson place!" Roy said as he jumped into the front seat of the cab.

* * *

J.W. turned off the paved highway onto a gravel side road before following an overgrown dirt trail. They soon approached the thick fence of evergreens where a group of young men had gathered.

The old, once-abandoned barn had been transformed into a small bootleg whiskey steel. The local sheriff knew it was there, but he didn't bother them and would, on occasion, join them.

Hubert had joined the group only a few minutes before J.W. and Roy pulled up, but he'd already managed to down half a Mason jar of moonshine. He recognized the new truck and walked over to greet them with a wide grin.

"Wa'al Ah'll be! Ah'm sho surprised tuh see yuh boys down heah!" Nodding at Carolyn he said, "Evenin' ma'am!"

Carolyn nodded and mumbled, "Evenin'."

"Whar's yuh car?" J.W. asked briskly.

"Whar's mah car? Whut the hell yuh thank? Ah walked down heah? C'mon boys," He yelled as he smacked the door with back of his hand and started staggering towards his loud friends. "Git on ovah heah an' have uh drank on me! It's uh damned good batch!"

J.W. looked away in disgust. "Huber', git yuh dumb ass back ovah heah. Ah said Ah need yuh car."

Hubert turned around. "Whut yuh want mah rusted ol' heap fuh' when yuh got this purty piece of machinery jist purrin' down da road...takin' yuh any place yuh want tuh go!"

Bonnie Blue

137

Hubert giggled as he turned up his jar of moonshine and wiped away the rivers of alcohol that splashed from the side of his lips.

"Don't ask so damn many questions! Jist git yuh damn car an' follow me!"

Roy surveyed the shadowy figures gathered in small groups and blurted proudly, "Yeah! We fixin' tuh take care of that problem we was talkin' 'bout earlier on tuhday!"

J.W. glared over at his excited younger brother. "Whut's the matt'a wit yuh boy?"

"An' Huber', whut the hell yuh still standin' thar lookin' like anybody's fool fuh! Ah said git yuh damn car, an' leave that shit alone! Yuh ain't got but uh piece of brain as it is!"

Hubert quickly tried to pull himself together. The moonshine must have been exceptionally strong, to allow him to be that familiar with J.W..

"Okay Dub," Hubert said as he screwed the top on the jar and staggered over to the side of the barn to his car.

"Whutn't no call fuh yuh tuh talk tuh me that way in front of folks," Roy said as he cut his eyes sharply at J.W.

"Shuddup, Roy! Ah don't know why yuh hang 'round the likes of that no-account no way! Yuh startin' tuh act jist like 'im! Hollerin' yuh damn bidness all out! Goddamnit, yuh act like yuh want evahbody tuh know! Might as well take out uh ad in the damn *Gazette*! From heah on out, yuh jist keep yuh damn mouf shut!"

Too Tight and Henry Lee sat listening quietly in the rear of the truck. They were careful to not even breathe too loudly or make any sound that would draw attention.

There was nothing more threatening to a Colored man than a group of liquored-up White men; some of whom were known Klansmen. Roy had just confirmed what Too Tight suspected. And if they were determined to take revenge on a Colored man, Too Tight was equally determined that it wouldn't be them; not tonight anyway.

Henry Lee cast his eyes down to the truck bed as he pressed his head firmly against the back of the truck.

Mama! I Should Have Stayed With You!

138

Too Tight could tell as the moonlight struck his friends face that he was terrified. As for Too Tight, the anger, which had been festering, it seemed from birth, was once again threatening to explode. His jaws clamped together so tightly that his teeth felt as though they would surely be reduced to dust. He squeezed his eyes shut as he struggled to regain control.

The truck lurched forward amid slurred shouts and greetings from Roy's drunken buddies. If Too Tight could have killed them all with a look, it would have been done at that moment, under the cloak of night as they pulled off down the road.

* * *

The deserted dirt road leading to the Hillard Plantation wasn't easily traveled. Both J.W. and Hubert, who followed closely behind, were bounced and tossed as their vehicles fell into and rocked out of potholes in the road.

The grounds had been deserted for years, and weeds had grown over the beautiful garden that once graced this huge white mansion, which itself, had long since deteriorated. All that now remained was the barn.

J.W. drove into the shadow of the barn, out of sight of the dirt road which led to the ruins. Hubert pulled in behind him.

J.W. and Roy got out and joined him.

After a short while, Roy came back to the truck, and told Carolyn to get in Huberts car.

"Ya'll git on out!" J.W. called out.

"Yassah," Henry Lee said as he released his grip on the tool chest.

"Ah ain't doin' dey dirt fuh 'em." Too Tight whispered as he jumped from the bed of the truck.

"Whut's that yuh say, Boy?"

Henry Lee's eyes shot past Too Tight and settled on J.W., who had walked up behind them. Too Tight slowly turned.

"Yuh heard me, Boy?"

"Sah?"

'Suh' mah ass! Niggah, yuh been gittin' uh mite 'sides yuhseff! Yuh bes' watch yuh step! Yuh heah whut Ah'm sayin' Boy?"

139

"Yassah."

"Now gowan an' git yuh black ass in the damned car. Henry Lee, yuh waitin' heah."

Roy's moonshine fog was slowly being replaced by clear-headedness. His attention was drawn to bright lights carefully dodging through the dense woods leading to the clearing.

"Hey Dub, who's that?" He asked nervously as he peered through the dark.

J.W. walked towards the truck as Melvin plodded through the jolting maze. "Ah told Melvin tuh meet me out heah. Huber', we gonna use yuh car. Ah ain't takin' uh chance on nobody seein' that white top on mah truck. Yuh ain't no use tuh nobody now, so yuh might as well stay heah wit Henry Lee 'til we git back."

Melvin joined the group and soon, they were weaving back out onto the highway leading to Money.

* * *

The bold brilliance of the full moon cloaked the delicate winks of the night's stars as they moved through the maze of roads. J.W. turned off the headlights as they drew nearer to their destination.

Too Tight occasionally stole glimpses of J.W. in the rearview mirror. The stoic face that stared out at the road seemed void of any emotion.

He turned to face the window, losing himself in the shadow of the trees, in an attempt to divorce himself from this place and these people. Angry, almost to the point of tears, he wondered how much more he could possibly take before he would lose his fight for self-control and strike out. He knew that it could only result in his own death.

His thoughts were interrupted when the car slowed to a halt under a cluster of persimmon trees.

* * *

It was near two o'clock and the Wright family was sound asleep. All was still, with the exception of the light rustling of leaves in the quiet breeze of the night.

"C'mon, boys!" J.W. commanded as he stepped out into the night.

"Dub, whut 'bout Car'lyn?" Roy asked as he opened the car door.

"She stayin' out heah wit Melvin. We brangin' 'im out. If we ain't got the right one, then we'll take hur in. But Ah don't thank we'll have uh problem."

Intoxicated with the certainty of his long awaited vindication, Roy darted ahead of J.W. and banged on the door. "Preacha! Preacha! Git on out heah! This heah Mista Bryant from Money! Ah want tuh talk tuh yuh an' that Ch'caga boy!"

J.W. rushed after him. "Whut the hell yuh doin', yuh damned fool!" J.W. growled.

Roy looked over at him confused and angered. "Whut? Whut yuh talkin' 'bout now? We come heah tuh set thangs right, ain't we?"

"Damnit! Roy, jist…," J.W. said as he forced back the urge to smack some sense into his brother.

Inside, Mose woke with a start. The memory of Emmett and the incident with the Bryant woman blasted through his mind. He shook Elizabeth fiercely and whispered, "Liz'bit! Liz'bit, wake up! We got trouble!"

She turned over to face him. It only took a second to snap out of her sluggish state.

"Lawd have mercy, Emmett!" she said as she sprang from the bed.

Mose pulled on his trousers and whispered frantically, "Quick! Git 'em out the back whilst Ah try tuh talk tuh 'em!"

"Help me Lawd!" He prayed quickly as he took a deep breath and walked slowly down the hall, giving his wife extra time to get Emmett out the back door.

Elizabeth fled down the darkened hall to the back room where Emmett and Alfie lay sleeping.

Mose legs felt weak and trembled. He fought hard to slow his short raspy breaths before entering his living room. Again, they pounded on the locked door. He knew that if he didn't respond soon, they would kick it down and probably rush in shooting, placing his entire family in even more danger.

Bonnie Blue

Mose mind whirled. His shotgun always lay propped in the corner behind the chair where, just a couple of hours ago, Emmett sat dozing. He strained his eyes in the dark to gauge rather or not he could make it to his shotgun. He nervously moved quietly across the unlit room.

Mose stretched his hand out cautiously towards his only source of protection. He held his breath as his hand crept closer to the muzzle.

Again, they pounded on the door. "Preacha! Open up this goddamn door!"

If Mose stepped any closer to the chair, he could be seen through the window; so he slowly pulled his hand away. With all the calm that he could muster, he took a deep breath and opened the wooden door.

He nervously unlatched the small hook on the screen door and stepped out onto the porch. J.W. aimed the bright beam from the flashlight into Moses' face, momentarily blinding him.

Too Tight stood back from the door and turned his face away, trying to hide.

J.W. towered over the old preacher, holding the pistol in one hand and the flashlight in the other. Mose looked from Roy to J.W., squinting from the light in his face.

"Suh? Kain Ah help yuh gent'men?"

"Niggah, turn on the goddamn lights!" Roy ordered as he pushed past the frightened little preacher and charged into the house.

"Sorrah suh, we ain't got no lights."

J.W. looked down at the thin frail Colored man. "Yuh got two niggahs down heah from Ch'caga!" he barked as he walked past Mose into the house, swinging the flashlight quickly around the living room and kitchen.

"Ah want the niggah who dun that talk in Money," J.W. said as he followed Roy down the flashlight lit hall to the darkened bedrooms.

The heavy pounding of their mud caked boots against the dull wooden floors vibrated throughout the hall, desecrating the sanctioned shield of slumber.

Mama! I Should Have Stayed With You!

Wheeler instantly sat up and violently shook Kelvin awake as he pressed himself against the wall at the corner of the bed.

"Move ovah, Wheeler!" Kelvin mumbled as he swatted blindly in the air. "Ah ain't got no room."

"Shhh! Be quiet!" Wheeler whispered frantically as he tugged Kelvin closer to the wall. "Somebody's here!"

Kelvin's eyes popped open as he scrambled over Wheeler, squeezing between the corner of the wall and his frightened cousin. Both boys were petrified. Fear locked their breaths deep in the portal of their throats. Their bodies trembled as they struggled to silence the raging palpitations in their chest that threatened to betray them.

A growing pulsating haze of lights moved through the hall, forcing back their protection of darkness. Suddenly, a blinding light whipped into the open doorway, smashing through the dark, flooding their bedroom.

"Ain't nobody in theah 'ceptin' mah own boys!" Mose called out loudly, warning Elizabeth; hoping that she got Emmett out the back door or was able to hide him somewhere.

"We only want the one that did all that talkin' in Money!" a voice from behind the light called.

Just as suddenly as the light whipped into the room, it swished back to fill the hall, leaving the two boys clinging to each other.

Elizabeth heard her husband's warning and fiercely tugged at Emmett's arm. "Emmett! Baby, wake up! Please wake up!!!" she cried frantically as she tried to pull Emmett to his feet.

Emmett stood for a moment and plopped back down on the edge of the bed. Dazed, he raised his head. "Huh? Okay, I'm awake," he mumbled.

"Emmett," she whispered as she grabbed him around the waist and desperately tried to pull him from the bed. "Emmett,

143

c'mon baby! We ain't got no time! Git up *now*! Emmett baby, *please*!"

She was too late.

Bonnie Blue

J.W. flooded the small room with light and caught sight of her attempting to haul the large child to his feet. He leveled the light on Elizabeth and the startled boy and easily snatched Emmett from her grasp; pulling him to his feet.

"Papa..." a tiny voice began and trailed off into silence.

"Git up!" J.W. barked, "Yuh the boy that did that talk and whistling at Ms. Car'lyn in town?"

Emmett was now fully aware of what was going on and who these men must have been. Shaken, he replied meekly, "YYY...Yes."

"Yuh ain't in Ch'caga, niggah! Yuh bes' say 'Yes suh' when yuh talkin' tuh me, or Ah'll blow yuh damn head off right now!" J.W. shoved him back against the bed. "Git dressed!"

Emmett sat on the edge of the bed and reached down to get his socks out of his shoes. Startled, Roy looked at the boy in disbelief. "Niggah! Whut the hell yuh doin'? Nevah mind the damn socks!" Roy yelled. "Jist put on yuh goddamned shoes, niggah!"

"I nnn...never wear shoes www...without my sss...socks," Emmett said nervously as he shook his socks out and slowly began to pull them on; hoping that his great uncle could do something to help him.

J.W. and Roy were temporarily shocked into silence. This boy was actually making them wait while he got dressed!

"Ah'm sorrah fuh any trouble he caused," Elizabeth pleaded as tears pooled in her large almond eyes. "We'll gladly pay fuh' any damages. Please don't pay 'im no mind. He's simple minded...ain't got good sense."

Roy raised his hand to slap her, but J.W. caught his arm, glared down at her and said, "Shuddup an' git back in bed befo' Ah knock all hell out yuh! An' Ah want tuh hear them sprangs!" he sneered as she backed away.

144

Emmett fumbled nervously with the buttons on his shirt when Roy snatched him away from the bed and pushed him out of the bedroom; towards the front door.

"Mista Milam suh, wheah yuh takin' 'im?" Mose asked humbly.

Mama! I Should Have Stayed With You!

"Nowhar, if he ain't the right one," J.W. said as Roy shoved Emmett off the porch into the yard.

Mose couldn't see Emmett's face, but he saw his silhouette against the moonlight turning back to look for him through the screen door.

Mose caught J.W. by the arm, hoping he could reason with him. "Please suh," Mose pleaded, "kain't yuh jist take 'im out back an' whup 'im? Ah'll pay yuh whutevah yuh ask. He ain't mean nothin' by it, suh! Please! He simple minded. Don't know no betta!"

"Old man! Preacha or no," he snarled, as he snatched his arm free, "don't evah put yuh hands on me. Now Ah dun told yuh, if he ain't the right one, we gonna brang 'im back an' put 'im in the bed." J.W. turned towards the door, "Yuh don't know nobody heah tuhnight, yuh unda'stand?"

"Yes suh," Mose mumbled.

J.W. kicked the screen door open and started to walk out when he hesitated and turned back to face Mose. "Do yuh know anybody heah?"

"No suh, Ah don't know yuh."

"Preacha, how old are yuh?"

"Sixty-four, suh."

"If yuh know any of us heah tuhnight, yuh'll nevah live tuh get be sixty-five." J.W. glared down at Mose for a long, silent moment, before joining the others into the night.

Mose stood helpless, watching Emmett struggling against the strangers.

Roy shoved Emmett into the open door of the car. "Bend down niggah. Ah want the lady tuh make sho that yuh're the right one."

Emmett obeyed.

"This the niggah?"

Carolyn peered over at him. "Yeah, that him," she said dryly.

"Git in on the other side!" J.W. ordered Too Tight as he slid into the driver's seat.

Bonnie Blue

Too Tight ran quickly around to the other side and climbed into the back seat.

Roy knocked Emmett into the open back door. He slipped and fell. Too Tight reached over to help him up, but felt J.W.'s cold glare. Emmett quickly climbed into the back seat next to Too Tight. Melvin climbed in afterward. Once Roy crowded into the front seat next to Carolyn, they sped away, headlights still off.

* * *

While Mose attempted to negotiate with J.W., Elizabeth slipped out of the back door and ran through the cotton field towards the large house where she hoped she could find help.

G.C. Fredricks was sound asleep when he heard loud pounding on his front door.

"Whut in tarnation?" he grumbled to himself as he got out of bed and turned on his bedside lamp. "Who the hell's out thar this time of night?" he yelled as he leaned out his bedroom window. "Damnit! Folks' tryin' tuh sleep!"

"It's me, Mista Fredricks! Liz'bit!" she called as she nervously rang her hands in her robe.

"Damnit, Liz'bit! Whut the hell's so impo'tant it kain't wait 'til mo'nin'? Don't come tellin' me somebody dead, 'cuz if they dead now, they still be dead in the mo'nin' afta Ah wake up!"

"Ah'm sorrah suh! But White men come an' took mah nephew!"

"Shit!" Fredricks yelled as he hurried down the long flight of stairs to the heavy front door where she stood waiting. "Ah ain't gittin' no damn sleep tuhnight!"

Ralph, his house help, heard all the commotion and came out from his room just off the kitchen.

146

"Is dey somethin' yuh be needin' me fuh Mista Fredricks, sah?"

"Hell, Ah don't know! Ah jist got down heah mah damn self," he grumbled. He opened the door and there stood Elizabeth, terror etched in her face, tears glistening as they streamed over her cheeks.

"Oh, Mista Fredricks suh! They come an' got 'im! They come an' took 'im away!"

Mama! I Should Have Stayed With You!

"Land's sake woman! Slow down! Now who come an' got who?"

"He say Mista Br'ant, from Money! They come an' carried off mah nephew that was visitin' out from Ch'caga!"

"Take it easy! Now wait uh minute! Ralph, yuh gowan check 'round back an' see whut yuh kain see!"

Ralph stood, staring into her panic stricken eyes. For a brief moment her fear spread to him and he was frozen.

"Didn't yuh hear me, Boy? Don't stand thar like yuh deaf!"

"Yassah," he said and disappeared around the side of the house.

"Whut happened Liz'bit?"

"Yes suh," she sobbed. "Yuh know we got them chil'ren down at our place visitin' out from Ch'caga."

"Yes! Yes! Ah know that! But whut happened? Whut'd the niggah do?"

Elizabeth held her head down. "The chil'ren went tuh town, an' they say Emmett whistled at Mista Br'ant's wife. But Mista Fredricks, suh, as God is mah witness, Ah know the boy didn't mean nothin' by it. He don't know whut tuh do down heah! He's jist uh boy!" Her body shook as she broke into uncontrollable tears.

Fredricks went around to the side of the house and bellowed, "Ralph, git back heah!"

He turned back to Elizabeth with a look of pure contempt. "Whistlin' at uh White woman?" he said briskly, "Yuh niggahs bought this down on yuh own seffs!"

147

Ralph ran back to the front as Fredricks continued to chastise Elizabeth. "It's yuh own damn fault! Ya'll shoulda leff that niggah up yonda! Ah ain't gittin' in them boy's affairs!" He abruptly turned and walked back into the house. Ralph quickly ran past her and closed the door.

Elizabeth stood quietly for a moment, as the subtle realization that she had darted out into the night alone, without Mose knowing, came to the forefront of her mind. But the fear

Bonnie Blue

for her own safety was quickly dissolved by the overpowering dread for her nephew's life.

"Lawd, whut mus' Ah do?" she said as she looked towards her home. "Please protect Emmett, Lawd," she prayed.

* * *

In the distance, a faint light flickered through the cluster of cottonwood trees, which separated Fredricks' house from the Wright's home. Mose had turned on the only light in the living room.

The boys quietly gathered in the bedroom where Emmett had just lay, sleeping.

"They gonna brang 'im back, ain't they?" Alfie cried, his eyes glistening in the dancing light that filtered into the bedroom.

"Shuddup boy," Kelvin said as he walked angrily out of the bedroom.

"Is they gonna brang Bobo back Ollie?"

Ollie joined Wheeler, who stood frozen and dazed against the wall.

"C'mon ya'll." Mose said whe he appeared in the door.

"Papa, is they gonna beat 'im an' brangin' 'im back home? Wheah's Mama?" Alfie's small shaken voice asked. "Is they got Mama too?"

"Ya'll hush up in heah! Ah got 'nough trouble widout ya'll gittin' riled! Now help Wheeler git packed! Ya'll heard me! Git his clothes tuhgetha! Don't matt'a if they clean or not, jist throw 'em in the bags!"

Kelvin ran around to the back of the house, searching for his mother. Finally, he ran to the front porch and out into the yard.

Nothing disturbed the ominous shadows of the trees that lined the road to town. Kelvin was terrified that the men might have returned and stolen his mother as well. But if they showed up now, he felt sure that he could whip them all. He was relieved when he saw her figure in the moonlight, moving slowly along the side of the road.

Mama! I Should Have Stayed With You!

He raced past the shadowy trees calling out to her, "Mama! Mama! Whut Mista Fredricks say? Is he gonna help look fuh Bo?"

She put her arm around his shoulder, sniffled and said quietly, "He say ain't nothin' he could do. We need tuh pray."

The tears, which he had suppressed behind his anger, fill the wells of his eyes and like water from a broken dam, rushed swiftly down his chin.

"Don't worrah child. Evahthang's gonna be alright."

They got back to the house just as the boys were dragging Wheeler's luggage into the living room.

When Mose saw the look in her eyes, he knew that she had already been down to Fredricks' and that no help was coming. He wasn't surprised.

Suddenly, Wheeler burst from the bedroom. Frightened and angry, he screamed, "We gotta go find Bobo! They're gonna hurt him if we don't go after them!" He looked around at his family scrambling to evacuate the house. "I'm not leaving here without him and I'm not gonna wait around for them to bring him back all beat up!" He looked around in disbelief, and near the point of hysteria, he begged, "Please! C'mon ya'll! We gotta do somethin'! How can you just stand there? C'mon!!!"

He darted across the room, but Mose grabbed him before he got out the door.

"Boy, we gotta git ya'll outta heah right now, in case they come back! Ah gotta git all ya'll out! It ain't safe! Now Ah knows how yuh feelin', but right now, theah ain't nothin' we kain do 'cept git outta this house an' pray!"

Wheeler jerked away from him and burst through the screen door.

"Liz'bit," Mose called over his shoulder as he rushed out after him, "ya'll go git in the car! Don't worrah 'bout no bags!"

Wheeler stomped up and down the road screaming at the top of his voice, "Bobo...I'm sorry!!! We shoulda just stayed home! I hate this stupid place! I ain't leavin' you ...Bobo!!!"

Bonnie Blue

Mose ran up behind him and grabbed him firmly by his arm. "Ah'ma find him! But right now, Ah gotta git ya'll somewheah safe jist in case they come back heah!"

"I want them to come back!" Wheeler yelled as he snatched away from his grandfather. "I ain't scared of them or nobody else! I ain't just gonna leave Bo! And I ain't gonna wait for them to bring him back all beat up! I told him..." his voice cracked. "I told him that we came together, and we're goin' back home together!"

Mose grabbed him firmly and held him by the shoulders. He looked unblinkingly into the Wheeler's angry eyes. "Look boy! Ain't nothin' Ah kain do fuh Emmett now! But Lawd willin', Ah kain git the rest of ya'll tuh safety! We all in uh dangerous place an'... Wheeler, look at me now! Ah need yuh help!"

Wheeler's body tensed as he struggled to breathe.

"Do yuh heah me boy? Ah need yuh tuh be strong fuh the lil' ones an' tuh do like Ah say. Now look at me," he yelled as he shook Wheeler's shoulders and squeezed his arms tighter. "Look at me!"

Wheeler's drained body surrendered. Gradually, his eyes met his grandfather's stone gaze. "I won't just leave him. I can't," Wheeler said quietly. "I can't leave without him. I promised him...promised him."

Mose paused for a moment, moved by the bravery and determination of his grandson.

"We ain't gonna jist leave 'im. Yuh grandma's gonna stay heah wid ya'll. Ah'ma go down tuh Money an' check at the sto'. Maybe they took 'im back theah. If they ain't theah, Ah'ma ride 'round an' see if Ah kain find 'em anywheah. If Ah kain't, then Ah'ma go tuh the law. They ain't gone tuh Fredricks' 'bout it, so theah's uh chance that they gonna jist let 'im go. Fact is, Ah thank it might be bes' fuh yuh boys tuh stay heah jist in case they do.

Mama! I Should Have Stayed With You!

Do yuh unda'stand whut Ah'm sayin' boy? Somebody need tuh be heah if they do let 'im go."

The old man looked into his grandson's stubborn, frightened face and knew, without a doubt, that Wheeler would listen to his grandmother and take care of all the boys if, and when the time came.

"Yes sir." Wheeler nodded as he tried to pull himself together.

"That means yuh boys gotta wait 'til Ah come back, befo' Ah kain carry the rest of ya'll out. Yuh jist keep watch. If they do brang 'im back, ya'll slip out the back way an' hide out in the field. Don't matt'a whut yuh see or heah, keep quiet. Wait 'til they good an' gone befo' yuh come out tuh help Emmett. Ah'll be back soon's Ah find out somethin'. Do yuh unde'stand me?"

"Yes sir. I understand," Wheeler said. "We're staying right here until they bring Bobo back. Don't worry about us. We're alright. Granddaddy, just find Bobo."

Mose held Wheeler in a tight embrace and led him back to the moonlit porch where the rest of his frightened family was huddled together.

BOOK FOUR

LORD! HELP MY CHILD!

No one spoke as J.W. sped over the blacktop, finally turning onto the gravel covered road that ran through the deserted town.

"Make sho the doors are locked!" J.W. ordered as he stopped the car in front of the store.

They waited until Carolyn ran upon the porch, vanished inside, and flicked the porch light off and on again, to signal that everything inside was alright.

Clouds began to gather and move ominously across the face of the moon. Eerie shadows and silhouettes of cottonwood trees became a blur as the crowded vehicle sliced quickly and silently through the darkness.

Every muscle in Emmett's body seemed to twitch as he stared out into the foreign blackness surrounding him. Terror, which churned violently in the pit of his stomach, made it impossible to remain still.

Too Tight looked cautiously over at him and, for the first time, saw just how young the boy really was. Under the cloak of night, he squeezed Emmett's moist hand which was pressing firmly into his thigh. Emmett's frightened eyes gratefully met Too Tight's, who quickly released his hand and turned away; fearing that his compassion might be discovered.

Lord! Help My Child!

* * *

The air became heavy as majestic rain clouds formed, secretly keeping watch as they rolled across the night's sky. Finally, J.W. turned down the deserted road which led back to the plantation ruins where Hubert and Henry Lee waited.

Bright headlights flickered through the cluster of trees, signaling J.W.'s return.

"They're back!" Hubert called, as he tossed his secret stash of moonshine behind an old tree and ran towards the leaning barn.

Henry Lee slowly rose from the tree stump where he had remained perched since they left. He somberly watched as the car bounced its way through the maze of unkempt grounds.

"Hey ya'll!" Hubert called, hurrying out to meet them as they poured from the car.

"Git his ass out heah!" Roy barked as he sprang excitedly from the car.

"Move! Move!" he yelled, snatching Too Tight away from the open car door. "Git the hell outta mah damn way!" He reached in and dragged Emmett from the back seat.

153

"Too Tight, yuh an' Henry Lee put 'im in the back of the truck an' keep an eye on 'im!" J.W. called.

"Roy, git yuh ass ovah heah!"

"Whut the hell yuh doin'?" Roy yelled. Frustrated and confused, he shoved Emmett to the ground. "We went tuh git 'im an' we got 'im! Now whut we got tuh wait fuh?"

Too Tight and Henry Lee grabbed Emmett firmly and led him quickly around to the side of the barn where the truck was hidden.

Emmett's frightened eyes glistened as he whispered, "WWW...What's ggg...goin' on? WWW...Where're they gonna ttt...take me? WWW...What're they ggg...gonna do? I wanna go home." Tears flowed as he looked over to Henry Lee for some response.

Bonnie Blue

Henry Lee avoided his eyes and said, "Ain't too much tuh worrah 'bout. Dey gonna whup yuh up an' make yuh walk home, is all."

Too Tight looked at his friend and mumbled, "Dat's all, mah ass." He turned his attention back to the bewildered boy.

"Yuh the one whut whistled at Mz. Car'lyn, ain't yuh?" he asked wearily. "So yuh tell me boy," he whispered angrily as he climbed into the bed of the pickup truck and reached over to pull Emmett in after him. "Yuh tell me why we heah!"

"I ddd...don't know." Emmett whimpered. "Because I www...whistled at ttt...that lady? Is ttt...that why they're mmm...mad at me?"

"Dey mo' den mad at yuh boy," Too Tight whispered as he cautiously looked around the darkness. "Don't matt'a now. Jist do whut Ah say. Keep yuh mouf shut an' do whut dey tells yuh real quick like. Efen yuh lucky, yuh might see da sunrise."

Henry Lee glanced curiously at the young stranger. "Ah 'spect dese White folks diffe'ent den dem up nawth, ain't dey?"

"Ah don't know why da hell yuh come down heah no way," Too Tight said angrily. "Ya'll don't need tuh be comin'

154

down heah efen yuh don't know whut da hell yuh doin'. Don't do nothin' but tuh serve up uh reason fuh des crackas' tuh cut loose on all us. Now do whut Ah say. Hold yuh head down an' nevah look 'em in de eye. Eben if dey holla all up in yuh face, jist keep lookin' at de dirt." Too Tight whispered quickly as he watched the small group of men talking by the car.

J.W. stared hard and spoke low to his younger brother.

"Yuh betta start actin' like yuh got some sense boy! Bellowin' out yuh damned name back thar! Whut the hell yuh tryin' tuh do, Roy? Yuh askin' fuh trouble!"

"Hell Dub. Yuh know niggahs," Roy said checking his Colt .45 to make sure that all of the chambers were loaded. "That ol' niggah know whut's good fuh 'em. He ain't openin' his mouf tuh say nothin'! Ah doubt the niggah even heard me. Now jist fuhgit it!"

"Fuhgit it? Roy, yuh crazy as all hell. Ah don't want the law knockin' at mah door, an' yuh sho as hell kain't afford tuh git

Lord! Help My Child!

caught up in no mo' shit!" J.W. said as he started walking back to his truck.

Hubert burst into a drunken giggle as he stumbled from behind the tree after retrieving his jar of moonshine. "That lil' niggah's got ya'll goin' at it like them roosters down at the cockfights!" He drained the last few drops of moonshine from the jar, wiped his mouth with the back of his hand, and said, "If it was mah woman, hell Ah'd jist git rid of 'em, an' gowan back wit the boys!"

J.W. turned, knocked the jar from Hubert's hand, and grabbed him by the collar. "This heah uh family matt'a. Ah thank yuh bes' stay outta it."

"Wait uh minute, Dub! Ah say Huber's right!" Roy ranted as he paced like a starving panther. "We kain jist make short order of it an' be dun! Won't take no time, an' yuh kain be back in yuh bed like yuh wanted tuh be anyway! Ain't that right, Huber'?"

J.W. shot a damning glare at Hubert, who promptly responded, "That's 'tween yuh an' yuh brotha," and walked away.

"Roy, be still an' stop talkin' like uh damned fool. Yuh dun already put us in uh bad way. This heah Nawthn niggah come up dead, the law will be at yuh door, guaranteed. Now, like Ah said, ain't gonna be no killin' tuhnight. Hell, yuh see he simple minded. It's them damned lib'rals, poisonin' them niggahs up yonda, then sendin' 'em down heah tuh stir up trouble. Ah b'lieve uh good long ass whuppin' is jist whut that boy need tuh set 'im straight on uh few thangs. It'll send word up tuh them niggah-lovin' pol'ticians too."

"Dub! Ah kain give less than uh hog's ass 'bout uh them damn pol'ticians up yonda! This heah ain't got nothin' tuh do wit nobody but me an' that damned niggah right thar!"

"Yuh bes' pull yuhseff tuhgetha boy," J.W. replied as he and Melvin converged somberly on the truck where Emmett, Too Tight, and Henry Lee sat, still and quiet, surrounded by the night. "Git on down from thar!" J.W. growled.

Emmett's legs felt heavy and throbbed with pain as he slowly climbed out the back of the truck. Roy jumped ahead and ripped him the rest of the way down.
Bonnie Blue

"Take 'im in the barn!" J.W. called as he pulled out his gun. "Henry Lee, keep watch. An' yuh," he pointed to Too Tight, "comin' wit me!"

Too Tight followed him into the barn.

By the time they got inside, Roy already had Emmett by the throat. Emmett's eyes bulged as he gagged and sank to his knees.

"Niggah, yuh let one drop of yuh nasty ass spit touch me an' yuh dead right heah! Yuh black mutha fucka! Ah'll teach yuh tuh shame me!"

J.W. took long hard strides over to Roy, pried his fingers from their deadly grip, and glared coldly into his brother's eyes. "Ah'm gittin' damn ti'ed of yuh hard headed ass Roy! Now Ah dun told yuh! Ain't gonna be no killin'! Not tuhnight!"

Emmett coughed and struggled to catch his breath. He was relieved that this big stranger was protecting him and that his ordeal was coming to an end. Silently, he promised himself and God, that when he returned home he would never think about going south of Chicago ever again.

156

"Git up!" J.W. commanded, pulling Emmett from the floor by his collar. "Unda'stand me, Niggah," he said coldly, "Ah ain't particular fond of niggahs, but Ah'ma patient man. Hell, Ah kain even tolerate Nawthn niggahs, long as they know they place, an' stay in it. But uh uppity niggah is jist itchin' tuh git the shit knocked outta 'im! Ah don't give uh damn whar the hell yuh come from! Ah dun seent yuh type befo', boy." J.W.'s face reddened as he twisted Emmett's shirt collar tighter around his locked fist. "Thankin' yuh kain go wharevah the hell yuh want an' do whut-in-so-evah yuh damn well please! Well, not wit me an' mine!"

Emmett squeezed his eyes as tight as he could and pleaded, "PPP...Please, sir. I'm sss...sorry fff...for everything I ddd...did. I sss...swear I'll nnn...never ddd...do it aaa...again."

J.W. shoved Emmett backwards onto the floor, shook his head and walked away.

"It's jist yuh an' me now niggah!" Roy giggled as he freed the pistol tucked in his belt.

Lord! Help My Child!

There was nothing in Emmett's world now; not home, not his mother, not even God. There was only the fraction of a second between the gun firing...and death.

"Git 'im out tuh the truck," J.W. said as he started out the door.

"Dub! Whut the hell yuh talkin' 'bout?" Roy yelled as he lunged in front of his brother. "Ah know yuh ain't takin' 'im back tuh the Preacha's place!"

"Don't worrah 'bout it." J.W. said as he easily pushed him away. "Ah got an idea. Too Tight, load 'im back up in the truck. We're goin' fuh uh ride."

Roy threw a powerful punch to Emmett's stomach and crashed the side of his head with the butt of his gun. Emmett's head whirled and his body trembled as his eyes fell upon the Colored man that caught him before he hit the floor. Roy glared at Too Tight, clutched his pistol tighter and rushed out of the barn.

157

"Ya'll put 'im in the back an' watch 'im! He git loose, yuh asses' takin' his place, yuh heah?" J.W. said as he lifted himself into the cab of the truck.

"Yassah."

Suddenly, Emmett jerked and tried to break free. Henry Lee snatched him back before he could dart into the darkness. Too Tight grabbed him, shoved him firmly into the side of the truck and said between clinched teeth, "Boy, yuh betta git yuh black ass up in dis heah truck fuh Milam cut dat fool loose on all our asses."

"I www...want my Mama!" Tears dripped from Emmett's quivering chin as he reluctantly climbed back into the rear of the truck. "I want my MMM...Mama. I www...wanna go hhh...home."

"C'mon! Let's roll!" Melvin bellowed.

"Yassah! We ready," Too Tight called. He leaped over the tailgate and fell into the bed of the truck as it lurched forward.

Emmett instinctively reached over to help him. Too Tight snatched away and sat across from him. "I sss...said I was sss...sorry. Please! Let me ggg...go! I jjj...just wanna go home!"

"Yuh shoulda thought 'bout dat befo' yuh come down heah actin' all high an' mighty." Too Tight's anger was quickly welling

Bonnie Blue

at this boy, who unwittingly stumbled into one of the biggest taboos in the South.

"Boy," Too Tight whispered angrily, "ain't nobody evah told yuh dese ol' crackas' will shoot yuh ass full of lead efen yuh look at dey damn dog sideways? Bein' uh niggah down heah don't mean shit. Rememb'a whut Ah told yuh. Keep yuh damned mouf shut, keep yuh eyes on da ground, an' pray daylight beat 'em tuh dey dirt. Crackas' ain't likely tuh do dey big dirt in da day wheah someone li'bul tuh see 'em. Now do whut Ah say, an' yuh might git uh chance tuh see yuh Mama again. Mess up, an' yuh'll see da Lawd, befo' day."

They continued their journey down dark, deserted back roads. Only the bright light of the full moon, which occasionally peeped through the dense clouds, lit their way.

J.W. had discovered a steep bluff while hunting deer last year. There were very few areas of this kind in the Delta. He knew that this would be the perfect place for Roy to vindicate himself after the blatant assault on his manhood.

The bluff is through a thickly wooded, secluded area and is over a fifty-foot drop from the edge right into the deepest waters of the Tallahatchie River. Melvin and J.W. planned to let Roy beat the boy, hold him over the cliff to frighten some sense into him, and leave him to find his own way home.

In the meantime, Emmett held a secret vigil of the night sky, searching diligently for any sign of fractures in the dark; a prelude to the coming of a new morning and his possible salvation.

They wandered diligently through the back woods for nearly 2 hours, but the dark of night continued to deceive them, steering them farther away from the their coveted cliff. It wouldn't be long before dawn overtook them. J.W. knew that if they were going to do something, they had to do it soon.

They were a short drive away from the tiny hamlet of Drew and the Clint Sheridan farm, where Leslie Milam, the oldest of the Milam men, worked and lived.

Lord! Help My Child!

* * *

Willie Reed, an eighteen year-old fieldhand on the Sheridan place, was already walking the few miles to Glenn Patterson's general store on the highway to get chewing tobacco before getting dressed for Sunday school.

Stubborn humidity was quickly robbing the air of the cool dew that caressed the grass under his calloused feet. Even with the hint of impending rain, his sweat soaked tee shirt was already clinging to his thin body. He was startled by the dust covered pickup, when it sped past him from behind. He quickly jumped off the road, into the shallow ditch.

A glimmer of hope flashed through Emmett's mind as this young man smiled and waved a greeting. His eyes clung to the symbol of freedom walking down the road, until the truck turned onto a wide gravel drive. He hoped that maybe they were taking him back to his Uncle Mose.

Emmett looked around seeking to find anything familiar. For the first time since his nightmare began, nothing looked ominous. Everything; the trees, cotton fields, and scattered shacks, all looked the same as they did around his great uncle's house. He cast his eyes towards the creeping sunrise and prayed for his odyssey to be over.

"WWW...Where are we?" he asked softly. "Are we ccc...close to my Uncle's? Are they ttt...takin' me bbb...back home?"

"Naw," Henry Lee said as he looked around from the back of the truck. "We ain't nowheah near Money."

Too Tight stared out across the cotton covered landscape.

"They ain't takin' yuh back tuh yuh kinfolks." He retorted. "Dat ain't li'bul tuh happen."

"That's alright," Emmett replied, "If I can get to a phhh...phone, someone can come pick mmm...me up."

Leslie had already begun his chores. He emerged from the shed pushing a wheel barrel when J.W. drove into the yard.

"Hey ya'll!" he hollered as he dropped his load and walked towards them. "Whut ya'll doin' way out heah this time of day?

Bonnie Blue

Francis' cookin' now! Ya'll gowan in an' git uh bite. Hey, Melvin! That you? Boy, Ah ain't seent..."

J.W. and Melvin jumped out of the cab and signaled for Roy to join them.

"Ain't got time now." J.W. said as he slapped his brother on the back. "Maybe later."

160

They stood talking in the middle of the yard for a short time. Suddenly, Leslie rushed into the house and J.W. returned to the truck to retrieve one of his pistols from under the seat.

Roy pulled Emmett from the rear of the truck. Too Tight and Henry Lee followed. The screen door slammed as Leslie came storming out of his house to join them.

Too Tight and Henry Lee stood just inside of the shed door as Roy shoved Emmett inside.

Emmett flinched and attempted to cover his head when he saw Roy take a gun from under his belt and raised his arm to swing. He wanted to run, but his legs pained him. Both legs were so weak and heavy that he could barely stand. As Roy drew nearer, Emmett began flailing his arms wildly.

"Grab hold of 'im, goddamnit!" Melvin bellowed.

Emmett struggled hard to fight back, to try to free himself, but to no avail. Roy threw a powerful blow to Emmett's abdomen, lifting him off his feet. His body collapsed around Roy's fist before he slumped to the ground.

The wallet, that Gene had given him before he left home, fell from his white jeans pocket. Melvin picked it up and noticed the dollar bills.

"Whut the hell is this?" he asked. "Dub, yuh might want tuh take uh look at this!"

J.W. snatched it from him. "Lemme see that!"

After jamming the three single dollar bills into his pants pocket, he flipped through the picture section. Blood flooded his face. His jaws tightened as he saw the pictures of the White woman and Emmett's grandmother.

J.W. snatched Emmett up by his collar. "Niggah, whut the hell's this?" he growled. "Goddamn, yuh black ass! Ah asked yuh uh question! Who's these White women, an' whut the hell yuh

Lord! Help My Child!

doin' wit 'em in yuh billfold?" he snarled through clinched teeth. "Ah'm warnin' yuh, Boy! Yuh bes' give me the right answer!"

"It's my ggg...grandmother," Emmett mumbled as blood dripped from his mouth; is tear soaked eyes, fixed on the floor. He gave no thought of the photograph of the white woman that came with all new men's wallets.

All that J.W. knew was that this boy, this product of a Yankee liberal society, had shamed his family, been disrespectful and now continued to mock them.

Melvin grabbed the wallet back from J.W. and looked at the pictures. "Niggah, jist who the hell yuh thank yuh are?" He yelled as his veins strained against his tense crimson neck. "So yuh tellin' me that yuh grandpa dun spoilt this heah White woman, too? Ah reckon that's the kinda shit they allow yuh niggahs tuh do up in Ch'caga! Yuh in Mississippi now, niggah!" Melvin cried out as his clinched fist smashed into the child's face.

Emmett heard himself scream as his exhausted body slammed to the ground.

"Whut the hell's goin' on heah, Dub?" Melvin asked in disbelief as he stepped away from the weak, crying boy. "Is the niggah crazy? He gotta be! He gotta be crazy!"

"He ain't crazy! Ain't uh damn thang wrong wit that niggah!" Roy yelled and kicked the huddled boy in the ribs. "Ain't no such thang as uh niggah don't know no betta!" he yelled angrily.

"Yuh black sonna-bitch!" Roy swung his leg so hard that he lost his balance and fell against the wall.

"I...I...I haven't ddd...done anything www...wrong," Emmett pleaded feebly as he fought the agonizing pain that throbbed through his entire body.

"Whut?" Roy stumbled as he charged back at him. "Who the hell yuh thank yuh talkin' tuh? Ya'll hear this heah shit? Yuh uh crazy niggah, alright!" Roy dragged the boy to his feet. "That ol' niggah bitch whutn't lyin'!"

Anger was beginning to overcome Emmett's pain. He had never heard anyone disrespect his great-aunt or any other woman in his family. He raised his swollen eyes to meet Roy's icy gaze but quickly turned away.

Bonnie Blue

"Maybe yuh jist plain confused," Roy said as he thrust his face close to Emmett's. "Maybe yuh thank yuh White? Maybe yuh thank yuh got one of them perm'nent deep down tans! Is that whut yuh thank niggah?" he screamed, hot stale saliva spraying from his mouth. "Niggah, yuh bes' talk wit respect when yuh talkin tuh uh White man!"

162

No one moved or spoke. It was all Roy and Emmett. Too Tight and Henry Lee were too afraid to move, dreading their own fate after death carried this boy, mercifully, on his journey.

"Niggah, yuh bes' look at me!" Roy yelled as he snatched Emmett's head around to face him. "Ah'm talkin' tuh yuh, niggah! Is that it? Yuh thank yuh as good as uh White man? Niggah, yuh ain't nothin'!" he screamed. "Yuh ain't nothin' but uh damn ape! Yuh got that, Niggah? Lissen tuh me good, Boy! Yuh niggah bitch mammie an' all the rest of yuh niggahs ain't no mo' then worms in mah dawgs shit!"

J.W.'s face rushed scarlet red. His fury boiled as molten lava erupting from the pit of his stomach. He shoved Roy aside. All of the rage that he'd attemped to contain over the North's chipping away at the institution of his beloved Mississippi, blasted from his huge clenched fist; smashing into Emmett's stomach.

A soul curdling, barbaric scream erupted from Emmett's tormented young body. He dropped to the floor; his body writhing in pain.

Emmett glared up at J.W. in a pain that most grown men would never know. Tears streamed down his face, mixing now with blood which oozed up from his throat. Anger mounted, overcoming even his excruciating pain and fear. Who were they to judge his worth, and more importantly, demean his mother.

"Look at that hunk of shit!" Roy screamed as he spit out the side of his mouth. "Ah bet he dun spoilt many uh White gal up yonda! This niggah ain't fit tuh take anoth'a breath!" All these goddamn niggahs an' mutha fuckin' Jews! Ain't nonna 'em worth shit!"

Lord! Help My Child!

Pain stabbed every inch of Emmett's body, His head was riddled with vertigo. His legs were numb and heavy, his eyes, swollen; his vision was so blurred that it seemed that he was looking through a fog. Despite this, he stared at Roy through the slit in his swollen eyes. He had never known that he could hate

163

anyone or anything as much as he hated these men at this very moment.

A flood of images flashed through his mind. His mother, small but strong, always expressed how proud she was of the man he was becoming. She taught him to stand up for what he thought was right. He remembered sitting in church as Bishop Roberts preached, *"We are all God's children, Colored, White, Yellow, and Red. He created us all equally and loves us all the same."* He could almost hear his teacher lecturing, *"The United States Constitution and our Founding Fathers wrote that 'All men are created equal."*

Fighting hard to control his words Emmett moaned, "III...I'm just as good...as yyy...you are."

"Whut?! Niggah, whut the hell yuh say tuh me? Ch'caga Boy," J.W. said angrily, "Ah'm ti'ed of 'em sendin' yuh kind down heah stirrin' up trouble!"

J.W. smashed Emmett so hard in the face that an explosion of the whitest light he had ever seen flashed in his head. He began choking on the tooth that had been knocked to the back of his throat.

In spite of the maniacal beating, neither unconsciousness nor death rescued him.

* * *

A small cluster of sparrows seemed to serenade the sun as it burst brilliantly through the dawn skies; host to growing mountainous storm clouds that drifted smoothly by.

Willie saunter leisurely back down the deserted red clay, dirt road towards his home; oblivious to the blanket of sharp rocks embedding themselves in the calloused soles of his feet.

Suddenly, his peace was snatched away by the undeniable scream of someone in terrible pain. He quickened his pace, not wanting to be seen or to witness anything. If you're Colored in these backwoods, it's best to be invisible.

Bonnie Blue

At first, he only heard the screams. But as he went closer, hiding in the weeds, he could actually hear the licks.

He turned and ran to the nearest house of a family that he knew; Mandy Bradley.

164

Mandy was frying fatback when Willie burst through the closed front door, nearly out of breath.

"A'nt Mandy," he called as he leaned one hand against the wall and double over to catch his breath. "Yuh heah dat? Dey got somebody out in da shed."

"Boy, yuh skeered me half tuh deaf runnin' in heah like dat," Mandy said as she quickly shoved the wooden door shut. "Now yuh jist hush yuh mouf. Yuh li'bul tuh git yuhseff in uh heap of trouble, mindin' somebody else's bidness." She turned her attention back to the thick pieces of fried meat, dodging the hot grease as it popped from the cast iron skillet.

"But A'nt Mandy, early mornin' Ah seent..."

"Yuh ain't seent nothin'. Now take dem pails 'round back an' brang me back some wat'a. An' Willie?"

"Ma'am?" he answered as he opened the door.

"Don't let yuh eyes git yuh b'hind in trouble!"

"No ma'am. Ah won't."

Willie hurried behind the shack to their water pump. He could still hear someone crying out from across the field. He knew that Mandy heard the licks and the screams as well. Even though the sounds were muffled, it was too familiar to be mistaken for anything else and besides, this was one of only a few times that he had ever seen her big door closed in the summer heat.

* * *

Inside the shed, they continued the assault on Emmett's body.

Emmett's eyes were so swollen that he could scarcely see at all. His lips, swollen and numb, nearly trapped the warm salty pool of blood in his throat. Blood crept from his ear and poured down his nose. Lights flashed inside his head with each blow. He could hear himself scream as white knuckled fists hammered fiercely into his flesh. It was like a nightmare, a terrible evil

Lord! Help My Child!

nightmare from which he would awake at home in his bed, with his dog Mike, asleep at the foot of his bed.

165

Henry Lee darted for the door. He couldn't bear to stand there watching this child's torture any longer. Too Tight grabbed him by the arm before he could make it out of the door.

He pulled him close and angrily whispered, "Man, whut da hell da matter wid yuh? Yuh want tuh be next? Dey'll kill yuh, kill both us befo' dey let yuh git outta heah like dat, an' Ah ain't ready tuh die!"

Whut yuh mean?" Henry Lee pleaded frantically. "Yuh know whut dey gonna do tuh us anyway! We's heah!"

The others were so preoccupied that they weren't aware of what was taking place across the room.

* * *

On the other side of the field, opposite Mandy's shack, lived the family of Frank Young, a forty-seven year-old fieldhand.

Frank had just completed his breakfast and was heading out to the fields. The blade on his hoe was loose, so he started towards the tiny shed at the back of his yard to get another. He stopped short, as soon as he heard the smothered screams emerging from the large shed in the distance. He crouched in the cotton field to see what was going on.

Willie had finished pumping the water and was carrying the full pail back to the shack when he heard the screams suddenly become louder. He turned and saw the shed door open and J.W. head towards the well near the middle of the big yard that supplies water to the main house. Willie flopped down on his belly and crawled into the cotton field.

Mandy kept watch from her kitchen window, but when she saw him disappear in the field, she panicked and darted to the door. She peered out and saw that J.W. had made no move towards the cotton field. Slowly, she eased the door shut and hurried back to the window.

Bonnie Blue

* * *

Leslie and Melvin joined J.W. at the well. "Whut'd yuh want tuh do wit 'im?" Leslie said, "Niggahs'll be in the fields soon, an' Ah got tuh start workin' mahseff befo' the damn rains come."

J.W. stood there, dazed, almost as if he was talking to himself, "Whut else kain we do? He's hopeless. Goddamn lib'rals dun poisoned his mind. Yuh heard that shit he threw at me. He really b'lievin' he's good as White folks. They really got 'im b'lievin' that shit!

"Yeah, Ah heard," Leslie said as he shook his head. "Damned shame too."

"Dub, yuh been talkin' 'bout this all 'long," Melvin said as he looked angrily at J.W. "Ain't no tellin' how mucha that shit they dun spread tuh our own niggahs! Befo' yuh know it, they all be talkin' crazy an' steppin' outta line!"

J.W. looked over at him, slung the cup of water across the yard and snarled, "Boy, kain't yuh see, that's already happenin'! Gov'ment talkin' 'bout lettin' niggahs vote an' go tuh school wit our youngins! Kain yuh imagine that?" He grimaced in disbelief.

"Niggahs ain't nevah gonna vote whar Ah live, 'cuz shit man, befo' yuh know it, they'll control the gov'ment! An' they damn sho ain't gonna go tuh school wit nonna mah youngins! Them damn lib'rals want tuh come down heah, mixin' mah youngins wit them niggah's! Talkin' 'bout they got some kinda rights! Hell, they ain't even human, damned sons of bitches! As long as Ah live an' kain do anythang 'bout it, niggahs gonna stay in they damn place! Hell, Ah dun fought too damned hard fuh this country, an' Ah got some damn rights too! Ah'll be damned if Ah'ma jist sit back an' allow some damn-body that don't know me, don't know nothin' 'bout me, take away whut's rightfully mine! An' uh niggah even come close tuh mentionin' uh White woman in that way…wa'al God help 'im 'cuz he's damn sho ti'ed of livin'! They gotta know whar me an' mah folks stand!"

"Ah'm b'hind yuh Dub!" Melvin exclaimed as he slapped J.W. on the back. "Whutevah yuh want tuh do! Now how yuh want tuh do this thang?"

Lord! Help My Child!

J.W. spat hard. "Roy went runnin' his damned mouf! Tellin' that damn niggah who the hell he is! Ah gotta thank this thang through." He headed back to the large tool shed with Leslie and Melvin following close behind.

* * *

As soon as they disappeared inside, Willie abandoned the water pail and ran back to the house. Mandy held the door open as he dashed up the dirt path, jumped onto the porch, and fell panting into a kitchen chair.

"Chil', Ah was skeered half tuh death! Is yuh alright?" Mandy asked as she stood back from the door and peered towards the shed. "Could yuh make out whut dey was sayin'?"

"No ma'am," he said as he gulped a mouthful of air. "Ah was too far away. But Ah thank they got one of them Colored boys Ah seent when Ah went tuh da sto' dis mo'nin'."

Mandy poured water from a jug into the chipped Mason jar and handed it to Willie. "Don't nobody deserve no beatin' like dat." She shook her head. "Lawd, please help dat po' soul."

After taking the rest of her breakfast from the stove, she pulled back the curtain that separated the sleeping quarters from the kitchen and living area. "Lonzo! Lonzo! C'mon eat!"

A muffled voice filtered from behind the cloth partition. "Ah'm wake. Ain't no need in yellin'!"

Alonzo, Mandy's husband, threw back the curtain, and dragged himself into the kitchen.

"Jist don't make no damn sense! All that damn hollerin'," he complained as his thick ragged nails dug through the nubby quill like stubs on his face.

"Yuh ain't eben got mah food on da table yet!" He turned to Willie and grunted out a greeting. "Mo'nin'. Kinda early tuh be callin' on folk." he said as he pulled a chair out from the table and eased his arthritic back down. "Ain't yuh got no home tuh go tuh?"

Mandy sat breakfast on the table and said, "Da boy been helpin' me, Lonzo. Ain't yuh heard all dat c'motion ovah yonda in Da big yard? Dem White folks dun gotta hold tuh some po' soul an' dey gittin' uh beatin' like nobody's bidness."

Bonnie Blue

168

"Most likely dun somethin' dey ain't got no bidness doin'," Alonzo said as he sopped his biscuit in the thick syrup from the pile of homemade preserves, and shoved it into his mouth.

"White folk jist plain low down!" Mandy said angrily. "Kain't uh body do nothin' bad 'nough tuh git dat kinda beatin'!" She returned to the window and gazed across the field towards the smothered cries. "C'mon, Lonzo," Mandy said as she removed her apron. "Maybe we kain fin' out who it is an' let dey kin know."

"Woman, yuh mus' be stone outta yuh min'! If dey don't know by now, dey fixin' tuh find out soon 'nough! Da only thang Ah gotta do is finish dis heah food an' mind mah own bidness."

Disappointed, Mandy looked away from him and shook her head. "Yuh act like da good Lawd ain't nevah give yuh no heart."

"Lissen tuh yuhseff, woman! Whut jist now fell out yuh mouf!" he said as he wiped grease and crumbs from his lips. "Da Lawd give me plenty good sense. Ain't no way in da worl' Ah'm goin' out dere meddlin' in dem White folks' bidness. Dat-a-way, dey ain't got no trouble wid me, an' Ah ain't got none wid dem. Efen da urge hit yuh tuh go out dere, yuh is welcome tuh do so, but don't fix yuh mouf tuh tell me tuh be uh fool wid yuh!"

Willie got up from the table and started out the door. "C'mon A'nt Mandy, Ah'll go wid yuh."

A long suffering sigh escaped her lips as she walked out to the porch. "Git dat hoe layin' upside da house theah," she said as she slung her sack on her back.

"Ya'll betta leave dem White folks 'lone! Ah'm tellin' yuh! Ah sho ain't comin' aft'a yuh!"

Mandy ignored Alonzo, and with Willie by her side, she crept into the field that separated her shack from Leslie's house.

"Mandy Mae!" he yelled. "Ah mean it! Dey come out aft'a ya'll, yuh on yuh own!"

* * *

Back in the shed, Emmett had finally reached unconsciousness. Sprawled on the floor, he lay covered with blood and motionless.

Roy kicked him in his side. His body rocked lifelessly.

Leslie knelt to one side of the child, to make sure the job was done. He saw no motion. Satisfied, he rested with his back against the wall and his legs crossed as he chewed on his fat, half-smoked, cigar.

Henry Lee stood paralyzed and nauseated. His unblinking eyes stared with disbelief at the heap of flesh. Too Tight's body was so tense with anger that it seemed his heart would shatter. There was nothing that he could have done. If he had interfered and tried to stop them, he knew what his fate would have been. Secretly, he prayed that the boy was dead. Suddenly, Emmett's finger began to twitch.

"Wa'al Ah'll be damned! Looka heah Dub! This niggah's still alive! Yuh stubborn sonna-bitch!" Roy yelled as he jumped up and aimed his gun at the bloody heap. "Yuh still tryin' tuh make uh fool outta me?!"

J.W. grabbed his hand as he pulled back the hammer on the gun and removed it slowly from his grasp. "Ah gotta betta idea," he said as he signaled for Too Tight and Henry Lee to join them.

He ordered Too Tight to find an anvil or heavy weight. Turning to Leslie, he asked coldly, "Yuh still got that old drill 'round heah?"

Leslie nodded towards the table in the far corner of the shed.

"Set it up," J.W. commanded of Henry Lee in a low monotone voice. Then he turned and saw that Too Tight hadn't budged. In an instant, J.W.'s scarlet washed face stood inches from Too Tight. His fleshy, clenched fist, blasted deep into Too Tight's stomach; knocking him to the ground.

J.W. scrunched his fingers firmly into the tight curls on Too Tight's head, pulled him up from the floor, and through clinched teeth said, "Niggah, mah mood ain't such that yuh should push me. Now, Ah'm 'bout ti'ed of all yuh mutha fuckas'! An' Ah'm damn sho sick of yuh black ass! Yuh bes' pay right close attention, unless yuh plannin' tuh join yuh friend thar," he said as he nodded towards Emmett.

Too Tight wanted to kill him. His fist tightened, his jagged nails cut into his calloused palms. Yes, he could kill him.

After all he wasn't a god. He was merely another man, flesh and blood. If the boy could stand up to him, then surely he could.

Too Tight stood straight and defiantly raised his eyes to meet J.W.'s, icy glare.

"Niggah, yuh got somethin' tuh say tuh me, boy? Ah'm jist 'bout ready tuh git rid of yuh ass right now."

For an instant, Too Tight stared unflinchingly back into J.W.'s soulless glare. Slowly, he became aware that no one else was speaking and that he was surrounded by Melvin, Leslie, Roy, and Hubert. Henry Lee cringed silently at the far end of the shed. A sick pain in Too Tight's stomach forced him to cast his eyes to the ground again as he replied meekly, "Nossah."

Roy noticed Henry Lee pressed against the wall, trembling. "Whut the hell yuh standin' thar lookin' crazy fuh? Yuh ass hard of hearin' too?"

"Nossah," he replied timidly.

"Well, act like it an' do what yuh was told!"

Henry Lee's hands shook as he attempted to assemble the rusted equipment.

Leslie chewed harder on his cigar stub as he squinted and looked out the side of his eyes at his younger brother.

Rumors of tortures used in the military to obtain information from some World War II prisoners of war, flooded Melvin mind, as fragments of sanity began to return. He grabbed J.W. by the arm.

"Dub! Jist take 'im out in the woods so Roy kain put uh bullet in 'im! He's damn neah dead already!"

"Naw Melvin. Yuh heard 'im. They drilled that Civil Rights shit intuh 'im," J.W. said sternly.

Leslie's eyes widened as he said, "Boy, yuh dun lost yuh mind. Ain't no need in...mean tuh say, it ain't gonna do nobody no good. Melvin's right. Jist let Roy take care of thangs his own way. 'Sides, who's gonna clean up the mess? Ya'll ain't walkin' outta heah, leavin' me wit it!"

"Don't worrah 'bout it! Mah Boys gonna straighten up yuh place, but Ah'll be damned if Ah'ma waste uh bullet on his ass!

Ah ought tuh throw 'im in uh crate an' ship his ass back tuh Eisenhower! Show 'im jist whut the hell Ah thank of 'im an' his niggah-lovin' ways!" With a swift forceful kick to Emmett's ribs, he spat and said, "This niggah an' evah goddamned one like 'im deserves evahthang he gits!"

Furiously, J.W. pushed Henry Lee away from the table as he made clumsy efforts to connect the rusted parts of the drill.

In the smaller tool shed, Too Tight noticed the rusted anvil under a pile of feedbags. He started to pull it out, but though again, when he realized that there was a slim chance that the boy could still live.

He hoped that maybe they would just take the boy out somewhere and dump him and that perhaps someone might find him in time to save his life.

"Dey treat me worser den dey damn dawgs, but Ah be damned if dey gonna make me help 'em kill dat boy. God, if Yuh up dere," he mumbled as he piled more bags on the anvil, making sure it remained out of sight. "If Yuh seein' dis, jist make sho all of 'em burns in de blackest part of hell!"".

When Too Tight walked back into the large shed, he saw Henry Lee struggling to scramble from the floor.

"Niggah, git yuh black' ass up!" Roy yelled, intoxicated with power. He grabbed Henry Lee firmly by his hair, dragged him from the ground, and hurled him against the wall.

"Too Tight!" J.W. yelled as he and Melvin finished bolting the brace to the table. "Ya'll brang that niggah ovah heah!"

Hubert looked nervously around the shed. When they first started on this venture, he was drunk. He'd been involved in beatings before, but now his heart pounded wildly, and he could feel the blood pulsating through his body. His friend didn't look the same. His face had turned a dark red that he'd never seen. The skin on his knuckles was bloody, bruised, and torn.

172

"Hey, Roy." he said with an uneasy laugh. "C'mon, ya'll jist foolin' 'round, right?" he asked as he pulled him to the side and nervously looked around. "Ah mean, ya'll ain't really gonna use that thang, are yuh?"

"Look, damn it," J.W. interrupted without looking up to face him. "Ah ain't got no time fuh hand holdin'! Now we gonna finish this thang tuhgetha, unless yuh one of them unda'cover boys fuh the damn NA'CP!"

"Naw! Naw! Dub, it ain't nothin' like that. Ah jist thought, Ah mean...like Melvin. . ."

"Ah'm tellin' yuh this jist one last time! Stay outta mah family's bidness!" J.W. growled as he continued working on the drill.

Their voices seemed to be coming through a tunnel somewhere far off in the distance. Emmett was reluctantly regaining consciousness. He was unable to move. His entire body throbbed with pain. But still, he frantically searched his mind for a way to escape this shed and save himself from these strangers that hated him so desperately. 'I should have stayed at home. I should have done what Mama wanted. But what have I done, for them to hate me so much? Why do they want to...to kill me? Oh God...what should I do??! Mama, God...please help me!'

Slowly, he realized that he was moving. Someone was dragging him across the floor. He tried to call out, but couldn't. He tried to squirm free, but his body felt heavy and numb and he couldn't move.

When they reached the table, J.W. propped Emmett against the wooden work table and started shoving his head into the brace.

"Ya'll hold 'im! Hold 'im goddamnit!" J.W. hollered as he began to lose his grip on the heavy boy.

Emmett was barely able to see through the narrow slit in his swollen eyes. Too Tight looked down at the helpless boy as he helped Henry Lee prop him against the table. With all the will and energy he had left in his body, Emmett, face bloodied and swollen beyond recognition, looked up at Too Tight.

Lord! Help My Child!

"PPP…Please…." He whimpered weakly.

Too Tight secretly eased his hand down to Emmett's side and clutched the boy's hand. Emmett's last tear etched a narrow path down the side of his blood-caked face and dripped onto Too Tights thumb.

J.W. signaled Roy to start turning the drill, forcing the bit to creep downward, towards Emmett's head.

With crazed excitement, Roy twisted the drill harder. The corroded bit squeaked as rust crumbled from the grooves, piercing Emmett's flesh.

"Oh, Mama…ppp…please help me!!! MMM…Mama!!! MMM…Mama!!!"

A sudden gush of blood splattered on Henry Lee's shirt. The warm red fluid of life seemed to penetrate through the cloth; deep into his own soul. He stood for a moment, frozen, staring down at the blood spreading like a sea over his shirt.

J.W. and Melvin pushed Henry Lee and Too Tight out of the way and held a tighter grip on Emmett as he kicked frantically; his arms flailing aimlessly in the air.

Henry Lee ran towards the door, vomit spurting from his lips with each step. Too Tight caught him before he could reach it and held his head down until he began choking with dry heaves.

Roy turned the drill harder. As Emmett's skull cracked further, J.W. attempted to take over, but Roy pushed him away.

"Naw…naw…this niggah's mine!" he said, turning the drill tighter and tighter. "Die, damn yuh! Die, yuh stubborn sonna- bitch! Yuh still thank yuh betta 'n me?"

"MMM…Mama! Mama! PPP…Please!" Emmett screamed as Roy laughed hysterically. "HHH…Help me! Oh GGG…God!"

The bit tore into Emmett's brain. His ear splitting screams rang through the shed and spread throughout the surrounding field. Emmett's body jerked in animal like seizures and then, was finally stilled.

"Whut's that yuh say, niggah?" A sick giggle laced Roy's words, as he danced around like a madman, his hand shading his eyes as he pretended to look far off. "Ah don't see yuh mammie!" He looked into Emmett's lifeless face and thumped him

on the side of his head. "Yuh heah me, niggah? Yuh mammie ain't heah! Maybe she's off somewhar wit that niggah-lovin' Eisenhower!"

"Roy, that's 'nough," J.W. said somberly. "It's dun."

Roy looked angrily over at his brother.

* * *

The shed stood engulfed in an ugly hush for what seemed an eternity. Their senses were suddenly assaulted by the sweet stench of spilled blood as they stared at the battered corpse hanging limply from the vice.

The squeaking of the corroded brace broke the silence as J.W. unscrewed the rusted bit. Sticky gray matter crackled lightly as the bit rescinded from Emmett's head; fragments of brain clinging in its grooves. The heap of flesh slumped lifelessly onto the floor.

"Git yuh ass up now, niggah!" Roy giggled as he kicked Emmett's lifeless body. "Whut yuh got tuh say now! Whut's that? Speak up! Aw, that's right," he giggled. "yuh kkkain't talk!"

The others stood silent and stunned. It was as if the cloud of rage began to dissipate and the reality of what they had actually done shone clearly in their faces.

"Roy," J.W. said quietly. "Gowan an' back the truck up tuh the door so we kain git outta heah."

"Ah ain't dun yet!" Roy replied angrily. His eyes widened as he searched through the tools that lay on the shelves and hung along the walls. "Stretch 'im out!" he yelled as he retrieved the heavy hedge clippers and stormed back to Emmett's lifeless body.

"Roy, whut the hell yuh doin'?" Melvin barked. "Stop! That's 'nough!"

"Aw, shit," Leslie whined as he looked over at Roy. "The niggah's already dead!"

175

He stood firmly in front of his young brother. "Heah me now Roy! That niggah's dead! Now git 'im the hell outta heah! Shit! Ah got work tuh do!"

"Git outta mah way," Roy growled through clenched teeth. "Ah said turn 'im ovah!" he screamed at Too Tight and Henry Lee as he shoved Leslie out of his path.

Lord! Help My Child!

Too Tight's head whirled and his hands trembled as he carefully rolled the child's body over on his back. Roy cut through the white denim of Emmett's bloodstained pants; down to the cotton underwear. His hate filled, hysterical laugh echoed throughout the shed as he reached his bloodied hands between the boy's legs and angrily yanked out his penis.

"Niggah! Yuh won't be spoilin' no mo' White gals wit this one!"

"Roy!" J.W. yelled as he snatched the hedge clippers and glared down at his flush faced brother. "Stop it! Whut the hell's wrong wit yuh, boy? We gotta git outta heah now! We ain't got no time tuh be assin' 'round!"

Roy drew his boot back and thrust one last powerful kick into Emmett's lifeless body. "Now we kain git outta heah," Roy said nonchalantly as he hurried out of the door.

"Aw, shit man! Damn!" Hubert said as he watched in disbelief as Roy left the shed as if nothing had happened.

"Ah don't know why they make yuh do shit like this," J.W. said quietly. His eyes remained transfixed on the body.

"Whut happened tuh yuh, boy?" Leslie asked, as he continued to stare at the body. "Ah ain't nevah hear tell of no mess like this. Ah'd 'spect somethin' like this from Roy, but yuh know betta! All yuh had tuh do was take his ass out somewhar an' put uh bullet in 'im!"

"Les, yuh heard 'im! Whut choice did Ah have? None, that's whut! That niggah ain't give me no choice at all! Hell, the gov'ment sent me ovah seas tuh fight fuh mah rights! They dun filled me wit all them metals 'cuz Ah ain't 'fraid tuh do whut's right! Ain't uh damn thang nobody kain tell me 'bout fightin' fuh me an' mah kinfolks right heah in mah own backyard!"

Melvin rushed out to find a tarpaulin in the small shed. In the meantime, in the large shed, Leslie stepped over Emmett's body and stood directly in front of his brother.

"Dub, don't yuh see whut happened heah? Yuh ain't in the army no mo'! Ah don't give uh horse's ass whut the niggah dun," he said as he pointed down at the bizarre mound of human

flesh. "But this? This shit heah is...! Dub, yuh know Ah don't care how many niggahs yuh bury, but damnit; thar's uh way tuh do it...an' this ain't it! Mean tuh say...this don't make no kinda sense! Yuh went way too damned far! Ah kain't hold yuh up on this one, Dub!" He threw his hands up as he turned to leave the shed. "Jist make sho yuh niggahs clean this mess up, an' leave me the hell outta it! Ah don't want nobody knockin' at mah damn door!"

"Too Tight, Henry Lee," J.W. said somberly, "ya'll git them clothes offa 'im. Hurry up!"

* * *

As Roy backed the truck up to the shed door, Frank looked out from where he was crouching and noticed that others were also in the field. In fact, many fieldhands had ventured out into the rows of cotton. Some hid in the field, while others nervously went about their business of picking cotton. They didn't want to take the chance of being beaten for not doing their chores but, they were careful to face away from the main yard and shed. Very few fieldhands remained behind the closed doors of their shacks, even though the air was heavy with humidity and the temperature was already well over eighty degrees. They knew that it would be safer to stay inside and claim that they heard nothing, even if it meant risking a beating for not working.

Frank stooped lower in the field and quickly crawled back to his house, but not before Mandy caught sight of him. When he came to the clearing to his shack he darted in and peered out of the window. Two of his teenage sons were already in the back yard preparing for the day's work. Georgia, his wife, stood at the table washing breakfast dishes in a large rust stained tin tub.

"Georgia, Ah don't want yuh outside dis mo'nin', an' git dem boys back in heah!"

177

"Whut yuh mean? Dey got uh heap of chores tuh do. 'Sides, it look like rain. Ah 'spect it'll be too mucha mud up in da day tuh do mucha anythang outdoors. Ol' Milam ain't beatin' nonna mine 'cuz Ah'm makin' sho…"

"Yuh heard whut Ah say woman!" he yelled. "Ah don't want nary one of ya'll on da other side of dis heah door 'til Ah tells yuh! Now, do as Ah say!"

Lord! Help My Child!

* * *

Roy walked back into the shed just as Henry Lee and Too Tight began carefully removing the clothes from Emmett's body. He had seen some fieldhands out in the surrounding cotton fields and for the first time, was getting nervous; worried that someone might see them.

"Hey Dub, yuh ain't gotta do that now! Why don't we jist wait an' take care of that when we outta heah?"

J.W. ignored him and instead turned his attention to Hubert.

"Whut the hell yuh doin' standin' ovah thar, actin' like yuh ain't gotta goddamn thang tuh do? Make yuhseff useful! Git ovah thar an'help 'em git them clothes off!"

"Dub, did yuh heah me?" Roy pleaded, "Let's git out now!"

J.W. was altogether weary. He couldn't understand how so many White men could have no idea what was going on right up under their noises. This wasn't just a killing. Their lives were falling apart and they couldn't even see it. Liberals and communists were destroying all that he and his ancestors worked so diligently to build. The glory of the South was, once again, under attack and he had no intention of standing idly by, watching and waiting for it all to collapse.

Hubert stood where he was; too frightened to move.

"Roy," J.W. growled, "stop whimperin' like uh damn woman an' help 'em load that shit on the damn truck so we kain git the hell outta heah!"

Roy looked over at the bloody mass on the floor and backed away. His rage had subsided, and now he was unable to bring himself to touch the body. He stood motionless; staring

178

down at Emmett's outstretched body. Blood that once flowed down Emmett's face, now sat in a pool on the floor; his swollen, accusing eyes seeming to stare through him.

"Boy, Ah kain't fuh the life of me figger out why the hell yuh come 'long!" J.W. said as he came up behind Hubert and shoved him towards the door. "Git yuh ass ovah thar! Hold the damn door!"

Bonnie Blue

"Yeah, Dub, Ah got it," he said as his trembling hands attempted to get a grip on the shed door.

"Lissen tuh me boy. When we leave up outta heah, Ah don't want tuh see yuh no whar 'round. Yuh got that? We got 'nough problems wit-out yuh fallin' apart. Now, all Ah got fuh yuh tuh do right now is tuh take them two Boys off somewhar an' make damn sho they bury them clothes whar ain't nobody gonna find 'em an' ain't no dog gonna dig 'em up; evah!"

Hubert stood motionless; his stare held captive by the blood stained floor.

"Huber'!" J.W. snatched him by the collar of his shirt. "Right now, it ain't gonna take nothin' fuh me tuh make fertilizer outta yuh ass too. Yuh bes' b'lieve me," he murmured in a low sinister tone. "Yuh mess this thang up, an' Ah'll kill yuh. Yuh unda'stand me?"

Hubert nodded slowly. "Whutevah yuh say, Dub. Ah'll make sho of it."

J.W. released Hubert's collar and smacked him across the face. His calloused chapped hands scrapped deeply across Hubert's cheek, nearly drawing blood. "Remember, when yuh leave heah, yuh don't know nothin'; ain't seent nothin' an' yuh won't hafta see me. Now yuh jist stand heah an' hold the door, an' evahthang will be all right."

* * *

In the field, now only a short distance from the tool shed, but still well out of sight, Mandy and Willie watched, as the men struggle to load Emmett's body into the back of the truck.

* * *

179

J.W. ordered Henry Lee and Too Tight to scrub the blood stained floor. "Ya'll git plenty cotton seed from 'round back an' cover the flo' when yuh're through. Too Tight, Ah want ya'll tuh bury them clothes an' yuh betta make damn sho nobody'll find 'em or nobody'll find ya'll! Yuh unda'stand Boy?

"Yassah," Too Tight replied humbly.

Melvin secured a large brown tarpaulin over Emmett's body in the back of the pickup and joined J.W. and Roy in the cab.

Lord! Help My Child!

Leslie called out to them as he took long strides to J.W.'s side of the truck, "Yuh boy's be careful now, yuh heah?"

Roy looked surprised that he was staying behind. "Why ain't yuh comin'?"

"Roy, git the hell on outta heah an' take care of yuh bidness," Leslie replied as he shoved his spit soaked cigar back in his mouth, turned, and headed back to the shed. "This ain't no goddamn church social," he mumbled as he headed for his house.

"Hey, Les! C' mere!" J.W. called.

Leslie whirled on his heels. "Goddamnit, Dub!" he barked. "Whut the hell else yuh want? Yuh come brangin' all this shit tuh mah door, an' now yuh tyin' up mah whole damned day cleanin' it up! This don't make no damned sense! Ah'm through now!" He said as he headed back towards his house. "Ain't nothin' but uh niggah! Now yuh gittin' me all behind...!"

J.W. jumped out of the truck and hurried over to his older brother. "Look, Les. Ah didn't 'tend fuh nonna this tuh happen, but it did. Mah Boys is cleanin' it up. Ah jist need one mo' thang. Let Huber' use one of yuh cars tuh take 'em out tuh bury them clothes. He ain't gotta wait fuh 'em, jist drop 'em somewhar. He'll brang yuh car right back."

"That's the last thang, Dub! Don't ask fuh anoth'a damn thang! Gowan boy! Git on outta heah!" he said as he stormed back to the shed.

J.W. sped down the driveway and disappeared in the gravel churned dust cloud.

"Huber'!" Leslie shouted as he poked his head in the shed door. "C'mon up tuh the house!"

Too Tight watched in silence as Hubert hurried out to meet him.

* * *

The furious whirlwind of hate and evil had finally ceased. The remaining silence was so complete that the buzzing of huge, thirsty, horseflies over the pool of blood was nearly deafening.

"Hen Lee," Too Tight whispered. Thick humidity held the gagging stench of death in his throat, nearly suffocating him.

Henry Lee remained in the shadows. Shame enveloped his fear. Had it not been for the sound of his own shallow, rapid

Bonnie Blue

breath and the salty elixir of tears and sweat that seeped steadily into the corner of his mouth, he might have clung to the illusion that this was just a hideous nightmare that held him captive.

Cautiously, Too Tight called slightly louder, "Hen Lee!"

Henry Lee could see Too Tight, but his body was unable to move.

Too Tight's steps creaked loudly against the silence as he rapidly made his way across the shed to his friend. "Look Hen Lee," Too Tight said frantically, "we gotta hurry up so we kain git outta heah! Hen Lee, is yuh hearin' me, Boy?"

He took Henry Lee's face in his hand and shook it from side to side. Panic started rising.

"Don't do this tuh me, Hen Lee!" He slapped him hard in the face. "Ah ain't plannin' tuh meet mah Mak'a tuhday! Yuh bes' pull yuhseff tuhgetha befo' dem damn crackas' come back heah! C'mon now! Yuh gotta help me clean up this place so we kain git as much land between us an' dem as we kain!" Too Tight shook him again. "Hen…"

"Ah don't b'lieve it," Henry Lee mumbled. "Lawd, please fuhgive me." He wailed. "Dey drilled dat boy's head." He whispered. "Yuh seent 'em, ain't yuh Tight?"

Too Tight pulled him towards the pool of blood and handed him an empty bucket. "Yuh worrah 'bout de Lawd later. We gotta stay on da sane side of dese crackas' so's we kain see anoth'a day. Now, c'mon. Yuh go git da wat'a from da well out front, Ah'll git da cotton seed out da lil' shed. Rememb'a, yuh gotta

181

play act like yuh ain't bothered so's yuh kain see Claire an' yuh chil'ren."

"Yeah," Henry Lee mumbled as he walked nervously out the door with the bucket.

Shortly after they scrubbed the area and were finally spreading cotton seed across the floor, Hubert came in for them.

"Ya'll dun?" He asked nervously.

"Yassah," Too Tight replied. "Soon's we spread da last of dis heah seed."

"Make sho yuh gather all them clothes tuhgetha, an' c'mon out tuh the car."

Lord! Help My Child!

They slung the remaining seed from the bag across the wet stained floor, rolled Emmett's sweat and blood soaked clothes into a bundle, and hurried out the door.

* * *

Dense dark clouds moved smoothly through the sky, bringing with it, the sweet clean scent of impending rain.

Rocks pounded wildly beneath the car as Hubert sped down the road. Too Tight and Henry Lee sat quietly in the back seat until it seemed that they were going deeper into the backwoods.

Too Tight looked frantically out the back window for any sign of familiarity. He glared over at Henry Lee, who stared blankly out the open window. Again, Too Tight turned around in his seat and searched out the window in an attempt to determine which direction they were traveling.

As the skies grew ever darker, Too Tight's suspicions intensified. Not only were the dead boy's clothes going to be dumped, but they too, had to disappear. Perspiration rolled in a steady stream down his neck, barely being absorbed in his already saturated tee-shirt.

The reflection of Hubert's nervous face in the rearview mirror caused Too Tight's gut to knot. He wasn't going to be taken down without a fight. There were two of them and only one White man now. The tables had turned and they now had a chance.

No more taking orders and cowling down. No more being treated with less regard than their hogs, cows, and dogs. Yes, now the tables had turned. If someone else was to be killed; it sure wouldn't be them. Not this time. Not today.

Too Tight glared over at Henry Lee, who still hadn't budged. By the lack of expression on his friends face, Too Tight wasn't at all sure that he would be capable of helping him fight, if it came down to that. "Hen Lee," he murmured as he slid his hand across the seat to nudge him.

Suddenly a loud, nervous voice broke the silence.

Bonnie Blue

"Ah don't want no trouble!"

Too Tight jumped and pressed his body hard against the back seat. He watched Hubert's arm for any movement towards the gun that surely lay next to him. He could grab him by the throat and squeeze the very life from him. They would run off the road, but he would have a better chance of living through a collision with a tree than trying to out-run a bullet.

"Nossah." A small shaky voice replied.

Startled, Too Tight shot a glance across the seat at Henry Lee.

"Ah'ma drop ya'll off up yonda thar." Hubert's voice trembled as he looked in the rearview mirror at Too Tight's cold, angry face staring back at him. "Make sho yuh find uh good spot tuh bury that stuff. Ah'll take yuh back tuh yuh place when yuh dun." His voice trailed off as he turned his attention back to the road. "Wasn't that the damnedest thang yuh evah did see?" he said quietly and sympathetically.

"Yassah," Henry Lee replied cautiously.

This White man trying to be nice frightened him, but the look on Too Tight's face frightened him more. He was afraid of what his friend might do. The night had been too much. The day had been too much. There was nothing else that he could live through on this day. All that he now wanted was the love in his wife's arms and the giggle of his children's innocence. It hurt him to know that this poor boy's Mama would never see him again.

"Now yuh niggahs know Ah ain't had nothin' tuh do wit all that. Not uh thang! Hell, ya'll did mo' than me! So if the law come askin' questions, ya'll jist remember that, yuh heah?"

"Yassah," Too Tight replied dryly, with just enough sarcasm to frighten this little man.

Staying alive was the strongest thought in his mind. If Hubert was going to try to kill them and he couldn't grab him by the throat, he was ready to jump from the car. But they were still speeding, and there were no trees that could protect them. He knew that Hubert would shoot them in the back for sure. Again, Too Tight looked at the face in the mirror.

"Damned shame though," Hubert said, talking more to himself than to his passengers. "Niggahs git outta line, yuh jist take

Lord! Help My Child!

care of it." He said shaking his head. "Ah sweah that was the damnedest thang."

He eased his foot off of the accelerator and turned off the gravel road onto a deserted dirt road and overgrown weeds. "Now whar the hell's this place?" Hubert mumbled to himself.

They rode in silence for another couple of miles before they turned onto a barely visible overgrown path that led to a wooded area.

"Okay, this heah's far 'nough," Hubert said cautiously as he slowed to a halt. "Ya'll git on out an' bury them thangs ovah in them trees somewhar. Now, ya'll gonna hafta be quick 'bout it! Ah don't want tuh be caught out heah when this storm hit! Hurry up, now! Make sho yuh git all that stuff out the car!"

Too Tight knew that this was where he would die if White folks had their way.

'Let dis peckawood git out dis car,' he thought to himself. 'Ah sweah befo' the Mak'a, Ah ain't gonna jist lay down an' die. An' Ah damn sho ain't gonna let 'im jist shoot me in da back!'

Henry Lee mechanically opened his door and slid out on his side, leaving the bundle of bloody clothes. Too Tight stared unflinchingly into the eyes in the rearview mirror staring back at him.

"Look, Boy," Hubert said anxiously, "Ah don't want no trouble, an' Ah 'spect yuh don't want none eith'a. Now jist do whut Ah say, an' be dun wit it."

Too Tight's bloodshot eyes, cold and dangerous, stared unflinchingly back at him.

"Yuh Boys know Ah ain't had nothin' tuh do wit it. It weren't right, but it's dun now. Kain't nobody do nothin' tuh brang that boy back. Ya'll jist gowan an' do as Ah say, an' git rid of them clothes so we kain all go home."

Roaring thunder shook the ground. Dark clouds holding the promise of heavy rains rolled across the sky. Too Tight and Hubert didn't release their gaze until Too Tight crunched the bundle of blood caked clothes together and carefully slid out of the car.

Bonnie Blue

Hubert's foot quickly slammed on the accelerator before Too Tight's hand had cleared the car door. Emmett's shoes, which rested on the back seat of the car, were thrown to the floor as the wide blue Chevy fishtailed down the path, disappearing around the bend.

* * *

Henry Lee crumbled to the ground and with his face lifted humbly to the heavens he called out, "Lawd! Why? Ah know Ah ain't got da right tuh question Yuh, but Ah don't unda'stand! He called fuh Yuh, but Yuh ain't answer! Yuh jist let da devil have his way! Ah know it's Yuh're will an' not mah will bein' dun but…"

Disgusted, Too Tight crushed his bloody burden to his chest, began backing away and yelled, "Prayin' ain't dun dat boy no damned good! Aw, fuck it!" He ran about a quarter of a mile before ducking into the dense thicket.

The skies turned dark green. A deluge of heavy rain and strong winds shook the trees, threatening to rip them from their roots. Thunder clapped loudly overhead as Too Tight ran deeper into the woods. His heart pounded fiercely, his curses could be

185

heard over the cracking of branches as he fought his way through the towering trees and foliage.

Henry Lee could see the occasional silhouette of his friend darting aimlessly through the massive underbrush beneath the trees ahead. He tried to catch up with him but fell further behind.

The sparse canopy of trees gave little protection against the relentless waves of rain that washed across the early morning skies. But still, for Too Tight, it felt like a haven; a refuge from things over which he had no control.

He collapsed breathlessly against the huge, timeworn trunk of a nearby tree. His bundle, heavy with blood and the peculiar stench of death, slid easily from his arms onto the exposed roots.

"Ain't no god!" He wept, "Niggahs talkin' tuh uh god dat ain't!"

Lord! Help My Child!

He kicked the small bundle of clothes over and over again, screaming up into the darkened skies. "Are Yuh up dere? Kain Yuh heah me? Why ain't Yuh strike 'em down befo' dey got tuh dat boy? Yuh coulda stopped 'em...stopped all dem evil mutha fuckas! Why didn't Yuh? Wheah da hell is Yuh?" He swung at the air and punched at trees with his bare fists. "Wheah is Yuh?" he screamed. "Didn't Yuh see whut dey dun tuh dat boy? Didn't Yuh know?"

The strong melody of raindrops gushing off the umbrella of foliage seemed to call out a divine reply. His voice cracked before he fell to his knees and wept. Suddenly, he heard Henry Lee's voice calling faintly from somewhere in the woods. He hurried to his feet and brushed the evidence of fear and shame from his face.

"Ovah heah!" he yelled.

Lightning clapped loudly overhead as he quickly gathered clothes that lay strewn across the ground. He reached for one of Emmett's socks, which rested apart from his other clothing. A large drop of rain fell heavily on his thumb, splattered, and was quickly absorbed into the white cotton, seemingly bringing the dried bloodstain back to life. He turned away and inhaled deeply, fighting off the anguish that he tried so desperately to control. His eyes slid back to his outstretched hand. He could almost feel the child's soft, moist hand in his as he squeezed and clung to the last thread of hope; pitifully begging for his help.

Slowly, carefully, he clasped the sock between his two fingers and rolled it with the other clothes. He heard Henry Lee and the crackling of branches approaching him.

"Tight! Why yuh leave me?" he asked out of breath.

Too Tight brushed insects, twigs, and leaves from a protruding root of an ancient tree and said nothing. Henry Lee looked up past the canopy of trees at the flashes of lightning that streaked across the darkened skies. Deep rumbles of thunder rolled overhead, but still the stench of death hung heavily in the air.

"Yuh thank he comin' back?" Henry Lee asked nervously. "Tight, Ah'm skeered. Eben dat White man skeered, an' he one of

Bonnie Blue

dem. Dey gonna come back. Dey prob'ly gonna git ridda us too, ain't dey?"

"Don't matter," Too Tight said dryly. "We already dead. All dey want tuh do is take uh niggah's manhood, one way or anoth'a."

A stabbing fear more frightening than the promise of a lynching, pounded away at Henry Lee's heart, as he watched his best friend dissolve into a state of hopelessness.

Too Tight had always been his protection from anyone and anything that he couldn't handle himself. His very presence gave him a measure of power, where there was none. Too Tight, who could stand up against almost anything now sounded; defeated.

He knelt beside Too Tight and began scraping frantically at the foot of the tree with a large sharp stone as the downpour forged through the layers of leaves. A puddle began to form in the bottom of the hole. They dug faster and harder.

At last, it was just deep enough to bury the clothes. Henry Lee pressed the clothes firmly into the ground and closed the tiny grave with mud, twigs, and a large fallen branch.

Too Tight crawled through the mud on his hands and knees searching the ground until he found a rock with sharp edges that suited his purpose. Nearly blinded by the rain and his own stubborn tears, he began to wildly chip away at the bark of the tree.

"Tight, whut yuh doin'? Is yuh dun gone crazy?" Henry Lee yelled, packing more mud and large stones securely over the internment site.

"Ah don't know!" he yelled over the thunder as he continued to chip away at the bark. "Maybe Ah is! Maybe Ah dun lost mah mind! Shit, man! Aft'a tuhday, we both shoulda been dun lost our mind! Ah don't know! All Ah know is we need tuh mark it fuh da boy! Hell, Ah ain't dun nothin' fuh 'im when Ah had da chance! Damnit! Ah owe it tuh 'im tuh mark somewheah on dis earf, dat he been heah!"

A bolt of lightning crackled just ahead of him striking a neighboring cottonwood; severing a large branch, which came crashing to the ground.

Lord! Help My Child!

Frightened, Henry Lee pleaded, "C'mon, Tight! Help me cover dis ovah real good so we kain git outta heah! Don't worrah 'bout da mark."

Too Tight continued chipping away and digging deeper into the face of the tree, even as his wet hands slipped across the sharp rock; cutting the palm of his hand. "Ah gotta do it fuh da boy! Shit, Ah gotta do it fuh all da boys ain't nobody say nothin' 'bout!"

"Ain't nothin' we coulda dun 'bout dat boy! Not den! Not now!" Henry Lee called as he forced the last large stone into place over the makeshift burial site. "We gotta git outta heah now!" he yelled. "The Lawd gonna take care of dem! He da only one dat kain take care of all da chil'ren, livin' an' dead!"

Too Tight shot a damning glare over to his friend. "Yuh need tuh stop dat prayin' shit!" he yelled. "Yuh always prayin' an' prayin', an' whut damned good did it do? Yuh prayed! He prayed! An' da Lawd? He ain't heard nary uh one of ya'll! Ah say theah ain't nobody up dere! If dey is, He uh White god fuh White folks! Yuh jist wastin' yuh prayin' on uh god dat ain't 'bout tuh heah no niggah!"

Henry Lee watched in disbelief as Too Tight spewed his anger and bolted out of the cluster of trees. He took one last look at the crude mark in the tree and the tiny grave and then followed Too Tight into the downpour on the open prairie.

"Tight!" he yelled as he ran behind the figure that darted ahead.

A jagged streak of lightening etched across the darkened skies as the growl of thunder quaked the ground below. Shaken, Henry Lee slid in the overgrown muddy tire tracks and lay trembling, waiting for the wrath from heaven.

Too Tight heard his childhood friend call from under the fury in the sky. He wasn't at all sure that it wasn't a gunshot. When he looked back and saw Henry Lee hit the ground, his heart beat so hard that he felt as if it would surely pound out of his chest. "Hen Lee!" he screamed, as his head darted in all directions for any sign of anyone, Colored or White, but all he saw was Henry Lee

Bonnie Blue

balled up. "Damn!" He screamed as he ran to his side.

Henry Lee drew his knees tightly beneath his belly. His slim back and shoulders shook as his own pain, anger, and guilt became unbearable. Too Tight sat on the muddy ground next to him.

Strong winds pressed against their stoned bodies, as heavy sheets of rain washed across their backs. They sat for what seemed an eternity, each man entrapped in his own hellish thoughts. Finally, Too Tight succumbed to the truth that there was nothing he could have done. He'd had enough. He had to put distance between him and anything that had to do with the lynching.

Thunder boomed relentlessly through the darkened sky as Too Tight screamed, "We gotta go! Gotta git away from dis place,

189

now!" He paused before he rose and glanced briefly back towards the area where the boys clothes lay, waiting to decay and return to the earth. "Hen Lee, c'mon!"

Henry Lee folded himself tighter into a knot, burying his head against his legs as massive waves of rain continued to pound against his body.

"Hen Lee! C'mon, Ah say! Ah don't want tuh leave yuh, but Ah gotta go!" He began backing away. "C'mon, man! Ah don't want tuh leave yuh out heah! C'mon, man!" He walked faster, stumbled over a downed limb, turned, and slipped on wet grass as he attempted to break into a full run.

Henry Lee heard Too Tight's pleas, but he was spent. He sat for a long while, letting the storm have its way with his body. It didn't matter to him if he was struck by lightning or hung at the end of a rope. There was no reason for him to live. The truth was; he wasn't sure that Too Tight wasn't right about God. That he could doubt God for even a moment, left him feeling unworthy of life. And he sat; alone, and conflicted.

* * *

The rains finally diminished to a light drizzle and the sun began to create heaven beams through the thick body of clouds

Lord! Help My Child!

that began to dissipate. Henry Lee remained planted in the spot where Too Tight had left him.

* * *

Henry Lee sat staring out at the vastness of the landscape, ignoring the sun biting relentlessly into his back. Then slowly, bit by bit, the vision of his wife entered his mind. "Claire...," he whispered as he exhaustedly unfolded himself and began walking, unaware of exactly how far from home he really was.

For much of the day, Henry Lee's body was protected by the shade of trees that dotted across much of the land. But there were many hours when the sun burned his back as he crawled secretly on his elbows and belly through rows of cotton and

190

beans, all the while spitting earth from his lips. He wasn't sure if he was traveling in circles, or not. But he couldn't take the chance of going out on the road and being seen. The one thing that he was certain of, was that the shadows were getting longer and Claire would be home from the fields soon; if she was still alive.

His thighs ached as he commanded them forward. Dust dried breath exploded from his lungs, further eroding his full, chapped lips as he finally ran through familiar woods praying all the time that Claire and his children were unharmed. He knew that she hadn't slept the night before and would have kept watch in the cotton field for any sign of him.

Until now, Henry Lee had given no thought to his bloodstained shirt which clung to his perspiration soaked body. He squeezed his eyes tightly, turned his face as far away from his chest as he could, and began ripping the shirt from his chest.

With his head turned away, he opened his eyes ever so slightly and peered down. Henry Lee could almost feel the warmth of Emmett's blood splattering on him all over again. His stomach shook in queasy waves. He frantically scraped through the carpet of tightly curled hair on his chest as he desperately attempted to remove what was left of the sweat moistened, sunbaked blood.

Henry Lee wanted to find a secluded place to wash himself, but the need to know that his family was unharmed forced him

Bonnie Blue

forward. Sweat poured down the sides of his face. He labored to move his numb legs and paining feet forward as he continued down the narrow dirt path that would ultimately lead him to Claire's garden behind their home.

"Claire!" he called as he commanded his body home. "Claire!" Panic rose in his heart. His house seemed too still. The children weren't in the yard playing, there was no fresh laundry hanging on the clothesline, and there was no sweet smell of food cooking. "Claire!" he screamed.

He had slipped through mud puddles and stumbled across her vegetable garden before Claire appeared in the open back door. She bolted over the two rickety steps and hurried out to meet him.

"Claire!" he screamed as tears of relief filled the wells of his eyes. It seemed that his feet never touched the ground as he fled to her arms.

"Hen Lee! Ah was so skeered fuh yuh! Is yuh alright?" She cried as her thin arms gripped him tightly around his neck. "Wheah yuh been? Jist been sick wid worrah! Ah been up most all night! Ah was skeered dat Ah nevah see yuh again, dat maybe ol' Milam come back again!"

He held her back and looked into her frightened eyes. "Wheah da chil'ren at? Is dey alright?"

"Dey's fine," she said quietly. "Jist sleep is all. Wouldn't go back tuh sleep aft'a ya'll leff. Ended up sleepin' in da fields." Claire's attention was suddenly drawn to his clothes. "Hen Lee," she gasped, "whut happen tuh yuh? Wheah yuh clothes at?"

He enveloped her tightly again. His family was all right. He would be all right.

"Baby, whut happen? Whut dey do?"

"Ain't nothin'," he murmured as he buried his face in her neck. "Evahthang alright."

* * *

Dense clouds that had cloaked the sky began to break away and before long, all evidence of the violent storms had faded.

Too Tight ventured within a stone's throw of the road as the day wore on, but he was careful not to be seen. He knew that, if Hubert had gone back to look for them, he would surely check every cotton field between Leslie Milam's place and Glendora.

Lord! Help My Child!

Bone dry red clay devoured the sweltering heat with a vengeance. He dredged doggedly along the trees that lined the roads. With the exception of an occasional growl of a tractor or cotton combine in the distance, the countryside was still.

Exhausted, Too Tight limped in pain as the crumbly earth burned through the thick layers of skin beneath his blistering bare feet. He wanted to rest, to soak his feet in a cool pond, or wrap them to protect against the ruthless jabs of twigs and rocks;

192

anything to give him relief. But he couldn't chance asking for help. Too Tight knew from experience that many of the men working in the fields, were the very ones that would have no problem turning on him, just to get the coveted 'atta boy'.

Finally, with the sun at his back, he began to feel confident about his bearings. A few more miles and he would be at his estranged wife's house. He needed to know that his family was safe.

Too Tight cautiously approached the massive field that led to the tiny segregated area just at the edge of the small town of Glendora. He carefully looked around to make sure that no one was in the fields before darting out from the security of the trees and into the waist high weeds that led to Triola's rundown shack.

Although the earlier torrential rains had rinsed some of the signs of the midnight raid from his clothing, Too Tight couldn't rid himself of the smell and feel of Emmett's hand. "Shit won't come off!" he cried frantically as he sniffed the back of his hands and scraped them firmly against his pants.

He panicked, ripped off his shirt, rolled it in a tight ball and cautiously dashed to the rusted water pump in the back of the yard, all the while watching for any sign of curious eyes. The pump clanked loudly as he primed the pump and repeatedly forced the handle down to suck the first splash of cold water from the underground well.

"Gotta git it off me!" he whined frantically as he fumbled to fill the dented tin cup and splashed it over his face, arms, and chest.

Bonnie Blue

Just then, his four young boys came running around to the backyard. "It's Papa!" they squealed as they ran to him. "Hey Papa! Whut yuh brang us dis time? Candy???"

"Git back!" he yelled. "Gowan! Do as Ah say! Git on! Wheah yuh Mama?"

Stunned, the children stopped and looked at their father and each other as they stepped away from him. "She in da house," his eldest son said quietly.

Triola stood at the kitchen table slicing fatback to fry for the children's dinner when he burst through the back door. She looked over at him and returned her attention to her task.

"Whut yuh want, ol' man? Yuh woman dun put yuh down?"

"Ain't got no woman 'ceptin' yuh."

"Well, yuh in uh sho 'nuff pitiful shape den," she quietly continued. "'cuz yuh ain't got me no mo', mist'a."

He wanted to hold her, to protect her and the children; to be a man. Slowly, he walked up behind her and slipped his arms around her slim waist and kissed her lightly on her slender, ebony neck. Triola jerked away from his grasp, careful not to look in his eyes. She gripped the knife firmly and slammed it fiercely into the slab of salt-pork.

"If yuh ain't took care of whut yuh need tuh ovah dat nasty heifa's house, ain't no need in comin' heah fuh it! Yuh ain't gittin' no mo' lovin' heah Tight, an' Ah means that!"

"Triola, baby," he pleaded as he backed away from her towards the door. "Ah needs yuh! Ah ain't lyin'! Ah really needs yuh! Baby, las' night, Ol' Milam an' dem made me an' Hen Lee..."

"Tight! Yuh bes' git on outta mah face wid yuh lies!" she yelled.

"Ah dun told yuh," he pleaded, "Ah ain't messin' 'round wid dem gals no mo'! Didn't mean nothin' tuh me, noway!"

She reluctantly looked up at him as he stood in the door with tears, filling his eyes. For too many days and nights, it had been her face soaked with tears; tears of shame, tears of pain, and tears of loneliness. No, she was determined not to give in. Better his tears than hers.

Lord! Help My Child!

"Don't matt'a! Dat whut yuh been sayin' since furst we took up tuhgetha! Yuh cut loose one an' pick up two mo'! Aw, naw brotha! Ah ain't takin' no mo'! Foolin' wid yuh, Ah'd be ol' befo' mah time wid worrah! So yuh might as well jist stay right wheah yuh is! 'Sides," she said as she returned to her slicing, "dere's uh plenty good lookers been payin' me some min' since yuh been playin' down da road! Tight," she retorted "Ah hopes yuh knows yuh ain't da only man dat kain warm mah bed! So yuh kain jist hit da door, mista! 'Cuz yuh don't live heah no mo'!"

Too Tight looked at her and saw the pretty young girl that he'd knocked up when she was only 14 years-old. Her flawless, ebony skin glistening from the sweat still excited him. He knew that too much time and too many women had passed through their lives for them to patch things up now. But the thought of her with another man just hurt too much, especially now.

"Yuh still mah wife, Triola! An' dem still mah youngins in dat yard back theah! Ah don't care whut yuh say, yuh still mine! Don't yuh evah lemme catch yuh wid anoth'a niggah or Ah sweah Ah'll kill yuh!"

"Tight," she yelled furiously, "Ah don't know who yuh thank yuh is! Poppin' in an outta mah life whenevah da urge hits yuh! Ah ain't..."

"Shuddup, woman!" he yelled as he slapped her across the room and stomped out of the house.

She ran after him screaming, "Ah ain't got no use fuh yuh! Yuh ol' no 'count dawg! None at all! Don't come 'round heah no mo'! Yuh heah me? Stay outta mah life!"

Neighbors came running out on their porches to see what all the commotion was. Too Tight ignored their curious stares as he took long strides down the dirt road towards Reid's Café.

Buck Albert, one of Too Tight's many drinking buddies, was driving down the narrow dirt road. "Hey, Tight!" Buck called as he grinned and hung out the window of his ragged, dirty truck. "Ah jist come out from Greenwood wid some sho 'nuff fine yella gals! Wanna c'mon out tuh mah house?" he asked as he drove alongside Too Tight.

Bonnie Blue

Too Tight looked back at Triola, who was glaring down the road at him. He needed somebody, anybody. Even a stranger's arms, would be better than no arms at all. "Fuck it man," he said as he hit the door with his hand. "Let's get outta heah!"

195

BOOK FIVE

The predawn storms reluctantly gave way to the birth of a new day. Deputy Ed Cocthran took this time to sit in his squad car, light a cigarette and bask in the fresh breeze of the rain washed air before opening, what should have been, his office.

Ed, a seasoned lawman, had run for the office of High Sheriff of LaFlore County. The election was close, but he lost to George Smith. Although he accepted the position of deputy he, more often than not, found himself working as though he was the High Sheriff.

The rich, melodic tones of Rosemary Clooney drifted softly out of his open window, filling the quiet morning. His serenity was suddenly shattered when a large black car stopped abruptly at the curb alongside his squad car, splashing pellets of mud through his window.

"Whut the hell?" he yelled as flying specks of mud came to rest on his shirt and cheek

"Hey! Whut's yuh dawg-gawn hurry Boy?" he called as he wiped dots of red clay off his face and threw open the squad car door.

Bonnie Blue

Mose hurried out of his car with Andrew, his eldest son, close behind. "Ah'm sorrah, suh," Mose said as he rushed over to the squad car. "Ah'll gladly have mah boys clean up yuh car an' have mah wife warsh yuh shirt, but we got uh mighty big problem, suh! Mighty big!"

"Don't worrah 'bout it. Ain't nothin' uh lil' wat'a kain't fix," Ed replied as he attempted to wipe the mud from his shirt. "Yuh might as well c'mon in," he said, slightly irritated that his

197

workday was meeting him before he could even get a sniff of coffee.

Ed tossed the keys on his desk. "Have uh seat." he said as he opened the windows and sat behind his desk.

"Whut yuh folks doin' out heah this time of mo'nin'?"

"Well suh, we in need of seein' the High Sheriff," Mose requested humbly.

"Ain't no tellin' whut time the sheriff's gonna be in," Ed said as he removed his hat and placed it gingerly on the edge of his splintering wooden desk.

"Gowan Papa," Andrew said impatiently as he nodded his approval to his father.

Mose identified himself and relayed what had transpired the previous night. He told the deputy that he hadn't seen Emmett since.

"Are yuh sho it was Roy Bryant?" Ed asked, sitting straight up in his chair.

"Yes suh. That's whut he say his name was when they come las' night. He say as clear as day, that he was Mista Br'ant from Money."

Ed reared back in his wooden chair, folded his arms across his chest, and thought back to the year before, when he and Roy collided under similar circumstances.

Andrew, who had been looking out of the window, turned to face the deputy. "Well suh, whut yuh gonna do? Emmett's been gone all night."

Annoyed, Ed glanced over at Andrew, but before he could say anything, Mose quickly spoke.

Mississippi Meets Ms. Mamie!

"That theah's mah son. He don't mean no harm, he jist worrahed 'bout 'im. We all worrahed."

"Looka heah, Boy," Ed said patiently, "Yuh bes' tuh take uh seat ovah thar." Then turning to Mose, he stood and said, "Rev'ran, Ah'll do whut Ah kain. But Ah gotta tell yuh, Ah know the family. Ah've had dealin's wit Roy befo'. Hell, the whole damn clan's mean as rattlers. Ah ain't holdin' out much fuh findin' 'im alive."

198

Mose lowered his head for an instant and looked back at Ed in stubborn resolve. "Emmett's alive. An' wid yuh help, we gonna find 'im."

"Rev'ran, like Ah said, Ah'll do whutevah Ah kain. Now, yuh say the other one was uh large, bald man?"

"Yes suh. It was Mista Milam, suh." He squared his shoulders in defiance. "Mista J.W. Milam."

For a moment, the two men locked eyes, each knowing that J.W.'s involvement made the situation as bad as it could get.

"How'd yuh know it was J.W.? Did he identify hisself too?" Ed asked, hoping that the old preacher wasn't absolutely sure of his identification.

"Oh yes suh! It was Mista John William Milam alright. Ah knowed him from when he brangs his Boys out tuh Mista Fredricks' tuh work the fields wid them cotton combinda's an' bean scratcha's."

"Was thar anybody else out thar that yuh kain remember?"

"Well, theah was anoth'a one Ah couldn't see plain. He kept his face hid an' kinda acted like uh Colored man. But like Ah say, the lights was out."

Ed took a pad from his desk drawer and scribbled notes. "Thar's uh hell of uh lot of them boys, but J.W.'s the only one stone bald on top."

Andrew leaped from his seat and rushed across the tiny office to Ed's desk. "Now yuh know who they are, kain't yuh go pick 'em up? At least call the sheriff in an' git some of yuh deputy's tuhgetha tuh look fuh the boy!"

Bonnie Blue

Ed abruptly stood, leaned over his desk and said impatiently, "Look, Boy, either yuh gonna sit yuhseff down ovah thar an' be quiet or yuh gittin' outta mah office!"

Andrew opened his mouth to challenge the deputy when Mose said, "Theah was somebody else. Uh lady Ah b'lieve. At least it sounded like uh lady."

199

Ed lowered himself back down, flashed a warning glare at Andrew and said, "Gowan, Rev'ran. Do yuh know who the woman was? Whut'd she look like?"

"Ah kain't rightly say as Ah know. Ah didn't see hur. But when they took Emmett out tuh the car, they asked if he was the right one. Whoevah it was that answered, had uh voice that was lighter than uh man. Ah 'spect it's Mista Br'ant's wife. The lady Emmett whistled at in town."

Ed jotted down his notes and asked, "Did yuh even git uh lil' glimpse of hur?"

"No suh. All Ah kain say fuh sho is that it sounded tuh be uh lady."

"Okay, that's good. Is thar anythang else yuh kain remember? Did yuh see the car?"

"Yes suh. But Ah kain't tell yuh whut kind or whut color it was. The only thang Ah kain say is that it weren't uh truck. It was uh car, an' they was parked und'a the shadow of the trees out front of mah house."

Andrew sighed as he turned his attention to Ed. "Okay, whut do we do now?"

"Well Rev'ran, we gonna start investigatin' soon's the Sheriff gits heah. We gonna do evahthang we kain tuh find yuh boy," Ed said, ignoring Andrew and continuing to address Mose. "In the meantime, ya'll gowan back tuh the house an' Ah'll call yuh if Ah need yuh. Ya'll gotta phone out thar?"

"No suh," Mose said as he searched his pocket for a pen. "Andrew gotta telephone out at his place, but he lives uh mite far from me. Ah'll give yuh Mz. Ony's numb'a. She'll send one of hur boys fuh me when yuh call."

Ed handed him his notepad and pen as he looked Andrew squarely in the face. "If yuh boy ain't back by late aft'a-noon, yuh bes' not let nightfall catch yuh out at the house. It'll be betta if yuh

Mississippi Meets Ms. Mamie!

hide yuh family somewhar 'til this is taken care of. Ain't no tellin' whut these boys got on their minds, 'specially after they find out ya'll come down heah."

"That's whut Mista Milam said last night, but Ah'm heah anyway, ain't Ah?" Mose said as he finished writing the number

200

on the pad and handed it back to Ed. "Ah got mah family out, but ain't nobody gonna skeer me offa mah land. Home is wheah Ah live, an' home is wheah Ah'll stay."

Ed looked at him firmly and replied, "Home may be whar yuh'll die if yuh stay out thar."

"Don't matt'a none tuh me now," Mose replied as he stood, with his shoulders just a little farther back than usual. "Ah went down tuh that sto', in Money in the middle of the night, right aft'a they took Emmett. Ah banged real hard on they door, but didn't nobody answer. Then Ah rode 'round lookin' fuh 'im. Ah'm black as coal an' ain't too big as uh grown man goes, but Deputy Ed, Ah ain't skeered of nary uh one of them men. They kain kill me, but they kain't stop me from lookin' fuh mah boy."

* * *

Hundreds of miles away, in Chicago, Mamie was cradled in the tranquil veil of sleep that enveloped her. The excitement of the previous day had relaxed her in a way that, for the first time in a week, she'd been able to really rest peacefully.

The day before, Mamie had received Emmett's letter, which really surprised her. Even though she'd packed stationary and stamps in Emmett's luggage, she really didn't expect that he would take time from his cousins to write her. So when Ruby, asked her to go with her to an event at the Grand Ballroom dance hall on 63rd street, she agreed.

As soon as they arrived, they ran into Ola Mae, Mamie's childhood friend, and other friends that she hadn't seen in a long while.

The group of friends spent the evening dancing the Bop, Madison and the Stroll. They talked and laughed about old times,

Bonnie Blue

well into the night. Mamie enjoyed herself so much, that she invited them back to her house for coffee.

The hours flew by and before they realized it, signs of dawn began to creep through the venetian blinds in the living room. Mamie decided to start an early breakfast.

Conversations buzzed and bursts of laughter roared through the connected rooms as the apartment filled with the heavy aromas of strong, fragrant coffee and thick hickory smoked bacon.

When Mamie told them about Emmett's letter, Ruby immediately jumped at the chance to get on her about smothering her son.

"Girl, I'm so proud of you! Letting that boy go *somewhere* by himself! I don't know about ya'll, but I didn't think Miss Mamie would ever let that child out of her sight!"

"Wait a minute now!" Mamie laughed. "I do let him go out to Argo."

"Girl, you're crazy as all get out! That's just right up the dog-gone street!"

"Well, I'm trying to give him some leeway! But if he thinks I'm going to send him that bike, he's mistaken. I can imagine how surprised he's going to be when he looks up and sees me down there, standing at the door!"

"Girl, I know you jivin'! You're not going all the way down to Mississippi!"

Mamie turned from the pancakes she was removing from the skillet to look at Ruby, put her hands on her hips, and said with an exaggerated Southern accent, "Shugga, come Monday mornin', I'm going to have myself a seat on the City of N'awlens, chug-a-luggin' my way to the big 'sippy!'"

"Besides," she said as she turned back to the stove, "Emmett isn't used to the South. Their whole way of life is different down there. You have to share everything and you better believe they work from sun up to sun down. He's probably ready to come home anyway."

Ola Mae took a deep drink from her coffee cup. "Mamie, please! You know it ain't Mississippi that's making you go get that boy. Ruby's right. You just don't want him outta your sight for

Mississippi Meets Ms. Mamie!

more than five minutes. Now tell me the truth. What're you gonna do when he grows up and gets himself a wife?"

202

Ruby threw her arm around Ola Mae's shoulders, looked her in the eyes, and said with a straight face, "She's movin' in."

"Was there ever any doubt?" Mamie said, trying to suppress the laugh that was rising in her throat. Laughter burst throughout the kitchen.

"I'm serious," Mamie said as she wiped the tears of laughter from her eyes. "If Emmett Till could get his feet back on Chicago soil, he would be one happy kid."

Perplexed, Mamie stopped for an instant, wondering why she had taken it that far. No one spoke for a brief moment and just as suddenly, conversations resumed.

Just after daybreak, shortly after everyfive o'clock in the morning, the party disbanded.

Mamie intended to take a nap on the couch before getting dressed for church. She slipped into her pajamas, set the alarm clock to wake her in three hours, and sank into a deep slumber.

* * *

The house lay still save for the soft chirping of sparrows, which drifted through her open living room window. Her sleep was soon broken by the loud ringing of the telephone. Mamie groaned as she stretched blindly across the couch to the end table, and awkwardly grabbed the receiver.

"Hello," she said groggily.

There was no answer.

"Hello...Hello?"

She was about to hang up when a voice on the other end responded, "Mamie...this is Willa Mae." She sobbed. "Ah don't know how tuh tell..."

Alarmed, Mamie sat up. "What is it? What's wrong?"

"It's Emmett." She paused. "He's...he's missin'."

Mamie leaped from the couch and yelled, "Missing?! What!? What'd you mean... missing?! Willa Mae," she said in a slow threatening voice, "Where's my son?!"

Willa Mae's voice trembled as she attempted to recount the conversation that she'd had with her mother just moments earlier.

Bonnie Blue

203

"Noooo...!" Mamie screamed. "Not my baby! Father, God, please anything but my little boy!"

"Mamie, Ah'm so sorrah Papa tried tuh stop 'em, but theah was too many of 'em an' he couldn't do nothin'," Willa Mae said, sobbing uncontrollably.

"God...! Why?! This doesn't make any sense! Willa Mae, where's my son?!" she yelled.

"Mamie, Ah'm sorrah," she pleaded. "Ah don't know nothin' else tuh tell yuh! They gonna find 'im, Mamie! They out lookin' fuh 'im right now!"

Mamie threw the telephone to the floor and screamed, "I want my baby back home! And I want him home now!"

She ran to her bedroom in confusion. Her eyes were so filled with tears and her mind was so jumbled that she didn't know what to do or where to start. "Father God! Why?!" She prayed as she paced quickly and aimlessly through the apartment. "I knew I should have kept him with me! I'm sorry, Lord God, for anything and everything that I have ever done wrong! Please send my baby home safely! Lord, please! Just let me hold my son again and I promise I'll never let him out of my sight!"

Mamie rushed back out to the living room. Her trembling fingers gently took the picture of Emmett from the piano. She had the photo taken for Christmas; just eight months earlier. She remembered telling him how grown up he looked and how much he resembled his father. Another sea of tears poured from her eyes, drenching the pink lace neckline of her pajamas. She pressed the framed photo to her breast and squeezed her eyes shut as tightly as she could, rocking back and forth in the middle of the floor.

"Emmett, I am so sorry!" Her voice cracked as she rushed to his bedroom, "I'm going to bring you home, baby! I promise!"

A burning pain ripped through her chest as her eyes roamed around his room. "Lord, I'll do whatever you want me to do," she whimpered. "Just tell me, and I'll do it. But please, Father, bring my baby home."

Mamie's fingers and toes began to tingle. Her knees weakened as she slid limply down the wall. Slowly, she became aware of a familiar scent filling the room. "Emmett," she whimpered, inhaling deeply; determined to hold on to the fragrance of her child.

She pressed her head against the powder blue wall, drawing her knees tightly to her chest, fighting her body's impulse to exhale. And then, just as suddenly as the fragrance came, it disappeared. "Emmett," escaped her quivering lips.

There she sat, rocking, staring blankly at the closed closet door.

Suddenly, she pounded her fist on the floor and screamed, "I should have *made* you stay with me! You are my responsibly! I should have done what I knew was right! Don't worry, baby! Mother's gonna find you!"

She covered her face with her hands; rapid hot breath burst rhythmically from her mouth as she struggled to compose herself. "Stop it! Pull yourself together girl!" she scolded. Okay...Okay... I can do this. I have to do this," she mumbled angrily as she attempted to put together the jumbled pieces of information from her cousin's telephone call.

"Emmett whistling at a White woman? That can't be right! Maybe they thought he was whistling at some...because..." An ugly realization suddenly stabbed her in the stomach. "Oh, my God!" she said as she pressed her head in her hands. "It's my fault!"

Mamie had no idea how long she sat there, treading in a pool of despair and confusion. Finally, she took a deep breath, wiped her eyes and pulled herself from the floor. "Baby, don't worry," she said as she kissed his picture and propped it up on his bed pillow. "Mother's going to bring you home and everything is going to be all right." She briskly wiped the tears from her face and inhaled deeply. "Everything is going to be fine. I promise."

* * *

She ran into the living room and retrieved the telephone from under the end table where she had slung it. Her body shook fiercely as she attempted to fit her trembling fingers in the rotary dial to call her mother. "Come on Mamie," she said as she took deep steady breaths to regain control of her body. After two failed attempts, the panic, which she had worked hard to suppress,

205

threatened to once again overtake her. "Come on...come on," she pleaded with her body. Her eyes were blinded by tears, and her hands shook so much that it took two more attempts before Alma's voice came through the wire.

"Good morning."

"Mother! Oh Mother! Thank God! Mother, Emmett's been kidnapped! White men came in the house and stole my baby!" she screamed. "Nobody knows where he is! We've got to get down there *now*! There's no telling wha..."

"Mamie? What are you talking about? Are you okay? What's wrong? What's going on?"

Mamie paced the floor as she told her mother of Willa Mae's call.

"No, no, that can't be right! I'm calling down there myself to find out what's going on! Mamie, you get over here right now! I'm going to call Willa Mae, to see where Elizabeth was calling from! Somebody's going to tell me something! Don't worry Mamie! I know he's alright! Just get on over here! We're going down there and bringing that boy home today!"

Secretions poured from Mamie's nose and her eyes, soaking her hand as she clung to the telephone. There was a glimmer of hope. Everything was going to be alright. "Okay Mother," she said, just above a whisper.

"Mamie? Mamie, are you there?"

"Yes ma'am," she sniffled, "I'm here mother. They thought that he was whistling at a White woman down there, and all my baby was trying to do, was clear his stuttering." The burning pain in her chest spread to the back of her eyes and a flood of salty tears once again, rushed down her face.

"Now Mam..." Alma started.

"Mother?! Mother, did you hear me?!" She screamed, "Willa Mae said Uncle Mose let a pack of White men come in his house and kidnap my baby! You know those folks down there don't give a care about anything! They hate Negroes! I know they're going to hurt my child!"

"Oh, my poor baby," she moaned. "Why did I let you go? I love you more than life itself."

"Mamie!" Alma commanded. "Stop it! We have to find out what going on down there! You aren't doing him a bit of good if you fall apart! Now, Emmett needs you. A *whole* you. It's hard. Believe me. I know it's hard. And you're right. Nothing's easy for Negroes in Mississippi or anyplace else for that matter. But these are the folks we've got to deal with. You've got to put what you feel aside as best as you can. You've got to be braver and stronger than you ever thought you could be if you want to find out what's happening and bring my grandson home. Even if you don't feel it, you've still got to act like you do! Do you understand me?"

Mamie knew that her mother was right. When Louis, Emmett's father, was killed in Italy, the military refused to disclose the circumstance surrounding his death. The pain of suddenly being alone with a toddler and no longer having the love of her life was more than she'd ever had to face. But, she managed to put her hurt and anger aside, and stand up to the armed forces until they gave an explanation for his death.

She took another deep breath, closed her eyes and mumbled to herself, "I can do this. I have to do this."

"Mamie?" Alma called quietly. "Do you understand what I'm saying? I know you're worried and scared. I am too. But, right now baby, it's important that we keep our wits about us. Before we get all excited, we have to find out what's happened. Emmett might just be at one of the cousins' houses or something. At this point, we just don't know. At any rate, we have to do the best we can for Emmett. Mamie, do you hear me?"

"I'm alright, mother. I've got to be alright." She felt her shoulders relax just slightly as she fought to focus on the business at hand. "Should I call Willa Mae back now?"

"No baby." Alma's tone softened. "Don't worry about that. I have to call her to find out where Elizabeth was calling from and get in touch with Andrew. Don't you worry about calling anybody. You just get over here and with God's help, everything will be fine."

207

Mamie hung up the phone and continue to pace through the apartment, fighting feverishly to clear her mind. "I can do this," she mumbled to herself while ringing her tiny hands. "Get yourself together girl and take care of your business."

She soon found herself back in the living room, mechanically folding the sheets that she had slept on.

"What's the matter with me?" She said, flinging the linen to the floor. "I can't wait around for somebody else to do anything!"

She threw her housecoat on over her pajamas, grabbed her keys, and ran down the back stairs.

* * *

Mamie raised the garage door with one swift pull and jumped into the driver's side of her car. The key was scarcely in the ignition switch before she floored the accelerator. Nothing happened. Once again, she turned the key in the ignition. The motor turned over. A second later, the car lurched out into the alley, just missing Gene's car by inches. "Get out of the way!" she screamed as she pressed her hand solidly on the horn.

"Mamie! Wait a minute!" He pulled his car on the side of the alley, rushed to her open window and said firmly as he opened the door, "Move over. I'll drive."

She scooted over to the passenger's side. "Emmett's been kidnapped," she cried.

"I know. Miss Alma called me. Don't worry. Emmett's smart and resourceful. I know he's alright."

As she retold the story of Willa Mae's call, her anxiety rapidly increased. "Gene, can't you go any faster?! I've got to get to Mother's!"

Gene glanced over at her as she strained to see around the car ahead of them.

"Pull over, Gene! Just pull over!"

"What? Mamie, I'm driving as fast as I can!"

"Gene, I mean it! Stop this car right now!"

He pulled over to the curb and walked around to the passenger's side. Before he could close the door, she shot out

208

into the Sunday morning traffic. She wove in and out; zipping past

moving vehicles as if they were immobile. She sped through stop signs and red lights alike. She hoped that a traffic cop would stop them. She planned to ask for a police escort, but none appeared.

* * *

They screeched to a halt in front of Alma's apartment in Argo. Mamie raced up the stairs, and burst through the open door.

"Mother! Did you get anyone? Did you reach Andrew or Archie? Where's Emmett?"

"No, baby," Alma said as she rushed towards her, arms outstretched. She held her daughter tightly as she secretly prayed for strength herself. "It's going to be alright," she said quietly. "Everything is going to be alright. I didn't get anyone down there yet, but I talked to Willa Mae and she's on her way over here now. You just sit down here and..."

Mamie backed away from her.

"Mother, what's the matter with you? We don't have time to wait around for Willa Mae or anyone else! Emmett is missing, and I'm not going to find him by sitting around drinking coffee!"

Gene grabbed her shoulders firmly. "Look girl, I know how you feel! We *are* going to bring him home."

Alma joined them and said softly, "He's telling you right baby. We're all worried, but like I told you, we've got to keep ourselves together."

Mamie surrendered and lowered herself into the overstuffed flowered sofa. She sat quietly for a moment holding her head in her hands. "This can't be happening," she said quietly as she squeezed her eyes tightly. "Not my baby."

With a deep sigh, Mamie opened her eyes and stood. "Okay. Alright. Since we can't get in touch with the family, let's try Mr. Fredricks'. Mother, do you have the phone number down there?"

"Wait a minute. Let me get my telephone book."

As Alma disappeared into her bedroom to retrieve her book, they heard a light tapping.

"That's probably your cousin," Gene said as he started towards the door.

Bonnie Blue

Mamie shot past him and flung the door open. Willa Mae stood limply before her. Dried streams of tears stained her slender, ebony cheeks as her frail body trembled. Mamie began bombarding her with questions.

Willa Mae stood silently in the doorway until Alma called from her bedroom.

"Here it is! Mamie, I've got the number!"

"I'm coming," Mamie said dryly, her cold gaze boring angrily into Willa Mae's defeated downcast eyes.

* * *

George C. Fredricks waited in a muddy cotton field for one of his tractor drivers to make his way back from the far end of the field. Massive rain clouds began to gather, rolling majestically through the humid skies, threatening yet another downpour.

"Damnit!" he mumbled to himself, exhausted, he looked around his rain-soaked fields. "Damned rains don't nevah come when yuh need 'em."

"Mista Fredricks! Mista Fredricks, sah!!!"

He turned and saw Ralph rushing clumsily through the muddy, yet neat, rolls of cotton.

"Mista Fredricks, Mista Fredricks, sah!"

"Yeah, whut is it? Boy, goddamnit! Be careful! Niggah, don't..."

"Mz. Fannie say come quick! Yuh gotta telephone call all dey way from up nawth! She say dey's waitin' on da line fuh yuh right now!"

He knew what it was about from the disruption of his sleep the night before, but he wasn't about to get into the Milam-Bryant boys' business. Whoever was calling had nothing but trouble and he had no desire to have any part of it. Even saying 'Mornin'' to them on his party line, could cause tongues to wag. Besides, he worked with the family and knew them well. Causing

210

them trouble could cost him, when it came down to renting their manned heavy equipment.

"Tell hur tuh find out who it is an' tell 'em Ah'm busy! Goddamnit, niggahs ain't got uh damn thang tuh do but sit on they lazy asses' causin' decent folk trouble. Ah'm in the middle of

Mississippi Meets Ms. Mamie!

somethin'," he said as he walked away. "An' don't dig up mah whole damn field wit them big feet!"

"Yassah! Ah means nossah!"

Ralph hopscotched his way quickly back through the field as Fannie trudged wearily across the length of the massive porch, awaiting Fredricks' arrival. When she saw that he wasn't coming back with Ralph, she went back into the house.

Fannie had never related to fieldhands, sharecroppers or tenant farmers. She had always worked as a cook in the 'Main House' as did her mother and her mother's mother, back through the days of slavery. In her own way, she felt more attached to the house than the current Fredricks family.

Last night, when Elizabeth came, Fannie had tipped out of her bedroom and eased her way silently through the vast kitchen, careful not to bump into the cast iron pots that hung on the knotty pine walls behind her. She stood rigidly in the shadows when Ralph ran past her, pulling the worn cotton robe tightly around his waist. She dared not go nearer, even though she couldn't clearly make out what was being said.

She waited until Fredricks called Ralph back to the house and started climbing back up to his bedroom before she whispered, "Ralph! Ralph! Ovah heah!"

He peered up the staircase to make sure that Fredricks was out of earshot and quickly tiptoed back into the kitchen.

"Hurry chil', an' take care," she sneer, "don't yuh go knockin' down nothin' wid yuh big ol' clumsy seff."

He slowed his pace and slipped into the darkness of the kitchen.

"Whudn't dat Liz'bit? Dat woman mus' be sho 'nuff outta hur min', wakin' up folk in da dead of night like dis. Whut she want, anyway?"

"She say one of hur youngins dun made dem White boys mad, an' dey come an' got 'im."

She shook her head self-righteously and slapped her hands on her full hips. "Dat be dey own fault! Lettin' all dem picka-ninnies go runnin' wild like dey do! Ah don't know whut she want us tuh do 'bout it!"

Bonnie Blue

Ralph shrugged his shoulders and replied, "Ah don't know. An' Ah sho don't know whut ol' Fredricks call hisself doin', come sendin' me out in da dark. Whutevah out dere ain't suppose tuh be, Ah sho don't want tuh run intuh it! Shoot! Ah sho ain't lost nothin' out dere! An' if Ah ain't lost it...Ah sho ain't 'bout tuh go lookin' fuh it!"

Now, after talking to Mamie, Fannie was sure that Ralph had it backwards. She wasn't sure who or what this woman was on the telephone. She talked proper, so she must be a White woman. But then again, she could be some kin to the boy she was calling about. That would make her some kind of uppity Colored woman. Either way, Fannie had no use for anything or anybody north of the Mason-Dixon Line.

She had seen the new boys with the Wright's sons on the road and in their yard numerous times in the last week. She was told that they were kin to Reverend Wright from up North, but she never said anything to them; never acknowledged that they were there.

Ralph returned to the hall where Fannie waited with her hand covering the mouthpiece of the candlestick telephone.

"Mista Fredricks want yuh tuh tell who eber it is dat he busy an' ain't got no time fuh talkin'."

Fannie looked down at his mud covered feet and the trail of red mud he'd tracked in. She rolled her eyes at him and said, "Niggah, if yuh don't git dem filthy dogs off mah flo', Ah'ma skin yuh alive! Now, git! An' clean dat stuff up! Yuh ain't turnin' mah house 'tuh no dawg-gawn pig sty, yuh ign'ant fool!" Then turning her attention to the telephone, she responded sharply, "Ma'am? Mista Fredricks kain't talk now! He in da field!"

212

"Please...," Mamie's voiced cracked. "Tell him this is very important! My son was kidnapped from his place! I have to talk to him! Please!"

"Ah'm sorrah ma'am, but like Ah say, he in da field an' ain't 'bout tuh come tuh no phone! If yuh want tuh call furtha up in da day, yuh welcome tuh do so!"

Mississippi Meets Ms. Mamie!

"Well take my phone number and ask him to call me! Call collect! I'll pay for the call!"

"Ah kain't write no numb'as, so yuh just gonna hafta call back! 'Sides, Ah got work tuh do! Kain't waste da whole day talkin' wid yuh! Call back later!" With that, she hung the ear piece back on its cradle.

"Nawthn niggahs always thankin' whut dey want's so almighty impo'tant," she mumbled to herself. "Whutevah happened tuh 'im, he prob'bly asked fuh. Folks don't come lookin' fuh yuh lessen yuh give 'em cause tuh."

"Wait! You don't understand! My son was there visiting Reverend Mose Wright! He sharecrops for Mr. Fredricks! You know my uncle, don't you? Would you please send someone over to get him? Tell him to call me collect if..."

The dial tone buzzed loudly in Mamie's ears. The receiver slid slowly from her hand.

"They hung up," she said in disbelief as she wandered back into the dining room. "He wouldn't even come to the phone or talk to me."

"Don't worry about him." Alma said. "Andrew should be home from church in a couple of hours. He might already know what's going on out there. If he does, you know he's out to Mose right now. We're going to find out what happened and where Emmett is."

Mamie laid her head on the table and said softly, "I have to get down there. I've got to find Emmett. He might be hurt. I know he needs me."

213

Willa Mae stood alone in the living room, staring at the picture of Mamie and Emmett that sat on Alma's piano. She tried to convince herself that he was all right, that he had somehow been rescued, but dread hung heavily and unyieldingly about her.

"Willa Mae! Come on in here child and tell us again, exactly what you heard."

Willa Mae walked slowly through the living room, feeling somehow responsible, and stood just inside the dining room.

Bonnie Blue

"Like Ah said this mornin', Auntie," she mumbled, "jist befo' Ah called yuh Mamie. Ah got uh call from Mama. She's out at Archie's. She said...she told me...Emmett whistled at uh White woman in town."

"That's a dirty lie!" Mamie yelled in disbelief, "Emmett would never do anything like that! They must have mistaken his whistle to clear his speech for a wolf whistle!"

"You're right Mamie. That just doesn't make any sense," Alma interrupted. "Who told her that?"

Willa Mae cast her eyes down to her feet and replied softly, "Ah don't know. Maybe one of the oth'a boys...Ah don't know."

"Well, where's the rest of the family? Are they all safe?"

"Yes ma'am. They all out at Archie's. They alright. Papa took 'em by theah early mornin' after he went out lookin' fuh Emmett."

Mamie turned to Gene, who sat quietly, trying to understand all that was happening around him. "Gene, that's it! That has to be what happened! They must have taken Emmett by mistake and when they found out they had the wrong boy, they let him go! He's got to be lost!"

He looked down at her and attempted to place his hand on her shoulder, but she turned away and searched her mother's face for confirmation. "Mother, you know he would never do anything like that. Emmett's a good boy. He'd never do that sort of thing."

"Mamie, hush now, and let her finish. Go on Willa Mae," she said, "What else did Elizabeth tell you."

Willa Mae closed her eyes, took a deep breath, and tried desperately to control her trembling voice as she unfolded the rest of her early morning conversation with her mother.

214

"So your father already went out to the police department to report it?" Gene asked.

Mamie grabbed the telephone. "Mother, what is that? Laflore or Tallahatchie County?" she asked as she dialed the operator for the connection.

* * *

It was still early morning when the screech of the long slender telephone on Sheriff Smith's desk shattered the uneasy calm in the tiny office. Ed was eager to begin investigating this Mississippi Meets Ms. Mamie!

case, but was unable to leave the office. He snatched the telephone from the desk.

"Sheriff's office," he answered, pressing the hard plastic earpiece to his ear.

"Hello. My name is Mrs. Mamie Bradley. I'm calling from Chicago. Is this the sheriff?"

The foreign accent immediately threw him, but for just a moment. "No ma'am. This heah's Deputy Cochran. Ed Cochran." He wasn't sure what the shaky voiced White woman on the other end was calling about, but he doubted that there could be two problems out of Chicago. "How kain Ah help yuh?"

"I really need to speak to the sheriff. When will he be in?"

"Ah really kain't say, ma'am. This time of day, he most likely still out at the church. Whut kain Ah help yuh wit, ma'am?"

"Okay, does your office have jurisdiction over Money, Mississippi?" Mamie asked, struggling to remain calm.

"Yes ma'am, Ah do."

"Do you know if Reverend Mose Wright has been in to see him this morning?"

Ed didn't quite know what to make of this call. He wondered why a White woman would call all the way from Chicago to check on the whereabouts of a niggra boy. "Ma'am, are yuh talkin' 'bout the Colored preacha?"

"Yes sir. He's my Uncle!" Mamie said excitedly. "Mose Wright. He lives in Money!"

"Well, he come by heah earlier, an' Ah took uh report on his kin from Ch'caga. Hold on uh minute," he said as he grabbed his notepad. "Uh niggra boy from Ch'caga, Emmett Till, 14 or 15

215

years-old thar 'bouts, got took las' night from his kin's house in Money. Is that who yuh askin' 'bout?"

Mamie sighed deeply. "Yes sir. Yes, that's my son," she said with a measure of relief. "Emmett Till, he's only fourteen years-old and was kidnapped early this morning. He and my other nephews were visiting my uncle, Reverend Mose Wright, in Money."

Ed plopped heavily in the sheriff's chair. "Yuh say that's *yuh* boy?" he asked, still confused. "Now Ah don't mean no harm

Bonnie Blue

but ma'am, like Ah said, this heah's uh niggra boy. Are yuh niggra yuhseff?

"Yes, I am Negro. Look, I would appreciate it if you would just have the sheriff call me as soon as he gets in! Please! This is very important! My child's life may be in danger! Remember, his name is Emmett, Emmett Till!"

"Yes ma'am," he said with authority. "Ah already know who prob'bly took yuh boy, an' if the sheriff don't show up soon, Ah'll gowan out an' talk tuh 'em mahseff."

"Oh, my God. Thank you," Mamie whispered humbly. "I thank you so much, sir." She said clinging desperately to the fine ray of hope she was just given.

"Here's my mother's telephone number. You can call collect. Anything that you think might help, any questions that you have, please, please call me." She gave him the telephone number to Alma's house and asked him to repeat it to make sure he copied it correctly.

* * *

It was nearly two o'clock in the afternoon before Sheriff George Smith finally pulled up to the jail.

He often came into the office late on Sundays. But, today of all days, he was more delayed than usual.

After losing the election, Ed had decided that it would be in his own best interest to allow George to continue his lackadaisical behavior. The next election would not be repeated.

216

Ed made it his business to hold his tongue and be as visible in the County as possible.

"Hey Ed! Whar yuh at, boy?" George called out, rushing through the open door carrying two wax paper covered plates. "Ah got us some eats!"

"Wa'al Ah'll be! George!" Ed said, swallowing the burning lump of aggravation and feigning excitement. "Yuh Mrs. sho do take care of folk!"

"Yes suhree, Bob," George said, a grin tearing across his face. "Inez's kinfolk come out from Ruleville an' went tuh church wit us. Ah looked up, an' the whole bunch trailed us down tuh Lula's an' Herman's fuh Sunday supp'a!" He laid the chaotic,

Mississippi Meets Ms. Mamie!

food filled plates on the rusty file cabinet. "Ah tell yuh, boy," George said as he eased down in his cracked leather chair, "Uh purty woman's good tuh look at, but when uh man's stomach gits tuh talkin', ain't nothin' like uh woman that know hur way 'round uh stove!"

"Yeah wa'al, right now, we got us uh situation. Early up in the mo'nin', uh Colored preacha down from Money, come by talkin' bout his kin from Ch'caga was took last night by Roy," Ed reported.

"Whut the niggah do? He had tuh do somethin'." George said offhandedly, his own distain seeping from his tone.

"Somethang else, uh woman called all the way down from Ch'caga this mo'nin', claimin' tuh be the boy's Ma. But Ah gotta tell yuh George, she sho ain't sound like no reg'lar niggra. That thar woman was White, if yuh ask me," Ed said, handing George the pad with the information that Mamie had given him.

"Ah flat-out asked hur if she's niggra! She said she was! Whutn't even shame! Yuh kain call hur up collect. She say yuh don't hafta pay fuh the call."

George glanced nonchalantly down at the paper and then up at Ed. "Alright, but like Ah said, the niggah musta dun somethin' he ain't had no bidness," he said self-righteously. "Hell, he was prob'bly in need of uh good ol', down home ass whuppin'. Somethin' his Pa shoulda give 'im befo' they sent him down heah."

"The Rev'ran said the boy whistled at Roy's wife, an' that's why they come got 'im."

"Ah knew it! Niggah come down heah actin' out an'..."

"George, it don't matt'a whut the niggra dun," Ed said impatiently. "Folk kain't jist go 'round, grabbin' youngins 'cuz they mad! Don't matt'a whar he from or whut he dun! It's jist plain against the law!"

"Alright. So whut else he say?" George asked halfheartedly."

"He say Roy, fuh sho."

"How'd he know it was Roy?" George retorted. "Yuh know Ray, an' Roy kain't be told apart. Hell, Ah don't b'lieve they own

Bonnie Blue

Ma kain tell which twin is which! Coulda been any damn body!"

"Why yuh fightin' me on this, George?" Ed asked, frustrated.

"The Rev'ran an' his boy come tuh the law an' reported uh kidnappin'! We gotta take this thang serious! Roy called out his own name fuh cryin' out loud! He say the tall bald man wit 'im was Dub! He say he heard uh woman in the car identify the boy! Kain't be nobody but Car'lyn since she's the one the boy whistled at!"

"Calm down, boy!" George smiled as he grabbed the slender base of the phone in his puffy pink hand, jiggled the switch-hook, and pressed the hard plastic earpiece against his ear. "Dub an' the boys most likely out tuh they Ma's place fuh Sunday supp'a. Ah'll jist give uh call out tuh Mz. Eula's, see if the boys are out thar, an' ask 'em whut they know 'bout all this."

A slow deep Southern voice dripped through the earpiece.

"Oparata."

"Aft'a-noon, Sadie Mae," George answered cheerfully.

"Aft'a-noon, Sheriff," she replied, a flirty pinch of personality quickly popped in his ear. "How's the family? Inez? She's well, Ah hope."

"The family's fine. Looka heah, Sadie Mae," he responded lightly, "kain yuh put me through tuh Eula Bryant's place?"

"Sho thang, hon'! Ya'll have uh good day now, yuh heah?"

"Yuh also Sadie Mae."

George looked impatiently at his deputy, whose arm was propped defiantly on top of the file cabinet, obviously passing judgment on his friends.

"Aft'a-noon, Mz. Eula ma'am. This heah George." He paused. "Fine. Jist fine." He paused again. "Yes ma'am. That was one pow'ful storm. Ah reckon it might of been the worst we dun had all summ'a." George sat down comfortably in his chair and listened to the voice on the other end. A light chuckle filled the room before he settled down to business.

"Yuh know thar ain't nothin' like it, that's fuh sho. Looka heah, Mz. Eula, we got uh lil' problem up this way, an' Ah need tuh talk tuh Roy. He anywhar's 'bout out thar?"

Mississippi Meets Ms. Mamie!

He paused. "No, ma'am. Ain't nothin' tuh really fret 'bout. Seems an ol' niggah preacha down the road in Money, claims Roy an' some of the boys come by his place las' night an' took his kin from up nawth," George said, looking nonchalant. "Like Ah said, ain't nothin' tuh worrah 'bout. Jist need tuh talk tuh 'im tuh see whut's goin' on."

He listened intently as the friendly tone on the other end of the earpiece immediately switched from casual to defensive. "No, ma'am, Mz. Eula!" George said quickly. "Taint uh thang tuh worrah 'bout Mz. Eula. Ah jist hafta ask 'im 'bout it is all."

He held the earpiece as the angry voice on the other end of the conversation continued to give him a severe tongue lashing about being blatantly disrespectful and calling decent folk on a Sunday afternoon over some 'niggah mess'.

* * *

The early morning storm had been unforgiving, making the assassins' ride from the backwoods back into town, even more treacherous. J.W.'s mud caked truck dipped in and out of water filled potholes. The crumpled rain and blood stained

219

tarpaulin, bounced chaotically in the truck's bed, threatening to expose the night's atrocities to the light of day.

It was mid-morning before the trio rolled back into Money. They had decided that Carolyn should stay out of sight until they knew if they had any trouble on their hands.

They cautiously made their way down the road that sliced through the tiny hamlet. The town was nearly deserted, as it usually was on Sunday.

Carolyn treaded anxiously across the storefront porch, as she had since just before daybreak. Her two little boys enjoyed the morning, chasing each other with toy cap guns.

The cracking of tires over the gravel road pierced the silence of the otherwise sleepy town. The truck whipped quickly around the corner, exposing the oversized bubble-hood pickup truck, its massive grill bearing a ravenous sinister grin.

Bonnie Blue

"Roy," she whispered to herself as she rushed off the porch to meet them; her floral cotton shirtwaist dress fluttering in the gentle breeze. "Roy," she said, relieved when the truck door open and he stepped out. "Whar ya'll been? Ah was worried 'bout yuh! Somebody come bangin' on the door late…"

"Git the boys, an' c'mon!" J.W. commanded.

For a fleeting moment, Carolyn wasn't sure who he was talking to. She looked into her husband's face.

"Yuh heard 'im," Roy said frigidly. "Git in the goddamn truck! C'mon, boys! Yuh goin' wit yuh Ma!"

Excitement boomed from the young boys as they scrambled to sit next to their uncle J.W. in the front seat.

Carolyn climbed into the truck without question, keeping her gaze on Roy's back as he disappeared into the store.

Roy walked inside, stood in the middle of his small business and looked around; finding himself oddly ill at ease with the stillness of the room. "Aw, this heah's uh bunch of hog shit," he mumbled as he fumbled around with the can goods

220

stocked on the wooden shelves. "Ah don't know whut Dub's talkin' 'bout," he smirked nervously. "Niggahs don't nevah say nothin' 'bout nothin'."

* * *

By early afternoon, Roy had finally fallen into a light sleep in the living quarters. It seemed that he had just closed his eyes when the screeching of a freight train on the railroad tracks just across the road from his home threatened to snatch him from his long awaited slumber. He flung himself over onto his stomach, groaning as he pressed the flattened pillow over his head.

"Hey, Roy!" A voice filter through the thin makeshift cushion. "Yuh in thar? This heah's Ed!" the deputy called through the latched screen door.

George's attention was fixed on the growing cyclone of dust moving quickly alongside the railroad tracks towards them. "Wa'al Ah'll be damned," he whispered to himself as he carefully removed his oversized sunglasses and laid them on the dashboard. "Hey Ed! Looka yonda!" George yelled from inside

Mississippi Meets Ms. Mamie!

the squad car; watching as the convoy of familiar pickup trucks quickly converging on their location. "Yuh still thank this uh good idea?"

Ed said nothing, but moved slowly away from the screen door and stepped down from the wooden porch onto the red dust covered rocks. His eyes stayed glued to the parade of vehicles rushing towards him; bracing himself for the confrontation that was sure to park at his feet.

The pickups whipped helter-skelter in front of the store. Menacing faced, sunburned men swung defiantly from the cabs; truck doors slammed shut in near unison.

Ed felt the rhythm of his heart beat faster as their unyielding glares washed over him.

"Hey, ya'll." He smiled and waved as he flit a glance back at George, who sat in the squad car like a spectator.

The newcomers ignored Ed and his greeting. Two men remained on the porch, while the others walked around to the back of the store.

221

"Good thang yuh boys come 'long when yuh did," Ed said lightly. "Me an' George been out heah fuh uh good lil' while callin' 'im." Ed looked hard at George, signaling with a light nod to join him. "Maybe ya'll kain git uh rise out 'im," he said as he joined the newcomers on the porch.

The two stocky men dismissed his clumsy attempts at small talk. Ed heard voices coming from inside. But when no one came to unhook the screen latch, he thought it best to retreat casually to the squad car.

"Look like Mz. Eula dun sent the whole damn brood out," Ed said as he leaned on the car door, keeping his eyes on the store.

"She jist lookin' out fuh hur kin is all. Kain't b'grudge hur that," George said sympathetically.

"Whut yuh thank George?" Ed asked, wiping his moist forehead with the back of his hand. "Should we go in or have 'im tuh c'mon out heah?"

"Naw, Ah thank it bes' he c'mon out heah. We go runnin' in thar wit all them boys, yuh ain't doin' nothin' but lookin' fuh Bonnie Blue

trouble. Yuh jist gowan in," George said as he looked cautiously at the empty porch. "Tell Roy Ah want tuh holla at 'im."

Ed headed back towards the store as Roy and his brothers poured out onto the porch.

"Hey, Roy!" Ed called cheerfully. "Been out heah knockin' an' hollerin' fuh yuh. Yuh alright, boy?"

"Jist sleep is all," he said lazily. "Kinda late up in the day fuh casual callin', ain't it Ed?"

"Yeah, wa'al," Ed drawled as he strolled up to the porch, pushed his hat off his forehead, and wiped the stream of sweat pooling in the creases of his brow, "Ah was plannin' tuh make mah way tuh the rivah tuh do some fisin' tuhmorrow daybreak. Need some of them big ol' worms Earl's boy be diggin' up tuh sell down the way thar. Ah'm tellin' yuh, wit all that rain, them night crawlers mos' likely jist jumpin' up out the dirt right up in the boy's can!"

Talk of fishing or hunting always made these backwoods men eyes glaze over with excitement. "Sheriff jist wanted tuh holla at yuh 'bout somethin' anyway," he said lightly.

"Now, yuh wrong thar!" Joey said authoritatively. He was one of the younger cousins that Ed had spent many mornings fishing with on the banks of the Tallahatchie. "Yuh need them big ol' fat juicy earthworms if yuh plannin' tuh do any real fishin'!"

"Joey, Ah dun told yuh, them the same kinda worm! Ain't no difference!" Roy said as he laughed and punched him in the arm. "Yuh don't know uh damn thang 'bout fishin' boy!" he called back to his cousin as he walked out to the squad car.

"Hey boy!" Roy greeted George as he smacked the roof of the squad car. "Ah know, ya'll ain't drive all the way the hell out heah fuh no damn worms!"

"Yeah, Ah wish that was all," George replied. "But Ah gotta ask yuh some questions 'bout uh niggah boy from out at the ol' preacha's up the way."

"Hell, thar's uh lotta niggah preachas out heah! Ah don't know nothin' 'bout nonna 'em!"

"C'mon Roy. Git in the car so we kain git this cleared up."

Mississippi Meets Ms. Mamie!

Roy slid into the front seat.

"Why'd ya'll go git the niggah?" George asked. "Ah know yuh got 'im! Now whut yuh do wit 'im? Whar's the body?"

Roy turned and faced George in disbelief. "Goddamnit, George!" he growled as he reared up and pounded his fist on the dashboard. "That niggah was outta line! No respect, goddamnit! Them goddamn uppity sons of bitches!"

"Hold on thar Roy! Now jist tell me flat out! Did ya'll go down an' git the niggah or not?"

"Whut the hell would *yuh* do? Sat down, pat 'im on the back, an' drank uh soda pop wit 'im?"

"Jist tell me. Whut'd yuh do wit 'im?"

Roy's mind was, once again, whirling with rage. Not only had that 'niggah' preacher called the law on him, but his family friend was here at his home, questioning him like a common criminal about a 'niggah'. All of this rage was overshadowing

223

the clarity of their alibi. He stared out the windshield as he struggled to push his feelings aside and clear his head.

"Yeah, Ah went out tuh the good Rev'ran's," he recited sarcastically. "He got uh bunch of niggahs down thar. So, Ah bought 'im back tuh the house fuh Car'lyn tuh take uh look at 'im. Wanted tuh make sure he was the right niggah. It was uh good thang, too!"

"Why?"

"She said he weren't the niggah!"

"Whut yuh do wit 'im, Roy?"

"Hell, Ah jist let 'im go is all," he answered nonchalantly. "Ain't mah fault the niggah's too damn dumb tuh find his way back home."

"Ah'ma hafta take yuh in, Roy."

"Whut? Whut tuh hell fuh?" he asked surprised, blood rushing to his face. "Whut's wrong wit yuh George? Ah told yuh Ah let the niggah go!"

"Look Roy, Ah don't want tuh arrest yuh, but when yuh took that niggah from his kin, that's kidnappin'. Now Ah'm as sorrah as Ah kain be, but that's the law. An' Ah'm sworn tuh uphold the thang. Now we gonna hafta really talk 'bout this thang."

Bonnie Blue

Another pickup truck drove past the store, made an urgent U-turn, and pulled up alongside the squad car.

"Aft'a-noon, boys," Sylas greeted cheerfully, his body nearly hanging out of the truck's window. "Hey Sheriff! Whut yuh doin' down in these parts?"

Word around the county was that if there was anything happening in or around the County Seat, Sylas Parnell would be the first to tell it. From the whole truth to the made-up truth, his would be the mouth spitting it out among the people.

Excited at the prospect of being privy to some gossip or news of any kind, he flung open the truck door and leaped to the ground.

224

Startled, Roy looked over at Sylas, who seemed to just appear at the sheriff's door; peering in at them through the opened window.

"Yuh want somethin' from the sto', yuh gonna hafta wait!" Roy barked impatiently.

"Hey Sylas," George said as he nodded a greeting. "We need uh minute."

The disappointment washing over Sylas' face couldn't be concealed. "Okay then," he replied and wandered over to where the others were gathered and effortlessly became the authority on whatever was being discussed.

George looked over at the group of men, who had moved out to the pickup trucks. They submerged themselves in lie swapping and fat talking as they eyeballed the fishing poles that different ones had in their flatbeds.

"Ah thank it'd be bes' all the way around, if yuh'd c'mon down tuh the office."

"Ah'm sorrah as Ah kain be, George, but Ah jist kain't go runnin' all ovah the county wit yuh! Ah gotta bidness tuh run heah!"

There was an uneasy pause before George looked over at Roy and said softly, "Roy, Ah gotta tell yuh, we dun already hadda call from up in Ch'caga."

Mississippi Meets Ms. Mamie!

"Is that whut all this 'bout? Yuh git uh call from some damn body up nawth, an' heah yuh come, skulkin' 'round!" He smirked. "Shit boy, they ain't had tuh walk all the way down heah!

"Wa'al Roy, the way Ah see it, yuh got two choices." George said, his patience drawing close to an end. "Yuh kain eith'a come on now, of yuh own free will an' git this cleared up, or wait 'til aft'a Ah drive all the way back tuh mah office, make out the pap'a work an' drive all the way back heah. An' Ah gotta tell yuh, it's too damn hot tuh be drivin' back an' forth. Now we gotta git this thang cleared up!"

"If it's alright wit yuh an' the law," Roy said smugly, "Ah need tuh git cleaned up furst an' take care of mah customer."

"Ah'll wait heah fuh yuh."

Roy saunter up to the porch and said to the group of men, "Ya'll kain gowan back tuh the house. Ah'ma jist go out tuh Greenwood wit George."

The crowd didn't seem to notice Roy as he walked back into the store, with Sylas nearly stepping on his heels.

"Whut's goin' on?" Sylas asked hungrily. "Whut the sheriff wantin' wit yuh?"

"None yuh bidness ol' man. Now whut yuh want?"

"Jist need uh lil' snuff! The ol' lady dun run out," he said as he slapped Roy playfully on the back. "Sheriff's got bidness wit yuh?"

"Ain't nothin'," Roy said as he went behind the counter to retrieve a can of Old Garrett's Snuff. "Yuh payin' fuh this or puttin' it on yuh bill?"

"Hell, yuh might as well bill it." Sylas hesitated before he continued. "Ah reckon yuh dun took care of whut folks been talkin' 'bout."

"Jist don't yuh worrah none 'bout mah concerns," Roy said as he continued writing.

"Now min' yuh, Ah ain't dippin' in yuh bidness. But Ah gotta tell yuh boy, ain't no way in hell Ah woulda thought yuh'd stand by an' let uh niggah git away wit that kinda goin's on! Now mind yuh, Ah ain't pryin', but damnit boy, yuh gotta know

Bonnie Blue

tongues been awaggin'! Hell, in mah day, niggahs knew they place an' by-god, they knew thar'd be hell tuh pay if they stepped outta it too! We didn't give uh damn if they come from as far nawth as the moon," he yelled as he pounded his fist on the counter. "They damn sho betta respect folk! Didn't nevah heah of no mess like this! No suh! We didn't tolerate it! Kill the fire befo' it gits outta hand! Ya'll young folks jist ain't..."

Roy finished making the notation when he noticed a patch of dried blood on the underside of his wrist. He quickly shoved his homemade ledger across the counter to Sylas.

"Jist sign fuh yuh stuff ol' man an' min' yuh own damn bidness."

Sylas smiled when he saw the smudge of blood, signed the ledger and walked out the door, shoving the can of snuff into his shirt pocket.

No sooner had Sylas reached the door, did Roy rush to the living quarters, rubbing frantically at the dried bloodstain, hoping that the sheriff hadn't noticed it. He scrubbed his arms so vigorously that it was difficult to tell if the red was the boy's blood or his own showing through his irritated skin.

"Hey Roy!" his twin brother Ray called as he came bursting playfully into the living quarters, a cold cola turned up to his mouth. "Whut George want?" He couldn't help but to notice his brother's bloodshot eyes, surrounded by dark sunken circles.

"Damn, boy! Yuh look like shit!"

Roy rolled his eyes at him and turned to get a shirt out of the pile of clothes stacked in the corner of the room.

"Okay Roy, whut'd yuh do? George ain't out heah jist tuh talk fishin'." He asked quietly.

Although they were identical twins, their appearance seemed to be the only thing they had in common. Where Roy was always ready to explode, Ray was a much calmer man.

"Shuddup Ray! Jist leave me the hell alone!" Roy said as he pushed past him. "Whut yuh doin' out heah anyway? Go home! All ya'll go home! Ah don't need no damn babysittahs!"

Mississippi Meets Ms. Mamie!

"We're goin'!" Ray said angrily. "Jist so yuh know, Ma made us come out heah an' check up on yuh," he said matter-of-factly as he walked through the store and out the door.

Roy could hear the anger in his twin brother's call to retreat.

"C'mon ya'll!" he yelled. "Ain't nothin' wrong wit that boy! Ma always holdin' 'im up in his mess! Ah'm hongry an' ain't 'bout tuh be wastin' no mo time foolin' 'round out heah!"

Vindication once again washed over Roy. Heavy with self-righteousness, he strolled behind the counter. With great

227

pride, he shoved the cigar box of coins and his ledger on the homemade shelf.

"Evahthang's alright. 'Sides, it's jist uh niggah's word ovah mine," he said to himself as a nervous smile slid across his lips.

He looked out the window at George sitting in the squad car. Suddenly, he wasn't so sure that the story was credible enough. Maybe he should change it all together. Maybe, he thought, it would be better to deny the whole thing. But, it was already too late. Roy cursed himself for admitting that he took the boy in the first place. He closed his eyes and with slow deliberate breaths, struggled to regain some semblance of composure before locking the door.

He snatched the large padlock from the bent roofing nail protruding from the side of the doorframe and with all the confidence that he could muster, locked the front door.

Most of his brothers were already heading down the road; convinced that Roy wasn't in any more trouble than usual. Only a couple of his brothers remained, continuing to swap fishing stories with Ed.

When Ed noticed Roy locking up, he slapped one of the younger men on the back and laughed as he began walking backwards towards the squad car.

"Wa'al, boys, Ah'ma hafta take yuh up on that fishin' hole sometime. But right now Ah gotta git back, or George's li'bul tuh leave me out heah, an' Ah'll hafta walk back tuh Greenwood!"

Bonnie Blue

Ed ran to catch up with Roy, who was already opening the front passenger's door. He assumed that Roy would sit in the back seat, but he wasn't sure what was going on, so he held his tongue and took his place in the back.

* * *

The bright glare of the afternoon sun danced off the hood of the squad car as George drove along the rock covered dirt road.

"Roy, we gonna go ovah this thang again," George said. "Ed tells me that ol' niggah preacha said yuh was by his place last night an' took off wit his kin. Yuh want tuh tell me 'bout it?"

228

Roy fidgeted with the soiled red bandanna he used to sop the perspiration from his forehead and neck.

"Was yuh out thar?"

"Ah already told yuh! Whut's wrong wit yuh George? He grabbed Car'lyn," Roy replied agitated. "Least ways Ah thought he was the one! But it turnt out he weren't, an' we turnt 'im loose!"

"Whut?!" George asked surprised. "Yuh didn't say he grabbed hur befo'! Now the whistlin' dun turnt intuh uh grab?! Who all went wit yuh?"

Roy stared out of the window at the long stretch of highway, sweat popped from his forehead like bullets when he realized that he had implicated another person. He didn't answer. George decided not to ask him anything more until they reached the office.

When they arrived, Charlie Weaver, an eager young deputy just out of his teens, rushed out to meet them. "Hey ya'll!" he called from the front door, broom in hand.

Roy continued to stare out of the front window, the glare of the sun flickering on his sweat soaked skin. "Yuh kain't lock me up. Yuh know that."

"We'll talk 'bout it inside." George said as he got out.

Roy's mind raced as he sat. Everything was getting mixed up in his head. He'd forgotten what he was supposed to say and wasn't sure what he'd told George already.

Charlie opened the door and touched his arm to guide him from the car.

Mississippi Meets Ms. Mamie!

"Take yuh goddamned hands offa me!" Roy yelled as he jerked his arm free. "Boy, if yuh don't want fish gnawin' on that damn arm, yuh bes' not touch me again!"

George turned back towards him. "Roy, yuh already got yuhseff uh heap of trouble. Now Ah don't thank yuh really want tuh threaten mah deputy."

Roy hesitated. He wanted to tell them both to go to hell but instead, walked unassisted into the office.

229

"Sit down," George said as he pulled a chair alongside his desk.

Roy ran his fingers through his thick black hair and sat nervously on the edge of the chair.

"Now let's take it from the beginnin'. Yuh say yuh went out tuh the house las' night?"

Roy jumped up and leaned over on the sheriff's desk. "Whut the hell's wrong wit yuh, George? Ah dun already told yuh Ah went out thar, but Ah ain't dun nothin'!"

"Whar'd yuh take the lil' niggah?"

"Nowhar!"

"Look, it don't make sense tuh lie now, Roy," Ed said as he walked over and pulled the chair out for Roy to reclaim his seat.

"Calm down. Yuh might as well gowan an' tell the truth so we all kain git back tuh our day."

"C'mon, Roy," George said. "If yuh hadda leff 'im at the sto', he'da been home befo' now, an' that preacha wouldn't of come all the way out heah this mornin'."

"Niggahs don't lie?! Yuh mean tuh tell me yuh'd take some ol' niggah's word ovah mine?"

"'Bout somethin' like this? Yes. C'mon now, Roy! Ah dun knowed yuh too long!"

"Okay! Alright!" Roy's temper flared. "He weren't propp'a wit Car'lyn! He tried tuh grab hur! Ah tell yuh, George, she damn neah did't git away! All we was gonna do was teach 'im uh lesson," he bragged. "Yuh know how uppity them damned Nawthn niggahs is."

"Who all went down wit yuh?" Ed asked.

Bonnie Blue

He had known Ed for a few years, and even though some of his family thought he was alright, Roy found himself at odds with the new deputy more often than he cared to remember. And now here he was; acting like he had some kind of power over him.

Roy's hands trembled as he subconsciously wove his bandanna through his fingers. He had slipped again.

"Yuh heard me, Roy!" Ed grilled. "Don't sit thar an' try tuh tell me yuh went by yuhseff! Hell, Ah doubt yuh evah did

230

anythang by yuhseff! Now, Ah'ma ask yuh again. Who all went wit' yuh?"

"Nobody! Nobody but me, Ah said!"

"Okay Roy," George calmly interjected, "whut happened then? Ah know yuh told me befo', but jist tell me again. Whar'd yuh take 'im?"

"Nowhar! Ah mean, Ah took 'im out tuh the sto'. Carl'yn said he weren't the one, so Ah let 'im go is all."

"An' yuh gonna sit heah an' 'spect us tuh b'lieve that nobody else went wit yuh?" Ed asked, his doubt, accented on each word.

"Ah dun already told yuh!" Roy's defiant glare accompanied his biting response. "Yuh kain b'lieve whutevah yuh want tuh, but Ah'm tellin' yuh, Ah was by mahseff!"

"Whut'd yuh do then?"

"Ah went out tuh Minter City an' played cards."

"At that hour of the night?"

"Yeah."

Ed paused as he stared Roy coldly in the eye. "Yuh want us tuh b'lieve that uh niggra attacked yuh wife, an' yuh jist decided tuh go out tuh Minter City an' play cards?"

Roy gazed smugly back at him and replied, "Whut yuh b'lieve is yuh own damn bidness, but that's whut Ah dun."

George reared back in his seat. "Look, Roy, Ah know thar was at least two oth'a boys wit yuh. Why don't yuh jist save me some time an' make it easy on yuhseff an' tell me who they are?"

"Ah told yuh! Wasn't nobody else!"

"Yuh say yuh was playin' cards. Who was yuh playin' wit?"

Mississippi Meets Ms. Mamie!

"Mah brotha's."

"Which brotha's?"

"Ah don't rememb'a, Ah was drunk."

"Whar was Dub?" Ed asked. "Try not tuh lie. 'Cuz right now boy, yuh got mo' trouble than yuh kain handle."

231

"Ah told yuh, Ah was drunk last night," Roy said smugly. "Yuh know, Ah kain't rememb'a one lil' ol' thang."

"Wa'al, Roy," George said as he tossed the large silver ring of oversized keys to Ed, "look like we gotta officially put yuh und'a arrest."

Shocked, Roy leaped from his chair. "Whut??? This ain't gotta goddamned thang tuh do wit that niggah, does it? Ed's jist out tuh git me is all! That's whut it is, ain't it?"

He glared at Ed, smiled and sat back in his chair. "Yuh ain't got nothin' on me Ed, so yuh bes' jist take me right on back out tuh mah sto'!"

"Yuh git uh phone call," Ed said as he slid the slender black telephone across the desk. "Yuh might want tuh make it now."

Rage again catapulted Roy from his seat. Throbbing veins in his forehead and neck bulged violently against his crimson skin. "Yuh goddamned, niggah-lovin' sonna-bitch! Ah be damned if Ah'ma let yuh lock me up ovah some goddamn niggah!"

George nodded towards the cells. Ed touched Roy's arm.

"Boy, Ah dun told yuh deputy thar, an' Ah'ma tell yuh," Roy said through clenched teeth, "don't put yuh damned hands on me, friend!"

George calmly wiped the back of his neck with a damp handkerchief. "Roy, yuh kain eith'a walk on back thar on yuh own wit Ed, or," he said, standing up and putting his hand on his revolver. "Ah'ma hafta take yuh an' Ah ain't in the mood tuh be tusslin' wit nobody. So yuh bes' thank befo' yuh act. Now whut's it gonna be?"

Roy's body was so tense that he stood stone still. Ed unsnapped his holster and began to slide his pistol from its resting place. Roy looked back and forth between the George and Ed. Slowly, he released his feet from their stance and swaggered back towards the cells with Ed following close behind.

Bonnie Blue

"It ain't gonna stick George!" Roy called as the cell door slammed shut.

"Hey George! Yuh ain't nevah gonna fine 'im! Yuh heah me?" He laughed. "Yuh kain't pin this niggah on me if yuh kain't fine 'im!"

George removed two rifles from the wall gun rack.

"Roy!" He called as he collected two boxes of ammunition from the drawer.

"Yuh kain't keep me locked up!" Roy barked from the cell in the next room.

"Charlie'll git yuh supp'a from the café if Ah ain't back soon! Don't worrah 'bout bein' lonely! Yuh li'bul tuh have comp'ny by day's end!"

"Hey George! Ed!" Roy laughed. "Ya'll ain't much fuh lawmen! R'memba last time? Yuh couldn't make it stick last time! Whut makes yuh thank yuh got somethin' now? Yuh might want tuh try gittin' work down at the Piggly Wiggly! Who knows, Ed," he laughed hysterically, "Niggah's might even let yuh mop up the hog shit from they chit'lin's!"

Ed marched angrily back to Roy's cell, stood silently glaring into Roy's wrath distorted face, and said firmly, "Ah'ma say this one time so that yuh ain't no way confused. If somethin's happened tuh that boy, Ah ain't gonna let yuh walk away. Yuh, an' evahbody else involved gonna have uh new home in prison. Ah don't give uh care how black he is or how white yuh are. If yuh dun it, yuh gonna hafta pay." He rushed back into the office.

"Yuh gonna hafta call the boy's Ma up in Ch'caga." Ed said as he emerged from the back and tossed the ring of keys on George's desk.

"Ah reckon so," George said somberly as he reached into his shirt pocket to retrieve the wrinkled slip of paper with Alma's telephone number. "Ain't no doubt they took 'im."

* * *

Mamie stood with her arms folded, rhythmically rocking back and forth as she tried to make sense of it all. "Emmett would never whistle at some grown woman," she reasoned with herself quietly. "We talked about White folks before he left. He knows

Mississippi Meets Ms. Mamie!

better than to say anything to any of those people down there, period."

The methodic ticking of the kitchen clock seemed to resonate louder and slower throughout the apartment, mocking her as she glanced repeatedly back at the silent, black desk telephone.

Gene slipped his arm around her waist and whispered to her as he led her back into the dining room, "Try not to worry too much, Mamie. Everybody knows Emmett. He's too afraid to talk to the girls at school, much less whistle at a grown woman in a strange town. I bet he's back at your uncle's right now and you might just be working yourself up for nothing."

Mamie wanted desperately to believe him. She needed to convince herself that it was all a mistake and Emmett was back at Uncle Mose.

"You're probably right Gene," she said as she joined her mother and cousin at the dining room table. "He could be back at the house, or they might even be at church."

Mamie forced an empty gaze across the table at Willa Mae, who continued to avoid her eyes but instead, engrossed herself in picking at the corner of the embroidered tablecloth.

"Willa Mae," Mamie said, harsher than she intended, "you know we won't know for sure what's going on down there until we get hold of Uncle Mose. I don't know why you haven't talked to your father about getting a telephone! He has to go, God only knows how far to get to a telephone! That has to be why we haven't heard anything! He has to know we're worried! Good Lord, it's 1955! It's not that hard to get a telephone!"

"Here, Mamie," Alma said, handing her a cup of fresh brewed coffee.

A puzzled look washed over Mamie's face as she gazed at the steaming cup and back up at her mother. "Mother, what are you doing?! I don't need any dog-gone coffee! What I need, is my son...here at home...in my face! That's what I need! Why the devil do you always want to shove food down my throat?! No..." she said sarcastically. "I don't want any coffee, I don't want any lemonade and I don't want any dog-gone Kool-Aid!"

"I'm sorry," Alma said as she placed the cup on the table. Her feelings were bruised, but she understood her daughter's anguish.

Bonnie Blue

A barely audible ringing penetrated the sound of their elevated voices. Gene was the first to bolt into the adjacent room.

"Gene, wait!" Mamie yelled, racing behind him. Frantically she snatched the receiver from his hand. "Hello? Hello? Who is this?" she blurted.

There was a moment of silence before a deep Southern accent slowly filled her ears.

"Good afta-noon, ma'am. This heah's Sheriff George Smith callin' from down at LaFlora County, Mississippi. Ah'm returnin' uh call from...Ah b'lieve the name is Mz. Mary Bradley?"

Mamie clutched the receiver firmly against her face. "No, no, it's Mamie, Mamie Bradley, and I did telephone your office earlier," she responded nervously. "I'm not even sure that this is the office that handles problems in Money. But, my son was kidnapped last night from my uncle's home in Money and I didn't know who else to call. I thought that they live in Laflo..."

"Ma'am!" he interrupted. "This the right place. Now, jist tell me whut yuh boy's name is."

"Oh, I'm sorry. His name is Emmett, Emmett Louis Till Jr. He's only fourteen. Have you heard anything? Have you spoken to my uncle, Reverend Mose Wright?" she asked anxiously.

"No ma'am. Ah didn't. But he an' one of his boys come by early this mo'nin'; daybreak, an' made uh report wit mah deputy. Have yuh talked tuh yuh kinfolk yet?"

"No sir. I don't know what's going on. Please," her voice cracked as she fought back the hysteria that was threatening to overcome her. "Can you help me? Please, tell me that you've found my son!"

George sighed. The bad news, he knew from experience, was only going to get worse.

"Wa'al ma'am, Ah got one of the men locked up heah now. He admitted takin' the niggah, but he claim he turnt 'im loose. We goin' out tuh talk tuh some mo' of his kin aft'a Ah git off the wire wit yuh."

Finally, Mamie saw a glimmer of hope. Emmett was alright and the police were already looking for him.

"Did he tell you where he released him? Emmett doesn't know anything about down there! He's probably lost!"

Mississippi Meets Ms. Mamie!

235

George shook his head impatiently. "Ma'am," he said quickly, "Ah ain't one tuh throw sug'a on uh hog's pile. The folks yuh boy had uh run in wit are uh mean an' spiteful bunch. Ah kain't sit heah an' let yuh thank that we gonna find yuh boy an' evahthangs gonna be alright. It prob'bly ain't. Now, Ah ain't tryin' tuh skeer yuh. Ah jist want yuh tuh be prepared. Jist in case the niggah's dead."

Mamie looked frantically at her mother and Gene. Her chin and lips quivered. "My baby," she whimpered.

"Mz. Mamie, ma'am?"

Gene took the telephone from her hand. "Sheriff, this is Gene Mobley. I'm a family friend. We know that you'll do the best that you can to find Emmett and return him to us safely."

George was relieved to speak to a man, even if it was a Colored man. "Like Ah told Mz. Mamie, thar's uh real good chance the niggah's dead."

"I understand," Gene replied quietly. "We'll be down as soon as possible."

"Naw, ya'll jist wait 'til yuh heah from me. Don't make no sense movin' around 'til yuh know whut direction yuh goin'. Ah'm sorrah the news ain't whut yuh want, but Ah'll call yuh folks when Ah got somethin' tuh tell yuh."

Gene lowered the receiver gingerly in its cradle and hesitated briefly before addressing Mamie and Alma. Their eyes bore urgently into his for an answer; any answer.

"The sheriff thinks we should stay put, just in case...just in case they find him."

Mamie's brow constricted, and her eyes squeezed shut as she reached for the edge of the table to steady herself. Her head became lighter. She felt her strength leaving her body and her knees began to buckle.

"Mamie!" Gene called as he caught her around the waist.

"Mamie!" Alma called, "Gene, take her in the front! Mamie, baby, you need to lie down for a while."

Alma knew all too well, the severity of the situation. She was born and lived most of her young life in Drew Mississippi,

Bonnie Blue

236

where it wasn't uncommon for Colored boys and men to be beaten, lynched, or simply disappear. This was the reason for her move to Chicago. Now, her only grandchild had unwittingly fallen into the lair of a malicious custodian of Mississippi's taboo enforcer.

Mamie was led, like a zombie, into the enclosed sun porch. Gene knelt beside her as she lay staring up at the ceiling in the stillness of the sun drenched room. An occasional breeze tickled the powder blue sheers which draped across the large picture window, caressing her perspiration soaked skin. A pool of salty tears collected in the back of her throat threatening to choke her. She turned to bury her head deep within the cushions of the sofa, attempting to drown out the muffled voices in the dining room as bits of conversation filtered through the French door. She fought back the tears and forced her head so deeply in the cushions that she could only hear the swooshing of blood pulsating through her temples.

Mamie was never one to sit by and let a problem resolve itself. She didn't know how. The one person that she loved more than anyone in the world was in horrible danger, calling out for her, and there was nothing that she could do but wait.

"Why did I let him go?" she whimpered. A deep moan escaped her lips, vibrated through her body and up Genes arm, startling him.

"Oh Mamie," he whispered. "It's going to be okay. Emmett's a smart boy. They'll find where he's hiding and bring him home. But, if you want to go down there right now, just say the word, and we'll be on the road in a half hour."

Mamie turned from the security of her cocoon. Her bloodshot eyes were so blurred that she could scarcely make out the features of his face. "Gene," she whispered hoarsely as he covered her tiny hand in his. "The sheriff thinks that they might have beaten him...or worse."

Mississippi Meets Ms. Mamie!

237

Gene gathered her in his arms and rocked her as he held her tightly. "The sheriff was just saying what he thought might have happened. He doesn't know for sure, but it looks like he's doing the best that he can. I mean, we're lucky. He's one of the good ones. He already has one of them behind bars. I know he's going to do everything he can to find Emmett. And you'll be hearing from your Uncle Mose and Andrew as soon as they can get to a telephone. You need to rest. Do you want me to stay with you?"

"No, I'm fine," she said as she pulled away. "I just need to be alone for a moment to get my head together."

"If you need me, just call. I'll be right in the next room." He kissed her forehead and pulled the doors together as he left.

Mamie lay back down on the sofa. This was the longest and most painful day of her life. She felt her heart was burning to a cinder. "God, why did I let him go?" She continued to moan.

A delicious scent of flowers suddenly filled the room. A fragrance so beautiful and intense, that she could almost taste it. She rolled over, glanced around the tiny room, looking for the bouquet that seemed to soothe her. There was none. She closed her eyes and calmly inhaled slowly and deeply; afraid to exhale for fear that if she stopped, even for an instant, the beautiful scent would be gone. After a short while, she was forced to breathe.

Mamie wasn't sure how long she lay there before the scent vanished. A river of tears had collected in her ears and had matted her hair.

She thrust her arms towards the ceiling, pressing her fingers upward as if to force her plea into heaven itself. "Father," she called loudly, "take me if You will, but protect my son, Lord! He's just a boy! I'm begging You now, Lord! Please show me the way! What would You have me to do?" She called out, "Tell me Lord, and I'll do it! My baby has got to come home! Father, please protect him!"

Gene rushed into the room when he heard her cries. Fear gripped him when he saw Mamie lying there, wounded and weak, her arms straining upward. "Mamie!" he gasped.

Bonnie Blue

238

He knelt beside her, wrapping his large, dark hands gently around her tiny, stiff outstretched fingers. He could feel her arms begin to relax as he lowered them to her chest and kissed her lightly on her puffy eyelids.

"I'm here, Mamie. I'm here."

"Father, God, help me. Show me the way," she begged rapidly and quietly. "I've got to think. I can't think straight. I've got to get myself together. My son..."

Gene gathered her into the security of his arms as he whispered softly, "God's not going to let anything happen to Emmett. You've got to believe that."

She sighed as she cradled her head firmly in Gene's neck, trying to mask the ugly thoughts that had been plaguing her since this odyssey began; thoughts that were eating away at her but too awful to voice.

'Was it really Emmett that they were after, or maybe one of Uncle Mose own sons? Why did Uncle Mose let gun toting strangers just come into his house and steal her child? Why didn't he do something to stop them?'

She knew that they were afraid. Negro's down south were always afraid. Good or bad, they always just 'took' whatever White folks threw their way. But not this time. Not with her baby.

Angrily, she pulled firmly from the security of Gene's arms, briskly rubbed the moisture from her face and said coldly, with a new harsh determination, "We're going to need more help. They're not getting away with this one. This is *my* child, and he is coming home to *me*!"

She jumped from the sofa and pushed through the double doors. Gene sat stunned for a moment before following her into the living room. She shot a damning glance at Willa Mae, snatched up the receiver and dialed the operator.

"Mamie, who are you calling?" Alma asked as she attempted to take the receiver from her. "We've got to leave the line open in case Mose or the sheriff calls."

Mississippi Meets Ms. Mamie!

239

A dull monotone voice broke through the telephone line. "Operator."

Mamie looked at her mother and said sternly, "They will call back." She paused. "Hello, operator?" She calmly addressed the voice on the other end. "I need to be connected to the National Association for the Advancement of Colored People (NAACP), The Chicago Tribune, The Chicago Daily News, and The Chicago Defender newspapers. But first, please put me through to the Federal Bureau of Investigation.

BOOK SIX

HUNTIN' WITOUT UH DAWG AIN'T EASY!

The large orange afternoon sun sat low on the western horizon. The earlier downpours that drenched the ground had now been absorbed in the intense heat of the day. Ed planned to go out to the Milam-Bryant homestead to question J.W. and Carolyn. He wanted George to have a couple of their deputies come in to watch the prisoner when they made the trip out to Eula Bryant's. But when George suddenly decided to busy himself with unnecessary paperwork; Ed ventured out there alone.

* * *

Ed drove through Money, to see if Carolyn had returned. But as he expected, the small general store stood quiet and abandoned.

He continued his journey down the highway through the thick dusk which began to settle over the countryside. Damp, telltale stains on his shirt, welcomed the constant breezes as they rushed through the open car windows. With the family in crisis, he hoped that he would be lucky enough to catch both Carolyn and J.W. down on the Milam-Bryant family farm. His mind raced as he cut past the outstretched cotton fields.

Experience had taught Ed that his best chance of recovering a Colored body would be to concentrate his search in the heavily wooded, secluded areas near the river.

241

He detoured off the main road to check a spot that held the unsavory reputation of being a bastard graveyard for Colored people who crossed the 'wrong folks'.

The road was nearly abandoned, which wasn't unusual for a late Sunday afternoon this far out. Ed hadn't seen another vehicle for miles. A chilling silence intensified his uneasiness. Cautiously, he pressed on down the muddy back road leading to the Bottoms, an ominous area that runs alongside of the Tallahatchie River, well out of sight of the main road and prying eyes. This lonely stretch of forest goes on for more than ten miles without a break and is one of the thickest woods in this part of the Delta.

Ed had traveled more than midway when a small clearing in the otherwise thick fortress of trees caught his attention. He pulled the squad car off to the side of the road.

His boots were quickly sucked into the saturated ground as he carefully navigated his way over layers of wet leaves, underbrush, and fallen branches. The air was so still, so quiet, that the sound of twigs snapping underfoot seemed to bounce from tree to tree. Ed slowed his pace as he artfully sliced through the sentinel of cottonwood and silver leaf trees.

He felt intrusive as he reverently and painstakingly scanned the ground around the den in this un-tampered world of nature's peace.

He saw nothing out of the ordinary. Tiny insects crept through the glistening clutter of greenery while small snakes slithered quietly about their journey. Streams of heaven's beams occasionally broke through the dense canopy overhead, exposing tiny droplets of moisture, which floated gently through the cool light air; such a contradiction from the smoldering heat that he had left behind.

"Damnit!" he cried as he lost his footing and slid across a large mushroom patch that poked out from the mist-covered blanket of leaves. A raccoon, picking through the foliage for food, was disturbed by the commotion, looked up at Ed, and darted out of sight. "Got-damnit!" He yelled as he regained his balance and attempted to brush water and leaves from his slacks.

Bonnie Blue

It was very easy to lose your bearings in these thick woods. Ed had gone just a short distance into the looming trees when the sunlight beaming through the clearing became cloaked, making it difficult to see. With sudden urgency, he quickened his pace and retreated back through the clearing to the security of his patrol car.

The day had been long and full since the old preacher came into his office to report the boy missing. Ed tossed his hat on the passenger's seat and massaged his slightly thinning temples. A dull ache began to throb in his head. He glanced down at his wristwatch and peered over his sunglasses at the huge golden sun as it began to slide voicelessly behind the edge of the western skies. Time was rapidly slipping away, but he was determined to question Carolyn and J.W. before the day was done.

* * *

Ed sped down Highway 3, slowing only when he neared the dirt turnoff which merged into Eula's private drive. Even though dusk crept like a thief across the cotton fields, the yard bustled with last minute chores. Shirtless children chased each other around the yard, sending chickens squawking in every direction.

One side of the yard was filled with pickup trucks and cars. From the looks of it, all of Mama Eula's boys and family had been summoned. Her people came from everywhere in and around the Delta after hearing of the trouble with one of the youngest of their clan and the law.

"Aw, shit," Ed drawled exhaustedly as he pulled into the mouth of her yard. "Looks like uh damn Klan meetin'."

He immediately recognized the prudence in staying within arm's reach of his squad car and keeping his conversation brief. He eased his pistol from its holster and placed it on the seat next to him. Having his gun drawn or even visible might provoke these men that he knew all too well.

243

As he slowly rolled to a halt, a throng of large, red faced men, most with shotguns at their sides, burst through the kitchen door spilling onto the carport. Ed exhaled heavily and slid out of the car.

Huntin' Witout Uh Dawg Ain't Easy!

"Evenin', ya'll! Sho was uh scorcha tuhday!"

Many of the same men that he had joked and laughed with earlier now met his gesture with silence and cold, unflinching stares. He didn't see J.W. in the group and now wished that he had waited until he had some kind of backup before venturing out here to ask about him.

"Lookin' tuh talk tuh Dub an' Mz. Car'lyn. They anywhars 'bout? Ah jist need tuh ask 'em uh couple of questions."

Again, silence.

Ed began to feel that perhaps he should have tried harder to get George to come out with him. They were, after all, friendlier with him. Suddenly, the kitchen screen door slam behind the wall of men.

A short, weedy woman appeared. Beauty, apparently, had never been a curse that plagued her youth. Her black and gray streaked hair was pulled loosely in a bun. Scraggly strands draped as ragged curtains around her narrow face, accenting the tough, leathery skin which housed deeply etched lines; evidence of the hard life of a matriarch.

"Whar's mah Roy?" she asked dryly as she looked past him into the empty squad car.

"Evenin', Mz. Eula ma'am. Ah wish Ah didn't hafta come out heah und'a these circumstances," Ed said as he took his white handkerchief from his back pocket and wiped the dampness from the nape of his neck. "but Ah 'spect yuh know by now, we got Roy down at the jail."

His attention was immediately drawn to the distinct clicking of a shotgun hammer being pulled back. Some of the men moved forward, leveling their guns at Ed's head. Eula raised her hand, and the men reluctantly lowered their weapons.

244

Relieved, Ed turned his attentions back to Eula and spoke as respectfully as he could.

"Well Mz. Eula ma'am, it seem yuh boy took uh niggra boy las' night an' ain't nobody seent no parts of 'im since."

"Uh niggah? Yuh got mah Roy b'hind bars like some kinda animal ovah uh niggah? Whar's George at?!" Eula barked as she moved a little closer to him. "Whut the hell's wrong wit yuh,

Bonnie Blue

boy? Yuh don't go lockin' up uh mah boy 'cuz of some damn niggah!"

Again Ed heard a click and some of the men standing behind her moved closer. "Ma'am," Ed replied somewhat uneasily, "the sheriff knows whut's goin' on. He's back at the jailhouse. An' Roy was identified by the boy's kin. Whut's mo', he confessed tuh takin' the niggra from the house. That's kidnappin' ma'am."

"Wait jist one damn minute," Eula said as she squint her eyes. "Ah ain't no fool! Ah know yuh boy! Ah nevah did trust yuh! Callin' yuhseff uh friend tuh mah boys! Ah told 'em yuh couldn't be trusted! Grinnin' all up in they face!" she yelled.

"Ah know whut this heah's really 'bout. Yuh been aft'a mah boy evah since that oth'a niggah got hisself killed las' year! Yuh tried tuh say mah Roy did that too, but yuh was wrong an' ended up lookin' the fool! Jist 'cuz yuh gotta badge don't mean yuh gotta right tuh go aft'a mah boy evahtime uh niggah git in some kinda trouble! Now yuh lissen tuh me real careful, boy!" She said pointing her crooked finger at his face.

Ed felt his body weaken as she walked up close to him and ordered in a low, cold voice.

"Ah knowd George was up tuh no good when he come callin' down heah. Now the bes' thang fuh yuh tuh do is ride that lil' fancy police car back tuh the jail an' tell that sheriff of yourn, Ah don't want tuh see nary one of ya'll lessen yuh brangin' mah boy home."

"Wa'al ma'am, when an' if Roy come's home, will be fuh the court tuh decide," he said, trying his best to sound secure and unshaken by his rapidly deteriorating bravado.

"Yuh talkin' back at me boy?!" she yelled angrily.

245

Ed made a silent, but clear pact with himself that he was never going to face these people alone again; not intentionally anyway.

"Now ma'am, boys, Ah ain't come all the way out heah tuh cause no trouble. Ah jist need tuh talk wit Dub an' Mz. Car'lyn."

Huntin' Witout Uh Dawg Ain't Easy!

Eula said nothing for a moment. She glared up at him. "Now whut the hell yuh be wantin' hur fuh?" she asked as she turned to walk away. "Yuh plannin' tuh lock hur up too? In case yuh didn't know, she got youngins tuh take care of, 'specally since they Pa's locked up like some kinda wild dog."

"No ma'am. Like Ah said, Ah jist need tuh ask hur some questions is all. Now, Mz. Eula," Ed replied calmly and with as much authority as he could muster, "Ah don't mean no disrespect ma'am, but Ah gotta ask yuh again. Is Dub or Mz. Car'lyn heah?"

"Wa'al, Ah tell yuh," she said smugly as she looked back at him, "fact is, she an' dem chil'ren off visitin' hur kin somewhar. Been gone uh while. Don't know when they be back. An' Dub? Mah Dub's uh grown man. Ain't no tellin' whar he's at. So yuh see, Mista Deputy Ed, she don't know nothin' 'bout nothin' an' yuh gotta fin' Dub on yuh own."

Ed knew that Eula was lying. He also suspected that she had Carolyn and the children hidden away someplace, maybe even in the house.

"Yes ma'am," he said as he straightened his hat back on his head and turned to open his car door. Until this moment, he was unaware that the yard had emptied except for the wall of men who, gratefully, had yet to move. "but like Ah said, Ah ain't come all the way out heah tuh make no mo' trouble than whut we already got. So, whenevah yuh see Mz. Car'lyn, Ah'd be much obliged if yuh'd let hur know Ah jist need tuh talk tuh hur."

"Deputy Ed," she said without turning to face him, "Ah dun already tol' yuh. Don't yuh nor that sheriff of yourn set foot back on mah land 'less mah boy's wit yuh."

246

Eula disappeared behind the wall of stone faced men, who remained motionless until the screen door slammed. The largest man in the group skeet a slimy brown stream of chewing tobacco through his teeth, past his heavily bristled red beard, raised his double barrel shotgun that was cradled under his arm and aimed it at Ed. The entire brood then raised their guns. Ed could hear the clicks as they prepared to fire.

"Wa'al Ed, yuh bes' be gittin' yuh niggah lovin' ass outta heah. The sight of yuh makin' me sick."

Bonnie Blue

"Boys, Ah dun told yuh, Ah ain't lookin' fuh trouble," Ed said as he slid into the opened car door.

Bamm! A bullet tore through the air, just missing the squad car.

"The hell yuh ain't!" The large man yelled as he reloaded his shotgun. "an' we gotta plenty of if right heah!"

Ed slammed his door, turned the key in the ignition, and prayed that it would start. With a sigh of relief, he called out the window, "Ya'll take care now!" He knew that if the bullet was meant to hit him, it would have. He quickly circled out of the yard and down the driveway.

* * *

Eula rushed out the screen door when she heard the shot. All that was left of the deputy's visit was a violent bellow of dust, which seemed to overtake the squad car as it vanished behind the cluster of trees.

"C'mon, boy's," she said as she watched the dust dissipate and settle back to the ground. "We gotta set this thang right! Sonna-bitch! He gonna try an' carry this thang out! He ain't plannin' tuh let mah boy go!" she said as she swiped the back of her hand across her forehead and flicked the collection of perspiration that threatened to drop into her eyes.

The group of men followed their mother back into the kitchen, where J.W., Melvin, and Leslie had been watching from the window.

"Harry, Ah'ma need fuh yuh an' Vern tuh gowan down tuh that jail an' check on yuh brotha. This ain't right." she said shaking her head. "It jist ain't right. He ain't got no right tuh be holdin' mah boy b'hind bars."

"Ma, whut yuh want us tuh do when we git thar? We kain take care of Ed an' George."

"Don't ya'll go down thar actin' out. Ah ain't nevah liked that boy. Ain't no tellin' how many folks he got sneakin' 'round," she said as she grabbed a plate from the tin tub filled with dirty dishes and soapy water and swished over it with a dingy dishrag. "He jist itchin' fuh uh reason tuh hurt mah Roy."

Huntin' Witout Uh Dawg Ain't Easy!

She sniffled as she wiped a tear from her cheek, dipped the plate in a bucket of clean well water, and filled it with the fried fatback and cold biscuits that were left over from dinner.

Frustrated, Leslie snatched his soggy cigar from between his teeth, glared over at J.W. who sat quietly at the large wooden table, and said, "This shit don't make no goddamned sense! If yuh gonna do somethin', yuh don't go tellin' the whole damned world 'bout it! Ah thank Ma's right! Look like tuh me he's gonna try tuh carry this thang all the way out! He goin' aft'a Roy like he dun somethin' tuh one of his own kin folk! Ah ain't nevah heard of such uh thang! Lockin' up White folks on uh niggah's say! Ah don't know whut kain be wrong wit that boy! Yuh know whut? Ah'll betcha uh dolla' tuh uh bucket of shit…he's one of them NA'CP'ers or he got some niggah blood in 'im!"

J.W. picked up his cup of cold coffee, looked at his older brother and said sternly, "Ain't nothin' gonna happen. Hell, he ain't even said nothin' 'bout uh body. He jist said the niggah was missin'. If Roy didn't go hollerin' his name all out when we got thar, he wouldn't be locked up now!"

"Dub, all Ah'm sayin' is, Ah don't need no shit comin' down on me!" Leslie said. "Mean tuh say…ya'll didn't hafta brang that shit tuh mah door! Ya'll know Ed dun hadda bad taste in his mouf fuh Roy! Don't ya'll fuhgit he's the same goddamned deputy tryin' tuh lock 'im up befo'! Now, Ah b'lieve he's hell bent on keepin' Roy locked up! Now, Ah'll do whutevah it takes tuh brang 'im home, but Ah ain't gittin' locked up next tuh 'im!"

248

"Hush up now!" Eula yelled angrily as she draped a towel over the plate of food and handed it to Harry. "Yuh boys stop an' git uh couple of soda pops fuh 'im."

"Yes, Ma'am."

"This ain't uh propp'a meal, but at least, he'll have somethin' decent tuh eat. An' boys, Ah don't want ya'll smartin' off at the law eith'a. Rememb'a, them boys ain't nonna yuh friends. Ah ain't havin' no mo' of mah boys b'hind bars, yuh heah me?"

"Don't worrah 'bout it, Ma," Harry said as he took the plate. "We ain't sayin' nothin'. We jist gonna make sho Roy's

Bonnie Blue

alright an' leave on out." Then he nodded at Vern and headed for the door. Eula continued to give instructions as she followed them out to the pickup truck.

"Ah don't thank Roy's gonna be able tuh do it," J.W. said as he stared somberly through the screen door. "Stick tuh the story Ah mean. That boy's too hot headed! He's gonna mess up! Sho as Ah'm standin' heah, he's gonna go runnin' his damned mouf!" J.W. looked coldly over to his older brother. "That's how we got in this shit in the furst place!"

"Don't be no fool," Leslie said as he took the last biscuit from the pan, shoved it into his mouth and licked his fingers. "It ain't nevah gonna reach no jury! Look at whut happened wit them oth'a niggahs ovah yonda! Damn agitata's up yonda had them niggah's thankin' they kain vote! Shit, Ah don't even thank that's legal! But they got put in they place propp'a! The law ain't even point uh fing'a at them boys an' evahbody know who blew they black asses' away!"

One of the younger brothers, which were crowded into the kitchen, wasn't sure which incident they were talking about. "Whut happen? Ah ain't heard of no trouble."

"One of them ol' niggah preacha's ovah yonda! 'Lee', Ah b'lieve they called him! Rev'ran George Lee or some shit. Ah know yuh had tuh heah 'bout 'im! One of them NA'CP niggahs, tryin' tuh stir up trouble! Makin' our niggahs thank they kain vote

249

or some shit like that! Hell, lettin' mah hound vote make mo' sense!" He laughed.

"Awww, yeah! Ah b'lieve Ah heard 'bout that uh bit ago, but Ah didn't know the 'ticulars! He got it in the middle of the day in front the courthouse, right? Bunch of folks saw 'em!"

"Naw, that thar was that Smith Boy! Lamar, Ah b'lieve his name was! Ah'm heah tuh tell yuh, them boys knew how tuh take care of all them goddamn NA'CP'ers! Blew them niggahs right on away from heah! Them boys made sho that 'stead of that niggah preachin' 'bout his Jesus, they sent his ass tuh have uh face-tuh-face wit 'Im!" Leslie laughed.

Huntin' Witout Uh Dawg Ain't Easy!

"Ah don't know," one of the other brothers said as he pinched off a piece of chewing tobacco. "Niggahs ain't as bad as them damn Jews!"

Leslie laughed and said, "Shit boy! Uh Jew ain't nothin' but uh niggah turnt inside out!"

Eula came back in the kitchen just as they burst into laughter. She angrily scanned the room and slammed the oversized cast iron skillet onto the wood burning stove, sending warm grease splattering across the wall and floor.

"Whut the hell's wrong wit ya'll? Yuh brotha's locked up, an' ya'll in heah laughin'? Ain't uh damned thang funny! So shut yuh damn moufs!"

A quick hush fell throughout the house as she pushed through the crowd of sweaty men, stormed down the hall, and slammed the bedroom door behind her.

The kitchen remained silent for a moment. And, for the first time, even the playful voices of her grandchildren, which constantly boomed through the house, were stilled.

"We gotta take care of this right now," J.W. said, breaking the silence.

"She gittin' too old fuh all this shit!" The bearded brother scolded as he stared down the empty hall. "Ya'll kain't be droppin' yuh shit in Ma's lap! Pa's dead! Roy's locked up! It's too much! Dub, unda'stand me. Ah don't give uh damn whut

250

yuh do tuh uh niggah; beat 'im or blow his fuckin' head off. Whut Ah care 'bout uh niggah ain't shit. All he gotta do is whut he's told. An', if he ain't got 'nough sense tuh do that, then yuh gotta do somethin' tuh git 'im back in line! Hell, if Ma weren't heah, Ah would'a sent that damn Ed, right on wit that niggah! All Ah'm sayin' is, yuh know Ma kain't take it if somethin' happen, an' Roy don't come home! An' ovah uh niggah? Shit, that'll be 'nough tuh put hur in uh early grave!"

Leslie removed his unlit, soggy cigar from his lips, looked up from the worn, green linoleum which blanketed the kitchen floor, and said coldly, "Dub, this heah's yuh shit! Ya'll had tuh go an' git all po'litcal, strangin' it out! Hell, all yuh had tuh do was

Bonnie Blue

take 'im in the woods an' put uh bullet in 'im propp'a! But, goddamnit, Dub!" he yelled as his temper flared. "Yuh had tuh go an' git messy, at mah place! Yuh trifflin' ass niggahs leff them damned bloody shoes in the back of mah damn car fuh god's sake! Mah niggahs was out in the field! Mean tuh say…ain't no tellin'! One of 'em might of seent somethin' or least, thank they seent somethin'! Now heah come the law, knockin' at Ma's door! Yuh shoulda..."

"Wait uh minute Les," Ray spoke up. "Whut the hell yuh talkin' 'bout? That niggah deserved evahthang he got. An' why ya'll jumpin' all on Dub? If Roy wasn't actin' uh fool, that preacha nevah would of even know who he was!"

"C'mon, we don't need tuh be heah," J.W. said as he motioned for his younger brother to come close. "It's okay, Ray. Gowan out back an' tell Frank, Ah said fuh ya'll tuh stay heah wit Ma. Ah thank it's bes' that ya'll stay. Ah kain count on yuh. If the law comes back, yuh know whut tuh do."

"Ah'll take care of it," Ray said as he hurried out the screen door.

"Ya'll gowan out tuh mah place. Ah'll catch up wit yuh. Ah need tuh talk tuh Ma."

"Yuh do that," Leslie said as he led the brood out the door.

251

J.W. walked quietly down the hall to his mother's bedroom. He could hear her sniffling through the door. "Ma?" he said as he knocked lightly on her door. "Ma? Yuh all right?"

She flung the door open. "Naw, Ah ain't alright," she said strongly as she pushed strings of hair away from her face and attempted to brush the mixture of perspiration and tears from her eyes. "Damnit Dub!" she said as she looked angrily up at him. "Yuh know yuh shouldn't of leff that boy by hisself! Ah'm proud he stood up like uh propp'a man an' took care of his bidness. But he ain't strong. He kain't hold up. Yuh brotha jist uh youngin an' uh lil' hot headed. Yuh know he's uh good boy. Sometime he mess up an' git in uh lil' trouble wit his friends. But the law comin' aft'a
'im fuh this heah? It ain't right. It jist ain't right. Ed been out tuh git mah boy evah since he got that star on his shirt. If yuh Pa was alive..."

Huntin' Witout Uh Dawg Ain't Easy!

"Ma..."

Her moist eyes squinted as her gaze bore through him. "Yuh do whutevah yuh need tuh do tuh make thangs right. Yuh unda'stand me?"

"Yes ma'am. Don't worrah. Ah'll take care of evahthang. We goin' out tuh the house. Ray an' Frank gonna stay heah wit yuh."

She ruggedly grabbed his thick forearm, her gaunt fingers and ragged nails nearly severing the hair on his arm. "Yuh be careful now, yuh heah me?"

"Don't worrah, Ma. Roy'll be home befo' yuh know it." He touched her hand, which was intensely embedded in his damp, crimson arm.

She unclenched her grip and patted him gingerly on his cheeks. "Yuh uh good boy, Dub. Ah know Ah kain always count on yuh tuh do the right thang."

"Ah gotta go," he said as he looked down at her and backed away. "Les an' some of the oth'a boys will be back later."

"Go git yuh brotha! Brang 'im back home whar he b'long!"

"Yes, ma'am."

* * *

J.W. hurried back through the kitchen and out to his truck, when he noticed Melvin sitting in the passenger's seat. He swung up into the cab and stared out the windshield.

"Ah gotta fix this." He shook his head thoughtfully, looked over at Melvin and turned the key in the ignition. "Les is right. Ah messed up. Ah don't know whut happened tuh me. Roy was right. Ah shoulda jist let 'im take care of it his own way," he said as he pulled out of the yard towards the highway.

Melvin looked out across the quiet fields of soft white cotton bolls and said nothing.

The pickup truck moved easily down the road as J.W. sank deeper into a muddled pool of remembrance.

Bonnie Blue

J.W. fought to control the nausea which threatened to erupt from his spastic stomach. He searched his mind to pinpoint when and why a simple beating evolved into a scene where he now seemed; a mere observer. He clung to his notion that the NAACP, Northern liberals, and communists had pushed him to such great depths. To him they were, without a doubt, responsible for the trouble that now confronted his family.

"Did we fuhgit anythang?" he asked Melvin flatly. "This mornin', Ah mean!"

"Ah sho hope tuh hell, not," Melvin said almost in a whisper as he stared out the windshield.

J.W. looked over at him and turned his attention back to the secluded road.

"Ah thank we alright." Melvin hesitated for a moment and continued quietly. "But Ah did see some blood back thar in the back. Ain't much tuh notice, but yuh Boys gotta warsh..."

"Damnit!" J.W. growled as he pounded his fist on the steering wheel. "Shoes in the car! Blood in the damn truck! Whut the hell else kain go wrong?" He slowly pulled to the side of the road and whispered hoarsely, "Melvin, we kain't tell nobody whut all happened. Not even the boys."

"Ah was thankin' the same," Melvin said dryly. "Ah'll talk tuh Les when we git tuh the house."

The drive through the somber dusk gave J.W. the time and solitude that he needed to make a decision; a decision that would leave nothing to chance. He was painfully aware that things had spiraled out of his control. Carefully, he reviewed each detail of the disposal of Emmett's body, making sure that nothing had been overlooked.

* * *

J.W. vividly recalled the dense, overcast skies that seemed to overtake them as they drove toward a deserted spot along the Tallahatchie River where he planned to dump the body.

Roy had become increasingly anxious as the clouds darkened and the air sweetened with the promise of a downpour.

Huntin' Witout Uh Dawg Ain't Easy!

"Whut we got tuh weigh 'im down wit?" Roy asked as he nervously scanned the cotton fields.

Melvin threw Roy an irritating glance and turned to J.W. "Look Dub, Marty jist got that new blow fan put in down at the cotton gin. The old one prob'bly still layin' out back. That'll be 'nough tuh hold 'im down."

"Yuh see thar lil' brotha? Ain't nothin' tuh worrah 'bout," J.W. said lightly as he made a sharp turn down another dirt road. "Wit that fan, they kain look all they want tuh, but they ain't nevah gonna find 'im!" J.W. laughed and turned back to Roy with a wide grin. "Boy, yuh bes' stop actin' so damned skeered. Jist relax. Ain't uh livin' soul 'round, an' Car'lyn's suitor back thar dun got real quiet. Guess he ain't got no 'jection now, does he?"

Roy's lips stretched tightly across his yellow teeth, and his face twisted into a contorted grin as he looked back at the tarpaulin covered body. Suddenly, in the distance, he heard the grinding motor of a tractor revving to life. His eyes shot over towards the Culpepper's farm. The old man's signature red cap was visible; even at that distance.

Willie Culpepper was eighty-two years-old and still drove his own tractor. Even though he'd hired some of J.W.'s manned tractors, he preferred to be out in the field to supervise them.

"Dub, look! Ovah thar!"

J.W. glanced over towards the sound of the tractor. "Roy, shuddup. Ain't no way in hell that ol' man kain see anythang from thar. 'Sides, he's in the Council. If anythang, he would'a give us uh hand."

J.W. had thought about joining the White Citizens Council when they formed last year, after the Brown –vs- The Board of Education decision, but he didn't like how they went about trying to stop the destruction of the Southern Institution; politically.

Trying to block the political march of Black folk and reasoning with Northern liberal agitators who were hell bent on destroying his sovereign state of Mississippi, was a waste of time.

He felt that the Klan was full of rednecks that weren't really fighting for anything; just killing because they could do it and get

Bonnie Blue

away with it. The militia would have been more to his liking, but J.W. wasn't a joiner of any group. He felt himself a patriot; fighting in the same way that wars were fought, and victories won. He may not have stopped the march of liberals, Jews, Colored people, and Communists from taking away all of his rights, but he felt that this was one battle that they didn't win.

J.W. pulled up alongside the mill.

"See! Jist like Ah said, thar's the fan!" Melvin exclaimed.

J.W. stopped the truck, got out and said to Melvin as they walked towards the side of the quiet building, "Ah feel good! Real good! Kinda like bein' back in the war!"

J.W. looked back and saw Roy still sitting in the cab. He took long hard strides back to the truck, jerked open the cab door and snatched him out.

He grabbed Roy by the scruff of his bloody tee shirt, and murmured, "Don't go gittin' soft on me now boy! Look 'round!

255

Ain't nobody heah!" He twisted the collar tighter around his fist and growled through clinched teeth, "Ah said, look 'round!"

Roy's eyes slid slowly to the side to see the empty road.

"Now, so far we ain't run intuh nobody, so yuh jist pull yuhseff tuhgetha an' help us load that fan on the damn truck!"

Melvin watched the road as Roy and J.W. struggled under the weight of the gin fan and tossed it onto the back of the truck next to Emmett's body.

"Hey, Dub!"

"Yeah!"

"Yuh got uh chain in yuh tool box?"

"Yeah, but Ah ain't 'bout tuh waste it on this niggah," J.W. grumbled defiantly. "Shit, Ah'd hafta go out an' buy anoth'a one. Roy, gowan 'round back an' see if yuh kain find somethin' tuh fasten 'im tuh that fan."

"Wait uh minute!" Melvin called as he ran back around to the side of the mill. There, in the weeds, he saw a discarded ball of barbed wire.

"Hey Roy! C'mon 'round heah an' git this!"

Huntin' Witout Uh Dawg Ain't Easy!

Roy rushed over to where Melvin was clearing away bushes. The tangled mass of barbed wire scraped across Roy's skin as he tossed it in the back of the truck.

J.W. lowered the tailgate and flung the tarpaulin back from Emmett's body.

Roy gasped, "Hey, Dub! Whut the hell yuh doin'? Keep 'im covered!"

J.W. glared over at him. Before Roy knew it was coming, his brother, grabbed him by the hair, and shoved his head down next to Emmett's mutilated, bloodied face. "He's dead, damnit! Dead! Now whut the hell's wrong wit yuh? Straighten yuh ass up boy! Ah'm warnin' yuh!"

Roy jerked his head away, careful not to touch the blood caked face. "Ah didn't mean nothin' by it," he said as he stood. "Ah jist don't like the way he's lookin' at me is all."

"Roy, Ah'm so goddamn ti'ed of yuh whimperin'," J.W. said as he carefully began to untangle the barbed wire.

Melvin stood silent for a moment. "Yuh sho yuh don't want tuh use the chain?"

"Whut the shit yuh talkin' bout? This was yuh idea!"

"Ah jist don't want tuh git all cut up on that rusted wire. Yuh got some gloves 'round heah?"

"Yeah, an' look in mah box an' git them wire cutta's outta thar too," J.W. said as he carefully threaded the knotted barbed wire through the spokes of the fan. "Roy, git up thar on the oth'a side. We ain't got much loose wire. Jist wrap it 'round his neck. Make sho yuh twist it tight at the base. Don't want it comin' loose."

Roy attempted to feed the barbed wire under Emmett's head, carefully reaching around his blood caked face.

"Lift up his goddamn head!" J.W. growled angrily. "Ah don't want his ass poppin' up in the river!"

"We need tuh leave some wire fuh his feet," Melvin said as he slid on the work gloves and handed J.W. the wire cutters.

"Ah don't b'lieve it's strong 'nough tuh hold that fan tuh the body. Dub, looks like yuh jist gonna hafta buy anoth'a chain."

"Ah dun told yuh. Ah ain't throwin' mah new chain in the damn rivah." J.W. said as he cut the remnant of wire for Emmett's

Bonnie Blue

ankles and attempted to wrap it around his legs. "Shit!" J.W. exclaimed when a barb scraped across his arm.

"Say Dub," Roy said as he twisted the single strand of barbed wire around Emmett's neck. "Yuh thank this heah's gonna be 'nough?"

"Goddamnit!" J.W. said as he tossed the remnant piece of tangled wire off of the truck. "If this niggah's body kain come up witout uh head, then his ass suppose tuh be fount!"

The cloudy skies turned a sinister green, and the sweet scent of impending rain blanketed the trio as they quickly spread the tarpaulin across their cargo and piled back into the pickup.

The road seemed to lead into a tunnel of darkness as the skies became more ominous and thunder rolled through the dense overcast. Thick pines lined the road on one side, and a glimpse of the winding Tallahatchie River was visible on the other.

"We gotta hurry up!" Melvin said as he looked up at the darkening skies. "It's 'bout tuh cut loose out heah! Whar yuh thankin' 'bout dumpin' 'im?"

"We ain't got much further tuh go," J.W. said confidently.

A huge jagged bolt of lightning etched through the clouds, bringing with it, large splatters of raindrops exploding on the windshield.

J.W.'s foot pressed solidly on the accelerator, catapulting the truck past forests of evergreens. His tires screeched as he turned onto a rarely used road etched out of the underbrush.

"They got that new bridge 'bout 5 miles out from the Point," J.W. said confidently, "The Tallahatcha's deep thar, an' that fan'll keep his ass down."

Blamm...! A deafening crackle of electricity streaked from the shadowy skies and found its mark in the nearby forest.

"Goddamn, Dub! Ah sho hope tuh hell yuh know whar yuh goin'," Melvin said nervously, squinting to look through the rain drenched windshield. "Ah kain't see shit!"

"Don't worrah 'bout it," J.W. said lightly as he sped through the torrential downpour.

"Ah thank it's bes' we jist dump 'im anywhar 'longside the river," Roy said as he too, squint his eyes and frantically wiped his

Huntin' Witout Uh Dawg Ain't Easy!

hands across the windshield in a vain attempt to clear the dense sheet of moisture which glazed over the glass. "Don't make no sense bein' out in this storm! We kain end up slidin' off the bridge!"

"Boy, stop smearin' that shit on the window, an' lemme handle thangs. Ah know whut Ah'm doin'. That bridge got them lil' cement walls on the sides, so we ain't slidin' offa nothin'," J.W. said as he maneuvered the truck off of the dirt road and continued up a wooded, debris covered path.

The men bounced chaotically as the large pickup climbed over fallen tree branches and splashed in and out of deep dips.

"Whut the hell yuh doin' boy?" Melvin demanded as he rose up to get a better look out of the window. "Whar yuh goin'?"

"We kain't take no mo' chances. Ah'm goin' up the back way. We almost thar," he said lightly. "Damn, this truck is rugged as all git out, ain't it? Ah hope tuh hell Ah don't tear it up in this shit!"

"Ain't nobody gonna be out in this storm," Melvin said as he drew his face closer to the window.

They had traveled a short distance when the rains began to diminish to a light drizzle.

Before long, J.W. emerged from the wooded shortcut and came to a halt alongside the narrow concrete bridge.

"We're heah!" he said as he jumped out of the cab. "C'mon! Hurry up!"

He quickly checked up and down the deserted road, unlatched the tailgate, and flung the tarpaulin from Emmett's body. Roy and Melvin climbed out the driver's side and jumped into the bed of the truck. They struggled as they awkwardly lifted the massive fan over the side of the truck and onto the low concrete wall.

"C'mon ya'll! J.W. bellowed as he strained to pull Emmett's body over the edge of the truck and onto the wall. "Roy! Lift 'im up! Lift 'im up!"

"Gowan Roy! Ah got this!" Melvin called as he held the fan steady.

"Ah got 'im!" Roy yelled as he helped J.W. push Emmett's lifeless body up the side of the truck.

Bonnie Blue

The skies again darkened. Low, threatening clouds once again began to clash and rumble.

"Git back! Move out the way!" Melvin yelled. With one big push, he shoved the fan over the side of the bridge.

Emmett's body was suddenly snatched from the truck, scratched across the railing and followed the fan as it plummeted into the dark river. They watched as the brown, murky waters of the

Tallahatchie exploded on impact and quickly and silently swallowed the newest member in its sinister legends.

* * *

That trip to the river seemed so long ago, and J.W. wasn't at all sure that there was nothing left to be found.

When he pulled into his truck cluttered yard in Glendora he was confronted by loud voices and laughter booming from inside his crowded house. Most of the pickups were his kin's. But when he noticed other trucks that belonged to staunch members of the Ku Klux Klan he knew that word had gotten out about Roy's arrest.

"Yuh alright?" Melvin asked when they pulled to a halt alongside the house.

J.W. stared intensely through the windshield, past the blackened cotton field, wondering how things could have gotten so sloppy; so out of control.

"Dub?"

"Let's go," J.W. said as he threw the truck door open.

* * *

They entered the house and saw Juanita scurrying around a flood of large, rowdy men who had spilled out from the living room into the kitchen. She had only prepared one jug of sun tea, biscuits, fried chicken and fried okra for J.W.'s dinner and was concerned that there wasn't enough food or drink for everyone.

"Ah'm sorrah, Dub," Juanita called out timidly as she pulled the large tin canister of flour from the pantry. "Ah didn't know nobody was comin' out heah tuhnight!"

"Ain't nobody 'spectin' tuh eat," J.W. said as he walked through the kitchen. Juanita replaced the canister and artfully weaved her way through the living room. Her quiet greetings went

Huntin' Witout Uh Dawg Ain't Easy!

unnoticed as she disappeared in the rear of the house with her children.

J.W. stood in the doorway and scanned the crowded, smoke filled room as he contemplated what had to be done.

260

Angry murmurs and conversations intensified as they discussed the actions of two of their own; the sheriff and the deputy, both supposed friends. And then there was Eisenhower, tearing down the South, paving the way for 'uppity niggahs' to do whatever they pleased.

J.W. made his way to a boisterous corner of the room where Leslie and some of his younger brothers were huddled; laughing with a group of Klansmen.

"Evenin' boys," J.W. said as he turned his attention to two very active Klansmen. "Byron, Ray Bob, whut brangs yuh boys out heah?"

"Hey, Dub!" Byron grinned and slapped J.W. on the back. "Ah'm right proud of yuh boys! Right proud! An' don't yuh worrah none 'bout Roy. We gonna take care of evahthang. We dun already..."

"Don't need no help," He cut him short and turned to Leslie. "C'mon outside. We need tuh talk."

Leslie followed his stoic brother as he stepped out into the night and the dead promise of a renegade wind. The two men distanced themselves from the small group gathered on the porch.

As they walked further away from the house, J.W. turned to face his older brother. "Why they out heah? Yuh ain't said nothin' 'bout this mornin', did yuh?"

"Whut kinda fool yuh take me fuh?" he whispered. Ah ain't tellin' nobody nothin'. Look Dub, Ah kain't say fuh sho whut happened mah damnseff. Hell, the last thang Ah want is fuh anybody, 'specially them Klan boys tuh know. They'd spread it all ovah Mississippi. All they know is the niggah's dead. Ah told 'em we beat 'im tuh deaf."

"That's good, but Ah ain't jist talkin' 'bout them. Ah mean the boys too. If Ma find out...Hell, Ah don't know. It's jist bes' if

Bonnie Blue

thangs stay 'tween us. Ah already told Huber' tuh keep his mouf shut. Me an' Melvin talked 'bout it on the way home."

"Whut 'bout yuh niggahs?" Leslie asked nervously. "Yuh gonna hafta take care of them niggahs befo' the law git tuh 'em."

261

"Ah don't know. Ah gotta thank," J.W. said as he rushed back towards the house.

"Dub, wait!" Leslie called as he ran to catch up with him. "Dub! Byron an' his boys kain take care of..."

"Ah don't need nothin' from Byron an' his boys. Ah already figured out whut gotta be dun!" J.W. called back as he leaped up the three steps of his front porch.

Voices thundered throughout the house. Accusations and murderous plots were rising to a feverish pitch.

"Hold on!" J.W. yelled above the thunder of voices. "Shit! Now, wait uh minute! One thang we kain't have is anoth'a dead niggah or the law comin' up missin'! Yuh gotta use yuh heads!"

"Yeah!" Leslie spoke as he held both of his hands up to motion for silence. "Ya'll need tuh hush up an' lissen! We gotta do this thang right! Gowan, Dub. Whut yuh got in mind?"

Silence fell throughout the room. All eyes fixed on J.W. as he coldly scanned the eager group that he now controlled.

"The only way he kain git this beat is tuh make sho Roy stick wit the story that we had. Well, we know that didn't happen 'cuz he's b'hind bars."

"Whut 'bout that, Dub?" one of his younger brothers asked. "They ain't suppose tuh have 'im locked up if they ain't fount no body. Yuh don't thank they fount 'im, do yuh? Ah mean, that ain't legal, is it?"

"Naw, they ain't gonna find nothin'! Fact is, somebody needs tuh check up on Ed, see if whut he's doin' *is* legal."

"Well, hell! Whut's George got tuh say 'bout all this heah mess?"

"George does whut he always do when it come down tuh that deputy of his. Not uh damn thang!"

Laughter spread throughout the house.

Huntin' Witout Uh Dawg Ain't Easy!

"Aw shit, man! Yuh ain't gotta worrah 'bout nothin'. Me an' mah boys'll take care of that in the mo'nin'," Byron said as he sucked his teeth.

"'Sides, Ah thank it'll be wise tuh have some of our boys keep their ears open. Ah'll make uh call tuh one of our men down at the County Seat tuh see whut George an' that deputy got already." His lips slid into a sinister smile as he leaned against the door. "Won't do tuh git caught wit yuh britches down, now would it?" Byron looked around the room at the other Klan members and then addressed J.W.

"Yuh know, Dub, we're heah fuh yuh. We kain make short order of yuh troubles. If the law ain't got no witnesses, they ain't got no case! Ain't that right, boys? Ah heah tell that niggah preacha's the one that bought the law in," Byron angrily looked around at his fellow Klansmen and continued.

"Hell! Me an' the boys kain take uh ride out thar right now, round up evah sangle one of them niggahs in that house an' yuh brotha'll be home fuh breakfust!"

"An' that damned deputy's got 'nough enemies 'round heah," one of the older men of the group said with a grimace, "his ass could disappear, an' folks'll jist thank he leff town. All yuh gotta do is say the word."

"Yeah," J.W. said with some relief. "We might need yuh down the line. But right now, Ah gotta plan. Melvin, Ah'ma need yuh in the mo'nin'."

"Whutevah yuh need."

"Yuh hadda couple of yuh own niggahs wit yuh, ain't yuh?" Ray Bob interrupted. "Gotta take care of 'em. Kain't jist leave 'em loose," he said as he leaned against the doorframe with his legs crossed. "Yuh bes' lissen tuh Byron. Yuh be uh damn fool sho 'nuff if yuh don't. Me an' some of the boys'll take care of that lil' problem an' that niggah preacha too. Ain't nobody tuh say nothin', ain't no body tuh be fount. Hell, it's like he said, yuh brotha'll be home fuh breakfust fuh sho. Won't be no problem."

J.W.'s bearded brother walked over to him and said gruffly, "Look Dub, it make sense tuh me. We make sho don't nobody find 'em, an' George or Ed won't have nothin' tuh hold Roy on. They'll

Bonnie Blue

hafta let 'im go. Ain't nothin' else we kain do! Ma kain't take that boy bein' put away! Yuh know that!"

263

J.W. bore his cold glare right into his brother's eyes and, without blinking, replied slowly and menacingly, "Ain't no mo' killin'. Not the preacha, an' not mah Boys. Do yuh heah me? The mo' bodies yuh got, the deep'a the shit gits. This is uh family matt'a," he scolded. "An' the family will take care of it, unda'stand?"

He turned to Byron and said sternly, "Ah 'preciate yuh boys comin' out, but Ah'm handlin' thangs mah way. That ain't tuh say that yuh boys kain't help. Ah know whut Ah gotta do, but Ah thank Ah'ma need yuh tuh check on some thangs fuh me."

"Howevah yuh want tuh do it, is fine by me," Byron said snidely. "Since yuh don't want us tuh git rid of 'em, whut yuh want us tuh do?"

Surprised, Leslie shot glances between his brother and Byron. "Whut the hell yuh talkin' 'bout, Dub?"

"Ah gotta plan," J.W. said calmly.

* * *

Meanwhile, Too Tight had just about had his fill of loose women and rotgut moonshine. Nothing dulled the images in his head for more than a moment.

"Hey, Buck!" he called as he looked over at his friend rolling around on a dirty mat in the corner with an equally nasty woman. "Ah gotta git da hell up outta heah." He struggled to stand to his feet, shoving the drunk, half-dressed young woman that sat on his lap onto the splintered, wooden floor. "Hey Buck!" he slurred as he staggered to the door. "C'mon, niggah! Ah'm ret' tuh go!"

Too Tight's stomach churned violently. The foul stench of stale moonshine and the dense fog of aged funk that sat motionless throughout the shanty, reintroduced the sickening scent of the lynching. He had to get out of there.

Buck rolled over on the filthy homemade pallet where he lay with his new found woman friend. He parted his liquor heavy eyelids as his full lips slid back exposing a very satisfied yellow, toothy grin. "Niggah, yuh mus' be crazy sho 'nuff, thankin' Ah'ma leave all dis heah," he said as he smacked his half-conscious

Huntin' Witout Uh Dawg Ain't Easy!

companion on her exposed butt. "Whut yuh need tuh do is git on ovah dere wid dat purty lil' ol' yaller gal yuh got."

Too Tight glared down at the young woman sprawled at his feet. "Naw, man. Ah'm feelin' like shit. Ain't uh damn thang 'round heah tuh eat. Ah ain't 'bout tuh be layin' 'round dis funky ass room all..."

Suddenly, Too Tight slammed his hand against his lips, leaped over the young woman, barely missing her, and quickly stumbled out the door. He'd just made it to the yard before his stomach squeezed into a final twisting seizure and vomit erupted from his gut.

"Wheah yuh goin', baby? Ah'll go wid yuh!" the young woman pleaded as she scrambled to her feet. "Is yuh gonna brang me back somethin' tuh eat, too?" she asked as she leaned against the wobbly, homemade banister; her slip strap hanging off her shoulder.

Too Tight made his way to the truck and turned the ignition. When Buck heard the motor, he yelled out the door, "Hey, Tight! Don't yuh fuhgit wheah yuh leff me! Yuh bet not be gone all damned night!"

* * *

The old truck rattled as it weaved erratically down the road. After a short reprieve from nausea, Too Tight's stomach was revisited by intense grips of convulsions. "Aw shit!" he moaned as he struggled to keep the truck out of the ditch and his fluids down.

The small town of Glendora is covered with nice homes of its White citizens. However, the back road of Glendora is crowded with leaning shanties for Colored fieldhands.

Reid's Café, is the Juke Joint on the back road where some fieldhands gather to dance and eat after picking cotton and working in the fields all day.

Too Tight followed the dirt road behind Glendora and finally jolted to a halt among the few vehicles scattered in the makeshift parking lot.

Bonnie Blue

He sat for a while, mustering up strenght to go inside. The moonshine still had him reeling. He looked down at his hand where Emmett's tear had landed. He began scraping the back of his hand against the tattered door panel; in an attempt to erase the memory of the child's last tear as it splashed on his thumb and absorbed into his skin.

"Hey, man! Wheah yuh been?" A slurred happy greeting boomed through his opened window.

Too Tight's heart suddenly felt as though it had burst from his chest. "Man, Ah'ma kick yuh ass! Don't evah do no shit like that tuh me no mo'!"

"Aw, niggah, yuh ain't gonna do shit," Black Jake said as he opened the truck door. "Wheah Buck at?"

Too Tight slid off the seat, nearly falling out of the truck. "Dat niggah's laid up wid some gal. Ah'm hongry as hell," Too Tight mumbled as he looked around and staggered towards the unadorned structure.

"Hey Tight!" A raspy voice bellowed from a loud carload of drunken men.

Too Tight ignored the anonymous voice and continued to make his way to the entrance of the small, wooden café.

The single, room was packed with young barefoot men and women whirling around the dance floor. No fresh air ventured to cut through the stubborn haze of musty workers, stale cigarette smoke, fried chicken, chitterlings and fatback. The patrons were all familiar with each other. They either worked together, grew up together, or became acquainted through their common situation.

Black Jake joined Too Tight as he fell into an empty seat at a table near the rear of the room.

"Man, yuh look like shit warmed ovah! Whut yuh need tuh do is take yuh drunk ass home," he said as he plopped into the chair next to him.

"Ah jist need somethin' tuh eat," Too Tight mumbled dryly as he flung his arm in the air to summon the young waitress. "Brang me somma dat goddamn chicken!"

Huntin' Witout Uh Dawg Ain't Easy!

266

"Yuh know somethin'?" he slurred, attempting to look Black Jake in the face. "Uh peckawood mutha fucka ain't shit."

"Niggah, yuh drunk." Black Jake laughed as he playfully slapped Too Tight on the back and raised his hand to beckon the waitress. "Hey Gert! Gib dis boy some chicken, some chit'lin's, or somethin'!"

Too Tight raised his eyes up at the woman and mumbled, "Chicken. Make sho yuh ain't stingy wid dem biscuits."

"Yeah, okay," she said dryly, and disappeared through the crowd.

Too Tight grumbled angrily into his arm as he laid his head on the table.

"Whut da hell wrong wid yuh?" Black Jake demanded. "Aw, shit on dis, man. Ah'ma go have me some fun!" He left Too Tight and joined a group of men and women playing cards and drinking at another table.

Too Tight nodded off to sleep until the waitress came back and let his plate of food drop on the rickety table next to his head. He woke with a start.

"Woman, whut da fuck wrong wid yuh?" He yelled, "Is yuh out yuh damn mind?"

"Yuh wan' some mo' biscuits, lemme know," she said slightly irritated and disappeared back through the crowd.

He started to yell something but instead, shoved a drumstick into his mouth and pulled out the bone. He rapidly devoured the plate of chicken and biscuits, barely tasting anything.

Too Tight's stomach was satisfied, but nothing else was at peace. His anger was not only at the men that killed the boy, but it was also mixed with the resentment at his own cowardice.

"Mutha fuckas'! Shit, Ah'm low-down mah damn seff!" he yelled. "Why da hell dey send dat boy down heah in da furst place?" His voiced rose to a scream as he pounded his fist on the small table, sending chicken bones flying from the plate. "Why couldn't dey jist shoot da damn niggah?! Why dey hafta drill uh goddamn hole in his head Jesus? Dat's evil! Evil!"

Conversation instantly hushed to a low buzz as attention immediately turned toward Too Tight. Black Jake looked around,

Bonnie Blue

saw some fieldhands that he knew couldn't be trusted, and rushed over to his friend.

"Hey, man! Whut da hell yuh doin'?" he whispered frantically. "Shut yuh goddamn mouf up, boy!"

Too Tight's tear soaked face looked pleadingly up at his friend. "Ah...Ah didn't know whut tuh do. Ah didn't know whut..."

"Whut da hell yuh talkin' 'bout, man?" Black Jake whispered as he held his head close to Too Tight.

"Ol' Milam an' 'dem," he said softly, as he looked down at his hands, "dey took dat boy, shoved his head in dat brace, an'...he looked at me. Me!" Tears dripped from his chin. "He looked dead at me. Begged me tuh help 'im. Ol' Milam! Dat crazy ass brotha of his! Dem mutha fuckas'! Dey jist kept right on turnin'! Didn't care one bit! Jist kept on!" Too Tight yelled as his fist crashed down on the table. "Dey ain't thought 'bout stoppin' 'til dat bit tore clean through dat boy's head! Da devil hisself was in dat room! Ah'm tellin' yuh true!"

The room became alive with murmurs.

"Whut da hell he talkin' 'bout?"

"Whut he say?"

"Dat niggah drunk. He jist talkin' shit."

"Aw shit! C'mon. Jist shuddup. We gittin' outta heah," Black Jake whispered as he tried to pull Too Tight to his feet.

"Ah let 'em do it!" Too Tight yelled as he snatched away. "Ah didn't help 'im! Dey drill dat boy's head like he weren't nothin'! An' Ah didn't do nothin' tuh stop 'em!"

* * *

A group of men rushed to help get Too Tight outside. They quickly shoved him into Black Jake's car, crowded in after him, and pulled off down the road to Triola's.

When they got to her shack, Black Jake jumped out of the car.

"Triola!" he yelled as he struggled to help a couple of other men haul Too Tight up the steps. "Triola!"

She appeared at the door, frightened and wide eyed.

"Whut's wrong?" she asked startled. "Who dat is?" She jump back in disbelief when they dragged Too Tight's drunken body past her. "Aw, naw! Naw! Hell naw!" she shouted. "Yuh crazy as hell! Come wakin' me up in da middle of da night fuh dis niggah!"

"He need tuh sleep it off befo' he git hisseff in trouble," Black Jake pleaded. "C'mon, Triola! He ain't gonna be no trouble. Jist need tuh sleep is all."

She softened as she looked at the tear soaked, helpless man who was unable to even hold his head up on his own power.

"Take 'im back in da room. An' be quiet. Don't wake up dem chil'ren."

They dragged him back to the bedroom and put him down on the bare floor.

"He kain stay da night, but ya'll betta come back early mo'nin' befo' Ah gotta git in da field," Triola demanded. "Ah ain't gittin' beat fuh nobody."

"He be 'right tuh leave by his ownseff in da mo'nin'," Black Jake call as he climbed back in the car with the other men.

Triola watched as they moved slowly up the road before going back into her house and crawling onto the small mattress with her children.

BOOK SEVEN

LOOKA HEAH BOY, IF YUH WAS UH WOMAN,
AH'D HAFTA SAY.... YUH SLIP WAS HANGIN'!

As the soft tranquility of night began it secret transition into dawn, Too Tight found himself, once again, in the stench laden shed where Emmett lay covered in blood; and lifeless. Distorted red faces of familiar men transformed before his eyes into evil, grinning serpents calling his name, taunting him and slithering toward him. He screamed, ran out of the shed, down the road and through the field. The fields were empty, tractors stood abandoned; and he ran. The stench from the shed intensified and followed him.

Horrifying voices became louder as they spat vile accusations. His chest burned, but screams got caught in his throat. Terrified, he glanced over his shoulder to see how close they were. The red faced demons were gone, but there were more, many more, battered faces that nearly filled the sky; Colored men, women, and children. Out of the pack of angry faces, one emerged larger, more grotesque, and closer than the rest. It was Emmett.

"Why didn't you help me?" The voice from the sky cried out. **"Why did you let them torture me? You should**

270

have let me go when you had the chance! You knew what they were going

Looka Heah Boy, If Yuh Was Uh Woman,
Ah'd Hafta Say...Yuh Slip Was Hangin'!

to do! I begged you to help me! Why didn't you help me? You were supposed to protect me! You'll never be a man!"

Too Tight tried to run faster; viciously kicking the floor. "Nooooo! Leab me alone!" he screamed. "Ah'm sorrah! Ah'm sorrah! God know Ah'm sorrah! Leab me alone! Ah couldn't do nothin'! Ah couldn't stop 'em!"

"Tight! Tight! Wake up! Yuh gonna skeer dem chil'rin!" Triola pleaded as she darted down to the rear room and shook him violently.

Too Tight continued to scream and thrash about, unable to escape his sleep of terror. Fear was rapidly overtaking Triola. She'd never seen Too Tight crying and screaming like this, awake or in his sleep. With all of the power that she could gather, she slapped him. The palm of her hand burned and instantly turned blood red, but he continued to kick violently, flinging his arms wildly in the air.

She slapped him again. "Tight, baby! Whut's wrong wid yuh? Wake up! Stop it Ah say!"

Suddenly, his eyes popped open. Frantic and trembling, he looked around the room and stared suspiciously at Triola. "Is yuh real, or is yuh uh hanck spirit come tuh git me?" he asked quietly as he lay motionless.

"Tight, baby! Wake up! It's me! Whut's wrong wid yuh? Ah ain't no hanck! It's me fuh sho!"

He lay still for a moment, afraid to breathe, convinced that even the slightest movement might summon the spirits that sought him.

Suddenly, a loud pounding on the door boomed through the tiny shack. They both froze and looked at each other.

"Too Tight! Git yuh black ass out heah!"

"Who dat is?" Triola whispered as heavy brogans pounded through the house towards them. "Whut yuh dun?"

"Niggah, Ah said git yuh black ass out heah!" J.W. commanded as he approached the back room.

271

"Hush up," Too Tight whispered as he got to his feet. "Stay heah. Don't say nothin'."

Bonnie Blue

"Ah'm comin' Mista Milam sah!" He rushed out the bedroom door and intercepted J.W. in the hall. "Ah'm heah, sah."

"Git out tuh the truck. Ah gotta road job fuh yuh up by Clarksdale," J.W. barked coldly. "Let hur know yuh won't be back fuh uh few days."

"Yassah," Too Tight replied as he turned back towards the bedroom, but Triola was already standing in the doorway, confused and afraid.

"Mo'nin', Mista Milam sah," she said timidly, her eyes cast to the floor. "He gonna be gone uh spell. Yassah."

"C'mon. We gotta long way tuh go," he said dryly.

Too Tight glanced back at Triola as he followed J.W. out into the dawn tinted morning and very possibly, his own death. He could feel Triola watching from the shadows.

* * *

J.W. leaped into the cab of the pickup and started the motor. Too Tight was about to climb into the back when J.W. called out to him, "Git up heah!"

"Yassah." Too Tight replied softly, hurrying around to the cab.

They rode in silence down the Colored section of Glendora and up through the main part of town leading out to the highway.

Too Tight kept his head down, but cast his eyes out onto the road, hoping to see a familiar face as small groups of fieldhands waved while making their way down the road to the cotton fields.

The silence was deafening. Never, in all his life, had he been so heavily laden with fear. Tiny white houses soon gave way to an empty stretch of highway laid atop the blanket of fields.

J.W.'s scarred knuckles whitened as he gripped the steering wheel.

"Ya'll was sloppy! Leff them bloody shoes in the car," he yelled as he abruptly jerked the truck to the side of the road. "Yuh tryin' tuh make trouble fuh me, Boy?"

Looka Heah Boy, If Yuh Was Uh Woman,
Ah'd Hafta Say…Yuh Slip Was Hangin'!

"Sah?" Too Tight's voice tremble as his eyes locked onto the dashboard; his heart pounding wildly. "Nossah, Mista Milam, sah. Ah ain't tryin' tuh make no trouble fuh nobody. Lawd knows Ah ain't."

"Whar was yuh las' night, Boy?" J.W. asked coldly as he turned to face him. "Yuh been talkin'?"

Too Tight searched his mind. He couldn't remember anything, not even how he got to Triola's. "Nossah. Ah ain't said nothin' tuh nobody. Dat's da god's honest truth."

"Fuh yuh sake, yuh'd bes' be tellin' me nothin' but the truth. Look at me, Boy." J.W. said dryly. "Niggah, Ah said look at me!" he shouted as he grabbed Too Tight by his collar. "Ah'm ti'ed of yuh worthless ass! If yuh tell anythang tuh anybody, Ah'll kill yuh, yuh woman, an' them lil' niggahs! Yuh unda'stand whut Ah'm tellin' yuh, Boy? Yuh unda'stand me?!"

Too Tight reluctantly looked directly in his face. "Yassah. Ah mean, naw, sah. Ah sweah Ah ain't nevah sayin' nothin' tuh uh livin' soul."

"Yuh betta make sho ya'll buried them clothes whar nobody'll find 'em! If Ah find out yuh didn't git rid of that shit propp'a, Ah'll git rid of both yuh damn niggahs! Yuh mo' trouble than yuh worth!" With that, he shoved Too Tight back and whipped the truck back onto the road. "Yuh gonna burn them shoes an' give this truck uh good warshin'. If anybody ask yuh 'bout the blood, tell 'em Ah was deer huntin' outta season an' didn't want nobody tuh know. Yuh heah me?"

"Yassah."

* * *

As the wink of a beautiful mauve daybreak continued to crack through the navy blue skies, Too Tight became keenly

273

aware that it was yesterday at this time, when they were headed down the same road. He was equally aware that the morning's end could find him and Henry Lee alongside the young boy.

Like the morning before, they turned off of the red dirt road onto the long private drive leading to Leslie's barren yard. Too Tight could feel his body begin to tremble in a panic. He secretly clenched

Bonnie Blue

his fists and pressed them firmly into the seat as he attempted to regain control.

"Git out!" J.W. barked as he flung his door open and leaped out the truck. "Them shoes in the trunk of the car. Gowan ovah tuh the back of the shed an' git uh fire started."

"Yassah," he said meekly and hurried out of the truck.

Too Tight quickly scanned the early signs of a new workday as fieldhands began dragging their burlap sacks out to the cotton fields. He ran nervously around to the back of the shed to gather kindling for a fire.

All signs of the previous day's downpour had vanished. Other than a hint of morning dew, the ground and wood were barely moist. He collected as many small branches as he could carry to stack on the gravel where the huge, red cotton combine was parked when it wasn't in use.

Suddenly, loud crunching of brogans and the vibrations of deep voices, cut through the peaceful songs of birds chirping in a nearby tree. Startled, he jerked, and the branches went spilling out of his arms. He whipped around in time to see Leslie and J.W. coming toward him carrying Emmett's bloodstained, corked soled shoes.

"Aw, shit," he mumbled as he scrambled to collect his tumbled load.

"Whut the hell yuh doin', niggah?" Leslie yelled. "Pile that shit up thar right an' brang that gas can out heah! Hurry up, goddamnit!"

"Yassah," Too Tight replied timidly as he scurried back to the shed.

274

"Whar's that oth'a one?" Leslie barked, keeping his eyes on Too Tight as he disappeared inside. "Ah'm tellin' yuh, Ah kain't have no mo' shit laid at mah door! Yuh need tuh have both them niggahs out heah cleanin' up this shit!"

"Melvin's on his way out thar now. Aft'a these shoes," J.W. said as he tossed them onto the pile of branches, "we'll be dun."

Too Tight clung to the can of gasoline and a box of stick matches as he crouched just inside the door, listening to the voices drifting in.

> Looka Heah Boy, If Yuh Was Uh Woman,
> Ah'd Hafta Say…Yuh Slip Was Hangin'!

"When ya'll takin' 'em out thar? Don't need tuh be wastin' time," Leslie said as he bit off the tip of his new cigar and spit it on the ground. "That's 'bout the smartest thang yuh coulda come up wit! Good thang them Klan boys come out las' night! They got folk spread out all ovah the place, ain't they?" he laughed.

Too Tight's foot slid across the cotton seed that he had scattered the day before, sending the metal gas can crashing to the floor.

"Whut the hell's he doin'?" J.W. rushed towards the open door.

Too Tight grabbed the can and clumsily caught the box of matches which had popped into the air.

"Whut yuh doin' in heah, Boy?" He shoved him back.

Startled, Too Tight looked in his face and quickly cast his eyes to the ground. "Ah'm sorrah, sah. Ah was jist gittin' the gas can fuh the fire like yuh told me, Mista Milam, sah," he said meekly and quickly darted around him to the pile of wood.

"Aft'a yuh burnin' them shoes, git that pail ovah yonda an' scrub out the truck! Make damn sho ain't nothin' fuh the law tuh find," J.W. said as he and Leslie went back toward the house. "Lemme know when yuh dun!" he called as the screen door bounced shut.

Too Tight's hands quivered as he quickly piled more broken branches, twigs, and rags on the heap. He nervously

275

scanned the cotton field to see if anyone was watching, before splashing gasoline over the stack and scratching the red head of the matchstick against the box. The lit stick landed lightly on the kindling. Bright flames instantly leapt into the air.

He couldn't bring himself to touch Emmett's bloody shoes. He scooped them up with a small crooked branch and let them slide into the fire. The top of the shoes began to wither as the heat intensified. But the stabbing blue flames quickly died down, giving way to a large plume of white smoke rolling up into the brightening dawn. He tossed another splash of gasoline onto the smoldering fire, but the dense cork sole of the shoes refused to burn; refused to even show signs of shrivel.

Bonnie Blue

Too Tight frantically surveyed the field when he realized that they wouldn't disappear in the ash.

A short distance away, Frank Young stood on his porch, watching the growing tempest of smoke. He could see that the yard was empty, except for the frightened man dousing fuel and skirting around in a panic. It was time to prepare for the day's work, but once again, the fields held an ominous stillness. He knew that his wasn't the only silhouette meshed within the shadows.

Frank caught sight of a cluster of heads just above the horizon of cotton bolls in the fields, peering toward the yard. Quickly, he slid back behind the safety of the barely attached wood-framed screen door.

Leslie looked out the kitchen window, saw the flames die down and became enraged.

"Yuh half-witted niggah kain't even start uh goddamn fire!" he yelled as he burst out of the house. "Ah ain't havin' this shit! Whut yuh bes' do is git rid of 'im! Git rid of both them sons of bitches! They tryin' tuh git evahbody b'hind bars!"

A rush of blood flushed J.W.'s face as he ran ahead of his brother and grabbed Too Tight by the collar. Too Tight caught the full blast of his fury square in the chest. His knees buckled, as he slumped to the ground. J.W. dragged him back to his feet and shot his clenched knuckled fist deep into Too Tight's belly. His body collapsed around J.W.'s fist as his breath was forced from his body.

"Not heah, goddamnit!" Leslie screamed as he grabbed J.W.'s arm. "Yuh bes' pull yuhseff tuhgetha boy," he said as calmly as he could. "We got 'nough damn trouble."

J.W. stared down at Too Tight as he gasped for air. "Burn the damn shoes," he said coldly.

"Yassah, Mista Milam, sah," Too Tight whimpered as he struggled to catch his breath and get out of striking distance.

"Hurry up!" J.W. boomed as he doused the shoes with more gasoline. "Git 'round back an' brang mo' wood!"

Looka Heah Boy, If Yuh Was Uh Woman,
Ah'd Hafta Say…Yuh Slip Was Hangin'!

Too Tight clutched his stomach as he ran around to the side of the shed, more afraid than angry. He looked out through the field and started to make a dash for it. But he knew that they would shoot him before he could get far.

"Aw, shit! Whut tuh do? Whut tuh do?" he mumbled as he stooped and clumsily grabbed scraps of wood. "God, efen Yuh up theah," he pleaded, "please help me. Dey stone crazy. Ah don't want tuh die. Not like whut dey dun tuh dat boy."

"Niggah, hurry up an' git that damn wood ovah heah befo' this fire go all the way out!" Leslie yelled.

"Yassah!" Too Tight called as he looked pleadingly upward into the new dawn and emerged with his arms full of branches.

"Go git some mo' gas! Hurrah up!" J.W. yelled as he grabbed a rake and jabbed feverishly at the kindling to reignite the fire.

"Yassah!" Too Tight said as he dumped the branches on the pile of crackling wood.

Sparks popped from the smoldering mass following the growing upward spiral of white smoke.

"Aw, tuh hell wit it!" J.W. yelled as he slammed the rake to the ground and hurried back to the truck. "We wastin' too much time! Jist bury the goddamned thangs!"

Confused, Too Tight grabbed the rake and continued to stab at the dying flames.

"Boy, Ah said bury 'em!" he barked.

Too Tight darted back into the shed and returned with a shovel. He hesitated to ask where he should dig. Instead, he scraped the charred remnant of Emmett's shoes from the mangled smoldering heap.

"Git ovah heah, Boy!" Leslie yelled as he rushed towards the shed. "Git that bucket of wat'a ovah yonda an' git this pump primed! Drop that shit! C'mon an' do whut Ah say! We ain't got all day! Yuh lazy sonna-bitch! Ya'll leff blood in the back of that damn truck!"

"Them damn shoes ain't stayin' heah!" he yelled over to J.W. "If they ain't burnt up, yuh gonna hafta take 'em wit yuh! Damnit! Ah got work tuh do! Ah'm ti'ed of this shit! Dub! Yuh heah me?"

Bonnie Blue

J.W. ignored his brother and intercepted Too Tight who was still standing with the shovel in his hand.

"Git the bucket an' start warshin' this bed out," J.W. said dryly.

"Yassah," Too Tight said.

"Yuh gotta git movin' on this thang!" Leslie yelled.

J.W. lunged towards his brother. "Whut yuh thank Ah'm tryin' tuh do, Les? Yuh thank yuh the only one that got shit tuh do? Yuh know whut Ah'm lookin' at! Damnit!"

"Ah know Dub! But niggahs suppose tuh be in the field right now! Look 'round! They ain't! Nary uh one! Why yuh thank that is boy?" Leslie bellowed as he shoved his distorted scarlet face a hair away from his brother's.

J.W. pushed Leslie aside and unlatched the tailgate. Too Tight stood invisibly next to the truck; afraid to move.

"Git up thar." J.W. said sternly. "Look in that toolbox an' git them rags. Make sho yuh git down in them grooves."

J.W. threw a strong glare at Leslie and signaled for him to walk with him out of earshot of Too Tight.

"Look, Les," he retorted. "Ah'ma drop 'im off out at Henry's place when he dun. Ain't nobody else gonna be out thar wit 'im. Then Ah'll gowan out, an' take care that oth'a thang."

278

"How yuh plannin' tuh git 'im out tuh..."

"Melvin, takin' ovah from thar," J.W. interrupted. "Jist make sho one of the boys git Juanita an' mah boys out tuh hur Ma's tuhday. Car'lyn's goin' down tuh Willie Clyde's out by Webb. He gonna keep 'em down thar. Evahthang's und'a control."

Leslie looked over at Too Tight, who was on his hands and knees, sloshing a large dingy towel across the grooves, working his way off the back of the truck. Suddenly, the old bantam rooster's crowing shattered the silence of the new day.

"Ah jist mean tuh have all this shit away from mah door. Do whut yuh gotta do Dub, but Ah got mah own work tuh take care of," Leslie said irritably as he whirled on his heels and went back in the house.

Looka Heah Boy, If Yuh Was Uh Woman,
Ah'd Hafta Say…Yuh Slip Was Hangin'!

J.W. rushed over to the smoldering mound, snatched out what was left of the shoes, and threw them into a pail. "Pour that wat'a out, an' git in," he called as he swung into the cab of the truck and dropped the pail on the floor.

Too Tight emptied the remaining water and ran to place the bucket back in the shed.

"Git back up heah Boy," J.W. yelled out the window as he turned the ignition.

"Yassah."

* * *

They traveled again in silence through the eminent crowning of the brightening countryside. Occasional pickups and cars honked a greeting as they passed along the highway. The grumbling of earlier abandoned harvest machinery could be heard in the distance as they came alive and began clawing their way through the crops. Fieldhands, reminiscent of their enslaved grandparents before them, began to trickle into the field to begin their long day under the new sun.

Too Tight felt safe for the moment and was able to breathe slightly easier. But then, he moved his foot. A dull thud resonated up from the floor of the cab. He couldn't feel his heart anymore, he was afraid to look down because he already knew. But he couldn't control his eyes. It was as though they no longer belong to him and against his will, they flitted down to the stubborn ash covered cork sole shoes that lay askew outside of the tin pail.

Too Tight's gaze was locked. He waited breathlessly for J.W.'s wrath to assault the fragile security that sunrise had given him. To his relief, J.W. hadn't noticed and continued to speed down the highway.

The truck jerked abruptly onto a gravel covered dirt road. He recognized the landscape and the looming old abandoned plantation house and barns standing out among the sea of cotton.

Too Tight and Henry Lee had driven the mechanical cotton combine on this piece of land before. He didn't know who actually held this land, but it was rumored that it belonged to a lawman and that he owned hundreds of acres across the Delta.

Bonnie Blue

His eyes strained to see if the Colored man operating the only moving tractor was Henry Lee. His heart curdled when he saw that it was Joe Willie.

Joe Willie epitomized the bitter taste of slavery's 'good niggah'. His life had been one of seeking the approval of White folks, playing the clown and grinning up in their faces. He sat atop that tractor like a king, looking out among his lowly subjects.

J.W. turned onto one of the many empty dirt access roads that snaked deeply through the fields, away from Joe Willie and the group of workers that filed into the grounds. Once again, Too Tight's heart began to pound fiercely; hot breath exploding from his flaring nostrils. He knew that this was where his final battle would be fought and lost. He struggled to contain his raging instincts, a toxic mixture of hate, fear, and fury whirling madly in his head.

'He da dawg gonna die tuhday,' he thought. 'Ah'ma send his cracka ass right back tuh hell! Efen da Lawd don't like it, den we gonna hafta speak on it come Judgment Day!'

Too Tight's body stiffened. He knew that J.W. always carried a pistol in his boots. He shifted his eyes carefully from J.W.'s waist to his boots, searching for any sign of the gun.

His eyes widened as they settled on the butt of a shotgun handle that had slid from its hiding place under the seat and rested, at the ready, behind the heel of J.W.'s outstretched boot. 'Low down mutha fucka thank Ah'ma jist let 'im kill me like uh mad dawg! He gonna hafta fight tuh put me down!' Too Tight's fist clenched with such ferocity that his jagged nails nearly pierced through his calloused palms.

J.W. slowed as he approached the end of the access road where a large red tractor sat unoccupied.

Too Tight forced his eyes away from the gun to search the fields. He knew that, if he didn't put this White man out on the first try, there would be no second chance.

Streams of sweat popped methodically from the thick stubble of hair jutting from his saturated chin. Blood swooshed loudly in his ears, and his fists trembled as he fought to keep them

Looka Heah Boy, If Yuh Was Uh Woman,
Ah'd Hafta Say…Yuh Slip Was Hangin'!

from striking out prematurely. In desperation, he quickly studied his surroundings to determine which direction to run.

The truck finally stopped. Too Tight stared fiercely ahead, ready for the confrontation.

"Take them shoes ovah on the oth'a side of that tree yonda an' bury 'em. Bury 'em deep. Make sho yuh cover 'em ovah good. Then yuh workin' this field. Don't talk tuh nobody. Yuh do, Ah'll know, an' *yuh* ass won't evah be fount."

Dumbfounded, Too Tight's face dropped. He cocked his head to the side, careful to keep his eyes no closer to J.W. than the steering wheel.

"Sah?"

"Gowan! Git out! Ah'll be back later tuh pick yuh up!"

"Yassah," he replied.

Too Tight quickly grabbed the shoes from the pail, jumped from the truck, slammed the door shut, and watched in unsettling silence as J.W. turned his truck around and made his way back down the narrow road.

281

In Chicago, dawn's delicate strokes of colors brushed the new day's sky as the giant city, cold and gray, began to awake. Clusters of sparrows perched secretly on their leaf cloaked branches, chirping a soothing morning sonata.

Once again, sleep had eluded Mamie. She lay next to her mother, watching the ivory lace curtains sway gently on each breeze floating through Alma's bedroom window.

The last time she'd slept in her mother's bed, she was 8 years-old, when the sky had exploded white with lightning and the house shook with thunder. She looked over at her mother, who had finally succumbed to exhaustion. She seemed much older and weaker than she was just one day earlier. Mamie watched in silence as her mother's chest rhythmically rose and fell.

Carefully, she eased from the bed and crept out of the room.

Bonnie Blue

Throughout the night, the telephone screamed out and the doorbell buzzed with family, friends and reporters alike. Many people had come and gone, but some remained; dozing on any piece of comfort that could be found. But the one call that would make her world whole again did not come.

Mamie moved quietly past the well-wishers, careful not to wake them. For now, she just wanted to be left alone with her thoughts.

She resigned to the sun porch and stared out the large window as an orange stripped cat dripped silently over the gray link fence and tiptoed down the sidewalk.

Andrew had called yesterday afternoon. Wheeler and Curtis were hidden at another cousin's home with Elizabeth, in Duckhill. But there was still no word on Emmett's whereabouts.

The authorities wanted her to stay put; not to come down until they knew something. But this perpetual state of helplessness was ripping a jagged hole in her very core.

Humbly, she knelt before the open windows and tilted her head as far back as she could, submitting herself as wholly as she knew how.

"Father," she prayed softly, clasping her hands together, "My holy Father. Help my son Lord. There's just so much hate...so much hate. Bring my baby home safe to me. Guide me. I don't know what to do, Lord," she pleaded as she squeezed her eyes shut and began
to rock gently from side to side. God, please, I'm begging You. Please protect my Emmett. He's just a baby."

She opened her eyes and searched the daybreak for a sign; anything to cling to. But nothing came. Her head sank heavily to her chest and she again closed her eyes as her lips moved faintly in deep prayer.

Alma awoke with a start when her door creaked as Mamie slid from the bedroom. She waited a moment to see if Mamie would return, but then went out in search of her.

Looka Heah Boy, If Yuh Was Uh Woman,
Ah'd Hafta Say...Yuh Slip Was Hangin'!

Alma tiptoed through the maze of outstretched legs in the dining room and into the kitchen, where two women slept at the table; their heads resting on their arms. There was no Mamie. She quietly dodged her way back through the dining room and poked her head into the bathroom. Still, no Mamie. But, when she crossed the threshold to the living room, she saw Mamie's kneeling silhouette through the open French doors.

Alma pressed her right hand gently to her heart and stretched her left arm out towards her kneeling daughter. "Lord," she prayed lowly, "You said where two or more are gathered and agree, it will be done. We abide in Your will, Father. I thank You for sparing the rest of the family and bringing Wheeler and Curtis home safely. I don't know where our baby

283

boy is or what's happened to him Lord, but I do know that whatever happened, You were there in the midst. Please Father, give my child strength and peace in the knowledge that Emmett was your angel first, ours for a time and yours forever more. Amen".

Light rustling etched through the calm of the apartment as the women in the kitchen began to stir. Alma quickly and quietly rushed back into the kitchen to make sure that Mamie wasn't disturbed.

The late summer sky settled on a clear blue canvas as remnants of the night's moon gallantly faded in the distance. Hat crowned Colored ladies gathered at the corner, waiting for the cable
car to take them to their day's work. Automobiles on the street below began to pass with increasing frequency as Chicago began to awake.

Finally, Mamie crawled up onto the sofa and watched as life went on for the people below. Somehow, it all seemed out of order.

"Did you get any sleep last night?" Alma asked as she extended a small glass of orange juice to her.

Mamie's glazed over eyes rose to meet her mothers. "I'm okay. I don't want anything. I'm okay," she said as she began massaging her temples.

Bonnie Blue

She'd accepted the relentless pounding in her head as part of the pain in her heart; which was far greater.

"I've got to get the newspapers. The reporters said the story was going to be in the papers this morning." She rose to leave, but paused when she saw the strain in her mother's face. "You need to drink this," Mamie said as she guided her mother's hand up to her own lips. "Don't worry about me, Mother. I'm fine. You know Emmett would have a fit if he came home and found his grandmother in the hospital."

Alma smiled. "No, we certainly can't have that." She began to swallow the juice.

"Okay, I'm going out to get the papers," Mamie said as she walked lightly back through the web of weary relatives to her mother's bedroom.

Alma followed her daughter and collected a small suitcase from behind the door. "Ruby went over to your apartment for some things last night. She and Ola Mae are in the kitchen. I'll have them come in here and lay down."

"Wait a minute, Mother. I don't think I'm ready for people yet. Just let me get myself together. I know everyone's trying to help but...," she said softly as she lowered herself to the side of the bed. "I just need to..."

"That's alright, baby. You just take your time," Alma said, rubbing her hand lovingly across Mamie's back.

"Mother, that's the problem," she said weakly, looking into her mother's puffy eyes. "We don't have any time. Emmett doesn't

have any time." She inhaled deeply. "Mother, they took my baby. I know he needs me, but...I ..."

"We're going to get him back," Alma said bravely as she fought the familiar burn behind her own eyes and retrieved Mamie's dress from the closet.

"Yes," Mamie said. "and we're going to keep it together and do what we have to do to make sure that Emmett does get home safely." She took the dress from Alma and started out the door to the bathroom, but turned and said, "I'm calling the FBI again. I don't care if they don't want to hear me! I'm going to keep calling them until they do hear me! Somebody's going to tell me

Looka Heah Boy, If Yuh Was Uh Woman,
Ah'd Hafta Say...Yuh Slip Was Hangin'!

something! If they can look for the Lindbergh baby, they can certainly look for Emmett!" She stormed from the room.

"I just thank God that the N-double-ACP has folks down there searching for Emmett!" she called from the small bathroom. "I'm calling him when I think they're in. What was that man's name?"

285

The shrilled scream of the doorbell jolted the apartment awake. The drowsy clan instantly began to collect their senses.

"I've got it," Alma called as she hurried to the door. "Who is it?" she asked anxiously. Perhaps it was some news about Emmett. Maybe he had been found, or worst.

"It's me, Miss Alma," the deep voice on the other side of the door replied. "Gene."

She immediately opened the door to find Gene standing in the hall, arms heavy with different newspapers.

"Oh come in, baby," Alma invited as she opened the door wide and stood back to give him room.

"Is it in there? Did they do the story on Emmett?"

"I don't know. I just went to as many newspaper stands that I could find and bought as many different papers that I could," he said as he piled them on the dining room table. "But with Mamie calling United Press International and the Associated Press, it could be in all of the newspapers across the country this morning."

"Gene, who is that N-double-ACP contact person in Mississippi?" Alma asked as she removed a couple of papers from Gene's arms.

"Medgar, I believe. Medgar Evers is the name. I wrote his phone number in both our books," he said as he pulled a small red telephone book from his shirt pocket. "I didn't want to take a chance on losing it. I think we need to call Mayor Daley too. I know he just got in office, but it can't hurt."

"Hey, man, let me help you with those," Edward, one of Alma's younger cousins said as he removed the floral centerpiece and candles from the table.

"Ya'll got to get up! It's time to get back to work!"

Bonnie Blue

"Where's Mamie?" Gene asked quietly. "How's she doing?"

"I'm fine," Mamie said, rushing past him and grabbing the first newspaper on the pile.

"Alright! Well come on everybody! Get a newspaper," Gene announced.

The apartment became abuzz with anticipation.

"Take your time. Read every little article. Read the ads if you have to. Look for any mention of a missing child," Alma said as she handed newspapers to everyone. "Then, after you're finished, pass it over to someone else to check. In case you overlooked it, someone else might see it."

"Miss Alma," Ola Mae said as she came from the kitchen. "while you're doing that, I'm going to the store for some more grocerie. Ruby's gonna start cooking. Is that okay? Mamie, do you need anything?" Ola Mae asked as she swung her purse onto her shoulder.

"My son," Mamie retorted without looking up.

"Yes, sugar, that's fine. Thank you," Alma said as she glanced over at her daughter. "Look in my purse on the dresser for some money."

"Don't worry about it," Ola Mae said as she flashed Alma a reassuring smile and headed towards the door. "I've got enough money. I'm not sure what's open this early, but I'll find something."

"Mamie, look!" one of the men called from the living room. "I've got something! It's in the *Chicago Defender*!"

"Bring it here!" she said eagerly as she frantically licked her index finger and flipped through the pages of another newspaper. "Mother, here! Look at this! I found another story, here in the *Chicago Daily News*."

They all crowded into the dining room, sounding off like roll call as they confirmed that their plight had gone out over the national news service. There were no front page articles. Most of the mentions of Emmett's kidnapping were small filler stories. But they were surprised and encouraged by that much coverage.

Looka Heah Boy, If Yuh Was Uh Woman,
Ah'd Hafta Say…Yuh Slip Was Hangin'!

"Take every story that you find and put them together over here so we can go through them," Gene called out as he began to organize the family.

"Ruby!" Alma called as she hurried to the kitchen. "Let's get started in here! We've got a lot of folks to get fed!"

* * *

287

The grandfather clock stood guard in the corner of the living room, impatiently thumping out each passing minute as an urgent angry call.

Mamie's scowl set deep in her brow as she retreated to the solitude of the overstuffed floral chair that sat in a corner of the living room next to the telephone. It was still too early to call any agencies.

Mamie hesitated before lifting the receiver from its cradle and slowly dialed Andrew's number. She pressed the receiver harder against her ear with each unanswered ring. Finally, a hoarse voice came through the line.

"Hello?"

"Andrew? Have you heard anything? Have they found Emmett?" Mamie fired, bracing for any news. "Have you heard anything from the sheriff?

"Mamie. Yes, me an' Pa went back down tuh the sheriff's office yesterday evenin'. He wasn't theah. But the Deputy said that they already got Mista Br'ant locked up. Ah ain't nevah heard of White folk gittin' locked up fuh doin' anythang tuh Colored folk. Ah guess we got lucky an' got uh decent White sheriff."

"Yes, he told me that he had already made one arrest and that he was going to keep looking for Emmett. But Andrew," she strained to keep her composure, "he doesn't hold out much hope that Emmett will be found alive."

"He could still be fount alive, Mamie. We jist hafta wait. They might of leff him somewheah. Theah's uh chance that somebody fount him. But, Mamie," he said softly, "yuh know how it is down heah."

"I know." She sighed. "But, he could have been found by some Colored people and they just don't have a way to contact anybody. That's possible," she said, drained. "And, as long as

Bonnie Blue

that's a possibility, that's what I'm hanging on to. Yesterday I called all the newspapers, UPI, and the AP news service. Gene brought in different newspapers, and some of them did have Emmett's kidnapping in them."

"Mamie," Andrew said as his voice perked up, "now they'll hafta do somethin'! Wid the sheriff on our side an' stories breakin' in the pap'as, we got uh good chance of findin' 'im!"

"I know," she said with a glimmer of hope. "I called the FBI yesterday, but they told me to call back today. Now I can let them know that the story has broken in the papers, and they'll have to get involved. I'm calling the mayor's office when it opens and the N-double-ACP said they had someone, a new boy that's going to help search for Emmett. They're the strongest Negro voice we have. With their voice and my voice, dog-gone-it, I'm going to be heard! I've got to wait a few minutes for the offices to open, but I'm going to ask that they send someone over. I don't want to leave the house. The sheriff might call with something."

"Yeah, that's good. The N-double-ACP does have that new office down heah. Ah'ma go ovah theah an' see if Ah kain talk tuh someone."

"Hold on Andrew," Mamie said as she called her mother for Medgar Evers phone number. Alma recited the information from her telephone book as Mamie relayed it to her cousin.

"Okay, Ah got it," Andrew said, his voice getting raspier as it began to fade out. "Look Mamie, Ah got tuh git back down tuh Duckhill an' check on the boys. It's gonna cost mo' money tuh change their train tickets an' buy Mama's, 'cuz she's goin' back wid 'em. We jist don't have it so they gonna hafta stay hid down heah 'til they kain use the return tickets they already got."

You go," Mamie said as she rose from the chair. "I have to start making calls myself. Where's Uncle Mose? Is he safe?"

"Ah'm goin' back out tuh the house an' try tuh git him tuh leave. Ah'm hopin' the White folk ain't got out theah furst."

"He's still at the house?!" she asked. "It's not safe! He shouldn't be there!"

"Yuh know he's tough, but he takin' too big of uh chance." Andrew said, "A'nt Lou want me tuh take hur out tuh talk tuh 'im.

Looka Heah Boy, If Yuh Was Uh Woman,
Ah'd Hafta Say...Yuh Slip Was Hangin'!

Maybe he'll lissen tuh hur an' leave. Ah'll call yuh when Ah git back."

Mamie hung up the phone, glanced over to the grandfather clock, and joined the group in the dining room.

"Mamie," Gene said as he rose from his seat at the dining room table, "sit here and take a look at this one." He slid a front page article across the table to her. There, in the lower corner of the front page; ***Chicago Negro Boy Kidnapped by Mississippi Thugs.***

"Thank you, Jesus," Mamie whispered softly as she read through the article.

Suddenly, the doorbell rang out. Alma pulled herself away from the kitchen table, and rushed to answer the door. She found no one; instead saw two bags of groceries sitting on the threshold.

"Miss Alma," Ola Mae called as she raced back down the stairs to her open car door, "can you have one of the guys come out here and help me with these things?"

"Howard, Robert, go on down and help Ola Mae. Ruby, we can finish up now," Alma called as she carried a bag back to the kitchen.

Gene and Mamie remained at the dining room table, devouring each story, making a list of each newspaper and reporter.

The apartment was soon overflowing with the heavy aromas of coffee, bacon, toast, grits, eggs, and cigarette smoke. Alma brought plates in for Mamie and Gene, who both slid them off to the side and continued their work. The group emerged from the kitchen, holding their plates and planning the day's options.

Mamie waved her hand without looking up and said, "You all are going to have to hold it down."

"You're right. I'm sorry," Howard said as he addressed the room. "Come on, we need to stay in the kitchen."

Surprised, Alma looked at the group as they converged back into the crowded kitchen. "What're you doing? It's hot back here."

Bonnie Blue

"We're distracting them," Howard said concerned, "I don't know that all of us being here is such a good idea right now." He laid his plate on the stove and looked around the room. "I mean, Mamie's got so much that she has to do. We can't do it for her. She knows we're here for her and Emmett, but we don't have to be *right* here. She needs space to think. Gene is here. We need to give her some air. If there's something that she needs any one of us to do, she'll call. We just need to go now."

Howard turned to Alma, gave her a full eagle hug, and whispered, "You call any or all of us whenever you need us."

The group began to scrape their dishes and file out of the house. Ruby and Ola Mae began to stack the plates and run the dish water, but Alma turned off the faucet.

"You know we love you all and appreciate you being here, but I think Howard's right. Right now, Mamie has to keep her mind on what she's doing. And, baby, don't worry about these dishes. It'll be good for me to have something to do later on."

"Are you sure, Miss Alma? It won't take any time," Ruby said as she placed a stray fork on the sink drain.

"You go on," Alma said calmly. "Everything is going to be fine."

"Know that we are all praying for Emmett, Mamie, and you too, Miss Alma."

"Baby, that's the only thing in the world that can help us now."

They took turns kissing Alma on her cheek as they passed her and quietly began collecting their belongings to leave.

Mamie was so engrossed in her work that she hadn't notice everyone leaving until the last person was crossing the threshold.

"What's going on?" Mamie asked. "Where's everybody going?"

"They thought it would be better if they left you alone. But if you want, I'll have them come back."

"No," Mamie said thoughtfully, "that's alright."

Looka Heah Boy, If Yuh Was Uh Woman,
Ah'd Hafta Say...Yuh Slip Was Hangin'!

"Mother?" she said as she rose and searched the photo albums on the bottom shelf of the cocktail table. "We need to look through all of these and pull out all the pictures of Emmett. The papers might need pictures to print in the next set of articles if..." Mamie faltered and inhaled deeply. "...if the sheriff still can't find him."

"Mamie," Gene said as he completed organizing the articles, "it's almost nine o'clock. We need to start making calls. Somebody's office has got to be open by now."

Mamie glanced back up at the grandfather clock and hurried into her mother's bedroom to find the writing tablet of telephone numbers that they had compiled the day before.

"I've got it," she said as she rushed to the telephone in the living room. "I'm calling Sheriff Smith first to see if he's found him yet'."

"Wait a minute, Mamie," Alma said as she pushed the photo albums aside. "We would have heard if he had been found already. The sheriff would have called Andrew or contacted Mose. I think we need to contact the N-double-A-C-P and FBI before calling down there. They need to know we aren't in this alone; that we aren't some frightened, helpless Negros that are going to stand by and do nothing."

Mamie nodded as she snatched up the receiver, stabbing her fingers angrily into the rotary dial.

"Operator." The light pleasant voice greeted her ears.

"Yes, please connect me to the FBI," Mamie said with just a hint of aggravation in her voice.

"Hold please," the operator responded urgently. Instantly, the telephone began to ring.

"FBI. May I help you?" asked a man's voice, void of personality.

"This is Mrs. Mamie Till Bradley. I called yesterday, Sunday, but was told to call back today."

"What's the problem, ma'am?" the man asked impatiently.

Bonnie Blue

292

"My son, Emmett Louis Till, was kidnapped yesterday from my uncle's home in Money, Mississippi. And he hasn't been seen since."

"Where are you calling from?"

"I'm in Chicago. This is where we live; in Chicago. He was down there visiting. He's only fourteen years-old. My uncle said that a group of White men came and took him from the house."

"Ma'am, was he transported across state lines?"

"I don't know where they took him."

"That sounds like a local matter. You need to call the law enforcement officer for that county."

Frustration began to well again, forcing Mamie to speak in a deliberate controlled voice. "Look, sir, I need to speak to an agent."

"I'll transfer you."

"Thank you," Mamie replied, a small layer of aggravation peeling away.

"Agent Beckley," a sharp, business-like voice nearly barked through the receiver.

"Good morning. This is Mrs. Mamie Till Bradley. I called yesterday and was instructed to call back today."

Agent Beckley remained silent.

"My fourteen year-old son, Emmett Louis Till, was visiting my uncle in Money, Mississippi. A group of White men came and kidnapped him early yesterday morning, and he hasn't been seen since."

"Are you Negro?" he asked as he scratched out notes.

"Yes sir. I am."

"Your boy is Negro as well?"

"Yes sir. He is," Mamie replied irritated that he would ask such a question.

"Have you people contacted the local sheriff? This is a local matter." He said as he crumbled the page of notes and tossed it into the trash can.

"Well yes, we have. He has one of the kidnappers in jail now, but they still haven't found Emmett. We need your help," she pleaded.

Looka Heah Boy, If Yuh Was Uh Woman,
Ah'd Hafta Say...Yuh Slip Was Hangin'!

"Look ma'am, it seems like you're already ahead of the game. The local sheriff is doing good by you people. The best way for you to help your boy right now, would be to work with the authorities down there."

"What does the FBI need to get involved?" Mamie asked as she attempted to suppress her growing frustration. "What do you need from us?"

"If you can show that the boy was taken across state lines that would be a start. But barring that, I don't see where there's a need for FBI intervention. Is there anything else I can help you with?" he asked impatiently.

"Bring my baby home," Mamie said strongly. "But, since you can't do that at this time, thank you for speaking with me."

"Have the sheriff in that county give us a call if he suspects that there has been a crossing of state lines. Good luck," he said as he discontinued their conversation.

She hesitated after hanging up the phone before speaking.

"Well, baby," Alma inquired, "What'd they say? Are they going to help us?"

"No, not now," Mamie said with a spark of reassurance, "He did say that Sheriff Smith could contact them if he thinks that they might have grounds to join the search. That was agent Beckley," she said as she scribbled his name in her mother's telephone book. "He said that, if they took Emmett across state lines, then they would definitely have grounds to intervene."

"That's good," Gene said as he sat beside Mamie. "Now, we can call the sheriff, let him know that the FBI has been notified, that the newswires have printed Emmett's story, and that the N-double-ACP is on the case. There are too many people on this for Emmett not to come home."

"I've got to call Mayor Daley's office first. Gene," Mamie said as she massaged the persistent pounding in her forehead. "I'm so glad that you're here."

"Mamie, you need to put something in your stomach before you call anyone else. You can't do much for Emmett if you lose your strength. Even if you aren't hungry, you need to force something down. It might help." He kissed her on the forehead and

Bonnie Blue

disappeared in the kitchen to prepare a small plate of sausage, biscuits and molasses.

Mamie laid her head on the arm of the flower pattern chair, fighting back the exhaustion that was stalking her.

Alma hurried from the bathroom with a small white envelope of 'Standback' powdered aspirin in one hand and a glass of water in the other.

"Here baby, take this."

"What is it?" Mamie asked without opening her eyes or looking up.

"A Standback. Open your mouth."

Mamie held her head back and opened her mouth. Alma emptied the small pile of crushed aspirin onto her ailing daughter's tongue and handed her the glass of water to wash it down.

Gene knelt next to Mamie with a plate of food in his hand. She pinched off a piece of biscuit and reached for the writing tablet.

"Let me try City Hall. The Mayor's office should be open by now."

"Here, I'll get the number for you," Alma said as she began scanning the list of agencies and telephone numbers.

"Mamie, we can use those pictures that you and Emmett had taken last Christmas." She said as she handed her the phone number.

"Thank you, Mother," she said dryly as she began dialing the number. "That would be good. If he is in one of those little hospitals down there, somebody might recognize him."

The telephone began to ring.

"They must not open until exactly nine o'clock," she said as she hung up. "I'm not waiting. I'm calling Sheriff Smith right now."

* * *

George sat alone in the office, with Roy locked up in a tiny cell in the next room. Charlie was across the road, getting

295

breakfast from the café for their prisoner while Ed took another trip to Roy's store in Money to try, once again, to catch up with J.W. or Carolyn.

Looka Heah Boy, If Yuh Was Uh Woman,
Ah'd Hafta Say…Yuh Slip Was Hangin'!

George didn't assume that things would stay this peaceful for much longer. He expected that very soon, truckloads of the Milam-Bryant clan would pull up in front of the jail, demanding that their incarcerated member be released.

He knew that with Chicago being involved, this investigation might become something bigger than what they're used to handling. He grabbed the slender telephone and clicked the switch hook until the operator responded.

"Oparata." A cheery, heavy Southern accented voice danced through his ear piece.

"Mo'nin', Sadie Mae."

"Mo'nin', Sheriff. How ya'll?"

"We fine out heah. Ah run intuh Ernie uh couple days back. He say he was takin' yuh boys out tuh uh new spot tuh do some fishin'."

"Yes suh, he sho did! They leff out well befo' day! Ah made sho tuh pack uh lunch fuh 'em! 'Cuz Ah ain't 'spectin' they gonna catch much of nothin' 'ceptin' maybe some bug bites," she laughed.

"Ah'm sho they'll be glad yuh did, come midday. Look Sadie Mae, Ah need yuh tuh put me through tuh H.C.'s, down at the Tallahatcha County Sheriff's Office."

"Sho thang. Ya'll be good now, yuh heah," she said as she made the connection.

"Sheriff's office." A thick husky voice barked in his ears.

"Mo'nin', H.C. this heah's George out at LaFlora."

"Mo'nin' George. How's thangs goin' down yuh way?"

"We gotta problem. Seem's uh niggah boy got snatched from his kin down in Money. Now, Ah got one of them boys locked up already. He claim he picked up the niggah, but said he was let go."

296

"Aw shit! George, Ah thought yuh said yuh had uh problem. Yuh know niggahs! He's prob'bly laid up wit some lil' niggah gal somewhar!"

"Naw, Ah don't thank so," George said as he leaned back in his chair and sipped from his cold cup of black coffee. "This heah's uh niggah boy down from Ch'caga. Ain't but fourteen an' don't know nobody down heah but his kinfolk."

Bonnie Blue

"Wa'al, yuh jist lookin' tuh make yuhseff uh problem, boy," Strider chuckled. "Lockin' up uh White man ovah this shit? That's whar yuh trouble's comin' from. Whut's wrong wit yuh, George?" he asked. "If he said he let the niggah go, he let 'em go! That boy ain't got no bidness b'hind bars, an' yuh know it!"

Charlie came back through the door carrying a plate of food.

"Ah know these heah boys. They ain't inclined tuh let no niggah walk away if they thank they dun somethin' tuh wrong 'em," George replied as he placed his hand over the mouthpiece, and signaled for Charlie to take the food on back to Roy.

"Whut the niggah do?" Strider asked.

"Well, furst Roy said he whistled at his wife uh few days back. By the time we got tuh the jail, he said he attacked hur. When Ah ask 'im whut he did wit the niggah, he told me they jist took im' out tuh his sto' out by Money fuh his wife tuh see if they got the right one. She said that he weren't the niggah an' he let 'im go. Then he went out tuh Minter City tuh play cards wit his brotha's."

"Naw," Strider laughed, "Ain't no God fearin' White man gonna let that go. He ain't suppose tuh! Ah tell yuh whut, Ah'll be up yuh way in 'bout an hour."

A sudden loud crash burst from the rear of George's office. "Ah'll see yuh when yuh git heah," George said as he hung up and rushed towards the cells in the back room.

Roy had knocked the tray from Charlie's hand sending steaming grits, eggs, and biscuits splattering against the cell wall.

297

His face reddened as he shouted vile obscenities from behind the bars of the small cool holding cell.

"Whut the hell's goin' on back heah?!" George yelled as he barged in the back room.

"Look at whut he dun sheriff!" Charlie yelled frantically as he wiped flicks of hot food from the side of his face.

"Roy, whut the hell's wrong wit yuh? Ah ain't yuh Ma! Yuh cleanin' this shit up yuhself! By the time yuh git somethin' else tuh put in yuh stomach, yuh gonna be good an' hongry!"

Looka Heah Boy, If Yuh Was Uh Woman,
Ah'd Hafta Say…Yuh Slip Was Hangin'!

"George, yuh betta open up this goddamn door an' lemme the hell outta heah! Yuh ain't got uh right tuh keep me locked up! That niggah is…"

"Ah ain't havin' this shit tuhday, Roy! So yuh bes' thank befo' yuh figga out whut kinda fool yuh gonna be!"

The persistent ringing of the telephone caught George's attention.

"Charlie, close that door back up an' git 'im uh towel! Roy, yuh clean it up, or yuh'll be sittin' in it 'til it dries up an' blows away!"

Ed had just walked into the office when George rushed from the back and snatched up the telephone.

"Find that niggah an' make *him* clean it up!" Roy yelled as Charlie grabbed a clean folded towel from the supply closet and tossed it into the cell.

"Sheriff's Office," George said as he shook his head and lowered himself in his cracked leather seat.

"Is Sheriff Smith in?"

"This is Smith."

"Yes, Sheriff, this is Mrs. Bradley, calling from Chicago."

George looked over at Ed, covered the mouthpiece with his hand and whispered, "It's that niggah's Ma from up in Ch'caga."

"Have you found my son? Do you have any more information?" She inhaled deeply, held her breath and braced for any news, good or bad.

298

"No ma'am. We still investigatin'. When Ah git anythang, Ah'll call ya'll."

"Well," Mamie replied, "I've already spoken to the FBI, an agent Beckley, this morning. He says that if Emmett was taken across the state line, then they can get involved. I think you should call and let them know how the investigation is going. Also, the newspapers have printed Emmett's story."

"Whoa! Hol' on thar Mz. Mamie, ma'am! Whut yuh talkin' 'bout? FBI? Newspap'as? We don't need all that! Ah jist need time tuh work on this thang!"

Bonnie Blue

"Well, I'm contacting our mayor up here, and I'm getting the N-double-ACP involved, also. I need to have as many people helping to find my son as I can possibly get."

"Mz. Mamie, ma'am, Ah'ma hafta call yuh back later on this aft'a-noon, earlier if Ah find out somethin'. We're doin' the bes' we kain ma'am."

"I appreciate all of your work, but I can't just sit by and wait."

"Ah unda'stand, but give me time tuh do mah job."

"Sheriff, please call me if you find out anything. I'll be waiting for your call," Mamie said as she hung up the receiver.

* * *

After George hung up the receiver, he signaled for Ed to join him outside. They sat out on the bench in front of the office to discuss what was happening in Chicago without Roy overhearing.

No sooner had they begun discussing how far they should take the investigation, did J.W. pull up in front of the jailhouse.

"Wa'al look yonda, Ed," George said stunned. "Look like yuh ain't gonna hafta go out an' face Mz. Eula an' the boys no time soon."

"Wa'al, Ah'll be," Ed said, standing up in disbelief.

"Ah come out heah tuh see mah brotha. Whar's he at?" J.W. demanded his; bass voice vibrating through their bodies.

"Roy's inside," Ed replied matter-of-factly as he walked back in the office.

299

This was certainly not what Ed expected; J.W., waltzing into the office without a brood of his kin, especially after the reception that he'd received the day before.

George remained outside the office to keep watch. Besides, he was in no hurry to confront J.W.

J.W. followed Ed into the small office.

"Yuh kain call uh lawyer or somebody whenevah yuh want tuh."

Looka Heah Boy, If Yuh Was Uh Woman,
Ah'd Hafta Say...Yuh Slip Was Hangin'!

"Whut ya'll got Roy locked up back thar fuh?" J.W.'s tone became harsher as his stoic presence filled the room with a sudden, inescapable foreboding.

Ed stood behind his desk, leaving his hand hanging in front of the drawer where his .38 lay waiting. "Was yuh wit 'im when he went out tuh git the niggra boy?" Ed asked as he looked up at J.W.'s sun baked, expressionless glare.

"Whar's Roy?"

"Roy's alright. Have uh seat." Ed nodded at the chair next to his desk. "Ah need tuh ask yuh uh few questions."

J.W. didn't break his glare as he lowered his large body into the wooden chair and fought to suppress the urge to grind this 'niggah lovah', under the heel of his boot along with the chicken shit that he'd stepped in earlier.

Ed cautiously took his seat behind his desk where he could grab his gun from the drawer; if the need arose. "Whar was yuh late Saturday night?" he asked, pulling his drawer slightly open. "Did yuh go out thar an' git that lil' niggra boy wit Roy?"

J.W. looked him straight in the face, but said nothing.

"Whut'd ya'll do wit 'im?

J.W.'s indignation was nearly more than he could control; to be interrogated like a common criminal!

300

"Whar was yuh late Saturday night? An', befo' yuh answer, rememb'a the boy's kin already reported that Roy an' at least three oth'a fellas' an' uh woman come out tuh the house. Who yuh thank that woman mighta been?" Ed removed his hat and placed it gingerly on the corner of his antique wooden desk. "Mah b'lief is that it might be Mz. Car'lyn. Whut yuh thank?"

J.W. couldn't believe that the old preacher had not only turned Roy in, but had recounted every single detail of that night. He had an idea of what his brother might have said. One thing was for sure; Roy had been talking and J.W. had to make sure that his brother didn't implicate everyone. He had no choice. He had to shut him up.

Bonnie Blue

"Whar's Roy?" he barked coldly, glaring at Ed. "Whar yuh got mah brotha?"

"He's locked up back thar," Ed replied, attempting to reclaim the interrogation. "But Ah need yuh tuh answer uh couple questions. Now, who was the woman?

"Goddamnit, Ed! Leave hur outta this!" J.W. extended his body upward, towering above Ed, his hot breath blasted rhythmically from his flaring nostrils. "Ah was wit 'im! It was me an' Roy! Whutn't nobody else!"

"Sit down, Dub," Ed said calmly. J.W. hesitated before lowering himself back into the seat. "Okay, whut ya'll do wit the boy?"

It took a moment for J.W. to pull himself together enough to remember why he was there.

"Okay! Roy an' me did go out tuh that niggah preacha's place. We went down thar and bought that Ch'cago niggah out tuh the car tuh talk tuh 'im. Then we leff 'im out thar."

"Okay, then whut'd ya'll do?"

"We went out tuh mah sto' in Minter City an' played cards."

"Yuh boys sho love tuh play yuh cards. Roy say ya'll took 'im back out tuh Money fuh Mz. Car'lyn tuh see if he was the one that disrespect hur. Is that so? Is that whut happened?"

"Yeah, it was like Roy say."

301

"Well, Dub, looks like Ah'ma hafta put yuh und'a arrest fuh kidnappin'. Ah gotta ask yuh tuh surrend'a yuh weapons," Ed said as he motioned for Charlie, who was quietly busying himself at the file cabinet. "Yuh folks kain take 'em home fuh yuh."

J.W. stood, pulled the Colt .45 from the waistband in the back of his pants and placed it on the desk.

"Yuh got anythang else?" Ed asked as he handed the heavy silver handled gun to Charlie.

J.W. propped his foot up on the sheriff's chair, and removed a pistol from in his boot.

"That it?" Ed asked, passing the weapon on to Charlie.

J.W. remained speechless as he reclaimed his defiant stance.

Looka Heah Boy, If Yuh Was Uh Woman,
Ah'd Hafta Say...Yuh Slip Was Hangin'!

* * *

Ed collected the cell keys from his desk drawer and led J.W. back through the door that separated the sheriff's office from the cells.

"Ah ain't cleanin' up this shit!" Roy screamed when the opening door flashed brilliant sunlight into the room.

"Quiet down back heah," Ed demanded calmly. "Yuh got comp'ny."

J.W. didn't turn to look at his younger brother. Instead, he walked straight to the cell across from Roy, which was the only other cubicle in the tiny two cell lockup. Ed unlocked the metal plate on the cell, and J.W. walked in unassisted. With a stern grimace, he grit his teeth as he faced Roy.

"Ah suggest yuh boys reconsider tellin' us whut ya'll did wit the boy or whar yuh dumped the body," Ed said as he closed the door and turned the large skeleton key. "Yuh know Ah'ma find 'im sooner or later. Yuh might as well make it easier on yuhseffs."

Both men's eyes quietly followed Ed as he walked back out to the office. The room dimmed as he pulled the door behind him, leaving it cracked.

As soon as they heard his footsteps fade away, Roy grabbed the bars and whispered, "Whut the hell yuh doin' in

302

heah? Whut's goin' on? He couldn't of fount the niggah that quick. He say they still lookin'."

"Ah had tuh come in heah tuh shut yuh ass up befo' yuh talk yuhseff intuh prison," J.W.'s raspy voice growled. "'Cuz of yuh shit, Ed's been out tuh Ma's lookin' fuh me an' Car'lyn. Whut the hell yuh been sayin', boy?"

"Car'lyn? Car'lyn? Whut he want wit hur? She ain't had nothin' tuh do wit nothin'! Goddamnit!" He raged as he paced back and forth. "He ain't even fount the body an' he goin' 'round lockin' up folks! Tryin' tuh lock up uh White woman, mah own wife! Ovah uh niggah? Soon's Ah git outta heah, Ah'ma take care of his ass, mahseff!"

J.W. strained to see through the crack at the end of the hall and grimaced. "Shuddup, Roy!" he demanded. "All this shit is yuh own damn fault! Yuh damn neah got caught when yuh killed that

Bonnie Blue

niggah las' year! If yuh didn't go stickin' yuh chest all out an' tellin' folk all yuh bidness, we wouldn't be sittin' in heah now! Don't yuh know that's why Ed's aft'a yuh dumb ass? Look at yuh! Yuh still ain't learnt uh damned thang! Talkin' loud an' actin' uh fool! Yuh behind bars an' Ah had tuh git mahseff locked up jist tuh keep yuh from diggin' uh deeper hole fuh yuhseff an' the rest of us!"

"Whut yuh talkin' 'bout? How'd he git yuh?"

"Shuddup, an' lissen," J.W. repeated as he pressed his face as close to the bars as he could and attempted to whisper, "Whut the hell did yuh tell 'im?"

"All Ah said was that Ah took 'im down tuh the sto' fuh Car'lyn to see. He weren't the one, an' Ah let 'im go. Then Ah went tuh play cards. Whar's Car'lyn an' mah boys?"

"That was all he needed tuh lock yuh up! Soon's yuh said yuh took that niggah from the house, he got yuh on kidnappin'!"

"Ed musta tricked me!"

"An' that ol' niggah preacha went runnin' straight tuh the law. He told 'im evahthang. Soon's Ah git outta heah, Ah'ma pay that sonna-bitch uh visit. Ah warned 'im. This shit's on 'im too," J.W. said as he paced impatiently in his cell. "An' yuh jist struttin' 'round tryin' tuh hold up yuh damn pride at the risk of brangin' the whole family down."

"Whar's Car'lyn an' mah boys?" Roy asked again, close to tears. "He kain't go aft'a mah wife."

"Don't make no mistake an' short change that man. Ah thank he'll do anythang tuh git back at yuh," J.W. said sternly. "Boy, yuh gotta start usin' yuh head. We got folks workin' on the outside. Willie Clyde's takin' Car'lyn an' the boys out tuh his place. He ain't nevah gonna find hur out thar, so that ain't uh problem."

"Whut 'bout yuh niggahs? We gotta git rid of 'em. Ain't no tellin' who all they been talkin' tuh," Roy said, wide eyed and rattled.

"Like Ah said, we got some boys on the outside that's takin' care of them too."

Looka Heah Boy, If Yuh Was Uh Woman,
Ah'd Hafta Say…Yuh Slip Was Hangin'!

* * *

Tallahatchie County was one of the Delta's most devout enforcers of the remaining slave culture, and Sheriff, H.C. Strider was the elected overseer. Strider had established himself as the iron law in this county for many years. He had the respect of White citizens and the fear of Colored ones. Not one single Colored person had ever successfully filed a report against a White person in the county.

When George called him about the missing Colored boy from Chicago, Strider was more curious than concerned. He had no doubt that, if the boy came up against any White men in the area, there would be nothing left to find, but a hollow shell.

Strider strapped on his gun and grabbed his hat. "Percy!" he called back to where his deputy was sweeping the empty jail cells. "Percy, Ah need yuh tuh stay heah! Ah got tuh go on out tuh LaFlora! They got niggah trouble, an' George kain't handle it!" he laughed as he eagerly headed out the door.

"Okay, boss! Yuh sho yuh don't want me tuh come wit yuh?"

"Stay heah!" he called as he pounded down the two steps from the sun-bleached, wooden sidewalk to the packed dirt ground. "Hey, Percy!"

"Yeah, boss!"

"When Bubba git heah, send 'im on down tuh LaFlora! We most likely be down at the Bottoms!"

* * *

Strider soon found himself parking alongside George's squad car. "Hey, ya'll!" he called.

"Hey, H.C. Glad yuh come out," George said as he slammed the trunk of his squad car shut and bent down to Strider's window. "Ah'ma tell yuh," he said quietly, "Ah gotta real mess on mah hands. This niggah's out from Ch'caga. His kinfolk been callin' down heah, an' now they dun foolt 'round an' got the Fed'ral BI, the newspap'as, that 'Sociation fuh niggah folk, an' God knows who all else involved!"

Bonnie Blue

"Goddamnit, George! Who is this niggah? Ain't no sucha thang as uh im'po'ant niggah, is it?"

"Hell, Ah don't know," George said as he walked over to his squad car, wiping the sweat from his neck with the handkerchief that he kept in his front shirt pocket. "All Ah know is, that niggah ain't 'bout tuh be fount walkin' 'round on this side of the grave. All we kain do is try an' find whar they dumped the body."

"Yuh had any visitors yet? Any of the boys come out tuh see 'bout junior," Strider said with a laugh.

"Wa'al, the damndest thang jist happened," George said almost to himself as he shoved the dampened cloth back in his shirt pocket. "Big Milam, Dub hisself, waltzed right in mah office an' turnt hisself in! Said it was jist the two of 'em. Him an' Roy."

"Yuh b'lieve 'em, don't yuh? Ah mean, it don't make no since tuh walk intuh uh jail jist tuh tell uh lie an' git yuhseff locked up," Strider replied confused.

"We'll see," George said as he slid into his squad car and turned the ignition.

* * *

305

They drove through the tiny business district toward the highway. Their tires crackled as they sped over the sun softened tar, which coated the blacktop highway.

Soon, they stopped their cars on the side of the road in the Bottoms and began their meticulous search through the wooded slopes.

They descended deep into the cool, dense collection of foliage along the banks of the Tallahatchie River. With each calculated step, the voiceless guardian of the thick, cool mud sucked at their boots; as vacuums. Occasionally, a partially unearthed piece of clothing or old shoe would draw their attention.

"Wa'al, George," Strider said as he became tired and hungry, "we been out heah fuh uh good lil' while now, an' ain't fount uh damned thang. Ah gotta git back down mah own way. Bubba was suppose tuh meet me out heah hours ago. Ain't no tellin' whut's happenin'. Yuh know they good men, but they ain't none too bright leff on they own."

Looka Heah Boy, If Yuh Was Uh Woman,
Ah'd Hafta Say…Yuh Slip Was Hangin'!

"Yeah, Ah know. An' lemme tell yuh, Ah sho 'preciate yuh comin' down heah," George said as he gazed across the wide murky waters of the Tallahatchie. "If he's down heah, we'll find 'im soon 'nough. Ah thank it bes' Ah git back tuh the jail, too. Gotta check on the boys. Been gone too long as it is," George said as he sighed, took off his hat, and wiped his forehead with the back of his hand. "Ain't no tellin' who all else dun turnt theyseffs in!"

"Yeah boy!" Strider laughed as he headed back up the embankment. "Yuh got some right cooperative criminal types down yuh way!"

"Ah ain't sho whut it means," George said as he trailed him up through the slick mud and weeds. "but yuh betta b'lieve, thar's somethin' b'hind it. Ah'm goin' out tuh Mz. Eula's tuh see whut Ah kain find out. Las' thang Ah need is fuh the Fed'ral BI tuh be tellin' me how tuh run mah investigation!"

"Lemme know whut else Ah kain help yuh wit. We kain't afford tuh have them damn lib'rals comin' down heah tellin' us how tuh run our own bidness. Befo' yuh know it, they'll be swarmin' all 'round down heah, jist takin' ovah! B'sides, Ah woulda thank they got bigg'a thangs on they mind then tuh be worrahin' 'bout one lil' niggah!"

Finally, they broke through the cooling shade of the Bottoms and began their trek through waves of heat, back down to their squad cars.

* * *

Sheriff Strider cruised easily down the highway towards his office. He couldn't understand what was actually happening. White men don't just turn themselves in for kidnapping 'niggahs'. And why would the Federal Government care? None of it made sense.

He parked once again in front of his office and was immediately met by his deputy, Bubba Garland.

"Whar the hell yuh ass been? Didn't Percy tell yuh tuh meet me down in LaFlora at the Bottoms? Goddamn!" Strider cussed as he slammed his squad car door. "Ah ask yuh tuh do one damn thang, an' yuh ass kain't even do that!"

Bonnie Blue

"Hold on thar, H.C." he whispered, "Yuh had uh call from Byron. He say he need yuh tuh give 'im uh call soon's yuh git back. He say it was impo'tant."

"Byron?! Wa'al, Ah'll be damned! That sonna-bitch! Did he say whut he want?" Strider laughed as he walked into his office, went straight to the telephone and tapped the switch-hook a few times.

"Aft'a-noon, Sheriff," the operator's thick accent greeted lazily across the line. "How ya'll?"

"We alright out heah, Sadie Mae. How's yuh folks?"

"Pa's foots is painin' 'im from the gout. But yuh know Pa. He ain't 'bout tuh let no lil' pain stop 'im."

"Ah know, stubborn as uh mule! Tell 'im Ah say 'hey'! Looka heah Sadie Mae, Ah need yuh tuh put me through tuh Frenchie! Byron De La Beckwit! Out by Greenwood, thar 'bouts!"

"All right, ya'll take care now," The operator said as she connected the call.

The telephone rang only twice before a harsh cautious voice answered, "Yeah?"

"Hey thar Frenchie. Ah got yuh message."

"Lissen. Me an' the boys need fuh yuh tuh do somethin' fuh us. We gotta couple of niggahs we gotta git rid of. Kain't have no bodies lyin' 'round jist now, so we need tuh hide 'im out. Jist at night. They asses' kain work durin' the day. Mah friend losin' money as it is."

Frustrated, Strider switched the telephone earpiece to his other ear and asked, "Now, whut the hell's goin' on out thar? George from out LaFlora way, had me lookin' fuh some lil' niggah an' says Big Milam walked in an' admitted takin' 'im. Is that yuh friend? Whut the hell's goin' on?"

* * *

Too Tight's throbbing headache had eased to a dull pain. He had been perched atop the tractor since the early morning. With the exception of Joe Willie and his tractor in the distance, he had only seen fieldhands working far from the remote plot that he was ordered to plow. But now, he was alone.

Looka Heah Boy, If Yuh Was Uh Woman,
Ah'd Hafta Say…Yuh Slip Was Hangin'!

It was just the day before that the boy was tortured and killed. But, he was still alive. Too Tight still didn't know if Henry Lee had been killed. He hadn't seen him since they buried the boy's clothes. Why had J.W. and Leslie not killed him when they had the chance? What were they waiting for? How were they going to do it…and when?

Almost as an answer to his mental interrogation, a cloud of dust chased a blue vehicle down the dirt access road towards him.

"Aw, shit," he mumbled as panic suddenly overtook him. He quickly whipped his head around the field, searching for anybody. Even Joe Willie would have been a reassuring sight. But the field was empty.

There was no one else out there except the stranger in the car speeding through the fields. He wanted to run, but his legs

308

were frozen. His onyx skin glistened from the day under the blistering sun, as turbulent rivers of sweat raced down his neck, disappearing into his saturated tee shirt.

Too Tight's eyes became transfix on the ominous cloud of dust barreling through the field, growing larger and drawing nearer. His chest pained as his stressed heart leaped about in a spastic frenzy. Suddenly, his pants became saturated with a flood of urine like a cow, peeing on a smooth rock.

The cloud abruptly stopped a short distance away from him and quickly began to dissipate; settling back into the tiny dirt road that birthed it. The loud slamming of the car door tore through the peaceful countryside. He remained frozen; unable to breathe. He knew that his end was nearing.

"Oh God, please help me." He moaned, "Dey 'bout tuh kill me, Lawd. Please don't let dem kill me, Jesus. Ah couldn't do nothin' tuh stop dem wid dat boy. Please Lawd, don't let 'im kill me out heah. Ah know Ah said some mean thangs tuh yuh Lawd, but Ah ain't mean it. Ah sweah, efen Yuh save me..."

"Git on down from thar Boy!" Melvin called as he came quickly upon the tractor. "We gotta go!"

"Yassah," Too Tight mumbled carefully.

Bonnie Blue

Too Tight inhaled deeply before casting his weary eyes heavenward and began his decent.

Melvin turned and walked rapidly back through the field to his car with Too Tight trailing close behind.

"Niggah, who yuh been talkin' tuh out heah? Yuh seent anybody out heah while yuh was workin'?"

"Nossah," Too Tight replied timidly. "Ah ain't seent nobody."

"Git in," Melvin said dryly as he climbed into the driver's side of the car and closed the door.

Too Tight looked around one last time, slid into the back seat behind Melvin, and closed the door.

They traveled quickly through the field and out onto the gravel road that led to Highway 3. Too Tight kept his face to the window, afraid to look in the rearview mirror; afraid of what he would see in this man's face. He had no idea where he was being taken, but he did know it would lead to no good. Many times along the road, he thought of escaping by jumping from the speeding car, but he knew that his temporary freedom would ultimately result in a bullet ripping through his body.

The late afternoon sun hung low in the skies as Melvin sped down the highway. They passed another town before turning onto a long private drive that led to a large dull, brick building set far back from the road.

Too Tight knew that he was in Charleston. He'd been in this town a few times before and knew that the foreboding structure
in front of him was the Charleston jail. He was flooded with conflict, as he began to fidget and look around.

A sinister aura looming around the building seemed to thicken as the duo drew nearer.

"Yuh gonna stay heah tuhnight," Melvin said coldly as he pulled to a halt just outside the jail. "Somebody'll pick yuh up early mo'nin' tuh do road work. Don't yuh talk tuh nobody. Yuh unda'stand me? If yuh do, yuh dead. Like Dub said, if anybody ask yuh whut yuh in heah fuh, tell 'em yuh und'a investigation fuh

Looka Heah Boy, If Yuh Was Uh Woman,
Ah'd Hafta Say...Yuh Slip Was Hangin'!

cleanin' blood out the back of uh pickup aft'a deer season was ovah."

"Yassah," Too Tight replied gratefully. "Ah sweah, Ah ain't openin' up mah mouf."

Bubba rushed out the front door of the jail. "Hey! How ya'll?" he called as he approached the car.

Melvin stepped out of the car and pulled Bubba to the side to talk.

"Yeah, Ah got word. Don't worrah, Ah'll take 'im from heah," Bubba said as he walked back to the car.

"Alright, niggah! Git out!"

310

Too Tight looked to Melvin for direction.

"Yuh heard 'im! Git out the car, an' rememb'a whut Ah told yuh!"

"Yassah," Too Tight said as he scrambled out the car and carefully shut the door.

Melvin made a 'U' turn and sped back towards the highway.

"Okay, niggah, move yuh ass!" Bubba barked as he pushed Too Tight ahead of him.

Too Tight had never been in this jail before, but he was thankful because he knew that being locked up behind bars was a hell of sight better than being nailed in a coffin. He had no idea what was going on, but at least, he was still alive…for now anyway.

BOOK EIGHT

MISSISSIPPI LAW…

The secret peace of midnight blue skies began to fade, making way for the awakening of the new day. Seventeen year-old Bobby Hodges was nuzzled in the corner of his living room draped in a dingy, worn out sheet. Unfortunately, Bobby's sweat plastered hair piqued the interest of a large green blowfly.

After the fly's many passes and landings, Bobby gave up the fight to return to sleep and lay in wait for his nemesis to buzz across his head again. When the amplified buzzing settled back on his head, he quickly thrust his hand out from under the sheet and swatted the fly against his covered ear. With his lifeless foe finally laid out on the floor, Bobby pushed the rest of the sheet off, tiptoed around his sleeping siblings stretched out on the floor, and left out the back door.

Bobby was the eldest of six children in the Hodges household. His parents, like many White tenant farmers, made a meager living doing odd jobs for the landlord and farming the grounds that had been overworked and under fertilized.

B.L. Mims, the owner of a motorboat rental business, had agreed to let Bobby use one of his motorboats for free; if he ran a trout-line for him.

Mississippi Law...Love Me, Love Mah Dawg!

Usually, Bobby let his thirteen year-old brother tag along, more to keep him company than to do any actual work. But last night witnessed another battle with his younger brother who was now feeling as grown-up as he was.

Bobby wanted a peaceful morning, so he left his brother sound asleep on the floor, balled in a knot with his thumb hanging out the side of his mouth on the slippery bed of spit.

He never liked running the trout-line alone on the river. The days were always long, the sun was always intense, and the mosquitoes were relentless in their quest to satisfy their thirst.

Between the thunderstorm and the field work that he did yesterday, Bobby had little time on the river.

But this day looked to be different. The scrawny young man quickly collected the can of night crawlers that he'd dug up the night before, grabbed his fishing poles, and set out on foot up the road towards the Tallahatchie River and Mims' dock.

Dew covered grass sparkled, as the brightness of the new day began to spread across the open blue sky. The two and a half mile walk to the dock went by rapidly, and as always, Bobby spent this time daydreaming about what his life would be like when he grew up and had his own boat rental business.

* * *

Soon, "BOAT RENTAL" with a crudely painted arrow pointing down a worn path to the dock below, appeared at the side of the road, nearly hidden by the overgrowth of weeds.

"Hey, ya'll!" A friendly voice called from behind an upturned motor of one of the small boats. "Whar's yuh co-pilot at?"

"Mornin' Mista Mims, suh!" Bobby called excitedly as he ran down to where B.L. Mims was repairing one of his outboard motors.

"Ah reckon Ah bes' gowan out on mah own tuhday. Them youngins don't do nothin' but git in uh man's way," he said as he put his can of worms in the boat that he always uses; the one that he fancied his own.

All of the equipment that he needed to run the trout-line was already loaded and ready to go.

Bonnie Blue

"Whar yuh plannnin' tuh drop yuh line at?" Mims asked as he stretched and cracked his back. "Gotta be uh heap betta then it was yesttidy. That was uh might sorrah haul. Didn't brang back 'nough tuh feed mah cat!"

"Yes suh. It was uh might po' day, but Ah b'lieve if Ah gowan out by Pecan Point, Ah'll have mo' luck. Ain't uh lotta folks goin' that far down rivah. But tuh make sho, Ah catch me somethin', Ah'ma toss in some of mah own lines right down rivah from yuh dock. Stick 'em in an' prop 'em up. Ah'm bound tuh catch somethin' by the time Ah git back."

313

"Yuh jist git started. Ah don't know whut yuh thank yuh gonna catch down thar. Them ol' catfish is feedin' way down in the bed of the rivah. Ah tell yuh whut," Mims said as he tossed two thick, hand sliced baloney sandwiches wrapped in wax paper towards Bobby, "yuh jist gowan an' git started. Thar's some old boys dun took off up the rivah uh lil' while ago. Ah'll set up yuh poles. Yuh jist git on out thar befo' all our fishs git snagged."

"Thank yuh, Mista Mims suh. Ah 'spect Ah'll be gittin' powerful hongry up in the day," Bobby said gratefully as he placed the sandwiches up by the steering wheel, next to the worms and the bucket of water where his catch would be kept until he returned later that afternoon. "An' don't yuh worrah none! Ah ain't comin' back 'til Ah dun caught 'nough fish tuh feed yuh Mizzus, all yuh chil'ren an' yuh cats!"

Bobby grabbed the wooden handle of the starter cord and gave it one hard jerk. After three tries, the motor roared to life. Smoke bellowed from its core as the small motorboat lurched forward.

"Make sho yuh go by the bend thar an' check them lines yuh already got runnin'!" Mims called after him. "Should be somthin' caught up on 'em by now!"

Bobby waved back at Mims as he glided across the smooth, wide and murky river.

He navigated carefully along the middle of the tainted waters; careful not to get floating branches or other debris caught in the small propeller.

Mississippi Law...Love Me, Love Mah Dawg!

Bobby called a friendly, "Hey ya'll!" as he past the old timers sitting in their rowboats; bating their hooks.

He quickly ate through two miles of the river's crust. The water was calm and empty, except for dragonflies that danced just above the surface and the occasional snake that skimmed lightly across the rivers skin. Bobby, like many of his peers, feared venturing too far out on the river alone. But there were times when he relished the solitude.

Bobby turned the motor off in the middle of the river and began to unwrap one of his dried sandwiches. Slowly, he became aware of a peculiar smell which rapidly became an overwhelming stench, settling as an iron hand over the still waters.

In the distance, damned up among the floating branches and algae, he noticed something jutting out of the brown water, swaying with the motion of his gentle wake.

He was curious, but didn't want to chance damaging Mims' motorboat. He stood to jerk at the starter cord to move further away from the smell, but his attention continued to be drawn to the odd looking object bobbing in the water.

Giving into temptation, he detached an oar from the floor of the boat and paddled slowly towards the small gathering of timber. As he drew near the pile, he pinched his nose and leaned to one side of the small boat. He knew it had to be something that died. Maybe a dog or some other large animal, but he couldn't get close enough to make out what it was. A piece of driftwood slowly worked itself loose from the dead tree stump which protruded from its watery dwelling. He strained to make out, what seemed to be waving to him.

"Good God Ahmighty." he murmured in disbelief.

Bobby made many clumsy attempts to pull the cord before the motor successfully spurted and began whipping the propellers. He had never operated the boat at full throttle, but he couldn't get away from that tree and its peculiar fruit, fast enough.

The turbulent wake that trailed him crashed violently against the bank as he sped around the bend. He quickly checked

Bonnie Blue

the lines and threw the fish, alive and still jumping, into the bucket of water. He carefully baited the poles and sped back up the river to Mims' dock.

Bobby was still a distance out in the river when he began waving wildly and screamed out to his father, who stood on the dock collecting money from a customer to rent a boat that he had just repaired.

"Pa!" He yelled frantically as he waved wildly. "Pa! Uh dead body! Up rivah!" But he was still too far out for his father to make out what he was saying.

His father quickly completed his transaction with the customer and waited for Bobby to come closer to the dock.

"Hey thar boy! Whut happen?" He smiled. "Yuh dun run up on one of them giant catfishs yuh always talkin' 'bout?"

"No, suh! Yuh gotta come! Yuh gotta come out an' see fuh yuhseff," he yelled as he came closer. "Ah'm tellin' yuh, Pa, thar's uh dead body out thar in the wat'a! Ah b'lieve it's uh niggah! Least ways, Ah thank it is! Might be uh White, but Ah kain't tell fuh sho! Legs look kinda funny color! But we gotta git the sheriff!" he cried out as he nearly fell from the boat.

"Whut's that yuh say? Uh dead niggah?" his father asked, slightly surprised.

"Yes suh! Right on the oth'a side of the bend! Could be uh White, though! Like Ah said, it look kinda gray! Kain't tell fuh sho," Bobby said excitedly as he leaped from the boat and pulled it onto the bank next to the dock.

"C'mon!" His father said, annoyed that his work had been interrupted.

They walked rapidly up the unpainted, wooden planks that led to Mims' handmade shack, which served as both his home and office.

* * *

Mims sat comfortably on his rickety wooden chair, balancing his breakfast plate on his lap while crunching on a thick strip of fried pig skin.

Mississippi Law...Love Me, Love Mah Dawg!

"Hey, ya'll!" he called, grinning at the couple running up his wooden walk. "Ah'll give yuh uh boat, but Ah ain't givin' yuh mah food!"

"B.L.! Bobby say he dun fount uh dead niggah up rivah! Maybe we outta call the law!"

316

B.L. Mims had inherited his motorboat rental business from his father. And like his father, he had conducted his business along this segment of the Tallahatchie. Over the years he had witnessed the recovery of many anonymous Colored victims, men and women, rising to the surface; floating face down in the brown waters of the river. Although this wasn't an everyday occurrence, it wasn't so unusual that the idea was unnerving.

"Wa'al, it appears tuh me, the dead don't do no whole lotta walkin' nor swimmin' 'round, so Ah thank Ah'll jist finish mah breakfust that mah Emma dun fixed me. Whut say Ah give the sheriff uh call aft'a Ah finish up heah," he said as he continued to gnaw on the tough fried pig skin. "Sheriff mos' likely ain't in yet, noway."

* * *

Bobby finished setting the lines, making sure that he stayed clear of the bend in the river and the peculiar looking body that seemed to wave for help.

By late morning, he was back home doing yard work. His younger brother listened eagerly as they pulled weeds in their mother's garden and he relayed the morning's adventure.

"Ooooh Bobby, yuh shoulda woke me up!" his brother said excitedly. "Ah woulda hauled that niggah up in the boat wit them fishs."

Suddenly, Bobby saw his father beckoning him from the road. He was flanked by Mims and a uniformed lawman.

"Mah god!" his younger brother said with excitement. "It's the law! Yuh sho 'nuff in trouble now, Bobby!"

* * *

Bobby tore through his mother's garden, through the weeds and dodged around the trees, to reach the road where the adults waited.

Bonnie Blue

"Slow down, boy," the Deputy Bubba said as he caught hold of the boy charging towards him. "Yuh the one say thar's uh niggah hung up out thar in the rivah?"

"Yes, suh! But like Ah told mah Pa, it was funny color," Bobby replied, still out of breath. "But Ah seent it plain as day!"

317

"Deputy, if yuh ain't needin' me, Ah got work tuh do," Bobby's father said as he walked away.

"Wa'al, befo' we go off halfcocked," Bubba said as they started walking back toward the dock. "we bes' jist take uh ride out thar tuh make sho whut we lookin' at."

As they got close to the dock, Mims called out to his youngest brother, "Fred!" he called excitedly as he looked back at the distress etched in Bobby's face. "Fred! Git on out heah, boy, we goin' tuh find that niggah! Yuh gonna wanna see this!"

"Mista Mims, we gotta hurry," Bobby pleaded.

"Aw hell, boy! If it's uh niggah, dead or lazy, it sho ain't goin' nowhar! Relax!"

A long, gawky young man appeared in the doorway. "Yeah, B.L.! Yuh catch somethin'?" he asked as he eased out of the door.

"C'mon down heah! We goin' down rivah tuh take uh look at that niggah Bobby caught this mo'nin'!"

"Mista Deputy, suh," Bobby asked as he grabbed at a wooden pole to anchor his motorboat to the dock, "ain't we gotta git the funeral coach down heah?"

"Now yuh jist hold on thar boy," Bubba said with rising aggravation. "Ah gotta make sho it ain't some oth'a kinda animal, got hisself caught up out thar. Don't make no sense callin' fuh the coach when it ain't nothin', an' Ah end up lookin' the fool."

Fred's long leisure gait seemed labored, as he made his way down the wooden planks to the dock.

"Hurry up, Fred!" Mims yelled as he climbed in the boat.

Fred increased his stride and cautiously stepped one foot into the side of the boat tipping it. His brother grabbed his hand and pulled him in the rest of the way.

"Okay, let's go find yuh niggah," Mims laughed as he took his position in the rear with the outboard.

Mississippi Law...Love Me, Love Mah Dawg!

* * *

The full boat skimmed across the opaque, brown water, while sunburned fishermen yelled obscenities at the speeding motorboat that created violent wakes, frightening the fish away.

318

"How far down?" Bubba called above the noise.

"Down rivah, right past the bend!" Bobby hollered as he pointed excitedly up the river.

Mims kicked up the power. The front of the small boat popped up as he sped around the wide bend in the Tallahatchie.

In the distance, the dead tree that dammed in driftwood from the earlier storms marked Bobby's curious find.

"Thar!" he called as he projected his arm towards the branchless dead tree. "It's ovah thar!"

Mims cut the motor as they neared the tree. The boat rocked as he stood to peer into the mound of wood.

"Kain yuh see it?" Fred asked as he clung to the sides and tried to steady the boat.

"Ah don't see it, but Ah kain sho as hell smell it. Somethin's dead in thar. Bobby, grab that oar an' brang me 'round tuh whar yuh saw it."

"Yes, suh," He eagerly grabbed an oar and gently propelled them towards the mound of debris. "It's right up in thar. Close tuh the tree wit them funny lookin' roots hoistin' it up out the wat'a."

"Kain yuh see anythang B.L.?" Fred asked again as they made their way past some dead wood.

"It's uh might hard tuh see anythang out heah wit all them branches bunched up thar." Mims said softly as he strained to see past the thick branches.

"Ah b'lieve it's one of them wild dogs dun got hisself caught up," Fred called as he peered around his standing brother.

"Ain't no dog smell like this. Ah smelt this befo'. It's uh body sho 'nuff. Gotta be uh niggah," Bubba said quietly as he leaned closer to the driftwood. "White folk don't end up in heah."

Suddenly, Bubba caught sight of the object that Bobby saw, swaying in the water.

Bonnie Blue

"Look yonda," Bubba said. "Ah thank Ah see somethin'. Help me move this stuff out the way! Looks like somethin's stickin' out!"

319

"That's whut Ah seent!" Bobby said excitedly. "We gotta go git the sheriff!"

"Yeah boy, Ah b'lieve yuh right. Somethang's dead. Don't know if it's uh niggah or uh White, but whutevah it is, it's sho 'nuff dead. Move that branch thar out the way. Ah gotta make sho."

Bobby and Fred took the oars and maneuvered the driftwood and a large branch away from the pile, fully exposing two swollen, grayish looking legs bobbing in the water.

"Aw, shit! Goddamn!" Mims shouted excitedly. "It's uh dead niggah, sho 'nuff!"

Fred's stomach gripped into a knot. He slapped his hand over his mouth, but it was too late. Chunks of undigested breakfast spewed from his convulsing stomach into the river.

"See? Ah told ya'll," Bobby called as he pointed excitedly at the two bloated legs bobbing among the rubble. "Ah knew it was uh dead body!"

"Okay. Alright. Ain't no need in gittin' yuh drawlz all balled up in a knot," Bubba said calmly. "We gonna need uh rope an' anoth'a boat tuh tow it back."

"Whutevah yuh need." Mims said as he ripped the starter cord. The motor once again began to roar. "Let's jist git outta heah befo' Ah git sick mah damned seff!"

Bobby fell back as the boat popped up and ripped through the serene tiny ripples that shimmered brilliantly in the sun.

* * *

Bobby's father rushed to the dock when he saw the small boat cut its speed and cruise into the wooden slip. He hated to get behind in his daily routine, but he could tell that his son must have discovered something.

He had to help move this thing along if he was going to get all of his own work done.

"Whut yuh need!" he yelled as they came nearer.

Mississippi Law...Love Me, Love Mah Dawg!

"Fred! Grab that rope out the shed!" Mims yelled as he stepped out of the boat onto the rickety dock. "Bobby, yuh an'

320

yuh Pa, git uh hold of that rowboat ovah yonda thar an' swang it 'round heah!"

The dock was soon busy with excitement. It wasn't long before the empty row boat, connected by a heavy rope, was skimming back up the river behind the group of men.

"Thar!" Bobby called to his father as they approached the legs sticking out from the debris.

"We see it, boy!" His father said as he cut the motor and began pulling the empty boat closer.

"Swang that boat ovah this way!" Bubba called. "Hey B.L., pull that branch out the way so Ah kain git tuh the legs!"

"Wait! Wait!" Mims called. "That ain't no lil' branch! Looka thar!" he said as he pointed. "It's still connected tuh that tree whut fell ovah in heah!"

After a considerable amount of time and sweat, they were finally able to get the rope around both of Emmett's legs.

"Goddamnit!" Mims called as they pulled hard on the rope to free the body. "This heah niggah's heavy as hell!"

Bubba loosened his grip on the rope and wiped the sweat dripping from his chin. "Gotta be some kinda weight on 'im."

"Whut'd yuh say we tow it down rivah tuh shallow wat'a?" Bobby's father asked. "Check an' see whut it's anchored tuh."

Finally, they were able to maneuver the body free from the dam of branches, stumps and logs. Slowly they dragged the body and its weight downstream. They cut the motor and rowed until they hit shallow water and the body was visible.

The men soon found themselves fighting to hold their balance as they slipped and sloshed around in the muddy water; refusing to succumb to the heat and overwhelming stench of the rotting corpse. Working as quickly as they could, they cut the barbed wire from the fan and loaded the heavy cotton gin fan and the bloated remains into the row boat.

Bonnie Blue

* * *

Sheriff Strider arrived at his office much later than usual and prepared himself to spend another day of futile searching with George. He wasn't surprised that they had found nothing along the bank of the river or in the wooded areas where so many other bodies have been discovered. The truth was; after talking with Byron, he didn't expect that the boy's body would ever be found.

He drove leisurely through the town, waving and calling out a greeting to merchants that were already open for business.

Strider caught a glimpse of one of his deputies, Ben Madison, leaning against the wooden beam outside of the office eating from a large Mason jar of buttermilk and cornbread; his morning ritual.

"Hey H.C.!" Ben called when Strider eased the squad car to a halt in front of his office. "Yuh want me tuh go out wit ya'll this mo'nin'?"

"Ain't no need," Strider said as he frowned at the Mason jar and brushed past him. "Ah'm goin' out tuh git Bubba. We meetin' up wit George down at LaFlora. Ah'ma need yuh tuh stay 'round heah."

"Yeah, but ain't nothin' happenin' out heah," Ben pleaded as he followed him in the office. "An' b'sides, Bubba dun already come in heah earlier on an' leff out uh lil' while ago. So uh extra pair of eyes kain't do nothin' but help. Ain't that right?"

"Yuh stayin' heah," Strider replied dryly as he rummaged through his desk drawers. "Whar the hell'd Ah put them...?"

The telephone rang out.

"Aw, Shit!" Strider cried as he accidentally jabbed his hand on the sharp point of an old can opener. "Goddamnit!" he yelled as he snatched his slightly punctured hand from the drawer. "Whut yuh standin' thar fuh? Git the damn phone!"

The telephone rang out again.

"Yuh alright?" Ben asked, keeping his attention on Strider. He lifted the telephone and crammed the earpiece to his ear. "Sheriff's office," he answered, just slightly interested.

Ben listened quietly and then intently. His attention went from Strider's slightly bloody hand to his face.

Mississippi Law...Love Me, Love Mah Dawg!

"Yeah. Yeah. Okay. We'll be right on out thar." he said as he hung up.

"Whut is it?" Strider asked gruffly as he wrapped a bandanna around his tiny wound.

"That was Bubba! Say they seent uh body caught up in the rivah down at Pecan Point! Say it look tuh be uh niggah! They goin' back down thar tuh see if they kain pull it out!"

"Move! Why didn't yuh give me the damned phone?" Strider asked, clearly irritated as he rushed behind his desk, snatched up the telephone, and joggled the switch hook. "Ah'm still the goddamn sheriff 'round heah!"

"Oparata." A high pitched Southern drawl squeaked through the earpiece.

"Mo'nin', Sadie Mae! Gimme George down at the sheriff's office at Greenwood!"

"Sho thang, H.C.," she said as she connected the call.

* * *

For Ed, the night meshed into the new day all too quickly. He was uncomfortable knowing that George had left only one man on duty at the jail with two prisoners, especially those two. He'd stayed at the office late into the night until exhaustion forced him home.

Ed had only slept a few hours before dragging himself back to the office and unloading the breakfast that his wife had prepared for the prisoners.

Charlie sat crumpled in the wooden chair; his head draped back and his mouth stretched open. Light gurgling bubbled up from his throat.

"Hey! Charlie!" Ed called as he kicked the chair. "Anymore of they kin come out whilst Ah was gone?"

"Aw shoot, Ed!" Charlie jumped with a start. "Yuh skeered the livin' daylights outta me!"

"Whut yuh doin' back heah already?" he yawned deeply as he stretched, lifted the towels that covered the prisoners' breakfast and retrieved a biscuit. "Ah jist dozed off mahseff. It's been quiet so far. Ah kept that back door wide open like yuh said, but Ah

Bonnie Blue

323

know them two up tuh somethin'. They been talkin' real quiet. When Ah went back tuh check on 'em uh bit ago, they tried tuh play act like they was sleepin', but Ah heard 'em talkin' befo' Ah got back thar."

Ed took his hat and tossed it on the desk before collapsing into his worn wooden, chair.

"Daggone, Ed, yuh ain't been gone but uh couple hours. An' if yuh don't min' me sayin' so, yuh don't look so good."

"Ah couldn't git no sleep noway. Ah gotta tell yuh," he said softly, "Ah ain't nevah talked tuh so many folks in all mah life. Ah 'spect fuh the boy's kin tuh call, but all them newspap'a boys from up nawth? Ah don't know why they callin'. Seems tuh me, they gotta 'nough trouble wit all them gangstas they got up thar in Chi'caga, tuh keep 'em busy," Ed looked puzzled over at Charlie, who was munching on the warm biscuit. "Why they care 'bout uh niggra boy? Thar mus' be somethin' 'bout 'im we don't know yet."

"Ah been wonderin' 'bout that mahself." Charlie said as he took a gulp from the near empty bottle of warm Nehi strawberry soda pop. "An' now, that NA'CP Boy showin' up, askin' questions. Kain't no niggah be that impo'tant, kain they?" Charlie paused, peered cautiously out the front door, and whispered. "Who yuh 'spect he really is?"

"Ah don't know," Ed whispered. "But, if we find this boy's body, it's gonna be one hell of uh mess. George need tuh be heah."

The loud ring of the telephone cut through the tense room. Startled, both men looked over at the slender black upright telephone. Ed quickly sat back at his desk, and lifted the earpiece. He hesitated before bringing it to his ear.

"Sheriff's office, Deputy Cochran speakin'."

"Hey, Ed. George anywhar 'round? Ah thank we fount ya'll's niggah."

Ed immediately recognized Strider's gruff voice.

"Jist gotta call from one of mah deputies. He say uh fella that rents out fishin' boats down heah say uh dead niggah's caught up in the rivah."

Mississippi Law...Love Me, Love Mah Dawg!

"Hey, H.C., George ain't made it in yet. Did they say if it was uh boy?" Ed asked as he stood and grabbed his hat.

"They ain't say. Ah'm on mah way up thar now," Strider said. "Yuh know the place?"

"Is that ol' man Walker or Mims?"

"Mims out by Pecan Point, 'tween Phillipp an' Tippo thar 'bouts."

"Ah thank Ah know whar it's at, but tell me whut it's out by," Ed said as he quickly grabbed a slip of paper from his desk drawer and began scribbling down information.

"Yuh got that?"

"Yeah!"

"Yuh bes' brang that niggah's kinfolk out tuh ID 'im."

"Okay, H.C., Ah'm on mah way." He said as he disconnected the call.

"They fount uh body down at the rivah," Ed said as he clicked the switch-hook twice and waited for the operator to come back on the line. "H.C. thanks it may be the one we lookin' fuh."

"Oparata." the cheery voice greeted.

"Mo'nin', Sadie Mae."

"Mo'nin', Ed. How ya'll?"

"Ah don't know yet. Git me George on the line, will yuh? He's out at his place."

"Sho thang, Ed. Ya'll take care now."

Ed placed his hand over the mouthpiece and said, "Yuh know whar they rent them fisin' boats out by Pecan Point? At ol' man Mims' place?"

"Yeah, Ah know the one," Charlie said excitedly. "Ah know exactly whar it's at! Mah Pa's been goin'...."

"Ah'ma need tuh go out tuh Money an' pick up the Rev'ran. It may be his kin. Are yuh gonna be...Hello?"

"Mo'nin'."

"Hey, George. It's me. They fount uh niggra's body out at the rivah. Ah'ma hafta pick up the Rev'ran tuh see if it's his kin."

"Alright. Ah was on mah way out the door anyway. So gowan, yuh ain't gotta wait fuh me."

Bonnie Blue

325

Ed thought about it for a moment. If the family heard about a body being found before they returned, there might be a problem.

"Tell yuh whut. Have Eli come down wit yuh. But Ah gotta git on outta heah right now, so yuh come on. Charlie don't need tuh be heah by hisself; in case thangs gits ugly."

"Ah'm putting' on mah shoes now. Be thar in less than ten minutes."

"They breakfust sittin' on the desk. Bes' not tuh tell 'em nothin'. Ah be back as soon as Ah kain."

* * *

Mose had been sitting guard alone at night in Elizabeth's rocker on the front porch. His shotgun rested across his lap, especially since receiving another threatening letter, warning him that he was next. Occasionally, the seduction of sleep would lull his eyelids shut and his head would drop to his chest. Each time, he would snap his head back up and stretch his eyes wide in an attempt to stay alert.

He'd been hiding the rest of his family with kinfolks in another town, except during the days. That was when he needed his sons to help pick cotton.

* * *

The day before, as the late afternoon sun began to set and the shadows of his persimmon trees began to stretch across the road, a timid cloud of dust crept behind the rumbling pickup that he knew was Andrew; coming to usher the boys back to Duckhill.

Mose had just emerged from the cotton field with his young sons. Exhausted, he trudged his way to the middle of the yard as Andrew's truck rolled to a halt.

"Hey Papa!" Andrew called as he rushed around to the passenger's side and opened the door for his 112 year-old aunt, Mrs. Lou Martin.

"Gurl, whut yuh doin' out heah? Andrew, why yuh brang hur out heah? Yuh know it ain't safe. It soon be dark!"

She stepped out of the truck, as old as time itself. Having been born in 1843, she had known the full evil of slavery. Her hair was a crown of pure white; her coal black skin, leathered under the

326

task masters whip; her eyes were as ancient, dimmed and worn as history itself. But, her words came as clear and true as the waters from heaven.

"Mose," she said as she dropped her homemade cigarette to the ground. "Ah know yuh trusting' in de Lawd tuh brang our youngin back an' tuh p'tect yuh whilst yuh wait. Now, yuh jis' wait 'til de Lawd speak tuh yuh befo' yuh does diff'ent. Ah knows des youngins is skeered fuh yuh, but de Lawd gots yuh an' dat lil' chil' in da palm of his hand. Yuh knows, an' Ah knows, dat po baby ain't comin' home da way he leff outta heah. Now yuh know Ah prays he do, but we knows da debel when he stompin' round tryin' tuh crush da life outta God's chil'ren. De Lawd let 'em git some, but evah time he do, we all git strong'a. De Lawd dun got mad now, an' He fixin' tuh take keer of evahthang! So Mose, yuh jis stay right whar yuh is an' trust in da Lawd. But take heed! When da Lawd send His own angel tuh tell yuh diffe'ent, den yuh ain't got no time tuh wait!"

"Lissen tuh me good Mose. Don't yuh move 'til de Lawd tells yuh so, but when he loose yuh feets…git tuh da woods wid haste! Fire don't ride no slow horse!"

"A'nt Lou, Ah thought yuh was gonna make 'im leave." Andrew said confused. "Ah thought that's why yuh sent fuh me tuh brang yuh out heah."

"Yuh keep right on thankin' baby, Ah still smell yuh Mama's milk on yuh breaf. Now, dis heah grown folk talk. Yuh Pa's uh grown man. Ain't no betta man walkin' dis earf. Yuh kain only take keer of yuh Pa uh hundred purcent of da time whilst yuh's wid 'im. But da Lawd take keer of 'im uh hun'red purcent, all da time!"

"Amen!" Mose said as he listened attentively to his aunt. "Lou, Ah know fuh mahseff the Lawd is good," he said as he embraced the eldest member of his family. "

Once again, Andrew pleaded with his father to come with him to safety. They both knew that it was never a question of 'if' it was solely a matter of 'when' another group of White men would converge on his home to retaliate. Knowing that, Mose steadfastly refused to heed the warning of the sheriff, his congregation and his family.

Bonnie Blue

* * *

After another sleepless night, Mose sat in Elizabeth's rocking chair, replaying the events of that night over and over again; searching for that one elusive moment that he must have missed…that one slim opportunity that could have perhaps changed the outcome. If he had enough money for gas he could have driven the boys to Memphis the night that he'd first heard of the whistling incident. They could have slept in the train station. But it didn't matter now. The only thing that mattered now was finding Emmett, and bringing him home.

Weary and moving much slower, Mose began gathering eggs from the chicken coop and placed them carefully in the homemade woven basket. Sweet Potato raised her head ever so slightly and thumped her tail lazily against the splintered, wooden porch as Mose walked past her into the kitchen.

"Hey gurl," Mose said as he reappeared with a plate of left over chicken bones and black-eyed peas that church members had sent to him the day before. "Ah ain't fuhgit 'bout yuh." He pushed the plate close to his aged companion's nose and stroked her head.

"Evahthang's gonna be alright. When Emmett gits back heah, that boy's goin' straight back home tuh his Mama. Liz'bit an' the boys be home fuh good, an' thangs gonna be jist like they suppose tuh be," he said as he stood and gazed around the quiet yard. His brow deepened with worry when he caught sight of his sons picking cotton in the adjoining field.

Slowly, he unhinged his sack from the rusted nail on the front porch, to begin his afternoon hours in the cotton field. "The Lawd gonna take care of evahthang. He gonna make sho evahthang alright."

He hadn't gone very far, before he noticed a whirlwind of dust speeding up the road. Fear immediately gripped him. He found himself wandering back towards his yard as the dust cloud grew larger and drew nearer. A squad car. He knew that it could only be carrying news about Emmett, bad news.

Ed whipped the squad car off the dirt road and into the yard. The dust cloud quickly overtook the car and settled back to the ground.

Mississippi Law...Love Me, Love Mah Dawg!

"Rev'ran'!" Ed called out to the old man as he emerged from the field. "Ah need yuh tuh come wit me!"

"Yes suh," Mose said as he walked unsteadily towards the squad car. "Yuh fount 'im? Yuh fount mah boy? Is he, alive?"

"Ah don't know who it is," Ed said as he shoved the front door of his squad car open for him. "But uh dead niggra was fount down in the rivah, an' Ah need yuh tuh come see if its yuh boy."

"Yes suh," Mose said as glanced back at his sons, and slid into the squad car.

* * *

Mose said nothing as he stared out the window and tried to quiet his trembling hands and palpitating heart.

The squad car raced down the highway and skirted over unmarked dirt roads. Mose felt like they had ridden for hours. He prayed that the poor soul pulled from the river wasn't his great-nephew.

As they turned down a secluded dirt road, he could see a carnival of flashing lights through the trees.

They quickly came upon official vehicles lining the road, and he prepared himself for the worst.

"Lawd, God," Mose murmured, as they slowed and pulled up behind the other squad cars, a hearse and several pickup trucks, "please don't let this dead body be Emmett."

"They gotta be down at the dock," Ed said as he flung the passenger's door open for Mose and rushed down to the plank lined path.

Mose stepped from the car and forced his legs to release the ground from where they were planted. Something in him resisted facing the dead body that may very well be Emmett.

Ed looked back and saw Mose moving slowly towards the trail that led down to the river.

"Ah'm sorrah, Rev'ran'!" he called as he ran back up the path, took Mose by the arm, and assisted him down the slippery wooden planks. "Yuh alright?" he asked as he led Mose down the path. "Jist take yuh time."

Bonnie Blue

Mose slowed as he neared the end of the mud covered planks that led to the cluttered dock. The smell of decaying flesh filled his senses, and his body stiffened. The dock was bustling with a mixture of men; Colored and White. Some of the officers milled around one of the small boats, attempting to get a look at the mass.

"Hey, Ed! Ovah heah!" Strider called as Chester Miller, the Colored undertaker from Century Funeral Home in Greenwood, opened a canned deodorizer bomb to suppress the odor of the decomposing flesh.

Ed released the tired old man's arm and rushed through the growing white chemical cloud, to join Strider and the other men gathered around the body in the boat.

Then, slowly, as the wind moved the chemicals across the river, Mose caught a glimpse of the huge, algae covered silver fan propped at the rear of the boat. And, bit by bit he began to make out the oversized, gray, naked body that nearly filled the row boat. He was sure that it couldn't be Emmett but still, his aged, sluggish heart began to pound fiercely, and a tear collected in the corner of his eye.

"Hold it, Rev'ran! Stay up thar!" Ed called over his shoulder. "Don't come down heah yet!"

Mose ignored the deputy. He had to see that body. He had to be sure. Carefully, he eased his own trembling body further down the last few muddy wooden planks.

"Goddamnit, Chesta," Strider yelled. "That bomb ain't dun uh damn thang! Ain't yuh got some oth'a kinda shit up in that coach that'll knock out this stank?"

"Yes suh!" Chester said as he ran around Mose and back up the planks to the funeral coach.

Mose fought through the stench as he made his way down to the dock.

Ed and the others had gathered next to an oversized wooden crate that read *Batesville Casket Co.* on the side.

330

Chester brushed past the unsteady old man, this time dragging a bulky roll of brown paper with a large brown glass bottle in hand.

Mississippi Law...Love Me, Love Mah Dawg!

"Well, Rev'ran," Ed said when Mose walked up alongside of him, "Ah know yuh kain't tell much 'til they turn 'im ovah, but does this look like yuh boy?"

"It could be him, but Ah ain't fuh sho," Mose said softly as he stared at the nude bloated remains.

They watched Chester pour the contents of the bottle over the body, amid Strider's curses.

"Maybe yuh should stand back up by that pathway thar. Don't make no sense fuh yuh tuh be down in this mess now," Ed said. "Ah'll call yuh when they got the body whar yuh kain see it propp'a."

"Goddamn if that niggah don't smell tuh high hell!" Strider laughed as he took his chewed cigar nub from his line thin lips. "That shit didn't do uh damned thang!" He shoved Chester out of his way and stooped down by the body. "Chesta, ya'll need tuh go back up in that wagon an' git somethin' else!"

"Sorrah suh, but we ain't got nothin' else. The body jis too far gone is all."

"Okay then," he said as he stood up. "Ya'll git 'im up outta thar! Turn that niggah ovah!"

A group of White men steadied the boat while Colored onlookers struggled alongside Chester and his helper, Simon Garrett, to lift the slippery body out of the boat. They lost their grip and the large, slimy mass splattered onto the wooden dock, propelling water, mud and other debris in every direction.

"Goddamnit! Would yuh look at this heah shit?" Bubba said to Strider as he snatched his tucked shirt out of his slacks and wiped off his arms.

Strider looked down at the corpse in silence. His thoughts seemed to leak from his lips. "Ah dun seent some shit in mah time, but Ah sweah tuh god! Ah ain't nevah seent no shit like this heah," he said as he wiped water from his cheek.

"Whew!" Bubba said as he backed away from the mound of flesh that beckoned large, green blowflies.

Bonnie Blue

"Ah b'lieve it's most likely the niggah ya'll been lookin' fuh," Strider said, wiping his hands on his pants. "This heah niggah look like he dun stomped on somebody's toes real hard." He paused and then yelled, "Bubba!"

Strider cocked his head to the side, and walked around the body to get a better look. "Gimme that twig ovah yonda thar by yuh foot."

"Whut yuh need this fuh?" he asked as he handed the twig to Strider.

"Whut'd yuh thank?" he barked. "This heah's uh official investigation. See that thar hole?" he asked, pointing to a small hole on the side of the corpse's head. "It's the smallest damn bullet hole Ah evah seent, but if thar's evidence in thar, Ah'm bound tuh git it out!"

Strider knelt beside Emmett's body. He forced the small knotted twig into the moist hole on the side of his head, sliding it back and forth, searching through the soft tissue for a bullet which should have been lodged inside. But, the hole wasn't deep enough, and there was no bullet or powder burns.

"Whut the hell?" he murmured as he examined Emmett's head, searching for an exit wound that wasn't there. Puzzled, he turned his attention up to Ed, who had glanced back at the frail little Colored preacher, standing alone at the foot of the path.

"Ah sho hope it ain't his boy," Ed said quietly as he shook his head and slowly walked back up to Mose.

"Okay, Rev'ran," he said calmly. "Ah'ma need yuh tuh take uh look an' see if this is yuh nephew. Ah gotta warn yuh, ain't much leff of the face, but it's uh male. He ain't got no clothes on tuh identify, but do the bes' yuh kain. Now, yuh jist take yuh time. Are yuh ready?"

"Yes suh," Mose replied quietly.

He walked alongside the deputy to the spot where the body laid; praying silently and summoning all of the inner strength that he could to keep his legs from collapsing.

Mose stood over the mutilated bloated body with Sheriff Strider continuing to probe in the hole with a twig.

"Oh, mah Lawd Jesus," Mose whispered in disbelief.

"Yeah," Ed agreed quietly.

Mississippi Law…Love Me, Love Mah Dawg!

"Ah don't know whut the hell this heah shit is!" Strider said confused. "But ain't no bullet in thar, less it fell out in the rivah! Well the niggah wasn't shot, that's for sho. That hole's jist too damn small!"

Ed's eyes shot bolts of anger at Strider as he tossed the twig to the side and stood coldly before the shaken little man.

"Okay, Preacha," Strider said impatiently. "This heah yuh niggah or not?"

Ed touched Mose lightly on the elbow and led him closer to the bloated remains. "Ah know thar ain't much tuh make out, but do the bes' yuh kain."

Mose sighed deeply and attempted to scrutinize what was left of the face. One eye hung out of the socket on the swollen cheek in a dull lifeless stare, while an empty socket sunk deeply into his skull. The deputy was right. There wasn't much of anything left of the face to identify.

Barbed wire, embedded deep into his neck, was only visible by the remnant piece of wire that hung alongside his face.

Mose was relieved that he couldn't absolutely make out familiar features on this horribly mangled body. But then, he saw the hand.

There, nearly buried in swollen fingers he saw a light reflecting from a piece of silver. All of the sounds surrounding Mose dulled as he knelt down next to the body and tenderly moved the soft flesh back, exposing the silver ring with 'LT' boldly engraved on the front. His shoulders slumped heavily forward, and his head fell in hopeless resignation.

"Preacha! It's hot as hell out heah, an' this stankin' niggah ain't makin' it no betta! Now, is this niggah yuh kin or ain't it?"

"Yes suh. It's mah nephew, Emmett Till."

333

"Whut 'bout that rang thar on his fing'a?"

"Ah thank that's his rang, but Ah kain't say fuh sho," he said meekly.

"Niggah! Whut the hell's wrong wit yuh?!" Strider yelled, his face close to Mose. "Do yuh mean tuh tell me that this heah niggah's been stayin' thar in yuh own damned house fuh uh whole damned week, eatin' at the same damned table wit yuh, an' yuh don't know if he had this rang on his goddamned fing'a?"

Bonnie Blue

"No suh," Mose said calmly. "Ah ain't fuh sho 'bout that rang. But mah boys would know. Ah'll carry it out tuh mah place an' ask 'em 'bout it."

"Hey Chestah! Ya'll git that rang off!"

Mose bowed his head and prayed softly as a river of hot tears flowed down his wrinkle etched, cheeks.

"Ah'm sorrah 'bout yuh boy, Rev'ran," Ed said as he laid his hand on Moses' shoulder.

Strider shoved his damp cigar butt back between his lips, shook his head and retorted, "This body's too bad off tuh keep out the ground fuh too long! We need tuh git his ass planted right now! Tuhday!"

"Yes suh," Mose replied as his attention remained transfixed on the small silver band shining up from the decaying body. "Ah unda'stand."

Moses' knees grew even more unsteady, threatening to topple his aged, lean frame as Ed led him back up the path to the road. Mose followed like a young child, looking back in silence as the group of Colored men struggled to wrap the brown paper around his great-nephew.

"Wait heah," Ed said as he ran back and recruited a couple of Colored men to load the fan into the trunk of his squad car.

Mose stood alone on the road, looking down at the men struggling to carry the oversized crate up the damp, grass covered embankment. When they broke from the foliage, he rushed to help carry their load to the funeral coach parked just up the road.

"Lawd, fuhgive me," Mose said as he grabbed the underside of Emmett's temporary coffin. After the crate was

334

finally shoved into the coach, Mose caressed the rough, wooden lid. "Ah should'a been able tuh keep 'im safe."

"Rev'ran, theah whutn't nothin' yuh coulda dun," Chester said quietly as he closed the rear door and slid into the driver's seat.

"Theah shoulda been somethin'," Mose said, standing in the open door of the coach.

Mississippi Law...Love Me, Love Mah Dawg!

"Rev'ran," Chester whispered and looked around. "Ain't no need in yuh blamin' yuhseff ovah somethin' yuh nevah coulda dun uh thang 'bout. Yuh know yuh kain't stop no crackas' when dey up tuh no good."

"Wheah ya'll takin' 'im now?" Mose asked softly as he stared back at the crate holding his young relative.

Chester leaned towards him and unfolded his clutched fist. It was Emmett's ring. He shook his head, grabbed Mose by the hand, and pressed the ring firmly into his palm. "We takin' 'im out tuh mah funeral home in Greenwood."

Mose thanked his compassionate brethren with his eyes.

"Hey Preacha! This heah niggah's fount in Tallahatcha County!" Strider announced loudly as he marched up to the rear doors of the hearse. "Ah'm the law heah, an' Ah'm takin' ovah this heah investigation!" He slapped the rear of the hearse. "We gotta hurry up an' plant this heah niggah," he called out, his newfound authority ringing out from the top of his voice.

Mose nearly bit through his lip fighting back a burning fury. He quickly snapped his hand shut, crushing Emmett's ring in his hand.

"Preacha? Yuh heah me?! This heah niggah boy of yourn stankin' tuh high hell! Yuh gotta plant his ass somewhar this aft'a-noon!"

As a young boy growing up in the South, Mose recalled working the cotton fields, where 'niggah" was used so much that it was just part of the vocabulary. And he, like all of the other Colored people that he knew, answered to it with no feeling one way or another. But then, one day, while he wasn't yet a teen, he overheard a group of White men talking. He couldn't recall what the conversation was about, but he always remembered that whatever it was, they used 'niggah' as a substitute for someone that was dumb, nasty, lazy, or low down; a waste of human flesh and below themselves. That was the first time that Mose realized, beyond a shadow of a doubt, that the word 'nigger' was the lowest form of disrespect that White men use.

"Preacha!" Strider yelled louder, his voice piercing Moses' soul.

Bonnie Blue

"Yes suh," Mose answered strongly as he lifted his head in quiet defiance and looked the stuffed scarlet faced sheriff squarely in the eyes.

Ed touched Moses' arm and said softly, "Rev'ran, Ah imagine yuh want tuh bury im' out at yuh church?"

"Yes suh," Mose said quietly. "Thank yuh."

"Ah'm jist gonna be uh minute. Then Ah'ma take yuh back out tuh yuh place."

Bubba shot a confused glare over at Strider. "Sheriff, seein' as this heah's our case, shouldn't Ah...?"

"Ed," Strider said dryly. "The case is mine now."

"Ah know, H.C. Ah know," Ed said as he led Mose past Strider, towards his squad car.

"Go wit 'em," Strider instructed Bubba as he turned back to Chester and the hearse.

"Niggah, whut the hell ya'll waitin' fuh?" He barked. "Git yuh asses' outta heah! Hose 'im down, box 'im up, an' meet us down tuh that niggah's church soon's yuh kain!"

"Yes, suh," Chester replied as Simon jumped into the cab of the hearse and pulled away.

* * *

Ed drove quickly across the network of red dirt roads with Bubba following closely behind; lights flashing and sirens screaming.

Mose stared silently out at the sun soaked fields, dotted with the children and grandchildren of former slaves.

"Ain't much else we kain do tuh help yuh, Rev'ran," Ed said as he glanced in the rear view mirror at the flashing lights and metal radiator grille that seemed more a sinister sneer than ventilation.

"Yes suh. An' Ah want yuh tuh know that me an' mah family 'preciate evahthang that ya'll dun. Ain't many White folk would of gone out the way like yuh folks."

"Well, we dun the bes' we could do. Now, it's up tuh Sheriff Strider. Ah know he'll take care of evahthang propp'a."

"Yes suh," Mose replied quietly.

Mose knew that with LaFlore County losing authority over the case, Sheriff Strider would do whatever he could, to protect

Mississippi Law…Love Me, Love Mah Dawg!

the killers. It didn't matter what they'd done. But he couldn't worry about that now. He only wished that he had more time for Mamie and Alma to come down and say a proper goodbye to Emmett. He deserved a proper homegoing and burial, surrounded by his family. It wasn't right. None of it was right.

"That's yuh turnoff up ahead, ain't it?"

Mose instantly snapped from his dimmed gaze to find himself surrounded by the familiar landscape of his home. "Yes, suh," Moses said just above a whisper. "Ah gotta git word tuh the boy's Mama." He wiped tears from his cheeks and cleared his throat. "She gotta know now."

Ed turned onto the dirt drive.

Bubba swerved his squad car around in front of them and skid to a halt in Moses' dirt yard.

"Whut the hell yuh doin'?" Ed yelled as he smashed his brakes hard to the floor.

"Preacha!" Bubba yelled from his opened window. "We gonna take 'im down at yuh church! If yuh plannin' tuh say some words, yuh betta git on down thar!"

He swerved the squad car around and sped back down the road, siren screaming.

Ed stared out at the cloud of dust from Bubba's car, shook his head and said, "We gotta make sho that rang b'long tuh Emmett."

"Mah boys' most likely still in the field," Mose said as he got out of the car. "Ah'll be right back."

He closed the door and walked out towards the cotton field, scanning the area for his sons.

"Papa!"

"Ollie! Kelvin! Wheah ya'll at?!" Mose yelled as he ran to the side of the house.

His heart pounded fiercely, terrified that White folks might have made good on their threats and converged on his land and beatened his sons...or worse. "Is ya'll alright?" he called as he ran to the house as fast as his pained knees could carry him.

Bonnie Blue

"Papa!" Kelvin called as the two scrambled from their hiding place under the house.

"Papa, we was skeered the White folk come an' carried yuh off like they dun Bo!" Ollie cried as he ran to his father and clung to his neck.

"Naw, naw. Ah'm alright. Ain't nobody come by heah did they?"

"Naw, suh," Ollie said as he wiped his dirt coated hands down his tears soaked face.

"Ah need ya'll tuh look at this heah rang. Both of yuh, take uh good look," he said, holding the ring out to them.

"That theah's Bobo's rang, ain't it?" Kelvin said reaching for his father's outstretched hand.

"Yes suh. That's Bobo's rang alright. Wheah ya'll find it at? Did ya'll find Bobo?"

"Ya'll gowan an' git in the car," Mose said as he walked back to the police car.

"They say it's Emmett's rang."

"Lissen, Rev'ran," Ed said troubled, "yuh bes' leave this place right now. The Milam-Bryant clan'll be knowin' we fount the body soon 'nough. Ain't no tellin' whut they li'bul tuh do."

"Ah'll keep mah boys down wit they Mama at Duckhill, but Ah'm stayin' right heah! Ah ain't lettin' them folks run me off mah land. All mah life, them folks dun walked all ovah me. But no mo'," he said as he stood erect. "If they come, they jist come. All they kain do tuh me now is kill me. They kain't hurt me no mo' than they already dun."

338

"Well then, be careful," Ed warned. "Be darn careful."

"Yes suh."

Ed turned his squad car and accelerated down the road, leaving Mose standing alone in his deserted yard.

* * *

In Chicago, early afternoon rays of sun washed through Alma's bedroom windows. Mamie's headache had been relentless. She hadn't been able to sleep through the night since Emmett's disappearance. Her mother had given her another Standback and some dry toast and encouraged her to try to take a nap.

Mississippi Law…Love Me, Love Mah Dawg!

Mamie lay quietly, listening to the sparrows that had found their home in the cottonwood tree outside her mother's bedroom window. It was then, when the house was still, that guilt threatened to paralyze her.

Mamie replayed in her mind, the last serious talk that she had with Emmett. That night before he left; she wasn't at all confident that he understood the severity of her directions. There was no way that he could have. There was also no way that she could dull the nagging guilt that she'd placed him in a position where he had to follow those instructions.

Ever since Emmett was kidnapped, Mamie had worked tirelessly to get nationwide coverage. Her mother's home had turned into media center as Mamie held interviews throughout the day and evening.

Richard Daley, the new mayor of Chicago, couldn't help in a Mississippi matter. But, Medgar and Mirlie Evers, the young Colored couple that worked out of the new Mississippi NAACP field office, had enlisted the assistance of other folks as they continued their own search for Emmett.

Mamie was hopeful that Emmett would be found, especially since she'd been informed by Sheriff Smith that two self confessed kidnappers were already behind bars. She continued to call the Chicago office of the FBI at least twice a day to see if they have found a way to intervene. It didn't matter to her that they reiterated each time that they had no jurisdiction in this situation.

339

Slowly, Mamie glanced over at the alarm clock and slid out of the bed. She stood before the open window, gazing out at the small birds hopping from branch to branch when the light aroma of fresh brewed coffee began to fill the air.

"Did you get any rest at all?" a rich deep voice greeted hesitantly, from the doorway.

Mamie turned to find Gene standing at the partially opened door, extending a steaming cup and wearing the same clothes that he'd been wearing since they got news of Emmett's disappearance.

Bonnie Blue

"As much as I could get." she said as she took the cup from his hand. "Gene, you need to go home and take care of yourself."

"I am where I need to be," he said as he studied her strained childlike face.

Mamie gazed into her coffee cup, losing herself in the swirling brown water until Gene touched her lightly on the shoulder.

"Mamie, you might want to reconsider letting one of your girlfriends stay here at the house to help out. Your mother...I don't know. I'm just afraid that she, well both of you..."

"Gene, we're okay. Mother has to do something. If she just sat idly by and did nothing, I'd really worry."

"Okay, you know her better than I do," Gene replied with a strained smile.

"And I know the girls want to help, but right now, there's just too much going on and I'm really trying to keep a handle on things," she said as she placed the coffee cup on the night stand.

Gene reached down and cradled her as she whispered, "All that I need right now, is my son back home."

"Everything is going to work out," he said softly as he rocked her gently. "Everybody is doing everything that can possibly be done and something is going to happen. I just know it."

"I'm glad you're here," she said as looked up at him. "I don't think that I could do it alone."

340

"I promise I will never leave you alone. Whatever we have to face, we will face it together."

She forced a nervous smile and stepped back. "You'd better get going. That reporter from the *Chicago Daily News* said he'd be back out here at around three o'clock."

"Gene!" Alma called from the kitchen. "Come and eat something before you leave!"

"Come on," Mamie said as she pulled her robe tightly around her waist and walked past him.

"Gene? Did you hear me?" Alma called, "I've got spam sandwiches and liverwurst sandwiches made. But, if you want some souse or hog head cheese and crackers, I've got that too!"

Mississippi Law…Love Me, Love Mah Dawg!

"Yes ma'am! I'll be right there!"

"Just eat something, Gene. It'll make her feel better," Mamie said as she disappeared into the bathroom. "It's late, and I've got to get dressed."

Gene joined Alma in the kitchen.

"Is Mamie up yet?"

"She's in the bathroom."

"I don't know how long she can go on like this," Alma said quietly as she removed the percolating coffee pot from the open flames of the stove. "Last night, she was fighting in her sleep again. I just don't know what to do," she said nervously as she filled his cup. "I'm glad she was able to get a short nap in, but she keeps having nightmares. I try to reassure her, but until Emmett comes home...I just don't know."

"Miss Alma," Gene said as he embraced her, "Mamie's going to be alright. She's a strong woman, and Emmett is coming home."

Alma's facade suddenly shattered. Her eyes abruptly filled with the salty tears that had been relentlessly stockpiling. Her seemingly impregnable show of strength had dissipated. She buried her face on Gene's chest to muffle the truth that she could no longer bury in the back of her mind.

"Emmett may never come home!" She murmured.

All of the fear and pain that she has suppressed for her daughter's sake erupted. Her small body shook as she sobbed uncontrollably.

"What's wrong?" Mamie called frantically as she ran into the kitchen. "What happened? Did someone call? Oh Jesus!"

Gene shook his head as he held Alma tightly. "No, Mamie. No one's called," Gene said softly.

Alma sniffled, wiped her eyes and pulled away. "I'm sorry. I'm sorry. I don't know what's wrong with me. I must...I don't know..."

"Mother?"

"Here, baby," she said as she quickly wiped her face on her apron, inhaled and busied herself back in the refrigerator. "Here, baby. You eat. Both of you, sit down and eat something." She filled a bowl with pudding and pulled out the plate of hog head cheese.

Bonnie Blue

Mamie put the bowl back in the refrigerator, and led her mother by the hand into the dining room.

"What are you doing? I'm fine," Alma protested.

"Mother," Mamie said gently as she sat beside her; holding her hand, "this is hard on all of us. I don't want you thinking that you have to be the rock. I know that you're afraid. We all are."

"Mamie, I'm telling you, I'm fine. You just stop worrying about me."

"What are you talking about? Emmett is missing. You can't be fine. None of us are fine. We're in this together. We're going to worry about Emmett and we're going to worry about each other because we're family. Besides," Mamie said as she smiled reassuringly, "God has blessed us, you know? He's paving the way. Reporters are working to get our story in the newspapers. Medgar and the NAACP have a lot of people helping look for Emmett in Mississippi, and I have faith that, sooner or later, even the FBI will help find my baby. And before you know it," she kissed her mother on the cheek, "Emmett will be back, running through your house, taking food from the kitchen and eating in the living room. You didn't know that I knew did you? You let him get away with anything he wants to over here, don't you?"

342

"Well, that's my only grandbaby," she sighed as she gave a sad smile to her only child. "My Emmett is a boy, and he does whatever boys are supposed to do at his grandmother's house. And I love every minute of it."

"Miss Alma," Gene said as he knelt beside Alma, covering both women's clenched hands with his own, "you know I'm here if there is anything that you need."

Suddenly, the telephone rang out. Mamie dashed to answer it. "Hello?" Mamie greeted anxiously.

"Hello. Is this Miss Bradley?"

"Yes, this is Mamie Bradley. Who's calling?"

"This is Dave Simmons with the *Chicago Daily News*. I was at your home yesterday. I have an appointment to see you a little later this afternoon."

Mamie glanced down at her wristwatch. "Oh, yes."

Mississippi Law…Love Me, Love Mah Dawg!

"Miss Bradley, have you spoken to anyone yet this morning. Have you gotten any word on your son? Has he been …found?" he asked cautiously.

"No, I haven't spoken to anyone since early this morning. I'll call the sheriff again after I hang up from you."

"Okay, well you make your calls. I'm going to be running a little late. Is three-thirty a good time for you?"

"Yes, that will be fine. I'll be here," Mamie said and hung up the telephone.

* * *

David Simmons, a young White reporter fresh out of college, had only been with the *Chicago Daily News* since the beginning of the summer. This was his first year as a newspaperman. The editor had assigned him this benign story of a missing Colored boy because there was no work involved and he would still be available to run copy for the seasoned reporters working on 'real' stories.

Initially, David was disappointed at being given a story that no one else would take. He knew that this, his first story, would end up as filler or possibly on the copy room floor. But he was determined to do his best.

343

Yesterday, during his initial interview with the boy's mother, she mentioned that she had contacted as many newspapers that she could, including the Associated Press and the United Press International news services. David hoped that one of the other news agencies had picked up the story as well.

He was excited when he pulled a story off the wire from the Associated Press, that a Negro boy's body had been found in the Tallahatchie River and that it had been identified by a relative as, Emmett Till. He knew that he would be the first to interview Mamie after the news was broken to her, but he didn't want to be the one to actually inform her that her son was dead.

David was surprised that the authorities in Mississippi hadn't already notified Mamie.

When he met with her yesterday, he had also been introduced to two other women. They were apparently close family friends. He had collected their names and telephone

numbers to contact them later for background information. Now, he searched feverish through the scraps of paper on his desk to find those telephone numbers.

* * *

Mamie finished getting dressed and sat at the kitchen table with her mother, snapping pole beans for dinner.

"How long has Gene been gone?" Mamie asked as she glanced up at the daisy clock, which inched its way to 2 o'clock.

"It hasn't been that long. I told him that, before he picks up the evening papers, he should go home and take care of himself. I can have someone else bring all of the newspapers when they come this evening. That boy has been in this apartment for as long as you have."

"Actually, I'll go down to the stand after I call the sheriff's office again. I think getting a little fresh air might help," Mamie said, her voice trailing off.

Both women stared without seeing, as they silently continued snapping their pole beans.

"You know, Mother," Mamie said, "I think everything will work out. With the sheriff already having those two behind bars, God only knows what else he's been able to find out since I

344

called him earlier. He said they were checking out something else."

"You go on Mamie," Alma said as she took the mixing bowl of unsnapped pole beans from in front of her daughter. "Don't wait for the sheriff to call. You go on and call down there now and see what's going on."

* * *

Mamie retrieved her writing tablet filled with names and numbers scribbled on the fronts and backs of the crinkled pages. The sheriff's phone number was the first on her list. She'd traced over it numerous times in pencil and blue ink. As she reached for the receiver, the phone rang.

"Hello?" she inquired anxiously.

"Mamie?" The voice, barely audible, cracked through the earpiece.

"Yes. Who is this?" Mamie asked slightly alarmed.

Mississippi Law…Love Me, Love Mah Dawg!

"Mamie, it's me, Ola…." The small nervous voice replied. "Ola Mae."

"Ola Mae, are you alright?" Mamie asked, alarmed.

"Mamie, is…is Gene there?" Ola Mae asked, nearly in a panic. "Where is he?"

"What is it?!" Mamie demanded angrily. "If something is going on, you'd better tell me! Now, what is it?"

"I'm on my way over there right now," Ola Mae said quickly.

"Ola Mae! Don't you hang up on me!" she yelled. "Don't you dare hang up on me!"

"Oh, my good Lord!" Alma cried out when she heard her daughter's voice boom from the living room. She leaped from her chair, knocking it to the floor. She bolted from the kitchen, through the apartment, to the living room where Mamie continued yelling into the telephone.

"You tell me right now, Ola Mae! I'm going through too much for this! What's going on?!"

"Mamie! What is it? What's wrong?" Alma asked in a panic. "What's happened?"

345

"Mamie," Ola Mae's voice cracked. "I wish...I wish I didn't have to tell you."

"Ola Mae," Mamie said quietly, her heart pounding frantically, "tell me. What is it?"

"Mamie, I'm so sorry." she struggled as she fought to steady herself. "I just got a call. He said...he said you didn't know! Oh, God, please help me!" Her best friend cried.

Mamie held her breath and closed her eyes for what seemed an eternity. "Is it my baby?" she whispered. "Is it Emmett?" The line seemed to go dead. Mamie froze as the toxic fog of silence threatened to choke her.

The burn behind Alma's eyes return as her trembling body clung to the living room wall. She knew in her heart that the relentless pang of truth that she had fought so diligently to squelch would soon pierce her daughter's ears.

"Tell me," Mamie repeated quietly.

Bonnie Blue

"Yes," Ola Mae replied her voice shaking. "I am so sorry, Mamie. A reporter just called and said you didn't know." she cried, "He said I should tell you!"

"Oh, heavenly Father! Where is he?!" Mamie screamed hysterically. "Where is my son?! Lord God! Please don't tell me he's dead! He's my baby! My son! He's got to be alive!"

"Mamie, I'm sorry. I'm so, so, sorry!" Ola Mae cried, at the threshold of hysteria. "Mamie...Emmett is dead! They found his body!"

"Noooooo!" she screamed. "Not my dear sweet baby! Not my Emmett!"

A stabbing pain ripped through her chest, sending exploding waves through every inch of her body. There was suddenly nothing left. Her body, her soul, her mind, all that she had been since her son's birth, was an utter void. She felt as though the core of her very spirit had been ripped from her body.

Mamie crumbled onto the floor, an abandoned shell; the telephone receiver sliding from her hand.

346

"They killed him," she whimpered in dazed disbelief. "They killed my Emmett. They killed my baby boy."

Mamie began to tremble violently. Her shocked eyes bulged as she fixed a gaze of disbelief towards her mother. She labored for breath as she began to hyperventilate.

"Mamie?!" Alma called out as she rushed to her fallen daughter. "Mamie! Baby, breathe! Come on, baby! Oh, Lord Jesus! Why?" she called out as she struggled to unravel the immediate conflict that cluttered her muddled mind.

She didn't want to leave her tormented child there on the floor alone, but she had to do something to help her. Mamie's strained face had already turned a deep red.

"Mamie! Mamie!" Alma called strongly. "I need for you to slow down! Just breathe! I'm not leaving you. I'll be right back! Baby, it's going to be alright!" Alma struggled to stand.

"Oh, my Lord!" she prayed as she ran back to the kitchen. "Sweet Jesus, give me strength! This can't be happening!"

Mississippi Law...Love Me, Love Mah Dawg!

Alma snatched a brown paper lunch bag from the sink drawer and nearly ran into the front door as Gene knocked and opened it simultaneously. He poked his head around the door when he saw Alma rush past. His eyes immediately landed on Mamie; her shoulders hunched up towards her ears. The veins in her neck distended as she strained to gulp air.

"Mamie," escaped his lips as he panicked and rushed to her side.

Mounting pressure in Mamie's head threatened to detonate. She wanted to die. She wanted to be with her son.

Alma knelt at her daughter's side, fighting desperately to control her own anxiety, and placed the paper bag over Mamie's mouth.

"Okay, Mamie," Alma said calmly. "Now, baby, take your time. Slow down. Breathe."

"What's happened to her? What's going on?" Gene asked.

347

Alma didn't answer, but continued coaxing Mamie to fight against everything that she was feeling; to live. "Come on, Mamie. Slow down." She pleaded, "We're going to get through this."

"I'm calling an ambulance," Gene said anxiously as he grabbed the telephone from the floor.

"Wait," Alma said cautiously.

The paper bag crackle as it began to inflate and deflate. Mamie's labored breath began to slow and the natural caramel color returned to her face.

Suddenly, Mamie violently shoved the bag from her face and her mother's hand.

"Noooooo!" A shrill death wail catapulted through the open window on the sun porch, frightening the sparrows which scattered from the nearby trees. "They killed him!" she screamed. "They killed him!"

Alma grappled with her own mounting urge to flee and scream past the top of her lungs. She gathered Mamie tightly in her arms and spoke lightly as she tried to soothe her, rocking her rhythmically.

Bonnie Blue

An excruciating burn in Mamie's heart flooded her quaking body. Anxiously, she invited her own death. "Lord, I can't...I can't do this," she moaned. "Not my baby. Please, God, not my baby. Not my little boy." She wanted to die, to fade away. She prayed for death to embrace her. She couldn't endure the pain. But the abyss didn't rescue her. "My baby was alone. Cowards! Evil devils! He is just a baby!"

Alma squeezed her tighter as she rocked. "I'm so, so sorry, Mamie," Alma said as her eyes released a river of salty tears that collected in the back of her throat. "It's all my fault. If I had just shut my mouth, Emmett would be at home right now."

Mamie looked up at her mother, confused; herself like a wounded animal. "Mother, he was alone. Nobody to help him. I wasn't there to help him." Mamie squeezed her eyes against the rushing flood of sorrow, shook her head hard, and began to sob uncontrollably.

348

Gene punched his fist into the wall. He had expected this. Both the sheriff and the deputy warned him that Emmett's death was more probable than possible. But the reality of it was nearly unbearable. Suddenly, he didn't know what to do. He was lost. What was left for him to do?

"I'ma kill them!!! I'ma kill every last one of those backwoods bastards!" he growled as his face constricted, distorting his features in a queer motley of emotion. "Those evil sons of bitches!" he screamed as he wept and pounded his fist into the wall. "I'll kill those cracker bastards!"

Mamie gazed blankly into the midst of chaos surrounding her. "I've got to see my baby," she said. "I've got to bring my baby home! Emmett is coming home to me!"

* * *

Down at the LaFlore County jail, Ed still hadn't returned. He radioed in to George that Mose had made a positive identification of the body and that he would be back after he dropped the preacher back to his place.

George's nerves were so frayed that a relentless throbbing had ignited in his head. Even though he had called in extra manpower, he knew that he would probably need to recruit even

Mississippi Law...Love Me, Love Mah Dawg!

more. With both brothers behind bars and finding the body, things could get really ugly, really fast.

Before he made anymore calls for help, George took a short walk down to the General Store for another bottle of aspirin, and to clear his head.

Even though Charlie was not in the office alone, he was still more nervous than the prisoners. He paced anxiously around the office; his hand covering his holster while periodically poking his head out the door to survey the street.

Two part time deputies, Eli and Sonny, had been sworn in to help. They were unseasoned lawmen who mostly made appearances during county celebrations to make their numbers look more impressive.

349

Eli, a lifelong farmer, sat behind Ed's desk, his hand resting at the ready on his shotgun. His alert eyes kept vigil between the propped open gray door to the cells, and the front door.

Sonny, Eli's son-in-law, who kept watch outside on the bench, called through the open door, "Hey ya'll! He's back!"

"Whut happened?" he shouted as he ran out to the squad car. "Was it the Ch'caga niggah?"

"Hol' it down and c'mon inside," Ed said as he looked around and rushed past him.

"Yeah, it was him. Whar's George?"

"Down at the General sto', Ah suppose," Eli replied as he relinquished Ed's seat. "Should be back terectly."

"Any of the boys come out heah yet?"

"Naw, not yet," Eli said nervously. "But Ah gotta tell yuh Ed, the only thang that skeer me mo' than uh mob of angry men, is the quiet. Yuh don't know whut folk's thankin', but yuh know they up tuh somethin'."

"Well, Ah 'spect thangs tuh git bad 'round heah," Ed said. Exhausted, as he plopped down in his chair. "The body was fount ovah on the Tallahatcha County side of the rivah."

"Was it the preacha's kin?" George asked, walking in the door and twisting the top off of his bottle of aspirin.

Bonnie Blue

"Yeah, it was him." Ed said, unable to bury his disgust as he relayed what had just transpired.

"Ah tell yuh George, that body didn't even look human. Whut they dun tuh that boy was lower than low. Ah don't know whut kinda meanness it take tuh do whut they dun. Yuh kain tell he was pistol whupped. Part of his skull fell off in the boat. Ah kain't even say fuh sho that he was shot. That hole was too small tuh be any caliber Ah evah head of. An' tuh make thangs worse, H.C.'s takin' ovah the case. Them boy's li'bul tuh be home befo' nightfall."

George sat somberly behind his desk and began scribbling information on a pad before retrieving a file folder of blank forms from his desk drawer.

"It's up tuh H.C. now. Ah kain't worrah 'bout that. The Fed'ral BI dun called out heah again. Ah hafta make sho Ah make out these warrants propp'a."

George was relieved that he wouldn't have to come up against the Milam-Bryant clan directly, but he hated that Strider was taking over the case. He knew that Strider had connections with the Klan. That didn't bother him as much as how he made him feel incompetent anytime that they were together.

"That's the law, ain't it Sheriff?" Charlie asked as he looked over George's shoulder at a document that he'd never seen before. "Him takin' ovah Ah mean."

The document listed the charges of kidnapping; naming Emmett Till as the victim and listed John William Milam with Roy and Carolyn Bryant as the accused. He paper clipped the document together to file with the county clerk in the morning.

"Whut yuh doin', Sheriff? If it's Sheriff Strida's case, Ah mean."

Irritated, George turned and looked him in the eyes and said. "Looka heah, Charlie. Ah need yuh tuh gowan ovah tuh the café right now an' fetch them boys somethin' tuh eat. Make sho they put it on the tab. Take Sonny wit yuh."

"Whut 'bout the boy's Ma up in Ch'caga?" Eli asked. "Don't yuh thank yuh bound tuh let hur know?"

Mississippi Law...Love Me, Love Mah Dawg!

"Naw, that's Tallahatcha County's job now," George said as threw his hat on his desk and wiped away the sweat that rolled so freely from his brow.

"Boy, whut yuh standin' thar fuh? Do like the High Sheriff told yuh!" Eli yelled. Sonny grabbed Charlie by the arm and raced out the door.

"Ah gotta git back out tuh the Rev'ran's church," Ed said as he walked quickly back towards the door. "Ain't gonna be long befo' the funeral coach brang the body back out thar tuh bury."

"All right," George said as he continued writing. "Ah gotta call that damned Fed'ral BI fella, tuh let 'im know we fount the niggah's body an' we got the warrants made out propp'a fuh them two an' Car'lyn."

351

George looked exhaustedly back at the open gray door to the cells. He didn't know when or if Strider would bring murder charges against the two. But for now, they were his prisoners. He already had a confession from both men, but he also wanted to gather as much information as he could to help solidify murder charges; in case Tallahatchie County pursued charges against the two.

* * *

George searched his desk for a slip of paper that held the FBI agent's name and telephone number that he was to use if and when Emmett was found or his body recovered.

"FBI. Agent Beckley." A dry voice announced.

"Afta-noon, Agent Beckley. This heah's Sheriff George Smith callin' from LaFlora County, Mississippi. Ah gotta tell yuh. We fount that niggah's body in the Tallahatcha Rivah down heah, bound up wit barb wire an' tied up tuh uh big ol' blow fan. Now, Ah ain't seent the body mahseff, but Ed, mah deputy said that, from the look of it, that niggah took one hell of uh beaten. Kain't tell fuh sho if he was shot but thar was a hol' in his head. The body was stripped naked an', wit it bein' in the wat'a fuh three days, it was bound tuh be broke down real bad. The only thang leff on the body was uh rang on the fing'a. That's the only way the boy's kin could identify 'im."

"Which of the relatives identified the body? I need a name."

Bonnie Blue

"That was Rev'ran Mose Wright. The niggah's Un'ka whar he was took out from. He's the one that identified the niggah by the rang on the dead body's fing'a."

"Do you think that his identification is reliable?"

"Yes suh. He was sho it was his kin."

"You said that the boy may have been shot? Have you found any more evidence? Did you find the boy's clothes, tire tracks, a weapon, a bullet, or gun powder burns at the wound site?"

"Well suh, Ah gotta tell yuh. We dun hadda lotta rain down heah an' ain't been able tuh find nothin'. Sheriff H. C. Strider, outta Tallahatcha, tried tuh find uh bullet in the head, but

352

weren't none in thar. Ah got the two brotha's both locked up down heah, but they ain't talkin'. The most they say is that they went down an' got the niggah. But they still sayin' they let 'im go. Now, Ah still got this heah warrant fuh Car'lyn, Roy's wife, fuh hur involvement. But we still don't know who the oth'a fella was. "

"Do you folks have a medical examiner down there to take a look at the body?"

"No suh. We ain't got nothin' like that down heah. 'Sides, we gotta git 'im buried tuhday."

"Do you have any idea what kind of gun was used? How big was the entrance wound?"

"Well suh, mah deputy say he kain't tell whut kinda gun they used. He say the hole was right small. He wasn't sho it was a bullet hole. Sheriff H.C. Strider, down in Tallahatcha County, is takin' ovah the investigation 'cuz the body was fount on his side of the rivah. Ah'll give 'im yuh telephone numb'a."

"No need. We'll get in touch with him if need be. We at the FBI appricate your cooperation, Sheriff."

"Yes suh."

* * *

Charlie and Sonny rushed back through the front door with two cloth covered plates of golden brown pork chops, cornbread, and a large bowl of turnip greens.

"We're back," Charlie said as he rushed to the sheriff's side.

Mississippi Law…Love Me, Love Mah Dawg!

George took the plates from his hand and whispered, "Ya'll gowan back out front an' stand guard. Ah don't want no surprises."

Both of the young deputies stood nervously on the wooden walkway in front of the jail. Once they were in place, George opened the gray door wider and entered the dimly lit space.

"It's 'bout damn time," Roy mumbled as he stood for his meal.

"Step back," George said as he unlocked the cell door and handed the plate to Roy.

He eagerly grabbed it, sat back on his cot and began to devour the fried meat.

"Ah got coffee out front," he said as J.W. stepped back from his cell door and quietly took his plate.

After George checked both cell doors, he opened the big gray door all the way and propped it open with a worn out doorstop.

"Yuh boys don't need tuh be closed up back heah. These windows don't give yuh uh real good cross breeze."

George filled two chipped cups with coffee, from the hot percolator that rested on the small stained hotplate on top of the file cabinet.

Roy had nearly finished sopping his cornbread in the pot likka when George extended the steaming cup out to him. Roy glared silently through the bars and licked cornbread crumbs from his fingers, sucked the remaining meat from the pork chop bone and slammed it onto the cleaned plate.

"We fount the niggah this mornin'," George said as he handed J.W. a cup of coffee and backed away from the cell.

Shocked, Roy leaped up, grabbed the bars, and screamed, "Yuh lyin'! Yuh uh lyin' sonna-bitch! Yuh ain't nevah gonna find that niggah's body!"

"Roy!" J.W. yelled across to his brother. "Shut yuh goddamn mouf."

"But did yuh heah whut..."

"Roy!" J.W. glared and ordered in a low calculated tone. "Sit yuh ass down, an' shut yuh mouf."

Bonnie Blue

"The preacha identified him," George said somberly. "Ah heah tell ya'll ain't made it easy fuh nobody tuh make out. Mah god, whut yuh do tuh 'im?"

J.W. stood silently, staring Roy sternly in the eye, daring him to say a word.

"Fount 'im down by Pecan Point of the rivah," George said, facing Roy. "Yuh want tuh tell me 'bout it?"

354

"Why don't yuh tell me?" Roy sneered. "Yuh thank yuh know evah goddamned thang."

George stared silently back into Roy's glare, turned, and walked over to the small barred window. He rested his forehead against the cool metal bars and closed his eyes.

"They tell me the body's so bad off, that at furst sight, Ah mighta thought it weren't uh real body." He paused for a moment and turned back to Roy. "Whar's the gun?"

"Gun? Weren't no gun!" Roy laughed sarcastically.

"We don't know nothin' 'bout no dead niggah," J.W. retorted as he stared hard at Roy. "We sho don't know nothin' 'bout no gun."

"Hey Sheriff!" Charlie called from the front door. "Yuh betta git out heah!"

"Well," George replied calmly, "if yuh boys happen tuh thank of somethin', Ah'm right heah. Jist holla."

He left his two prisoners, unsnapped the gun in his holster, and covered it with his hand, making it ready to draw before joining Charlie outside.

As soon as George was out of sight, Roy's whitened knuckles gripped the iron bars. "Dub," he whispered frantically, "He's bluffin'!"

"Shhhh," J.W. whispered as he held his finger to his lips and pressed his ear through the bars.

* * *

Outside, Andrew slammed his car door and sprinted up the step to the sidewalk.

Mississippi Law...Love Me, Love Mah Dawg!

"Sheriff! Yuh fount 'im?" Andrew asked as he rushed past the threshold, his face drenched in panic. "Yuh fount Emmett?"

"Hold on thar!" George said, somewhat surprised by his boldness. "Yuh don't give so much as uh how'd yuh do?"

"Ah'm sorrah, suh. Good aft'a-noon. Ah didn't mean no harm. Ah just heard that yuh might have fount Emmett Till, mah kin."

355

"We fount 'im alright," George said calmly. "C'mon inside."

Andrew quickly glanced around and followed George into the office.

"We jist hauled 'im out the rivah uh lil' while ago, down by Pecan Point," George said. "Yuh Pa was took down tuh identify the body. They say it was hard tuh make out, but the body was wearin' uh rang that he identified as yuh kin's."

Andrew noticed the gray door open, and turned back to George. "Yuh let 'em go?"

"Naw. They still back thar. But Ah don't know fuh how long. The body was fount in Tallahatcha County. It's their case now. But Ah'm still holdin' 'em on kidnappin' the niggah."

"Thank yuh suh. Kain Ah ask Wheah Emmett's body is?" Andrew asked quietly, keeping his gaze fixed on the open door.

"They brang 'im back down heah tuh the Colored unda'taker's. Then they takin' 'im right on out tuh yuh Pa's church tuh be buried. Hell, they might even be down thar now."

"Buried?!" Andrew said louder than he intended. "He kain't be buried down heah!"

Andrew's gaze shot from George to the open gray door. "Look Sheriff, Ah dun already talked tuh Emmett's mama an' grandma. They wanna bury 'im back home in Ch'caga! Heah's the boy's grandma's telephone numb'a! Mrs. Alma Spearman! Emmett's mama is theah wid her! Please call her collect! She'll tell yuh herself!"

George was taken aback and pulled him closer to the front door. "Look, Boy," he said as he looked back at the silence of the gray door. "The body's in too bad uh shape tuh keep 'im out the ground. Truth is, Ah don't thank the niggah's Ma should see 'im

Bonnie Blue

like that. From whut Ah heah, it's the worst folks dun seent in uh while."

"It don't matt'a, Sheriff. His mama still wants 'im home. Please suh, call her collect an' talk tuh her! Please!"

George had the operator put the call through collect and spoke in hushed tones for only a short time.

356

When he was finished, he stared Andrew in the eye, sighed, and said, "Ah told his Ma Ah'ma let yuh take 'im, but ain't uh soul need tuh see that niggah like that, least of all, his own Ma."

"Thank yuh Sheriff," Andrew said gratefully. "Me an' mah family sho 'preciate evahthang yuh dun fuh us."

"Yuh gonna halfta sign these papers b 'fore Ah kain release the body." he said as he thumbed through the file cabinet for the document that would allow him to legally release the body.

"Sign heah." He said, shoving the documents across the desk.

"Yuh bes' git goin'. If they throw one shovel of dirt in the grave, it'll be too late."

* * *

"Roy!" J.W. growled angrily as he strained to see down the short hall into the sheriff's office. "Ah thank he's gone. We gotta git word tuh Byron an' his boys. This thang dun gone too far fuh me tuh fix. We gonna need help."

"Whut we got tuh worrah 'bout? Yuh heard 'em. Even if they do send that niggah tuh Ch'caga an' bury his ass up thar, ain't nobody gonna open that box. Ain't nobody gonna know nothin' but the niggah's dead."

"Shuddup!" J.W. yelled before he caught himself. "Jist shuddup! Ah gotta thank."

By late-afternoon, Highway 3 was busy with pickups and the usual scattered foot traffic of Colored men, woman and children; hugging the side of the road. Massive stretches of fields were filled with oceans of soft white cotton bolls. Huge green combines ground methodically, as tractors took full commanded of their tasks.

Andrew raced through the familiar highway onto the dirt roads that led to his father's tiny whitewashed church.

Mississippi Law…Love Me, Love Mah Dawg!

The churchyard was crowded with pickup trucks and official vehicles, among them, the ominous black funeral coach.

Andrew pulled up alongside his father's car, sitting dust covered and worn at the foot of the church stairs; oddly reflective of its owner.

He heard voices coming from around the back of the church, in the tiny graveyard where most of his family and church members had been laid to rest.

Andrew bolted through the maze of police cars and pickup trucks. As he rounded the side of the tiny structure, he saw his father standing under the shade of a weeping willow tree near the end of the tiny graveyard. Moses' head was bowed at a shallow grave, looking more frail and weaker than Andrew has ever seen him.

"Papa, whut...?"

His eyes were suddenly drawn to the large pine wood box on the ground next to the freshly dug grave.

Immediately, Andrew stopped, bowed his head, and tried to pray silently with his father. But his heart pounded with anger, and his hands constricted in a death grip, blocking any notion of forgiveness.

"Oh, merciful Father!" Mose called out. "We don't know why Emmett was given tuh suffer at the hands of the devil. But Lawd..." His pain was evident in the cracking of his voice and the depth of his sorrowful, carved into his brow. "...we know that Yuh created our b'loved Emmett an' now he's restin' in the hollow of Yuh lovin' hand wid all the oth'a..."

"C'mon! C'mon!" Bubba called out impatiently as he pried his thin, sweaty back from the peeling, whitewashed wooden church. "We ain't at no damn Sunday service! Shit! It's too damned hot tuh be standin' 'round out heah!"

"Bubba, whut yuh doin' out heah anyway, boy?" Ed asked as he walked up from the side of the church. "Let these folks do whut they need tuh do."

Andrew peered over at his father, who looked to have aged greatly within the last few days, and announced out loud, "Ah'm takin' Emmett home! His mama's givin' 'im uh propp'a funeral an' buryin' him back in Ch'caga!"

Bonnie Blue

Frightened and confused, Mose turned his gaze from his son to Ed.

"Hell naw yuh ain't!" Bubba yelled back to Andrew. "Ah don't b'lieve that's even legal!"

358

"Yes he kain; an' it is!" Ed yelled. "Ah jist got word from the sheriff on the radio. The boy's gonna be shipped back tuh his Ma, in Ch'caga!"

Four burly, sunburned, strangers stood shoulder to shoulder beside the church bearing menacing gazes at Mose and Andrew.

"Preacha!" Bubba yelled as he stormed towards the drained little preacher. "Yuh try movin' that niggah anywhar oth'a then that damn hol'," he pointed down to the shallow grave. "an' thar be sho nuff hell tuh pay! Ah'm tellin' yuh right now! That ain't the way it gonna go! That stankin' corpse ain't leavin' heah!"

Andrew quickly stepped in front of his father.

"Bubba, jist calm down," Ed said as he approached the enraged deputy. "Yuh kain't stop the family from buryin' their boy wharevah they want tuh."

"Who said?!" Strider barked as he pounded his way along the dirt path that led to the preacher's tiny graveyard. "Keepin' that stankin' niggah out the ground is prob'bly the thang that ain't legal! It's uh goddamn public health hazard is whut it is! Ain't nobody shippin' that niggah outta heah! His ass is goin' in that hole right now!"

A finely dressed outsider had been standing at the edge of the graveyard as anonymous as the trees, his arms folded firmly across his chest, observing the individual scenarios that played out before him. After it seemed that he'd heard enough, he took long strides towards the tiny group.

"Now, who the hell are yuh, boy?!" Strider yelled when the stranger joined them. "This heah's mah case! The State ain't got no jurisdiction down heah! Who all told yuh tuh come out heah?! This heah's mah case!" Strider screeched at the top of his voice, as the red in his face intensified.

Mississippi Law…Love Me, Love Mah Dawg!

"Sheriff H.C. Strider?" The stranger addressed him dryly, his voice oddly void of the rich singsong rhythm of Southern speech. "I'm not here to take over your case. But I must tell you, there is no legal reason that Mrs. Bradley cannot have her son's body returned to Chicago for burial."

359

The stranger's clear, gray eyes pierced past his thick black brow as he stepped closer to the irate sheriff. He stopped within a breath's distance of Strider, his imposing, thin stature looming over the overstuffed man.

"The fact is sheriff," the stranger continued in a tone as cold as his glare, "it's an issue of public health that makes it necessary for the remains to be prepared properly before burial anywhere. I already spoke to a Doctor Otken, who was called to examine the body. The body wasn't autopsied. He did a visual examination and signed the death certificate. I expect that you will have someone take pictures of the body and the fan before it leaves here. The family will make the necessary arrangements to have the body prepared for shipment. I trust that your office will assist as required."

Strider looked up at the stranger and then fixed his eyes on the small group of men who quickly disappeared around the corner of the church.

"Whut should Ah do, now?" escaped Andrew's lips, as he stared at the pine box.

Confused, Mose closed his bible and stood quietly alongside Andrew at the gravesite under the shade of the weeping willow tree.

"Ah 'magine ya'll gonna hafta ship 'im by rail," Ed said softly as he walked up beside the frail, bewildered minister.

"Yuh really lettin' us take 'im home tuh his Ma?" Mose asked, still not quite sure what was going on.

"Yes, Rev'ran," Ed said as he laid his hand on the old man's shoulder. "Yuh takin' yuh boy home tuh his Ma. But yuh betta make sho yuh take yuh family an' leave outta heah wit 'im. It's jist flat out foolhardy tuh make yuhseff uh sittin' target."

The stranger walked over to Mose, who continued to stare mournfully into the hole that he'd helped to dig for his great-nephews remains.

Bonnie Blue

"Reverend Mose Wright?" The stranger asked respectfully. "I am sorry for your loss, sir."

"Thank yuh fuh yuh kind words, suh," Mose said, still unclear as to what had just happened. "Me an' mah family 'preciate it."

"Be careful, and take care of yourself," the stranger said as he lightly nodded his head to the deputy. His long strides carried him swiftly down the narrow dirt path to a waiting vehicle.

"Well," Ed said, "Ah know Ah ain't gotta tell yuh, but ya'll ain't gotta lotta time. Fact is, Ah'd be surprised if them boys ain't on the move right now. Ya'll gotta hurry up an' git this body ready tuh be shipped outta heah."

"Don't matt'a," Mose said quietly. He slid his gnarled thin fingers into his pant pocket and clutched the cat-eye marble that Emmett had given him just a few days earlier. "Emmett's goin' home."

"Chesta!" Andrew called as he rushed over to the undertaker. "Chesta, we gonna need yuh tuh embalm the body an' git 'im ready fuh the train. Kain yuh drive 'im down tuh the Batesville station? Ah gotta take care of shippin' 'im."

"Now, wait uh minute," Chester whispered frantically. "Don't thank Ah don't feel bad 'bout yuh sit'ciation, but Ah kain't have that body in mah shop ovah night. Come mo'nin', Bossman won't have no bidness. Hell, they li'bul tuh have me laid up in uh box next tuh yuh kinfolk theah!"

"Please Chesta! We've gotta git 'im back tuh Chicago," Andrew pleaded.

"Ah'm sorrah, but yuh know Ah gotta look out fuh mah own family. Ah jist kain't put mahseff out like that," Chester said as he turned away. "Yuh bes' call down tuh Advent's in Tutwiler. They gotta Colored section."

"Ah'm beggin' yuh! Please," Andrew pleaded as he grabbed the man by the arm and looked him in the eye. "Please! Ah ain't askin' yuh tuh even touch the body. Please, jist take im' back tuh yuh place whilst Ah make the arrangements in Tutwiler tuh pick up the boy. He kain't stay in this heat no mo'! It's fuh the boy's Ma. Please!"

"Jist fuh uh hour. If Ah don't heah back from yuh in uh hour, Ah'm droppin' this body right back out heah."

Mississippi Law…Love Me, Love Mah Dawg!

"Thank yuh, Chesta! Thank yuh! God Bless yuh," Andrew said gratefully as he shook his hand and rushed back over to his father and Ed.

"Ah want tuh thank yuh, Deputy Ed. Chesta's takin' Emmett back tuh his place whilst Ah git in touch wid Advent down tuh Tutwiler an' talk wid 'em mahseff. Papa, yuh gonna hafta come wid me."

"That's uh good idea, Rev'ran. Make sho yuh stay wit yuh boy. It ain't nowhar near safe out at yuh place."

Ed pulled Andrew to the side, "Now lissen. The case is Tallahatcha's now. Ah kain't do much else. But Ah want yuh tuh know, Sheriff Strider might try an' stop yuh from shippin' the body, so yuh bes' hurry up an' git it outta heah. Sheriff Smith's still goin' out tuh the Milam place tuh try an' pick up Mz. Car'lyn. Ah 'spect all hell tuh break loose once they know the boy's body's been fount and he's goin' back home."

"Ah want tuh thank yuh again, Deputy Ed," Andrew said as he took Ed's hand in both of his own and squeezed them tight. "Yuh a good man. God Bless yuh, suh."

"C'mon, Papa. We got tuh hurry," Andrew said as Chester and his helpers loaded Emmett's body back into the hearse.

BOOK NINE

The long awaited serenity of dusk was suddenly shattered by screams of sirens searing through the air; alerting Mississippi that her evil seed continued to flourish as undeniably as the ever broadening fields of King Cotton.

Brilliant lights of blue and red, pierced the early evening skies as the caravan of Tallahatchie and LaFlore County police vehicles marshaled the dust covered pickup truck quickly across the narrow, two lane highways. Even the freight trains seemed to cooperate; clearing their paths as they traveled the highway and back roads.

Andrew struggled to keep up in his old pickup that was weighed down with the crate that held his young cousin. He was mindful that the police cars wouldn't be stopped in speed traps as they whizzed across county lines. He on the other hand, was a Colored man, in itself an offense, speeding through the backwoods of Mississippi. He was grateful that Ed trailed him in his squad car giving him some measure of safety as he at times, fell behind.

Although Andrew was aggravated that Chester had refused to bring Emmett's body down to Tutwiler, he understood. In a way,

Bring My Baby out of Mississippi!!!

this dusty journey gave him a sense of honoring what was left of their fallen innocent.

Mose rode silently next to his son, staring out the window at weary fieldhands who, just moments ago, were an undeniable part of the Mississippi landscape.

They seemed curious, though exhausted, as they made their way through the sea of cotton bolls toward their days end in their wooden homes. With his hand in his pocket, rolling Emmett's cat-eye marble in his fingers, he remembered that less than week ago, that could have been his family.

* * *

Moses' mind wondered back to Emmett's time on the farm with him, remembering one day in particular.

Mose had been working through what seemed a never ending day of stagnant humidity. When he returned home, his clothes were drenched in the salty moisture which coated his body. He'd sought refuge out on the small porch at the back of the house. He recalled stepping just outside of the doorway, feeling his body surrender to the shaded cool air, before his attention was drawn to the cotton field bordering his yard.

The boys were unaware of his presence as they played tag, ducking and dodging down the manicured rows, snatching bolls of cotton from the drying tan stalks, bombarding each other with the soft white puffs.

Mose knew that his sons and grandsons had spent more time playing in the field than actually working when he wasn't standing over them.

Earlier that day, Mose had asked Emmett if he would rather be working in the cotton field with the other boys instead of staying in the house doing women's work with Elizabeth. Emmett grinned excitedly and assured him that he would be careful and that he knew how to pick cotton. But, Emmett also asked Mose to not tell his mother.

Mose recalled the mischievous glint in Emmett's eyes when he confided that Mamie would have a fit if she knew how much

Bonnie Blue

he'd played baseball and dodgeball, when she wasn't looking.

* * *

Suddenly, the fleet veered off of the main highway onto the red clay road that slithered through the countryside toward the tiny town of Tutwiler. All of Moses' thoughts and prayers for a life so recently robbed, were abruptly shattered; replaced by a sharp pain that stabbed deeply and silently into his chest.

Mose could feel the pressure in his chest pounding harder and faster. For the first time since this ordeal had begun, he became painfully aware that the strain on his own aging heart just might lay him out before he could complete this one last act of respect for Emmett. In truth, he felt that he deserved to suffer.

Sweat rolled down the side of Andrew's face as freely as waterfalls, as he kept a nervous eye in the rearview mirror for any potential trouble.

"Papa," Andrew said quietly, touching his father's knee with his free hand. "Papa, did yuh heah me? Are yuh alright?" he asked as he trailed closely behind the speeding sheriff's car just ahead of him.

For the first time in many miles, Mose faced his son and whispered, "Whut'd Ah do?" His dimmed, moist eyes peered aimlessly past the aged creases that set deeply in his face. "Mamie trusted me wid Emmett. Ah shoulda leff him theah is whut Ah shoulda dun. Leff him in Ch'caga wheah he was safe," he said weakly.

"Papa, it ain't yuh fault. Theah weren't nothin' yuh coulda dun once them crackas' made up they minds. We're blessed they didn't kill yuh, Mama, an' evahbody else in the house. 'Sides, yuh jist didn't know," Andrew said more to himself than to his tormented father. "Weren't no way yuh coulda knowd whut happened."

"Ah knew," Mose said softly. "That night, befo' they come."

Andrew choked the steering wheel with both hands, juice from his sweaty palms oozed out the sides, his brow constricted

Bring My Baby out of Mississippi!!!

365

in confusion. "Papa, whut yuh say?" he asked, not at all sure that he heard his father right. "Papa!"

"Mista Fredricks ain't sent fuh me 'bout nothin'," he said meekly.

"Papa, yuh sayin' yuh knew this an' ain't said nothin', didn't leave the house? Nothin'?"

"Ah ain't heard nothin' 'til las' Friday, when Cleotha told me whut he been hearin' 'bout some boys from up nawth makin' trouble down at Money. Ah went straight home an' talked tuh the boys. Emmett even told me whut he dun. He ain't even try tuh lie. Mah furst mind was tuh put all of 'em back in the car an' head on out tuh Memphis an' try tuh git the train folks tuh let 'em leave on the furst thang headin' tuh Ch'caga. But Ah ain't had 'nough money fuh gas tuh git theah. Ah knew yuh ain't had no money neith'a. Ain't nobody had no money. Ah went down tuh Batesville tuh git they tickets changed, but they say they kain't jis change 'em down heah."

As Mose continued to explain, his voice became nothing more than a penetrating inaudible buzzing, igniting a pain that threatened to bore through Andrew's forehead.

"That was the same night, when them White boys come bangin' at the door..."

"Papa, why didn't yuh tell me?" Andrew asked, struggling to hide his anger.

"Don't matt'a now. Ah ain't had no money eith'a," he said limply. "Theah weren't no way of stoppin' 'em. That's why yuh ain't heard nothin' from Mista Fredricks. But Papa, are yuh stone sho this heah dead body is Emmett's? No doubt in yuh mind?"

"It's Emmett. Lawd knows Ah surely wished it wasn't him." he said somberly, " All the time whilst Ah was in that car wid Deputy Ed, drivin' down tuh the rivah, Ah was prayin' tuh the Lawd, tuh let that po' dead body not be Emmett's. Andrew, Ah ain't nevah been so torn up 'bout uh soul in mah life. Ah was so skeered it might be Mamie's boy. But then when Ah seent it, Ah was relieved that the body looked tuh be uh grown man."

"Well, how'd yuh know it's Emmett? This might not be him! It might be..."

Bonnie Blue

366

"Ah wished it weren't so, but he had on his rang. Emmett's rang. The boys say it was Emmett's Pa's. That's when Ah knew fuh sho that body was him."

It seemed that the remnant of sunlight hurried to leave the face of this day as the car fell quiet. Both men stared blankly through the windshield as the countryside whizzed by. The looming fields defining the landscape were dotted with islands of shacks. Friendly residents waved as the motorcade sped past. Only, the whirling Mars Lights and bright headlights sliced through the new darkness, marking their paths. And then, there it was, sitting comfortably along the side of the road past a cluster of trees, a sign that read:

'WELCOME TO TUTWILER

Mose clenched his eyes shut and took an unsteady, deep breath. He struggled to control the anger, guilt, and defiance that had been a budding blister of pain; forcing it deep into the core of his spirit.

Andrew knew that there really wasn't anything that he or his father could have done. And he was torn, knowing that he had added to his father's grief and guilt. "Papa," he said softly when he saw his father eyes closed, surely in prayer. "Ah'm sorrah. Yuh did evahthang that anybody could do. Truth be told, sometimes, evil jist gotta do whut it's gonna do."

Mose was afraid to open his eyes, afraid that the malice which filled his heart would spill out and his son would see that his spirit was indeed fractured. He pleaded with God to strengthen him, to order his lips to say the words that He would have him to say; to stifle the toxic emotions churning wildly in his heart.

"Papa?" Andrew repeated as the convoy burst onto the gravel covered red clay, that would carry them the short distance to Advent and Advent Funeral Parlor.

The pleas that Mose forced heavenward became so passionate and desperate that they seeped out as a low murmur from his lips.

"We'll be theah in uh minute," Andrew said, placing his hand gently on his father's.

Mose continued to beg God to strengthen him and help him stand strong and straight. The dignity he commanded was for his fallen nephew, not for himself. Moses' eyes reluctantly opened as the train of cars slowed just enough to turn onto the gravel coated dirt drive behind the funeral home. Both men fell silent as the tires of the caravan crackled to a standstill and the officers filed out of their vehicles.

* * *

Ed rushed over to Andrew and directed him to back his truck up to the oversized delivery door on the shabby, wooden addition behind the funeral parlor. Mose turned his eyes away from the sign that he knew loomed above the flimsy whitewashed door; 'Colored'.

Suddenly, the delivery door swung wide. Holding the door was H.D. Malone, the local mortician who had arrived from his farm, just moments before. His sweat drenched overalls swung limply from his razor thin frame as he ordered his Colored helper to get something to prop the door open.

C.F. (Chick) Nelson, the manager of the funeral parlor who is also the mayor of this tiny town, separated himself from a group of men that were already gathered in front of his furniture store next door.

"This heah the niggah ya'll fished out the rivah?" Chick called abrasively as he walked leisurely over to the open entrance.

"Yes, suh," Andrew replied as a group of men helped him slide the crate from his truck.

"This heah's, Emmett Till," Mose said as walked ahead and looked Chick straight in the eyes. "Mah kin."

Andrew led the procession to just inside the entrance of the tiny white structure and watched nervously as his father faced this White man; more dignified than was safe to do in this small Southern town.

Andrew quickly intervened as he came to a halt next to the tall heavy mayor. "Yes suh, Mista Nelson."

It took a moment for Chick to move his baffled gaze away from the little preacher that stood so defiantly before him.

"Evenin' suh. Ah'm Andrew Wright. Ah'm the one that called yuh earlier on tuhday."

"Now, yuh say ya'll plannin' tuh ship this niggah outta heah on the train tuhmorrow daybreak at Batesville?"

"Yes suh, Ah am."

"Ah ain't sho if whut ya'll doin' is Christian or not, but Ah reckon yuh niggah's got yuh own way," Chick said nonchalantly as he headed back to his tiny office. "C'mon back heah. Ah got some pap'as fuh yuh tuh sign. Elmer!" he called down to the anxious, old man waiting at the end of the hall. "Gowan an' git ready down thar! Make sho yuh open one of them deoderiz'a cans!"

Elmer quickly rushed to the end of the short hall and swung the heavy, mystery stained door wide open.

"Yes suh. Thank yuh suh." Andrew said, straining under the weight of the crate; even with three other men helping.

"H.D., ya'll kain git started on him when yuh ready!"

Chick stopped and faced Andrew. "Now, Ah dun put uh call in down tuh that insurance comp'ny tuh make sho ya'll kain pay fuh all this heah. Ah'ma git mah money one way or anoth'a. Now, Ah'ma say this real slow so as ya'll unda'stand real good!" he said as he deliberately slowed his speech and raised his voice. ***"Ah ain't runnin' no sto' house fuh dead niggahs!*** Ah don't give uh shit if yuh take his ass outta heah on the train, bus, or on yuh damned back! He gittin' outta heah furst thang tuhmorrow mo'nin'! Now, H.D. gonna take uh quick look at the body. Ain't nobody got no time tuh be foolin' round wit this thang. The niggah's dead. That's all."

Mose and Andrew stood quietly and listened.

"We gonna make sho the body be prepared propp'a fuh shippin'," Chick said nonchalantly. "Then we gonna seal this niggah up. That's the only way ya'll gittin' this heah niggah. Ya'll unda'stand yuh gonna hafta sign this heah pap'a. Now, this heah's uh true legal document that says ain't nonna ya'll heah nor in Ch'caga kain open up that box when it git thar. Now, kain yuh do that?"

"Yes...suh." Andrew grunted under the weight of the crate.

"Yuh know, if any of yuh niggahs *do* break this seal, don't matt'a who, all yuh asses goin' tuh jail."

"Yes, suh. Ah unda'stand," Mose said as he signed next to the X. "That seal will nevah be broken."

* * *

In the deserted Bottoms of the Tallahatchie River, the setting sun left its legacy of stifling heat as it began its descent behind the horizon. Sweat flowed doggedly down the exhausted lawmen as they painstakingly scoured through the grass covered ground, examining anything that looked as though it might be out of place or perhaps even, a clue.

Slowly and carefully, they made their way down and along the slippery embankment that bordered the Tallahatchie River. The torrential downpours the night of the murder and the thick underbrush seemed to work as co-conspirators in the lynching, hiding any hint of evidence in the thick mire of the Mississippi woodlands. No shell casings, no tire tracks, not even a sign of the boy's white pants or cork soled shoes could be found.

"Hey George!" Strider called from within a sparsely wooded landscape, which skirt the shoreline. "George! Whut the hell we out heah fuh? One of mah boys jist told me he heard the Fed'ral BI dun called down tuh mah office, askin' questions 'bout this heah dead niggah; wantin' tuh know whut Ah was doin'!"

"Ah 'spect that's prob'bly that Fed'ral BI boy outta Ch'caga. Beckley's the name. Ah told yuh, he been callin' regular since this niggah disappeared. Ah tell yuh H.C., when Ah called tuh let him know we fount the body. He weren't surprised. It almost look like they knew 'bout the body befo' we did!"

"Whut?" Strider asked surprised "C'mon George, yuh kain tell me. Yuh know Ah'ma keep mah mouf shut. This heah ain't no regular niggah. He come from some kinda uppity niggahs up nawth, ain't he?"

"Ah'd tell yuh if Ah knew. All Ah know is they been checkin' tuh make sho we investigate this thang propp'a."

George looked out across the silent river and said quietly, "Ah thank Ah'ma gowan back down tuh Mz. Eula's, see if Car'lyn dun showed up yet. Ah want tuh serve this warrant befo' thangs git any hotter."

"Whut?!" Strider stopped and look at George in disbelief. "Whut the hell yuh tryin' tuh do, boy? Whut the hell yuh want tuh arrest that gurl fuh? Jist tell me! Why yuh out tuh lock up women folk!" he yelled. "Yuh already got the brotha's locked up! Now, Ah tell yuh, Ah don't give uh shit nor holla who this damn niggah really is! Ain't no need in goin' aft'a that po' gurl, too! Ain't no tellin'! That niggah most likely did try tuh git aft'a hur like Roy said! Goddamnit, George! That po' gurl dun gone through 'nough as it is!"

"The law is the law," George said calmly as he climbed carefully back up the slippery embankment.

"Remember," Strider called behind him, "that niggah was fount in mah county! Ah'ma do mah own damn deaf certificate! Now that's the law! Tallahatcha law is *mah* law! Yuh remember that, yuh heah?"

"Ah know," George said more to himself than to Strider. "But the boy was taken in Laflora County, an' that means Ah have jurisdiction in the kidnappin'."

"Whut's that yuh say?" Strider asked as he slipped in the mud.

"Nothin'', H.C. Ah got work tuh do. Ah'll call yuh if Ah find anythang an' Ah 'spect yuh'll do the same."

* * *

George soon found himself alone in his squad car, riding down the familiar road to Eula's farm. This time, he wasn't just coming to socialize. He was coming as the law.

The sun was already sitting low, and the day was nearing its slumber. George didn't expect the Milam-Bryant clan to willingly turn Carolyn over to him. Then again, he hadn't expected J.W. to jump into the silver platter of justice either.

Things seemed peaceful as he slowly wove his way through the sentinel of giant pine trees. When he emerged from the shaded drive, the yard was bustling with children and fieldhands finishing their chores, unaware and unmoved by his presence.

Bring My Baby out of Mississippi!!!

The yard was bare of vehicles with the exception of the two pickups that sat sedately beneath the pine trees bordering the yard and the fields.

Eula's dust covered, pickup looked abandoned as it rested in its coveted spot in the carport and the scent of fried catfish and cornbread lingered in the air. He knew that someone had to be in the house.

George scanned the yard and waited as he watched the screen door. He opened the glove box and removed the warrant that he had with Carolyn's name on it, took a deep breath, and stepped from the safety of his car.

He expected a flood of red faced acquaintances to pour from the house, but no one appeared. After unsnapping his holster, he began to walk towards the door.

"Yuh that niggah lovah, ain't yuh?" a chastising tiny voice asked from behind him. "Mah Pa say yuh is. Whut yuh doin' at us house?"

George turned and looked down to see a thin, dirty faced child sneering up at him. "Yuh grandma or A'ntee Car'lyn at home?"

"Ah ain't tellin yuh nothin', niggah lovah! Now git off us land 'fuh Ah shoots yuh! Mah Pa say Ah could!"

George gave the little boy a sarcastic half smile and walked carefully to the kitchen door, his hand covering the handle of his gun. He stood to the side and knocked on the flimsy, wooden doorframe.

"Hello? Mz. Eula? Anybody home?"

The air was quiet. No hint of any activity, in what's normally a very busy household. The boy was joined by four other children, all under the age of eight years-old, piling up behind him on the small stoop.

"Ain't nobody heah fuh yuh! Yuh bes' gowan back whar yuh come from!"

"Mz. Eula," George called again through the darkened mesh. "It's me! George! Sheriff Smith! Ah need tuh talk tuh yuh!"

Still, the house remained quiet.

372

"Whut yuh doin' out heah?" a large raspy voice demanded from behind George. "Ain't yuh dun 'nough dirt? Whut else yuh want?"

George turned to see a big man; 290 pounds and at least six foot four, with deep hazel eyes leering at him through a hedge of thick black brows. The children instantly disbanded, but kept a watchful eye on the sheriff.

"Hey, Willlie Clyde," George greeted cautiously. "Ah ain't seent yuh 'round these parts in uh while. Ah was jist lookin' fuh Mz. Car'lyn. Is she anywhar heah 'bouts?"

"Ma already told yuh deputy, she gone off wit hur folk. Don't 'spect hur tuh be back heah anytime soon. Now, yuh kain tell me whut yuh need hur fuh, an' Ah'll be sho tuh pass it on, friend." Willie Clyde said stone faced.

"Well, Ah'd be much obliged if yuh'd ask Mz. Car'lyn tuh come by mah office when she gits back in town. Ah jist got uh couple questions tuh ask hur."

"Ah'm sho yuh got mo' sheriffin' tuh do somewhar else up the road." He said harshly.

George thought that he noticed someone standing just inside the screen door, but out of clear view. He knew that even if Carolyn was inside, there would be no way to serve the warrant; not now.

"Ah'm sorrah as Ah kain be 'bout all this," George said as he walked back to his squad car, not sure why the man didn't ask about Roy or J.W.

The children stood next to Willie Clyde and watched, as George turned his vehicle respectfully and made his way down past the fence of pine trees.

* * *

The feeling of contentment that usually greeted George as he drove through his town had changed. The smiles and friendly waves that usually greeted him were replaced with angry glares. Some of his neighbors even turned away, refusing to look at him at all.

George's attention was suddenly drawn to the gathering of lawmen from neighboring towns, milling around just outside of

Bring My Baby out of Mississippi!!!

his office. He wasn't quite sure what to expect. He cautiously pulled up in front of the jail.

"Hey, ya'll!" he called.

"Hey thar George! We heah tell yuh got some kinda mess down heah! Figger yuh kain use uh lil' help!"

It was RJ Sheridan, the retired Greenwood High Sheriff and one of George's longtime friends.

"Me an' the boys, heard 'bout yuh trouble. Ah dun seent the pap'as. Look like yuh troubles is all our troubles. They tryin' tuh make out like evahbody south of the Mason Dixon's dumb as dirt."

"RJ! Boy, am Ah glad tuh see yuh! Yeah, Ah tell yuh, it's some kinda mess fuh sho. C'mon inside. Ah'll brang ya'll up tuh snuff," George said as he patted Sheridan on the back and led them through the door.

"Hey, George," Ed called as he shut the gray door leading back to the cells and his now nervous prisoners. "Ah been back uh while," he spoke in low tones, looking back over his shoulder at the steel barrier between the jail cells and the office, "an' them boys dun had mo' kin an' friends' marchin' in an' outta this place than uh lil' bit. Yuh'd would'a thought it was uh parade or somethin'."

"Ah guess it's safe tuh say the word's out. Charlie, any of 'em try an' make trouble?"

Charlie, skittish as a calico, continued to stand guard at the front window, eyes flitting from truck to pedestrian, hand firmly on his holster.

"Charlie," George called. "Hey Charlie! Yuh heah me, boy?" he called again, louder.

"Yes suh?" Charlie replied, his attention still locked on passersby.

"Who all been out heah, Eli?" George asked as he walked around to his seat to read the messages that were piled on his desk.

374

"Kain't say fuh sho, but Ah b'lieve most of the younger fellas an' some trouble makers musta been Roy's friends. Funny thang, though," Eli said somewhat puzzled. "Yuh'd uh thought they was in church, they was so quiet."

Bonnie Blue

"Yuh ain't let 'em all back thar did yuh?"

"Didn't let nobody back thar but uh couple of the brotha's. But Ah gotta tell yuh," Eli whispered, "Ah 'spected 'em tuh act up when Ah wouldn't let all of 'em back thar, but they jist turnt 'round an' leff right on out. Ain't said nothin', but they made damned sho Ah knew they wasn't happy."

"Whut yuh thank all this means, George?" Sheridan asked as he leaned back and looked out the front door onto the street. "Seems like tuh me they up tuh somethin'."

"Tuh tell yuh the truth RJ, Ah don't know whut the hell's goin' on. The Fed'ral BI been callin', so Ah 'spect we kain git some help down heah if we need 'em."

"Fed'ral BI?" Sheridan asked, while the group of newcomers looked around at each other.

"Yeah. Ah ain't nevah..."

Suddenly, the telephone screamed to life. For a brief moment, the room froze. George cautiously reached for the narrow telephone.

"Sheriff's office. Smith speakin'," he said cautiously, not quite knowing what to expect.

"Sheriff Smith, this is Mrs. Mamie Bradley again," she said quietly. I was calling to see if my cousin Andrew was able to get custody of my son's body."

"Yes ma'am. We stopped the burial. Yuh kin's down at Tutwiler right now, gittin' the body ready fuh shippin'. Now, Ah 'spect they had tuh sign uh legal paper down thar too, sayin' kain't nobody break the seal on that coffin. Did yuh know that?"

"Yes, Sheriff. I'm aware of it."

"Mz. Mamie, ma'am, Ah gotta tell yuh. Keepin' that box sealed, is the bes' thang all the way 'round. Yuh gonna want tuh rememb'a yuh boy the way he was, not laid up in uh box."

"Thank you for your concern, Sheriff, and you may very well be right," she said, more curtly than she realized. "I've just gotten off the telephone and have made the necessary arrangements for my son to come home on the City of New Orleans tomorrow morning from the Batesville Station."

Bring My Baby out of Mississippi!!!

"Yes, ma'am," George said, taking no offense. "If thar's anythang else that yuh that yuh need help wit, yuh gonna hafta take it up wit Sheriff Strider in Tallahatchie County. We kain't step on no body's toes. But I wish yuh good luck ma'am."

"I will. Thank you, and good bye."

"Well, it's official." George said as he eased down into his worn, leather seat and blew a puff of exhausted air through his lips. "They shippin' the niggah's body outta heah furst thang, befo' daybreak."

"Yuh know, somebody's li'bul tuh open up that box," RJ said as he looked around at the men that accompanied him. "From whut we heah, it was uh right ugly affair, an' George, somethin' like this heah..."

"Whut Ah want tuh know is why they sent that niggah down heah," one of the older men in the group interjected, "an' why all the sudden, the gov'ment so damned all-fired consumed wit the welfare of some niggah boy! They ain't nevah give uh damned one way or anoth'a 'bout no niggahs befo'! Ah don't trust 'em! Ah'm tellin yuh, somethin's stankin' tuh high hell!"

"Yeah!" Oscar, one of RJ's deputies chimed in, "thar's uh whole lot ain't right 'bout this thang! Ah thank this heah's them damn commies doin's! That's all that 'Sociation of Coloreds need tuh stir up our own niggahs!"

"We keepin' uh cap on this thang," Sheridan said as he addressed the entire gathering. "Ain't nobody stirrin' up nothin'. This heah uh niggah, true 'nough, but we gonna check evahthang, an' Ah mean evahthang, high an' low. Killin' uh youngin ain't right in nobody's book. If them boys back thar the ones whut dun it, then they gonna hafta stand in front the bullet they shot. That's God's law! We gonna show the Fed'ral BI we know how tuh take care of our own bidness down heah! Ain't got no need fuh no outsiders nosin' 'round, actin' like our

376

lawmen kain't tell they ass from uh hole in the ground. So evahbody jist calm down. Ain't nobody gonna make mo' outta this thang than it is."

RJ paused, turned to George, and said, "Ah ain't sho whut tuh make of this, but one of mah boys scraped it off one of them Bonnie Blue

new bridges when we did uh sweep of the back bridges earlier on this mo'nin'."

He reached into his red plaid shirt pocket and removed a neatly folded packet of wax paper. "Look like tuh me, tuh be uh patch of blood an' maybe some hair, caked 'cross one of them lil' concrete walls," he said as he handed the packet to George. "Whutn't uh lot leff. 'Spect the storm warshed most all of it away. But I was thankin' that maybe that's whar they dumped yuh niggah."

"Thanks RJ, Ah sho 'preciate it," George said as he unwrapped the wax paper and examined the contents. "Ah'ma drop uh line tuh that boy from the Fed'ral BI. Maybe they kain make heads or tails out it. Ah gotta tell yuh, wit all them storms runnin' through heah, Ah'm surprised that evahthang ain't got sloshed und'a the mud."

"Yeah, wa'al, yuh know bes', George. Yuh bes' jist send it right on, so's they kain run some kinda test on it. Me an' mah boys goin' back out mah way. Checkin' up an' down the rivah, see kain't we turn up somethin' else. Later on this evenin' Ah'll go down tuh Rosedale see if Ah kain dig up somethin' down that way. Some of Roy's drankin' buddies likely know 'bout the killin'."

* * *

In Chicago, the early evening traffic on the busy city streets began to subside as straggling commuters forged their way home. Mamie's foot barely touched the gas pedal, as she crept down the busy street, oblivious to irate motorist speeding past her. She struggled to push aside the million tiny details that crowded her mind as she neared her neighborhood on St. Lawrence Street.

Emmett, Wheeler and Curtis' round trip tickets were already scheduled to return home tomorrow on the 'City of New

Orleans' to begin a new school year. How ironic, it seemed to her, that she only had to change Emmett's ticket for the same day of travel from passenger to cargo. She thought of the hurt Wheeler had to feel, riding for hours with his best friend and cousin not playing beside him, but instead, boxed up in the baggage car.

Bring My Baby out of Mississippi!!!

Mamie and Alma had made plans to take Emmett shopping up on 63rd Street when he returned home, to select school clothes and supplies for the new school year. Mamie had already stocked up on his notebook paper and pencils, but she knew that Emmett wanted to pick out his own three ring binder notebook and book satchel. That had been the plan. It was always the plan. Instead, they spent all day, picking out his casket and burial plot. And instead of picking out school clothes, she had to buy the clothes that he would be buried in.

Mamie finally turned onto her street. Her eyes scanned the sidewalk, searching for any sign of Emmett's friends, but the neighborhood seemed unusually quiet for this time of day.

She parked in front of her apartment building and sat. She couldn't bring herself go into their empty apartment or to even face the front stoop; the place where Emmett and Wheeler had spent so much of their time. She had no way of knowing how unprepared she really was to return to her home and see the stoop empty; knowing that she would never again see Emmett hopping up and running down to the car to greet her. She wasn't ready for that.

Mamie had no idea how long she has sat there, replaying all of the, 'what if's' in her mind.

The sun was beginning to set when a gentle tap on the passenger's window startled her.

"Mamie," Miss King's gentle voice called, barely audible through the partially rolled up window.

Mamie was instantly jerked from her mental wandering. "Oh, Miss King," she said as she caught her breath. "I'm sorry. I didn't see you there."

"I wouldn't imagine you would dear," she replied softly, her own eyes, sad and sunken.

Miss King rarely ventured off of her front porch. Mamie could tell that the old woman was also mourning.

"I saw the news," she whispered somberly. "And baby, I can't tell you how sorry I am." The frail woman hesitated, inhaled deeply and shook her head slowly. "Umph, umph, umph. It's just

Bonnie Blue

a sin and a shame," she said softly. "I just don't know what to say. Emmett was just so sweet. I just don't..." Her slim frame became unsteady as she fell forward and caught herself on the car door.

Mamie hurried out of the car and quickly wrapped her arm around Miss King's waist.

"Take it easy," she said as steadied the tiny lady and began leading her back towards her apartment building.

"I'm sorry dear. I'm alright," Miss King said as she attempted to collect herself and walk weakly at Mamie's side. "You don't need to look after me. I'm fine," she said as she straightened her back.

"It's okay. Let's get you in the house," Mamie said as she led the shaken lady up the steps of her home.

"So much meanness," Miss King whispered sadly as she firmly gripped her open doorway and entered her apartment. "It's a comfort to know that the Lord will take care of what the law won't."

"Emmett's coming home tomorrow," Mamie replied quietly as she cast her eyes next door, staring blankly at her own empty stoop. "I sent my baby away," she said softly. "He's the love that pumps my very heart. Now, he's gone. All that's left is his empty body."

Both women stood solemnly for a moment, before Mamie gave her a firm hug and turned to go.

"Baby," Miss King called as Mamie began walking down the short steps, "why don't you stay a while? I'll fix you something to eat."

"Oh no, thank you Miss King. I think I just need to be alone right now."

"Well I'm here if you need me," her voice trailed off as Mamie walked slowly down the sidewalk to her own apartment building.

* * *

The mud brown painted steps moaned as she slowly and steadily ascended the stairs to her apartment door. She held the keys in her hand. Her head dropped, in exhausted resignation.

Bring My Baby out of Mississippi!!!

After standing briefly in the hall, she took a deep breath and slowly unlocked the door.

Mamie needed to be alone in the home that she shared with her son, away from well-wishers, photographers, NAACP representatives, reporters, and friends and even her family. She needed, if only for this one night, to be away from the cold, calculating business of being the mother of a victim of racism. Right now, she simply needed to be a mother that had lost her child.

It had been three days since Willa Mae's fateful call desecrated the life she shared with her child.

The heavy wooden door creaked as she slowly pushed it open and entered the portal. The room was familiar yet, unreal. It was as if she was stepping into a still-life oil painting; a snap shot of her previous life.

For a fleeting instant, things seemed to be as they should. Her breath caught in her throat, as she expected Emmett to come running out of his room. But the rooms remained still.

She laid her purse on the coffee table in the living room. The light tapping of her flat shoes against the hardwood floors echoed throughout the rooms, drowning out the occasional street noises that crept through the cracked windows, as she walked through her apartment.

She was careful not to glance towards Emmett's bedroom. She was aware that, not only had her friends straightened her

380

house, but they had also closed the door to Emmett's bedroom. She was grateful.

Even with the windows cracked, the heat in the apartment was stifling.

Mamie opened the kitchen door and stepped out on the back porch. She leaned against the gray, banister as she gazed out at the half painted garage that Emmett and his friends had left unfinished earlier this spring. A sad smile crept across her lips as she recalled threatening Emmett with no more baseball if he didn't finish that chore before the end of summer.

Bonnie Blue

"Lord," she whispered, "why did I let him go? Why did I teach him to whistle when he stuttered? There must have been something else that I could have taught him to do," she said, searching the sky. She eased her weary body down onto the top step. "It was me," she said in timid disbelief. "I did it. I turned my baby over to them. I've killed my own child."

Mamie sat quietly, searching for peace in the delicate wisps of God-kissed colors of the late afternoon sky. The large orange sun began to slide discreetly beyond the western sky, taking with it, all unspoken secrets.

Suddenly, the intrusive ring of the telephone's screaming out from the living room, jolted her back to cold reality.

Mamie ran back into the dimly lit apartment and snatched up the telephone receiver. "Hello?"

"Baby, oh thank God! When you didn't answer...I just wanted to make sure that you're alright. I really don't think you should be alone."

"Mother, I'm fine. Really, I am."

"Baby I don't think..."

"Mother, there's nothing more that anyone can do for me or Emmett now. I just need to be alone tonight."

"Alright. Okay. But I still don't think it's a good idea. I just want to come over for a little while to make sure. I have to look in your face to know for myself that you're alright."

"Mother, trust me. I just need to do this for myself. I'll call if I need someone." Mamie paused, took a deep breath, and said quietly, "Mother, Emmett...they're shipping my son...he's coming home tomorrow, and I have to be ready."

The other end of the phone was silent.

"Mother?!" she asked alarmed, "Mother, are you alright? Who's there with you?"

"Mamie, it's me," Gene's baritone voice vibrated through the earpiece. "I'm staying until she goes to sleep, but some of the cousins are staying with her overnight."

"Thank you," Mamie replied gratefully.

"Do you need anything?" he asked patiently.

"No, not now." She paused again. "Gene?"

Bring My Baby out of Mississippi!!!

"Yes Mamie."

"You'll be here early?" she asked timidly.

"I'll be there whenever you need me. If you need me at two in the morning, don't think twice. Call me, and I'll be on my way before you can hang up."

"I couldn't do this without you."

"I wouldn't let you. Mamie, try to get some rest, and I'll be there first thing in the morning. And remember, you call me even if there's a slight possibility that you don't want to be alone."

"I will."

"Don't worry about Miss Alma. She's being looked after."

"That's good. That's good."

"Mamie?"

"I'm going to go now. I'll see you in the morning."

Mamie felt like a lost little girl as she stood in the middle of the living room, alone. She soon found herself wandering into her bedroom, unsure of what she should do. She sat on the edge of her bed and looked lovingly at the cluster of framed pictures on her dresser. Each intricately tooled, silver frame, garnished photographs of Emmett from a tiny, happy baby in his light blue suit, giggling back at her, to his most recent taken just a few short months ago at Christmas; wearing that same smile.

"My baby boy is not gone," she whispered as she began rocking gently from side to side.

"No," she said rising from the bed, joining the collection of Emmett's silent smiles, "God gave you to me, and no one on this earth can take you from me."

She lovingly lifted the Christmas picture with the two of them together. She closed her eyes and pressed the hard glass covered photograph that protected that moment in time, to her breast. The gripping pain in her heart that had become so familiar to her was oddly absent. There was one more thing that she had to touch. One more piece of her 'living' Emmett that she had to see.

Mamie replaced the photograph on the dresser and began to reverently slide her top dresser drawer open. She hesitated, but then allowed her tiny, unsteady hands to complete their task and slid the drawer all the way open.

Bonnie Blue

There it was, sitting right where she'd left it; the letter from Emmett. She reached for it. Her body tensed as she snatched her hands away, squeezed her eyes shut, and allowed the pain to consume her heart. Silently, she rocked back and forth.

"Father," she whispered as she shook her head. "Father, Father, Father..."

Finally, she timidly reached in and with great reverence, lifted the envelope from its resting place. "Emmett...," Her voiced cracked as she held the envelope in her outstretched hand and gently pressed her other hand over the address that Emmett had written, not long ago; the last thing that she had of her living son.

She gathered all of Emmett's pictures with his letter and walked to the closed door of his bedroom.

A sudden shiver rattled her body as she stood before the door and wrapped her damp, glistening hand around the diamond cut glass doorknob. Even it, felt cold. It was as if the door was an oracle, holding back some ugly truth that had yet to reveal itself. She released the doorknob and quickly stepped back. She took a deep breath and again reached for the doorknob and firmly pushed his door open.

His room was exactly as she'd left it, with his picture propped on his embroidered bed pillow that his grandmother had made. Mamie stood in the middle of his room and looked around at everything that was a part of her son's young life. She slowly stooped to pick up his favorite old Red Ball Jet sneakers sitting, neatly just inside his closet door.

Emmett had pleaded with her for the whole summer, to not throw them away. He was convinced that he had worked them into the shape of his foot and that they fit him perfectly. And besides, he had christened them, his lucky shoes. Now, she was glad that she had always given in. She carried her memories to Emmett's bed, sat down, laid the shoes and pictures on the bedspread, and stared at the envelope.

"My little baby. My sweet baby boy. Is this all that I have left of you?"

She sniffled, fighting back the urge to cry as her fingers lightly caressed the pencil inscription.

Bring My Baby out of Mississippi!!!

The envelope flap easily gave way as her fingers crept inside to retrieve Emmett's letter. '*Hi Mama*,' she read out loud. '*Having fun, but I miss you.*'

"Oh baby, you will never know how much I miss you."

She gently nestled his dirty red gym shoes, pictures and his letter on one of his cool, white pillows and sank her head soothingly into the other. The pale green ribbed bedspread embraced her weary body as she stretched out across Emmett's double bed. She looked over at his bat and worn baseball mitt and at his clothes hanging neatly in the closet.

"Emmett, I am so sorry, baby," she said, her voice cracking. "It's all my fault. I never should have taught you to whistle. But baby, I never in a million years, thought that trying to help your stuttering could put you in harm's way. I never should have let you go in the first place. I should have come right down there and brought you home as soon as I got your letter. I should have known that..."

Mamie's body shook uncontrollably as she wept. Her knees drew tightly to her chest as her hands clutched at the bedspread, crushing it into her face. Suddenly, the light scent of her son filled her nostrils. Every nuance of her surroundings rewound the sound of his laughter, the mischievous twinkle in his light brown eyes, and the many times that she saw him try to hide the pain in his legs and she pretended not to notice. It all rushed to her in an instant. Her heart was broken, but now there was peace; a peace that she didn't fully understand. Somehow, she knew that her son was with his father. She could feel them both there with her. She could hear herself whisper into Emmett's bedspread, "Louis, I'm so sorry I didn't protect him."

* * *

Hours had passed before Mamie became aware that she had fallen asleep. It was the first deep sleep that she's had since this nightmare began.

The morning was still in its infancy, and the birds had yet to awake to begin their serenade in the trees outside of Emmett's open window. The light, cool breeze danced across her damp skin.

Bonnie Blue

Mamie didn't want to open her eyes. She knew that the moment she did, she would be faced with the undeniable truth that Emmett was indeed dead, and that only his body was coming home to her.

This day was not at all what she had imagined it would be, just a few days ago. She imagined that her son would excitedly leap from the train, and run to give her a tight hug, all the while rambling on about his trip to the country. But now, there would be no smiles and hugs. Instead, she would take that somber drive down to the Illinois Central Station with a claim ticket to collect the crate that was labeled; Emmett Till.

Mamie's eyes slid open. She found herself surprisingly at peace. There was no recollection of how she ended up cradled on Emmett's crisp white pillows, garnished with delicate needlepoint that her mother had embroidered.

She knew that Emmett had never liked the tiny lavender lilies and green leaves winding lightly across the face of the pillowcases. He had complained to her that they were 'too girly', but happily accepted them from his grandmother.

385

Mamie wasn't sure if the visit from Louis last night actually happened. Perhaps, it was just a very vivid dream. Either way, she was comforted by it and decided to keep it to herself.

She became aware of a sharp object sticking lightly in back. She rolled slightly away, reached down, and dislodged the silver metal frame from her flesh.

Mamie sat up in the still darkened room and felt around frantically for the letter. Her hands felt the paper clumped together with Emmett's shoes that lay with her in the bed. She sat for a moment in the middle of his bed with the selected bits of Emmett's life gathered in her lap. She didn't have much more time to be alone. She lifted both of his worn gym shoes to her face, longing for another scent of her son, but the sweet smell that seemed to have had lulled her to sleep did not return.

The moon began to surrender its reign, to hints of lighter shades of night. Mamie slid from the bed, leaving all but the letter

Bring My Baby out of Mississippi!!!

behind, and lifted Emmett's window all the way open. She gazed out past the trees into the dawning sky.

"Baby, I know you're with your father now. Louis, take care of our baby for me." She looked back and could barely see the red gym shoes that lay on his bed in the dimly lit room. "I know how much you love those dirty, little gym shoes. And I don't care what anybody says," she said with a sad smile, "I know that you'd want to take them with you. It'll be our secret. Besides, it will just be your family and maybe some of your friends from school. I don't know...it might be too much for them." She sniffled back another wave of tears and took a deep breath. "But they love you, your family loves you and...," she said as the back her eyes once again threatened to succumb to the familiar burn. "I hope you know, my precious boy," her voice cracked. "that you are my whole heart, my whole soul, my whole spirit and my whole being."

A deep moan escaped Mamie's lips. Her head fell back as she looked unseeingly up into the ceiling. "Baby, even before you were born, you were my purpose. You were the only thing that made sense in this world. I love you so much! I don't think..." She cried. "I don't think that I can live without you! Father," she pleaded, "please take me with him! There's nothing here for me now! Pleeease..." Mamie steadied herself against the window sill as she pressed the letter fiercely to her chest. "Father, I just..." She said weakly. "I just don't know what to do. I can't let him go. He's my baby. He can't be...it's all just an ugly, obscene lie. He's my baby. He can't be...dead."

Through her tear blurred eyes, she watched the delicate curtain of navy blue sky, graciously make way for the unwrapping of the sun.

Her shaking hands released the crumpled letter from her chest. Her eyes widened as she saw two tear stains on the light pencil writing.

"Oh, no!" she cried as she rushed to the bathroom and carefully spread the single sheet of stationary out on the closed toilet seat. She grabbed a long sheet of toilet paper from the roll, quickly

Bonnie Blue

folded it and gingerly dabbed at the moist droplets that had already been absorbed. "No, no, no! Please don't fade!"

The telephone rang out from the living room. Frantically, she shot a glance through the open bathroom door and back down at the letter. She opted to save the letters on the paper and continued to press lightly over the tear swollen damp circles.

Meanwhile, the telephone continued to impatiently beckon her through the open door; demanding her full and immediate attention.

She was painfully aware that the ringing wouldn't stop. She also knew that, if she didn't answer it, an alarm would sound; possibly pushing her mother off of the emotional tight wire that she was already walking.

Mamie quickly examined the sheet of paper, dashed into the living room, and snatched up the receiver.

"Hello!" she said, nearly out of breath. "I'm here! I'm here!"

"Oh thank goodness!" her mother's excited voice cried. "Mamie, are you alright? What took you so long to answer the phone? Where..."

"Mother, I'm fine. Why are you up so early?"

"Gene is on his way over there! He stayed here again all night and when you didn't answer the telephone, I gave him my set of door keys!"

"Yes Mother, that's okay. But why are you up so early? Are you alright? Did something else happen?" Silence flooded the telephone. "Mother, what's wrong? Is there someone else at the house with you?" Mamie asked, trying to quiet the stirring ball of panic that had found its home in the middle of her gut.

"Mamie," Alma replied with a voice so soft that her daughter could barely hear her, "there is nothing more that man can do to make things more wrong than they are right now. Emmett...our precious baby is coming home in a box. Nothing can be more wrong than that."

Again, there was silence; a chilling painful silence that, for the two women, seemed to last an eternity.

"Mother, I don't think that you should come to the station. It'll be better for you to stay at the house. Mr. Raynor is going to

Bring My Baby out of Mississippi!!!

meet me at the train station with the hearse. We're going to follow him out to the funeral home, and then I'll come back over to your house. Is Ruby or Ola Mae there with you?"

"Mamie, I don't need a babysitter!" she retorted. "I am perfectly capable of taking care of myself! Furthermore, I will definitely be on that platform when my grandson arrives!"

"But Mother," she began but thought better of it. "I know Mother. The sun's not up yet, and I was just concerned that you haven't been able to sleep."

"I don't need to sleep," she replied curtly.

"I know Mother. I know. May I speak to Ruby, please?"

"What do you need to speak to her for? I'm not a child!"

"Mother, I know. I just need to ask her where they put something when they were over here cleaning up."

Alma remained silent.

"Mother," Mamie said softly, "I'm sorry. I didn't mean to upset you."

388

"I'm not upset," Alma proclaimed. "You just need to understand that I can hold my own. Here's Ruby."

"Mother, I..."

"Hello?" Ruby's timid voice came through the line.

"Ruby, act like you're telling me where you put a dress or something that I can't find."

"The blue and white shirtwaist dress?"

"Do you think that Mother's strong enough to go down to the Illinois Central Station?"

"I don't know where the purple one is. But if push comes to shove, I think that would do okay. I really do."

"So you think that she'll be able to handle it?"

"Yes, I really think that would look nice."

"Thanks so much. You all just keep an eye on her."

"You get dressed, and we'll be at your place around noon. Okay?"

"Yes, that's fine. Thanks again Ruby," Mamie said as she hung up the telephone and ran back to the bathroom. She was relieved to see that the penciled script wasn't affected by the tear dimpled paper.

Bonnie Blue

Mamie returned to her bedroom, carefully carrying Emmett's letter in her open hand. She laid it down on her bed as gently as a newborn baby, emptied all of her slips from her top drawer and placed them on top of her chest of drawers.

Carefully, she retrieved the letter, placed it flat on the bottom of the empty drawer and slid it shut. Exhausted, she laid back down on the bed, clinging to Emmett's picture.

"Mamie?!" Gene called as he burst through the front door and rushed towards the back of the apartment. "Mamie! Where are you?!"

Mamie woke with a jolt. She had no idea how long she'd been laying there or that she had fallen asleep at all.

"Mamie! Mamie, are you alright? What happened? We couldn't reach you!"

"I'm fine," Mamie said as Gene rushed to her and gathered her tightly in his arms.

"Don't ever scare me like that," he whispered. "I didn't know what to think."

"I'm okay," she whispered as she found solace in his protective arms. "I'll be okay," she said as she buried her face in his chest and sought to somehow, replenish her strength.

"I'll be with you every step of the way," he said, stroking her mussed hair.

She sighed deeply and pulled herself lightly from his chest. "I've got to do it," she said softly. "I've got to bury my son. This is just not the way that it's supposed to be. Mothers should never bury their children. It's just not right."

"I know," he replied. "It's not going to be easy, but we'll get through it."

She knew that he was trying to be helpful, but there was no way that life was supposed to be like this. Her son was not supposed to be dead. She was not supposed to be burying him.

"I've got to get cleaned up," she said as she walked towards the bathroom.

"What do you need me to do?"

"You probably want to go home."

Bring My Baby out of Mississippi!!!

The telephone rang again. "I'll get it." Gene called as he rushed into the living room. "Hello?"

"Gene," Ruby's frantic voice answered", the telephone has been jumping off the hook with news people! I don't know what to tell them! They know that Emmett's coming home today! What should I do?"

"Calm down," Gene said reassuringly. "What'd they want?"

"They wanted to know what time Emmett's train is due in! And they were asking me all kinds of questions! I don't know what to say!"

"Don't worry about it. If anyone calls from the news again, give them Mamie's number. I'll take care of it."

"Gene, who is it?" Mamie called over the water filling the tub.

"When do you think you all will be here?" Gene continued.

390

"Miss Alma is getting dressed already. I got the phone so she that doesn't know what's going on."

"That's good. Give my brother a call, will you? The number is Hudson 3-1276. Tell him to bring my black suit over here. I don't want to leave Mamie right now."

"I've got it. I'll call him as soon as we hang up."

"Gene," Mamie called. "Who is it?"

"I'll see you when you all get here," Gene said before hanging up.

"It was Ruby!" Gene called as he stood outside of her bathroom door.

"How's Mother?" Mamie asked as she opened the door.

"She's getting ready. But Ruby was telling me that reporters have been calling the house. I told her to have them call here if they had any questions. No need in upsetting Miss Alma anymore than she already is."

"I have to get Emmett's clothes together," Mamie said quietly as she came out of the bathroom in her house dress; the water still running.

Bonnie Blue

Gene quickly turned off the water, and followed her. He suddenly stopped in middle of the doorway. Seeing Emmett's bedroom gave him an unexpected jolt in his gut.

"I'll let him wear his new black suit, the one that we had our picture taken in. He looks so handsome in it. You know he doesn't like any suits period." She said rapidly. "It's the same old story every Sunday, negotiating which suit to wear to church and fighting to keep that tie on straight. I swear, if he could, that boy would walk into church with his blue jeans and those horrible old red gym shoes."

Gene worked to pull himself together before walking slowly into Emmett's bedroom.

Mamie carefully laid his suit out on the bed, draped a starched white shirt next to it, and placed his narrow black tie in its place down the front.

391

"Mamie," Gene said lovingly, "what do you need me to do?" He tried to hide his confusion as he watched Mamie flit through Emmett's closet, retrieving one thing and then another. He'd gone shopping with Mamie and Alma to buy the clothes that Emmett was to be buried in.

"Oh, I don't need any help," Mamie replied lightly. "I'm fine, Gene. I've been laying his clothes out for him all of his life." She collected his underwear and socks and laid them next to his suit on the bed. "And, I'm going to let him wear those red gym shoes. He would want to wear them, don't you think so?"

Gene stood there, stunned. He didn't quite know what to do or say.

"Everything is going to be fine," she said as she rushed back into her bedroom to gather her own clothing and ran back into the bathroom, leaving Gene standing in Emmett's empty bedroom.

"Don't you need to go and get ready?" she called through the door.

"I'm getting changed here, if it's alright with you."

"That's fine!"

Gene didn't quite know what to make of all this. On the outside, Mamie seemed too calm, almost as though nothing was

Bring My Baby out of Mississippi!!!

wrong. It was as if they were picking Emmett up from the train station and going out to a restaurant. He knew how Mamie had crafted her entire life around her son and how his death had shredded her heart. He also knew how she was able to adapt to nearly any situation. Finally, he thought it best to just follow her lead and not intrude on how she wanted, or needed to handle this day; one minute at a time.

It wasn't long before the apartment was filled with relatives and friends dressed in their Sunday best. Mamie lingered in her bedroom alone with the door closed. Occasionally, a light tapping mixed with muffled voices would threaten to catapult her into a place that she wasn't yet ready to face.

"Mamie, you need some help?"

"No," she called. "I'm almost ready."

She sat on the edge of her bed in her black shirtwaist dress and white lace collar with her black pillbox hat. The delicate sheer black veil draped just past her chin. She held her bible opened to the 23rd Psalm; the first scripture that Emmett had learned and recited in Sunday school.

Her white lace gloved hands lightly caressed the tissue pages as she recited quietly, *"The Lord is my Shepherd. I shall not want."* She mouthed. *"He maketh me to lie down in green pastures."*

She closed her eyes, and fought back the tears as her voice began to crack, *"He leadeth me...besides the...still waters. He restoreth...He...restoreth...my soul."*

She shook her head as she laid the bible on her bed, fell to her knees, and began to pray.

"Father, please. I can't. I can't. They're saying my baby is dead. He can't be. I know he can't be. It's got to be some horrible mistake. But Lord...my God. If it is my Emmett, please give me Your strength. I cannot endure without Your power, Your perfect peace."

"Mamie," Gene called softly through the door. "It's time to go."

She paused before picking herself up from the floor. "I'm ready," she said as she cast her tear filled eyes out the open window, past the leaves, into the clear blue sky.

Bonnie Blue

* * *

Moments later, Gene, Mamie, and Alma led a convoy of cars through the Southside of Chicago toward downtown and the Illinois Central Station.

The sounds that paraded through the car's opened windows eluded her senses. Mamie took comfort in the realization that she was totally numb. The strong pounding of her heart, which had become such an uncomfortable mainstay since the news of Emmett's kidnapping, was now eerily silent. For now, she couldn't even feel her heart beating. Perhaps, she thought, she too was dead.

Mamie rode in silence and felt gratefully protected as only a faint glimpse of life flash past her sheer black veil. And then, there it was; looming right in front of her with its mammoth, imposing cement pillars. The gateway to Illinois Central Station, where a train was racing to deliver cars full of happy travelers and a single baggage car; a baggage car of luggage and a lone wooden crate which encased the corpse of her baby.

She stared unblinkingly at the pillars as they whizzed past. Suddenly, she was very aware of every movement that the car made. Dread became nearly overwhelming as Gene turned the corner to come around to the rear of the station. She could feel the intense vibration of the powerful train engines and could hear the screeching of metal on metal as a train pulled to a halt at the platform.

* * *

Gene parked the car next to A.A. Raynor's hearse, which was already sitting parallel to the tracks. And like an explosion, before the car came to a complete stop, the iron wall of strength and control, which Mamie had so carefully attempted to build, abruptly crashed.

She bolted from the car and sprinted towards the incoming train, tripping over the steel rails, searching frantically for the car that held her beloved son.

Bring My Baby out of Mississippi!!!

"Emmett! Emmett! I'm here baby! I'm here! Where are you baby? Mother is here!" she screamed. "Emmett, where are you?"
"Mamie! Noooo! Waaaait!" Gene and Alma screamed from their windows as he threw the gear into park.

The undertaker dashed from his hearse and raced after her. Tears blurred her vision as her white laced gloves snagged across the rough wooden cars, frantically searching for the lettering painted on the outside as they rolled to a halt.
"Emmett! Baby, I'm here! Where...where are you?"

Finally, a large wooden box car with no windows, displayed large white lettering which met her fingertips; **BAGGAGE**.

"Emmett! Emmett! My baby!" She clawed at the large sliding door. It didn't budge. She shoved, she pounded.

"There she is! That's her!" a voice boomed from a crowd of photographers and reporters that stampeded from the platform toward her.

Mamie's head fell hard on the door. "Baby...my baby..." Her voice cracked as her body succumbed to the vacuum in her heart and she began to slide.

Gene dashed to her side and caught her before she hit the ground. Mamie was unaware of the crowd of reporters filling in around her; bulbs from their cameras flashing in her face. Her head fell back. Her tear soaked face sparkled in the sunlight as she screamed, "Noooo! Not my baby, Father! Pleeease...take me!"

"Mamie," she heard a voice whisper quietly in her ear, as a soft ample body enveloped her and began to rock her gently. "God isn't punishing you or Emmett. We don't know why this evil came to him, and right now, we aren't expected to. The most important thing for you to remember baby, even in the midst of all of your pain, is that you must stop believing 'In' God and 'Believe' God."

"Mother! But it's my baby!" she screamed. "They killed my baby! He was all alone!" Mamie was numb to the wild clicks and popping of flashbulbs as photographers reached over and around the group of family and friends that surrounded Mamie as she knelt on the ground.

Bonnie Blue

"Baby," Alma whispered as she held her tighter, "don't you know? He was never 'your child'. Emmett has always belonged to God. You were blessed enough to have been given stewardship over him. Every single child that's born belongs to God."

"Miss Bradley!" Reporters shouted. "Miss Bradley, do you have a comment?"

"Miss Bradley! Tribune here! What do you think about the people that did this to your son?"

395

"Larry Crowley! Daily Herald! Do you hate all White people now?!"

Suddenly, from the chaos, a stranger pushed through the crowd with a wheel chair.

"Thank you sir," Gene said as he lifted Mamie's weak body and placed her gently into the high back wooden wheelchair.

"Mamie, I think we should go back to the car and meet Mr. Raynor at the funeral home."

"Why, Gene?" she asked, her voice weak and low. "Why did they do this to my baby? He could have stopped them. He could have stopped them."

Flashbulbs continued to explode in her face, and reporters continued shouting questions as Mamie's family and friends held them at bay and made way for Gene to push her wheelchair back to the car.

Suddenly, the mob of reporters that were following them retreated and ran back to the boxcar.

"What's happening?" Alma asked.

"I think they opened the baggage car," Gene said quietly as he glanced back beyond their compact entourage and continued pushing the wheelchair at a steady pace towards their car.

Railroad workers yelled for the reporters to step back as they rolled the heavy door of the baggage car open.

The passengers' luggage was unloaded first, followed by the shipping boxes. Finally, as the crowd thinned, one of the conductors signaled for the hearse to be backed up to the platform.

Bring My Baby out of Mississippi!!!

Raynor, the mortician, guided the hearse carefully over the metal rails to the open door of the boxcar.

He hurried out and darted artfully around reporters as they yelled out questions.

"Get back!" one of the White conductors demanded. "We've got work to do, so you reporters are gonna have to take it somewhere else! Don't make me have to call the police out here! Nothing's coming out of nowhere until this area's cleared out!"

"Is Emmett Till's body in there?" a reporter shouted.

"I ain't saying!" the conductor replied as he held his arms up and signaled for the throng to back up. "Now you folks are gonna have to leave here!"

Suddenly Gene and a group of men in suits emerged from the crowd and formed a barrier between the reporters and the entrance to the boxcar.

Raynor signaled for his assistant's to retrieve the gurney from the rear of the hearse. When he leaped up into the boxcar, he saw no coffin, only a huge pinewood box pushed up against the rear wall. He stooped down and whispered to the conductor, "There's no coffin in here."

"That's it," the conductor said as he swung up into the entrance of the car. "That's what they loaded up at Batesville station. According to the shipping papers, it's a body. Here, take a look at this paperwork. See if you recognize the name on it."

Raynor examined the shipping document. He didn't recognize the signature but then, there it was, 'Negro Body; Emmett Louis Till'. He looked down at the gurney that was being wheeled up to the door, and he looked back at the huge box. He needed more manpower.

"I'm gonna need some help up here!" He called down to the group of men guarding the entrance.

Mamie sat quietly in the car with her mother, Ruby and Ola Mae while four men from her church stood outside of the car to protect them from whatever might arise.

"The last time we were at this train station," Mamie said just above a whisper, "was with Emmett, rushing to catch the train to begin his big adventure. We missed it here." She turned to her

Bonnie Blue

mother and asked "Mother, do you remember? Do you remember? I told you we missed the train and had to catch it on Stony Island. Remember?"

"Yes, baby, I remember."

Mamie looked sadly over at the growing mob of reporters in front of the boxcar that held her child; nearly crawling over each other to get a photograph. "I wish we had missed it there, too." She couldn't stop picturing the other mob of White men;

the ones that Emmett saw coming after him, taking their turns at him.

Gradually, the mass began to shift, making way for the hearse as it drove slowly through the crowd.

"Emmett...," Mamie whispered as she pressed her hand lovingly against the window.

Gene ran ahead of the hearse, snatched the car door open, and started the motor. The men from her church dispersed as the hearse drove past, with Gene following close behind.

* * *

The motorcade made its way down State Street, and turned into the A.A. Raynor Funeral Home parking lot.

Gene and Alma held Mamie's hands as she walked unsteadily towards the black hearse. The rear doors swung wide as a group of men pulled the oversized box from the rear of the hearse and struggled to balance it on the waiting gurney.

"Please, be careful with him," she said gently as she freed her hand and rushed to the side of the box to help steady it.

"Mamie!" Alma called. "Let them do what they need to do!"

Mamie ignored her mother and continued to hold her hand on the crate as they wheeled it through the back door of the funeral home into the preparation room.

"We've got it from here, Mrs. Bradley," Raynor said as he signaled for Gene to move her back. "I'm gonna need you to step back. I don't want you to get hurt."

"Yes, of course," she said as she felt Gene's hand surround hers and pulled her gently towards him.

"Mr. Raynor, what's that smell?" Gene asked as he held Mamie's tiny trembling hand.

Bring My Baby out of Mississippi!!!

"The body been in the water for three days," he said as they slid the box onto the preparation table. "I'm gonna need for you all to wait in the waiting room out front."

The group of reporters and onlookers that crowded in the doorway filed silently down the hall to the funeral home's lobby.

398

After the door was closed, Raynor turned to Mamie who hadn't taken her eyes off of the box that encased her son.

"Mrs. Bradley, I know that you and your mother had picked out a casket. But as you can see, by the size of this crate that they shipped the body...sent your son home in. What I'm trying to say is that, your son's body probably won't fit inside of the casket that you've selected. We might even have to have one made.

"Open the box," Mamie said quietly.

"I beg your pardon?" Raynor asked, not sure that he heard correctly.

"I said, open the box," Mamie repeated slowly and sternly as anger began to churn from the pit of her stomach.

"Mamie, we can't open it," Gene said as he turned her to face him. "Remember, that was the condition that was set when they released him to you. Your uncle had to sign papers, promising that the family wouldn't open this box."

Fury was shooting from her squinted eyes as she snatched away from him. "I didn't sign anything. If they didn't respect the life of my son, then to hell with them and their papers! Give me a crowbar! I'll do it myself!"

"Mrs. Bradley," Raynor exclaimed. "I cannot open that box! A legal document was signed forbidding the opening of this coffin!"

"I said, give me a crowbar! He is my son, and it's my right! I won't say goodbye to a piece of wood!" she yelled as she looked around the room for something to pry the top off of the crate. She grabbed a handheld steel instrument from the metal counter and attempted to shove it between the lid and the box.

"Mamie, no." Gene said as he gently, but firmly pulled her away from the table.

Bonnie Blue

"This is *my* son!" she screamed as she tried to shake loose from his grip.

399

"Mrs. Bradley," Raynor said as he rushed in front of her, "I think that it would be better if you went home and gave me some time to prepare the body before you see him."

"Mr. Raynor! That is not, *the body!* This is my son, Emmett Louis Till! I owe it to him! I have to see him!"

"Okay Mrs. Bradley. Okay, since you insist."

He left out of the room and returned with another assistant and a crow bar. The men struggled as they slid the crate onto one of the steel preparation tables. The nails screeched out against the wood as they pried them apart.

Suddenly, the toxic stench of decaying flesh erupted from the crack in the pine coffin, instantly filling the room. They retreated from the table, choking, coughing, and grabbing anything to cover their noses and mouths.

"Oh my God!"

"Mrs. Bradley, you really should go out front," Raynor pleaded through his white handkerchief. "The more nails I take out, the worse it's going to be. And when that lid comes off, there's no telling what we're going to find."

"I'm not leaving," Mamie said defiantly. "I am not leaving him."

"I cannot, in good conscious let you stay in this room!"

"Mamie come on out front for a minute," Gene said as he took her by the arm to lead her out. "You shouldn't be in here. You need to get some air. We'll be right out front."

"Gene, I'm not leaving! Mr. Raynor, you can either open up that box, or I'll do it myself!"

Raynor studied Gene's face and then Mamie's. "Okay, I'll do it. But I have to ask you to stand over there by the door."

Mamie and Gene stepped back, while Raynor and the other morticians once again approached the preparation table.

With every screech of a nail being removed from the crate, Mamie felt a strange, unnerving tingle in her heart. Finally, they had all been removed. Raynor turned back to the door where Gene stood with Mamie, her lace gloved hand over her mouth.

Bring My Baby out of Mississippi!!!

"Are you ready?" He asked.

"Yes, open it."

400

As the men lifted the lid away, the heavy odor seemed to catapult from the box, engulfing the entire room. Mamie walked slowly across the room to the table and the box that held her baby. She touched the edge lightly and peered over. She gasped. A floodgate of tears quickly etched a stream of salty water over her cheeks, dripping as a faucet; the pine absorbing each painful drop. She hadn't been prepared for what she saw.

"Oh, my poor baby," she whispered as she reached her hand out to touch him. "My poor poor baby, what have they done to you?"

Raynor snatched her hand back. "Don't touch anything in there. That's lye. Please Mrs. Bradley, just go home and give me a chance to get him on the table and get him cleaned up. You shouldn't see him this way."

"Mr. Raynor, he shouldn't be this way," Mamie said as she stared down into the box at the white powder that all but covered the mangled face that was, just days ago, brimming with innocent life.

"Mrs. Bradley..."

"I'll be right outside of this door."

Raynor threw a helpless glance over at Gene.

"We will do whatever and however she wants," Gene said, forcing the anger from his voice. "Like she said, we will be right outside of that door." With that, they left the room.

Inside, the morticians began the task of disassembling the pine box that held Emmett's body. One by one, as the planks were pried away, chunks of lye broke away and crumbled onto the floor.

Finally, after some time and much effort, they began to rinse the lye from Emmett's body. As the water dissolved the white powder, the hose slid from Raynor's hand. The frightening thing that covered his table couldn't be a boy; couldn't even be human.

The team in the room was stricken with confusion and fear and for a moment, the room became death still.

Bonnie Blue

"What the...?"

"What'd they...?"

"How..."

"That's a damn shame!"

"No wonder they wanted to keep his body sealed away!" Mr. Raynor said as he walked across the large room. "I wish I didn't have to do this."

He pushed the wide wooden door open just enough to slide through, and said, "Mrs. Bradley, I'm asking you as a friend. Please, just go home for a while and give me time to try to fix him up for you to say a proper goodbye."

"Mr. Raynor, I know he's gone. I know that they beat my baby. And I also know that he's no longer in his body. But that body is how I talked to my son, played with my son, and raised my son. I will pay respect to all of my son, including his body."

Raynor looked over at Gene for support, but he held Mamie's fragile hand and said, "She's ready."

Raynor reluctantly pushed the heavy door open. Mamie's eyes were suddenly filled with the enlarged gray body. The stench had intensified, nearly overwhelming, but she couldn't help herself. She released her hand from Gene's; drawn towards the mass that she'd been told, was her son.

"Mamie, maybe you shouldn't...," Gene said as he followed behind her, his eyes transfixed on a body that he hoped was not the young boy that he loved as much as any father.

"Mrs. Bradley, do you think that this is really your son?" Raynor asked as he stood guard at the door.

Mamie said nothing as she walked slowly to the head of the table. There were no tears, no fear, no anger, only a mother carefully searching for her son inside this cold, decaying corpse.

She removed her white church gloves and placed them carefully on the table beside Emmett's head.

"Mrs. Bradley, don't touch it! The lye isn't all off."

Emmett's face was horribly mangled. She ran her fingers lightly across his hairline. Silently, meticulously, she examined every inch of her child's distorted face. One of his teeth was missing. She touched the front teeth that were bared on his distended

Bring My Baby out of Mississippi!!!

tongue, which covered his swollen lips. One of his beautiful light brown eyes was missing, and the other, cold and vacant of life, rested on his cheek. The eyes that cried as they looked into the face of evil.

"My poor, poor sweet boy. What have they done to you?" she asked as she lightly stroked his cheek. Then she noticed on the side of his head, just above his ear, a hole.

"They shot him," Mamie said as she leaned down to see more clearly. She held her small hand over the hole, closed her eyes, and fought back the floodgate of emotions. She had never felt such hate. Hate for the animals that had done this to her child, anger at God for letting this happen, guilt for sending him and teaching him to whistle when he stuttered and pure love for her son, blood of her blood. "They beat him without mercy. Why did they have to shoot him too?"

"Mamie, that's enough," Gene said, concerned that seeing Emmett like this was finally too much. "We need to go now. Let Mr. Raynor do whatever he can for Emmett. You shouldn't be seeing him like this."

"No," she said as she caught a glimpse of light shining from the hole. She leaned in closer to the hole on the side of Emmett's head and could see light coming through from the other side. A chunk of skull was missing from the back of his head. "What kind of animals could do this to my child?" she asked as she stood straight up.

"Mamie, we should go," Gene said as he took her by the hand to guide her away.

"Look what they sent back to me!" she said, staring at the barbed wire marks that cut through her son's neck. "Look what those evil, evil devils did to my baby!" She spewed. "Satan is racism! There is no difference! They will all burn in the deepest, pit of hell!"

"Are you sure that this is your son?" Raynor asked. "The body looks too big to be a fourteen year-old."

"It doesn't matter what they did. I know my son. They cannot take that away from me. His hairline. His perfect teeth. I made sure that he brushed them well. This is my son. This is my Emmett," she said as she tenderly scanned the nude body.

Bonnie Blue

403

She reached down and touched the hand that once warmed his father's ring. She stroked her index finger along the lingering crevice where the ring was once embedded.

"They aren't getting away with this one," she said as she stared down at his face. "They thought they could bury what they did to my son. They just knew that they got away with killing another Negro and no one would see." Anger and defiance rose from her heart. Her forehead banged with sudden pain.

"No! Not this little Black boy!" she said angrily. "The world will see and the world will know that race hate is alive and well in the great state of Mississippi! He will have an open casket funeral!"

"Mrs. Bradley," Raynor interrupted as he cleared his throat, "I don't know how to say this. I'll be as delicate as I can. The body is decomposing so quickly at this point, that there is no way that I can possibly do anything to curtail the...odor or the decomposition. Probably, the best thing to do is go home and rest. All of this is too much for anyone to take in. Let me get started on him. I don't know what I can do, but I'll try to fix him up as best as I possibly can."

"No," she said as she looked up at him. "No, no, no! You will *not* fix him up! I want the world to see what they did to my boy! Folks don't need to just hear about racism! They need to look at this evil to know that it's real! The men that did this to my baby, are pure evil! They are cowardly, evil dogs that need to be shown for what they are!"

"Mamie," Gene said, his gaze transfixed on the body, "I don't know if they can even embalm him like he is now! Can you Mr. Raynor?"

"I'll have a casket made and encase him in glass if I have too!" Mamie exclaimed harshly as she wiped a reluctant tear that seeped from the corner of her eye. "Can we get a glass casket made for him?"

"I'll make some calls and do what I can," Raynor said as he escorted the couple towards the door.

Suddenly she stopped. "I want a photographer in here!" She said with clear determination. "Emmett's body can say much

Bring My Baby out of Mississippi!!!

404

more than I ever could! I want the world to see what racism truly is!"

* * *

Mamie got part of what she wanted. Her son, Emmett Louis Till Jr., was encased beneath a custom made, vacuum sealed, glass covered coffin. And the world did come. Jews and Gentiles, African Americans and Whites joined together with the global community in voicing their outrage. For the first time, many Whites witnessed for themselves how a passive stance could contribute to racism.

African Americans were all too familiar with these stories, which came through word of mouth via the back roads or the front-stoop news. But now, they felt that for the first time, the world would know the plight of African Americans living in the South. Their tale would finally be told through the unknown suffering of this innocent young boy from Chicago.

The lynching of Emmett Till was, in fact, the spark that ignited the Civil Rights Movement. A conservative estimate of 50 thousand people filed past the open casket from September 3rd thru September 6, 1955.

News services from around the globe came to witness how America would attempt to defend democracy when one of its most blameless citizens had been so brutalized. Racism had a written definition, but now it also had a face. This face has become synonymous with the heinous manifestation of racism. This face is in the personage of fourteen year-old, Emmett Louis Till Junior.

GLOSSARY

A'nt	Aunt	Dun	Have/Finish
Aft'a	After	Earf	Earth
Aft'a-noon	Afternoon	Eben	Even
Ah	I	Efen	If
Ah'm	I'm	'Em	Them
Ah'ma	I'm going to	Evah	Every
Aira-one	Anyone	Fine	Pretty
An'	And	Fixin'	Getting ready
Antee	Aunt	Flo'	Floor
Anythang	Anything	Fount	Found
B'hind	Behind	Fuh	For
B'lieve	Believe	Furst	First
Befo'	Before	Gal	Girl
Bes'	Best (should)	Gonna	Going to
Betta	Better	Gowan	Go on
Brotha	Brother	Goin'	Going
'Cept	Except	Gurl	Girl
Ch'caga	Chicago	Hafta	Have to
Chil'ren	Children	Heah	Here
C'mere	Come here	'Im	Him/God
C'mon	Come on	Impo'ant	Important
Comin'	Coming	Jist	Just
'Cuz	Because	Kain	Can

Cuz	Cousin	Kain't	Can't
Dawg gawn	Dog-gone	Leab	Leave
Deaf	Death	Leff	Left
Lemme	Let me	Prob'bly	Probably
Li'bul	Likely	Propp'a	ProperL
Lib'ral	Liberal	Purty	Pretty
Lil'	Little	Ret'	Ready
Lissen	Listen	Reckon	Think
Liz'bit	Elizabeth	Regrest	Regrets
'Lone	Alone	'Round	Around
Mah	My	Sah	Sir
Matt'a	Matter	Seent	Saw
Mista	Mister (Mr.)	Shuddup	Shut up
Mo'	More	Skeered	Frightened
Mo'nin'	Morning	Sorrah	Sorry
Mouf	Mouth	'Spect	Expect/Think
Nary	None	Sto'	Store
Nawth	North	Suh	Sir
Nawthn	Northern	Teefs	Teeth
Nevah	Never	Terectly	Directly/soon
Nonna	None of	Thang	Thing
Nossah	No sir	Thar	There
'Nough	Enough	Theah	There
Offa	Off of	Theyseff	Themselves
Ol'	Old	Ti'ed	Tired
Onna	On a	Tuh	To
Oth'a	Other	Tuhgetha	Together

Outta	Out of	Tuhmorrow	Tomorrow
Ovah	Over	Un'ka	Uncle
Po'	Poor	Uh	A
Pol'ticians	Politicians	Wa'al	Well
Preacha	Preacher	Wat'a	Water
Warsh	Wash	Ya	You
Whar	Where	Ya'll	You all
Wheah	Where	Yonda	Over there
Whilst	While	Yuh	You
Whut	What		
Wid	With		
Wit	With		
Worrah	Worry		

GLOSSARY OF PHRASES

Ain't big as a gnat's ass:	Very small
Behind:	Posterior/rear end
Boo Boo:	Child's terminology for bowel movement
Chicken coop:	Fenced area for chickens
Chit'lins:	Chitterlings - hog intestines – a slavery survival – a very pungent meat that is boiled until tender
City Slicker:	City dweller
Conk:	Chemical permanent hair relaxer
Corporal punishment:	Beat the livin' daylights outta yuh – snatch a knot in your behind - whuppin'
Cracka:	Referring to the mindset of slavery's task master (cracking sound of the whip used to beat Black enslaved people) Racist
Down tuh the white meat:	Down to the bone
Feet hit the flo':	Get out of bed
FBI:	Federal Bureau of Investigation
Git on mah nerves:	Get on my nerves/irritate
Git rid of yuh nightly dirt:	Take a bath or wash up in the morning

409

Hold down the fort:	Stay behind to protect the home or location
In the doghouse:	In trouble
Kain't see tuh kain't see:	Can't see to can't see (Slavery's terminology for slaves work day: before sunrise to sunset)
Nary uh one:	Not one/no one
Niggah:	A derogatory demeaning, racist label for African-American
Negro/Colored	Legal category to describe African Americans in the 1950's
Niggra	Terms used by liberal Whites to describe African Americans in 1955
Peckawood:	Derogatory term used by African-Americans to describe White racist
Pot likka	Pot liquor: the juice that is made when boiling greens for food (turnup, mustard, collards and dandelions)
Pot shaken:	Cooking
Right nice:	Very nice
See ya later alligator After while crocodile	Term used by African American children in the 1950's to say goodbye to their friends
Sho 'nuff:	Sure enough

Shooter:	Sling shot
Showing out:	Misbehaving to impress others
Slop:	Hog food
Slop the hogs:	Feed the hogs
Sooner:	Sooner be on bred as another/mixed breed dog / cur
Spider leg:	Small amount of remaining liquid left the corner of a container
Teenonchy:	Little/small amount
Yardbird:	Chicken
Yuh slip is hangin	Your slip is hanging / undergarment is unbeknownst to the woman, hanging lower than the skirt. What one thought was hidden is now seen by everyone that comes into contact with you.

SAMPLES OF RALLIES AND POLITICAL RESPONSE TO THE LYNCHING OF EMMETT TILL

August 29 - Detroit, Michigan
24 hour mass meeting – 1,000 in attendance

August 31 – New York, New York
A. Phillip Randolph, president of the AFL – Brotherhood of Sleeping Car Porters called for investigation into the disappearance of Leroy (Too Tight) Collins and Henry Lee Login, who were to testify in the trial (murder trial) – Wired United States Attorney General, Hubert Brownell Jr.

A. Phillip Randolph, one of two Black AFL-CIO Vice-Presidents and Michael Quil, President of the AFL-CIO Transport Workers Union, joined in calling on President Eisenhower to send Federal troops into Mississippi and South Carolina to protect American citizens.

September 23 – Washington D.C.
William Faulkner, Nobel Prize winning author from Mississippi wrote a special dispatch from the United Press Service, condemning the kidnap-slaying of Emmett Till.

September 25 - Chicago, Illinois
Metropolitan Community Church, 4100 South Parkway (Dr. Martin Luther King Drive) 6,000 in attendance. Willie Reed, Congressman, Charles Diggs. Those in attendance approved the resolutions calling on President Eisenhower to halt the 'Wave of Terror' against Black citizens of Mississippi. The resolutions also asked that Governor Hugh White of Mississippi, protect the rights of Blacks and urged Attorney General Brownell to investigate White terrorism.

September 27 - Detroit, Michigan
10,000 persons call for Federal intervention to punish the killers.

September 28 - Baltimore, Maryland
2,500 persons rally at Sharp Street Methodist Church. In attendance were activist, Dr. TRM Howard; NAACP Speakers: Mrs. Wilbur Halyard, State President of the NAACP – Rev. B.G. Gordon; Dale Phillips, President of the NAACP, Milwaukee Chapter; Circuit Judge Michael T. Sullivan; former Circuit Judge, Elmer Roller, and Rev. J.C. Huges, pastor of the Friendship Baptist Church.

Copies of a resolution calling upon the Federal government to: intervene to secure justice in Mississippi, demanded federal legislation to end the poll tax, and to prevent lynchings were sent to: Mayor Frank Z. Zidler and the Common Council of Milwaukee, to Governor Walker J. Kohler as well as to President Eisenhower and the Human Rights Commission of the United Nations.

September 28 –Detroit Michigan
Walter Reuther, CIO and UAW President stated: "The CIO and UAW would do everything in their power to protest and correct this miscarriage of justice.

October 2 - New York, New York
Lawson Auditorium – 3,000 in attendance – Shad Polier, chairman of the National Executive Committee of the American Jewish Congress – Main speaker, Roy Wilkins

October 5
American Civil Liberties Union stated: "This taking of human life, because of a person's color, is a shocking departure from democratic ideals.

October 8 - East St. Louis, Missouri
2,500 in attendance Medgar Evers speaks at NAACP rally. "We must resolve our difference of opinion and combine our efforts."

October 9 - North Jersey (Montclair)

2,000 in attendance - Hubert Hill, NAACP attacked the Republican administration of the Justice Department and particular heads of both parties for not taking a stand on the Till case. Rev. D.C. Rice declared that America is on trial before the world.

October 9 - St. Louis, Missouri

Masonic hall – 3,000 in attendance

October 11 - New York, New York

Labor anti-lynch rally sponsored by District 65 of the CIO Retail Wholesale and Department Store Union in cooperation with the NAACP attracted many thousands of trade unionist and other New Yorkers. Police roped off the entire area between 7th and 8th avenues of West 36th street. Full mobilization of the 65 shops was mapped out for this rally. This was the first large-scale rally protesting the lynching of Emmett Till in a predominately White community.

Speakers included Adam Clayton Powell (Democrat-New York); Rabbi Israel Goldstein, President, American Jewish Congress; Roy Wilkins, Executive Secretary, NAACP; Max Greenberg, President, RWDSU-CIO; Mrs. Ruby Hurly, NAACP Southern Director; and Cleveland Robinson, Secretary/Treasurer, District 65; David Livingston, President, District 65; Shops and crews of District 65 have sent protest to Governor White of Mississippi and to U.S. Attorney General Brownwell in Washington. Among these were: Button Sample card, General Office, Mital, knitwear, and apparel. Other unions in the garment area have acted on the Till case included: The 25,000 member Local 22 of the AFL International Ladies Garment Workers Union.

October 12 - New York, New York

Eleanor Roosevelt stated: "The Till case may make more propaganda for Reds (communist). The jury allowed itself to be persuaded that no one really found and identified the body."

October 19 - Washington D.C.

Line Arena – 9,500 in attendance –Fire marshals and police turned thousands away – sponsored by Reverend Smallwood Williams, Bible Way Church – Founder and Director of the National Prayer Mobilization Association Against Tyranny and Intolerance in Mississippi and Elsewhere - Senator Henning's, democrat from Missouri, demanded that Mamie Bradley and other witnesses be called before the Senate Subcommittee on Constitutional Rights.

October 22 - New York, New York

American Jewish Committee – Stated: enormous damage to American prestige abroad – Called upon Congress to stiffen Federal Civil Rights laws and throw the Attorney Generals Offices and the FBI behind their enforcement.

Some critics condemned all of Mississippi, others condemned the entire south and the entire United States – Such criticism was not limited to Communist or Communist controlled groups.

October 25 - Newark, New Jersey

A Resolution to challenge the seating of every congressman from Mississippi when congress convened January of 1956. Congressman Hugh J. Addonizio supported this move. His congressional district includes many thousands of Blacks citizens.

October 25 - Pittsburgh, PA

Soldiers and Sailors Memorial Hall – over 3,000 in attendance. Dr. T.R.M. Howard, Mayor David L. Lawrence, members of the CIO United Steelworkers Civil Liberties Committee, other city and county officials – W. Carter, Publisher of the Courier.

Oct. 25 – Albuquerque, New Mexico

Fred M. Strait, Pres. of Albuquerque Chapter of the NAACP protested the rising pattern of terrorism in the South. Both Democrats and Republican leaders were invited. Democrats declined – Republican County G.O.P. Chairman and Republican National Committee woman were in attendance.

415

Oct. 29 – Chicago, Illinois

Theatre – 1225 N. Clark St., film and stage star, William Marshall – featured at a single performance – Also in the program was Simeon Booker, Jet magazine editor, who gave eyewitness account of Mississippi trial of Bryant and Milam – Sponsored by the NAACP

Princeton University

Undergrads students signed a petition terming the Till murder a "resurgence of racism in the most virulent form" Among the students signatures, were four department heads.

Albany, New York

Brooklyn N.Y. Assemblyman called on the New York State Legislature to ask for the expulsion from congress of Senator James O. Eastland (D. Miss.). (Senator Eastland made what many would call, inflammatory and racist statements during the trial) Samuel I. Berman, a democrat, charged that Eastland is "palpably unfit to uphold the law of the land. He called for a full congressional and Department of Justice investigation into the slaying of Emmett Till.

Deputy Attorney General William P. Rogers branded the kidnap-murder a "serious black mark against the nation".

In the sharpest criticism of the Till case yet heard from the Justice Department, Rogers said the savage killing of the Chicago youth while in Mississippi "did much harm to our country". Rogers said his recent membership on a U.S. delegation to a United Nations conference in Geneva showed him the foreign spotlight is on discrimination suffered by American minority groups.

Illinois Governor, William G. Stratton requested the Federal Government investigate the Emmett Till killing. Stratton's announcement came a day after the Leflore County Grand Jury refused to indict Bryant and Milam on kidnapping charges. In a letter to Attorney General Herbert Brownell Jr., Stratton wrote; "As Governor of Illinois, I would like to call your attention to the disposition of the Emmett Till case in Leflore

416

County Greenwood, Mississippi. Emmett Till, a citizen of Illinois, was abducted and brutally murdered. It now appears that those responsible for this tragic crime are not being brought to justice. As Governor of this state, I feel it my duty to respectfully request the United States Government, through your office to investigate the violation of the rights of this Illinois citizen in another state."

Stratton told reporters that he didn't believe the case should be dropped "at this point. Somebody murdered that boy and should pay for it. We have a responsibility here in Illinois to protect our citizens. It is clearly within our duty to ask for an investigation."

In Washington, D.C., a Look article in which Bryant and Milam confessed to the murder of Emmett Till, hit the Congressional chambers with impact through a speech delivered in the House of Representatives by Congressman Charles Diggs Jr. of Detroit.

Diggs claimed that "there is no doubt that the information (in the Look article) came directly from the killers themselves. The killers were safe within the legal confines of immunity from another trial by the very constitution which they and others of their breed have challenged. These men apparently grasped at the opportunity of selling this exclusive story for an undoubtedly handsome financial award."

The article, written by William Bradford Huie, pictured Milam as having fired the shot that killed Emmett Till.

Roy Wilkins (NAACP Executive Secretary and Activist) stated, "The whole nation is horrified and stand humiliated in the eyes of the civilized world that these vicious men should walk free and unashamed while boasting of their depravity. If nothing is done to make them pay for at least one of the crimes, not only is Mississippi disgraced, but our country will be held up for international ridicule.

The storm of protest over the unpunished murder of Emmett Till whipped up by revelations in Look magazine, continued to develop. The American Veterans Committee called for the establishment of a 'Radio Free Mississippi,' implying that the clichés about 'freedom in the blurbs for Radio Free Europe' be translated into meaningful actions for freedom at home. "We ought to set up a committee to strengthen the voice of freedom so that it may penetrate behind the Magnolia Curtain."

Mickey Levine, AVC Chairman wrote the editors of Look. Levine also urged an economic boycott of Mississippi products and federal intervention, through which Mississippi residents would learn 'that they are part of the United States and are subject to our federal laws."

In Mississippi itself, the 'solid' Dixiecrat front began to crack under the strain of the sustained campaign for justice in the Till case. Mississippi Governor, J.P. Coleman, who is reported to have privately express concern over the economic consequences of the anti-Negro terror in his state, took a step or two away from the secessionist position of Senator James O. Eastland and supporters of 'nullification'.

INTERNATIONAL REACTION

A memorandum from The American Jewish Committee, Paris Office, to their National Office in New York, New York, dated October 7, 1955, summarizes the European reaction to the Emmett Till case.

It reads in part:

Europe's reaction to the trial and verdict in Sumner, Mississippi, was swift, violent and universal. There was total and unqualified condemnation of the court proceedings, of the weakness of the prosecution, the behavior of the jury and the judge, and at the verdict of acquittal.

Europe's condemnation came from all sections of public opinion, all political directions, and was expressed immediately and spontaneously. Surprisingly, on this occasion, the Communists were less vociferous than many of the liberal and conservative elements. These protestations were expressed in hundreds of newspaper editorials, statements by public leaders in every country of Western Europe, and by men in the street.

The proceedings of the trial were reported prominently and at great length in the daily newspapers. Seldom has a trial at such distance been reported so extensively. The descriptive and detailed reports were accompanied by dramatic photos of the court session.

The first reaction was astonishment that such a trivial beginning should have such tragic results. A typical expression of this reaction was the short inscription under a series of pictures in the Parisian illustrated weekly, *Radar*. Under the headline - Lynched for Having Admired a Woman - this paper said, in part: It is impossible to believe, but, alas, like many other exceptional crimes, this one is authentic. At Sumner in the state of Mississippi, a young Negro, Emmett Till, 14 years old, whistled in admiration at the young white woman, Mrs. Bryant. In Europe, this is a homage which provokes a smile.

Here (in the United States of American), it was the equivalent of a death sentence.

AUTHORS NOTE

During the murder trial, the Sumner courthouse lawn was flooded with national and international news crews. The United States suffered a major black eye on the global political scene. For months, after the lynching and acquittal, of Roy Bryant and his half-brother, J.W. (John William) Milam, news reports on the case continued to blanket the front pages in countries around the world.

According to J.W. Milam, the account of the lynching that he and Roy Bryant gave to William Bradford Huie was a lie. He claimed that they told Huie and their friends that they shot Emmett Till because shooting a Black person was more acceptable. But, when the truth of what they actually did to the child leaked out, they were ostracized by the very community that had supported them. They could no longer be trusted. Their peers were afraid that the Milam-Bryant clan was capable of committing great acts of evil toward any one of them, or their families.

My personal truth is that the lynching of Emmett Till is more than the story of a helpless 14 year-old child that encountered pure evil. The lynching of Emmett Till was the spark that ignited a sleeping consciousness. Suddenly, the truth of inalienable racial value of all humankind was before, not just the United States of America, but the world. This is an awakening that was needed at that time in human history.
I cannot help but to believe that in the face of ultimate evil, even greater honor, love and bravery stands irrepressible; changing the intended outcome.
There will always be those that fight against the wave of change; sometimes violently. I believe that it is the charge of the more evolved, to stand up against those that would oppress, harm or kill the most innocent in the world. And in so doing, those who think themselves all powerful by destroying the will

420

and at times the lives of any that would dare think themselves worthy of human status, will ultimately be exposed as weak and cowardly by their need to swarm in groups.

Mankind is evolving. This is not a choice. In this regard, our permission is neither required nor requested.